ADOLESCENT CASEBOOK

Adolescent Casebook

Jack Novick

Kerry Kelly Novick

IPBOOKS.net
International Psychoanalytic Books

International Psychoanalytic Books (IPBooks)
New York • http://www.IPBooks.net

Adolescent Casebook

Published by IPBooks, Queens, NY
Online at: www.IPBooks.net

ISBN: 978-1-956864-08-3

This volume brings together 19 psychoanalytic treatments of adolescents from pre-puberty to emerging adulthood. With the freedom and confidentiality of anonymity, the 58 contributors of cases and commentaries from around the world offer a state-of-the-art compendium of adolescent treatment and technique. Contrary to conventional opinion, this volume demonstrates that adolescent psychoanalysis is alive and well, and also directs us to consider radical revision of theory and clinical interventions.

This volume is dedicated to the many adolescents we have enjoyed and learned from over the years and to those professionals all over the world who care for and appreciate young people.

ACKNOWLEDGEMENTS

We want to thank all the contributors to this volume; in sharing their experience they are helping others learn and become better able to offer young people and their families hope for the future. We offer them our deep appreciation for the opportunity to be part of their thinking, their devotion, and their creativity.

Special thanks to Denia Barrett, friend, colleague, support, and proofreader extraordinaire!

TABLE OF CONTENTS

Contributors xiii

Introduction 1

I   PASSAGE THROUGH PUBERTY 7

    1. RADHI – age 9 9

    2. KEVIN – age 10 33

    3. CLAIRE – age 12 69

    4. JOHN – age 12 93

II   EARLY ADOLESCENCE 119

    5. KAITLYN – age 12 121

    6. NINA – age 13 141

    7. MARIA – age 13 169

III   MIDDLE ADOLESCENCE 201

    8. NICK – age 16 203

    9. JAKE – age 16 235

  10. CLAUDE – age 16 251

  11. ANNE – age 17 277

  12. KELLY – age 17 299

  13. JIM – age 17 325

IV   LATE ADOLESCENCE 349

  14. FRED – age 18 351

  15. KARL – age 19 375

  16. MEGAN – age 19 399

V   EMERGING ADULTHOOD 425

  17. CHRISTIAN – age 20.. 427

  18. MARK – age 20.. 467

  19. JULIAN – age 21 497

Conclusions and Future Directions 521

References 533

CONTRIBUTORS

David M. Abrams, PhD, is a Certified Child, Adolescent and Adult Psychoanalyst. Director of Training Harlem Psychoanalytic Family Institute (HFI); member Contemporary Freudian Society Institute; New York University Postdoctoral Society; and China American Psychoanalytic Alliance (CAPA). He is the author of four books and many articles.

Shoshana Shapiro Adler, PhD, treats children, adolescents, and adults in psychoanalysis and psychotherapy. On the faculties of the Denver Institute for Psychoanalysis and the St. Louis Psychoanalytic Institute, she also teaches at the School of Professional Psychology, University of Denver; the University of Colorado School of Medicine; and in Chengdu and Yichang, China. Dr. Adler coordinates the Schools Committee of the Denver Psychoanalytic Society.

Denia Barrett, MSW is a child and adolescent supervising analyst on the faculty of The Chicago Psychoanalytic Institute. She is Co-Editor-in-Chief of *The Psychoanalytic Study of the Child* and a past President of The Association for Child Psychoanalysis.

Thomas Barrett, PhD is a Child and Adolescent Supervising Analyst on the faculty of the Chicago Psychoanalytic Institute, Adjunct Professor in Infant and Early Childhood Mental Health (IECMH) at Chicago's Erikson Institute, and President of the Association for Child Psychoanalysis. Executive and Clinical Director of the Hanna Perkins Center in Cleveland, OH from 1990-2010.

Meryl Berlin, PhD, is a child and adult psychoanalyst and clinical psychologist in Ann Arbor, MI. She works with individuals over the lifespan, and is actively involved in psychoanalytic teaching and supervision.

Gertie F. Bögels, MD, is a supervising, and training psychoanalyst. Former psychiatrist Radboud UMC, co-editor of the Dutch *Tijdschrift voor Psychoanalyse*. Editor: Freud Letters to Jeanne Lampl-de Groot; Publications on biography and psychoanalysis, narrative and imagination, child analysis, and intergenerational symptomatology.

Paul Brinich, PhD is a retired child and adult psychoanalyst; past President, Association for Child Psychoanalysis; faculty member of the Psychoanalytic Center of the Carolinas and of the San Francisco Center for Psychoanalysis.

Peter Bruendl, PhD is a psychoanalyst in private practice, working with infants, children, adolescents and adults. Training- and Supervising Analyst (MAP, DGPT, VAKJP).

Donald Campbell is a training and supervising analyst, Distinguished Fellow, past President of the British Psychoanalytical Society, former Secretary General of the International Psychoanalytic Association. Past Chair of the Portman Clinic in London, he has published papers and chapters on adolescence, doubt, shame, metaphor, violence, perversion, child sexual abuse, and horror films. Co-authored with Rob Hale, 2017, *Working in the Dark: Understanding the pre-suicide state of mind.*

Monica Cardenal is a Training analyst, Buenos Aires Psychoanalytical Association, Consultant of IPA Child and Adolescent Committee, Chair of IPA Committee on Psychoanalytic Assistance in Crisis and Emergencies, Associate Professor in Clinical Psychology and Infant Psychiatry postgraduate training, Director of Infant Observation Seminars, Italian Hospital. Author and Co-editor of international publications.

Kimberly Chu, LCSW, is Co-Chair of the Child & Adolescent Psychoanalytic Training Program and Chair of the Diversity Initiative of the Psychoanalytic Association of New York (PANY) Affiliated with NYU School of Medicine. In addition to private practice, she has worked in hospital-based child & adolescent psychiatry as a bilingual Spanish/English clinician, supervisor, lecturer, diversity educator, and has been a consultant to public and private schools in NYC.

Herman Daldin, PhD, is a Child and Adolescent psychoanalyst. Trained at the Hanna Perkins Center and the Anna Freud Centre. Member of several psychoanalytic societies with offices in Birmingham and Wyandotte, Michigan.

Minnie Dastur, BCOM, LLB, MIPS, is a Training & Supervisory Analyst (Adult & Child), Indian Psychoanalytic Society. She has presented Keynote papers at the Asia-Pacific Psychoanalytic Conferences and presented at other conferences, teaches in China as part of IPA's China Committee, and conducts programs linking Psychoanalysis to Art, Literature, Cinema as part of Continued Professional Development for the Mumbai Chapter of the IPS.

Jennifer Davids, MSc, Clinical Psychology UCT trained as a clinical psychologist in South Africa and in child and adolescent psychoanalysis at the Anna Freud Centre, where she then worked as a staff and teaching member. Consultant to a looked-after children and adolescent team; trained as an adult psychoanalyst at the British Psychoanalytical Society (BPAS); Supervising child and adolescent psychoanalyst at the BPAS and internationally; *IPA in Health* and the *ACP grants* committees.

Enrico DeVito, MD is a psychiatrist and psychoanalyst, member of the Italian Psychoanalytic Society and the IPA, with a private practice in Milan, Italy. He founded and directed Progetto A, Center for Consultation and Psychotherapy of Adolescents. Formerly President of the International Society of Adolescent Psychiatry and Psychology (ISAPP).

Susan L. Donner, MD is a Training and Child, Adolescent and Adult Supervising Analyst; Chair of Child and Adolescent Psychoanalytic Training; Director, 0-21 Child and Adolescent Clinic, New Center for Psychoanalysis, Los Angeles; Associate Clinical Professor, UCLA Departments of Adult and Child Psychiatry; Director of UCLA Child Psychiatry Fellowship Area of Distinction: Psychoanalytic Perspectives; Director of APsaA College Externship program. Private practice in Woodland Hills, CA.

Joshua Ehrlich, PhD, is a psychoanalyst who practices in Ann Arbor, MI. He's Faculty at the Michigan Psychoanalytic Institute and supervises psychiatry residents at the University of Michigan Medical Center. Dr. Ehrlich published a book *Divorce and Loss* in 2014 and is currently completing a book on male sexuality.

Karen Gilmore, MD is Training and Supervising Analyst at Columbia University Center for Psychoanalytic Training and Research, where she served as Director of the Child Division for 15 years. She is Clinical Professor of Psychiatry at Columbia University School of Medicine. She co-authored books and chapters on development with Pamela Meersand, PhD and published papers on play, development, ADHD, and emerging adulthood.

Susan E. Goodman, LCSW is a Child and Adolescent Psychoanalyst with private practice in Westport, CT and NYC, working with young children through young adults and their parents, individual adults, and consultant to local pre-school. Teaches at The NYU Graduate School of Social Work, the CAP program at the Institute for Psychoanalytic Training and Research (IPTAR), and The Harlem Family Institute. Has written on a variety of topics related to children, adolescents, and parenting.

Jim Herzog is a child and adult psychoanalyst and psychiatrist.

Paul C. Holinger, MD, MPH is Professor of Psychiatry, Rush University Medical Center, Chicago IL; Faculty, Chicago Psychoanalytic Institute; Dean, 2011-2014; Training and Supervising Analyst; and Child and Adolescent Supervising Analyst.

Theodore Jacobs, MD is a Training and Supervising Analyst at the New York and PANY Psychoanalytic institutes.

Justine Kalas Reeves teaches at Contemporary Freudian Society, Washington Baltimore Center for Psychoanalysis, and is Affiliate Assistant Professor at Howard University's College of Medicine. Trained at the Anna Freud Centre, and the CFS, she has published on child and adolescent analysis.

Bernadette Kovach, PhD practices in Farmington Hills and is a clinical supervisor for several area universities. A teaching and supervising analyst at the Michigan Psychoanalytic Institute, Chair of the Child and Adolescent Psychoanalysis Program, Co-chair of Candidate Progression Committee, she was named teacher of the year for her course on psychoanalytic research, and has published on child analysis.

Jacqueline Langley, PhD is a psychologist and child, adolescent and adult psychoanalyst in St. Louis, Missouri. On faculty at the St. Louis and Michigan Psychoanalytic Institutes, she teaches and supervises, and presents to St. Louis schools and mental health agencies. She has published articles describing psychoanalytic treatment of children and adolescents with concurrent parent work.

Marsha H. Levy-Warren, PhD is a Training and Supervising psychoanalyst at The Contemporary Freudian Society, the International Psychoanalytical Association, and the Confederation of Independent Societies; and Faculty and Clinical Consultant at the NYU Postdoctoral Program in Psychotherapy and Psychoanalysis. In private practice seeing adolescents, adults, and parents in New York City.

Era A. Loewenstein, PhD is a Child, Adolescent and Adult Psychoanalyst. She is a Training and Supervising Analyst at the San Francisco Center for Psychoanalysis (SFCP). Era was the Founder and Chair of the *Preschool Consultation Project* at SFCP and in this capacity she has been collaborating with Early Childhood Educators in various projects for the past 20 years.

Mali Mann, MD, FIPA is training and supervising psychoanalyst, adult and child at San Francisco Center for Psychoanalysis. She is clinical professor at Stanford School of Medicine, Department of Psychiatry and Behavioral Science.

Ellika McGuire, MD is a child, adolescent, and adult psychiatrist and psychoanalyst in private practice in Seattle, working in community mental health. Teaches and supervises fellows in the University of Washington Child Psychiatry Residency Program.

Marina Mirkin, MD is a Faculty member of the Psychoanalytic Association of New York where she is also Chair of PANY Program Committee. She is in private practice working with Adults and Children in NYC.

Elissa Baldwin Murphy, PhD, LCSW is a child, adolescent and adult psychoanalyst in private practice in Durham, NC where she provides psychoanalytic treatment, parent consultation, and clinical supervision to individuals and groups. She has been a lecturer and research advisor at the Smith College School for Social Work, and as a faculty member of the Psychoanalytic Center of the Carolinas, she has taught multiple courses and coordinates a study group on race and psychoanalysis.

Monisha Nayar-Akhtar, PhD is an adult and child/adolescent psychoanalyst who practices in Philadelphia, Pennsylvania. She is interested in cultural issues especially as they impact the adolescent years of development. She has a keen interest in understanding and exploring issues that impact identity development especially in complex cultural environments impacted by both immigration and trauma.

Jack Novick, PhD, (Editor) is an Adult, Adolescent, and Child Training and Supervising Psychoanalyst; Co-founder: Allen Creek Preschool, MPI Child analysis and Integrated training programs, Alliance for Psychoanalytic Schools. Former President, Association for Child Psychoanalysis and IPA Board and Executive Committee member. Author and co-author of papers on termination, sadomasochism, technique, and six books.

Kerry Kelly Novick, FIPA, (Editor) is a Child, Adolescent, and Adult Psychoanalyst, former President of the Association for Child Psychoanalysis, Founder of Allen Creek Preschool, author of publications on development, defenses, two systems of self-regulation, sadomasochism, integrated curriculum, and other topics, and co-author of six books.

Deborah Offner, PhD is a clinical psychologist specializing in adolescents. She consults, teaches and writes about adolescent development and mental health for middle and secondary school educators and parents.

Laurie Orgel, MD, graduated from Washington University in St. Louis. She trained at Sheppard Pratt Hospital, and the Baltimore Washington Institute. She practices Child and Adult psychiatry and psychoanalysis, and is on the teaching faculty of the Washington Baltimore Center for Psychoanalysis and the University of Maryland Department of Psychiatry.

Deborah W. Paris, LISW, BCD, is a child psychoanalyst in Cleveland, OH. She has worked with children, adolescents and families for over 40 years.

Purvi Patel is a graduate in Bachelor of Commerce and Economics, and Psychoanalytic Psychotherapist working with children, parents and young adults. She is also a candidate for Adult Psychoanalysis.

Daniel W. Prezant, PhD, is a child, adolescent, and adult Training and Supervising Analyst at the New York Psychoanalytic Society & Institute and the Secretary of the Association for Child Psychoanalysis. He is in private practice in New York City.

Timothy Rice, MD, is a child, adolescent, and adult psychiatrist and psychoanalyst in New York, NY. Associate Professor of Psychiatry at the

Icahn School of Medicine at Mount Sinai, and Chief, Child and Adolescent Inpatient Psychiatry Service of the Mount Sinai Health System.

Rachel Z. Ritvo, MD is Assistant Clinical Professor of Psychiatry and Behavioral Science, George Washington Univ. School of Medicine; Lecturer, Children's National Medical Center. Teaching Analyst, Washington Baltimore Center for Psychoanalysis. Founder, AACAP Psychodynamic Faculty Initiative.

Samuel Roth, PhD studied sociology and clinical psychology. Trained at the Massachusetts Institute for Psychoanalysis, and the Boston Psychoanalytic Society and Institute, he teaches, supervises and practices in Newton, Massachusetts.

Janet C. Rotter, MS is a Psychoanalyst in private practice in New York City. She works with adults, adolescents, children, families and couples. Head of School at the Studio School and Vice President of Alliance for Psychoanalytic Schools. She writes and speaks on psychoanalytic techniques and child, parent, and teacher development.

Majlis Winberg Salomonsson, PhD is a Swedish training and child psychoanalyst in private practice and at the Mama Mia Child Health Centre, Stockholm. A Lecturer at the Faculty of Psychology, University of Stockholm and researcher at the Karolinska Institutet, Stockholm, she has published several papers and books on psychoanalysis with children and adolescents.

Edgard Sanchez Bernal, MD Psychoanalyst, London, UK. Co-founder of Freudian Study Group (FSG).

Jani Santamaría Linares, PhD, is a Child and Adolescent Training Analyst, Mexican Psychoanalytic Association (APM); Latin American Board Member of the IPA 2019-2023; Director, A-Santamaría Psicoanálisis México; Member, International Advisory Cttee. Routledge Bion Studies; Chair, International Bion Conference México 2022.

Maxim de Sauma, MD is Director of the Brent Centre for Young People in London, and leads projects in Schools and Youth Offending Services and Adolescent Suicidality. He leads a collaboration between the Brent Centre and the Institute of Psychoanalysis, and is a Training and Supervisory Analyst and a Child and Adolescent Analyst.

Jill Savege Scharff MD, FABP is co-founder of the International Psychotherapy Institute (IPI), founder of its adult analytic and combined child analytic and child psychotherapy training programs; Clinical professor of psychiatry at Georgetown University; author; editor of *Psychoanalysis Online* volumes 1-4; and recipient of the 2021 Sigourney Award.

Erika Schmidt MSW is a child, adolescent and adult psychoanalyst practicing in Chicago. She is on the faculty of the Chicago Psychoanalytic Institute where she served as President from 2013 to 2022. She is also on the Board of Directors of the American Psychoanalytic Association, the Board of the Psychotherapy Action Network and the Editorial Board of the Journal of the American Psychoanalytic Association.

Caroline M. Sehon, MD, FABP is Director of the International Psychotherapy Institute (IPI) where she is a supervising child and adult psychoanalyst and past Chair of IPI's International Institute for Psychoanalytic Training. She writes articles and book chapters on child, couple, and family therapy, and teleanalysis. She is Clinical Professor of Psychiatry at Georgetown University School of Medicine and in private practice in Bethesda, Maryland, USA.

Merton A. Shill, JD, LLM, PhD, FIPA (Ann Arbor, MI) is an adult analyst with supervised experience in child and adolescent analysis. His publications include ADHD, signal anxiety, affect, intersubjective ego psychology and relational analysis.

William Singletary, MD is a child, adolescent, and adult psychiatrist and psychoanalyst, a member of the faculty and supervising child analyst of the Psychoanalytic Center of Philadelphia, and President of the Board of the Margaret S. Mahler Child Development Foundation. He is in private practice in Philadelphia, PA.

Donna Roth Smith, LCSW, FIPA is a child, adolescent, and adult psychoanalyst in NYC working with parent-infant dyads, children/ adolescents, adults, couples, families, clinical supervision, and consults to private and public schools. Training and Supervising Analyst at The Contemporary Freudian Society, faculty at CFS & IPTAR, the Anni Bergman Parent-Infant Program, formerly at Bank Street Graduate School Infant and Parent Development and Early Intervention Program.

Ann G. Smolen, PhD is a Training and Supervising Analyst in child and adult at the Psychoanalytic Center of Philadelphia

Angelika Staehle, Diplom-Psychologin is a Training Analyst for Child-, Adolescent- and Adult Psychoanalysis (DPV /IPA) and for Group-Analysis (GAS/London). She works in full private psychoanalytic practice. Her publications focus on: Psychoanalytic technique, especially disturbances of symbolisation of children, adolescents and adults, integration of adult- and child analysis, group processes in institutions, psychoanalytic education.

John Tisdale, D.Min., holds a B.A. from High Point University, a Master's of Divinity degree from Duke University and a Doctorate of Ministry degree (D.Min.) in Pastoral Counseling from the Graduate Theological Foundation, South Bend, Indiana. As a part of his 25+ year clinical career, he is an ordained United Methodist minister and a Child and Adolescent psychoanalyst in practice in Durham, North Carolina.

Elizabeth Tuters, MSW, RSW, FIPA is a Child,Adolescent, Adult Psychoanalyst; Co-Director Infant Mental Health Studies; Board of Directors Canadian Association for Psychoanalytic Child Therapists; Faculty/ Supervisor Canadian Institute of Child/ Adolescent Psychoanalytic Psychotherapy & Toronto Psychoanalytic Society/ Institute.

Peter Wilson, BA, Dip. Applied Social Studies, MACP is a Consultant Child and Adolescent Psychotherapist, qualified as a child psychoanalyst with Anna Freud in 1971. Senior child psychotherapy posts in the NHS and Voluntary Sector; Director of a community service for adolescents and Director of a national child mental health organization, Young Minds. He has been in private practice and served as a teacher and supervisor in various institutes.

INTRODUCTION

On the site of the biblical city of Ur, a four-thousand-year-old tablet was discovered with the following inscription carved on it: "Our civilization is doomed if the unheard-of actions of our younger generations are allowed to continue" (Lauer 1973, p.176). Some historians, however, claim that adolescence is a modern invention, a post-industrial phenomenon (Aries 1965). There is controversy about this view but all agree that the scientific study of adolescence started in the 20th century, with two salient works, G. Stanley Hall's monumental two volumes on adolescence (which he called the "Ephebic transformation") (1904) and Sigmund Freud's "Three Essays on the Theory of Sexuality," (1905) one section of which is devoted to the Transformations of Puberty. Despite the differences between these two seminal thinkers, it is striking that each describes the phenomena of adolescence in Hall's terms of "sturm und drang," a reference to German Romantic ideas, as described, for instance, in Goethe's novel "The Sorrows of Young Werther" (1787).

Certainly the concept of adolescence as a central developmental phase is firmly established in current North and Latin American and Western European cultures, but it may be shortsighted or ethnocentric to assume universal importance or focus on adolescence. Elisabeth Young-Bruehl suggested that adolescence takes on importance in any culture to the degree of that culture's reaction or response to the fact of puberty (1996). There are many conceptualizations and perspectives on adolescence, spanning multiple fields of study, but they are beyond the scope of this

1

book. In this volume we will focus on psychoanalytic descriptions of adolescent development and functioning and the psychoanalytic treatment of teenagers and emerging adults.

We are doing this against a background of a century in our field of ambivalent thinking about adolescents. The fundamental outline of the classic psychoanalytic view of adolescent development is contained in Freud's essay: the increase of sexual drive intensity at puberty breaks down latency defenses, including the incest barrier. The major tasks of adolescence are the repudiation of infantile relationships and desires, the detachment from and opposition to parental authority, and the establishment of non-incestuous sexual relationships and a mature set of ideas, values and morals. These momentous changes take place initially and mainly in fantasies and often under the impetus of masturbation. During puberty, infantile sexual impulses become fore-pleasures under the dominance of the genital urge for heterosexual intercourse and procreation. Interferences with genital aims can lead to perversions.

This is the basic psychoanalytic model of adolescent development; the contributions of later writers add important details but do not alter much. Ernest Jones (1922) borrowed the theory of recapitulation of early phases from G.S. Hall (1904) to extend Freud's idea of the revival of oedipal wishes at puberty. However, Jones's view is more far-reaching, as he claims that all of the infantile phases are recapitulated at adolescence, a view that has influenced most psychoanalysts since, for instance, Peter Blos, Sr., who wrote about adolescence as a second separation-individuation phase (1967).

Anna Freud, in her classic "The Ego and the Mechanisms of Defense" (1936), and her work on adolescence 20 years later (1958), elaborated many of the details in her father's model. In particular she described with dramatic vividness the struggle between id and ego, the increase not only in libido, but also in aggression. This was a most important addition. She underscored that a major anxiety in adolescence is the fear of being overwhelmed by the instincts, a fear of the quantity rather than quality of instincts. Noteworthy in that description was her understanding of the traumatic impact of helplessness; in the Discussions in the 1980's (Sandler and Freud, A.), she elaborated on the idea that fear of helplessness underlies all the other anxieties in the classical sequence.

In 1958 and again in 1969 Anna Freud graphically described a so-called "normal" state of adolescent turmoil. She said that adolescent reactions are intermediate between mental health and illness. Adolescence, she averred, is a developmental disturbance. Anna Freud decried the paucity of psychoanalytic understanding – "The position with regard to the analytic study of adolescence is not a happy one, and especially unsatisfactory when compared with that of early childhood" (1958, p. 255). She not only called the study of adolescence a "stepchild," but, like most of her contemporaries, considered adolescents unanalyzable (DeVito, Novick and Novick 2000). She is quoted as saying, "Analyzing adolescents is like trying to run after an express train" and "we may have to face that adolescents are not truly analyzable" (Panel, 1972, p.135).

Winnicott said, "There exists one real cure for adolescence and only one… It belongs to the passage of time" (1961). Notice that adolescence is described as a disease needing a cure, and that cure has nothing to do with psychoanalytic treatment. Blos (1980) summarized his years of experience with adolescents with the statement that a transference neurosis cannot be formed until the end of adolescence, a remark that echoes a view stated earlier by Berman that "the adolescent does not have the capacity to regress and develop a transference neurosis" (Panel, 1972, p.135). Our theory was taken over by conflation of categories of health and pathology, and a potential risk turned into an actuality. Thus it was not only Anna Freud who described adolescence as a developmental disturbance.

We question the psychoanalytic view that normal adolescence is "a developmental disturbance," that adolescent reactions are "intermediate between mental health and illness," that extreme fluctuations of mood, affect, behavior, modes of thought, drive discharge and relationships are normal and to be expected, as are extreme negative reactions to parents and their values. In fact, according to that model, the *absence* of such adolescent turmoil would be worrying. The database of the psychoanalytic model of normal adolescence has been derived primarily from the intensive study of severely neurotic adolescents in life, in art, and sometimes through psychoanalysis. We suggest that the standard psychoanalytic model vividly describes *disturbed* adolescents.

For a large segment of the twentieth century, psychoanalysis offered the dominant theory and model of development. Thus the psychoanalytic descriptions of adolescence, which we contend are really about pathology, entered the cultural mainstream and were assimilated as delineating the norm (Devito et al 2000). Analogously to Young-Bruehl's description of "childism," we suggest that there is an active strand of "teenism," a prejudice against adolescents that operates unconsciously in the culture to attribute out-of-control sexuality and aggression to all young people.

Nevertheless we all have to acknowledge that the *capacity* for sexual and aggressive action in adolescence is a reality we must integrate. Adolescence is indeed a time at which troubled youngsters are at high risk of serious, even lethal, harm to themselves or others. Analysts feel at risk engaging with these dangerous potentials. In addition to the host of alternative treatments offered currently for dealing with adolescents, ranging from wilderness camps to CBT, DBT, MBT, ACT, and the continuing exponential increase in psychopharmacology, and so forth, we suggest that it may be hard for analysts to contradict the ongoing cultural and theoretical prejudices against adolescents embodied in the negative images described above. These "teenism" prejudices intensify therapists' own unconscious biases and fears, and the need to maintain repression of their own adolescence also contributes to a general reluctance fully to engage with adolescents.

In order to deal effectively with that real potential for feeling overwhelmed by work with adolescents, we need to revise the standard classical theory of adolescent development and technique. We must construct a theory that robustly supports the observable range of phenomena and offers us a framework for expanded technical options.

To do this we have to ask some fundamental questions:

1. Are people treating adolescents psychoanalytically?
2. Is psychoanalysis an effective treatment for adolescent disturbances?
3. How do the contributors to this volume think about adolescence as a phase of development?
4. What are the techniques being used in adolescent treatments?
5. Does the material in this volume point us to useful revisions of the psychoanalytic model of adolescent development and our understandings about adolescent treatment?

This book is a collection of examples of psychoanalytic clinical work with adolescents, with commentaries on each vignette by other child and adolescent analysts around the world. Throughout, we as editors, will reflect on what we can glean from each case, using the material of the book as a pool of data to help us answer the above questions.

Readers will note that the contributions are printed anonymously, with contributors to the volume listed alphabetically at the front of the book.[1] This format, which originated with the Parent Work Casebook (eds. Novick, Novick, Barrett, & Barrett 2020), provides a further layer of confidentiality

---

1 Where an author included a title, we have retained it.

to the clinical material and affords authors increased freedom in describing the work.

I

PASSAGE THROUGH PUBERTY

CHAPTER 1

RADHI – age 9

From Dead Mother to Internal Mother – The Journey into True Adolescence

This case presentation is of a girl who started treatment at the age of nine. She was seen in her school, where I worked as a Psychoanalytic Psychotherapist as part of the community work being done by our Psychoanalytic Society. The school is an ancient, stone structure spread over junior and senior sections. The school has allotted rooms to conduct our sessions for students, who on their own would not have access to psychoanalytic therapy. The therapy room is like a one room cottage a few steps away from the school building. It was earlier used as a storeroom facility.

The reason for the referral was that her grades had fallen miserably and, according to her teacher, she was exhibiting inappropriate sexual gestures during class. The inside child was covered by a patina of precocious adolescence trying to make believe that she was a woman in charge of her own destiny. What emerged in the consultation was a rather tragic history. What has saved her is a consistently caring aunt/mother and a supportive 'father' to form a good parental couple. Most of all it was her ability to adapt to the exigencies of her external circumstances and 'latch on' with full force to whatever good is given to her.

When the teacher had referred the case, the parent therapist had a meeting with the adoptive parents who were appreciative and eager to explore the option of therapy for Radhi. There were also bi-monthly meetings with the parents conducted by the parent therapist to give them a confidential space to talk about their difficulties in dealing with a disturbed child and keeping them informed of Radhi's development in therapy. Initially I saw Radhi once a week, and then, seeing her eagerness, in a couple of months, we moved to 4 times a week.

History

At the age of 8 months, Radhi lost her mother who was from the North, but had eloped at the age of 18 with a boy from the South. On the death of Radhi's mother, the maternal grandfather and maternal aunt adopted her and put their names as her Father and Mother, forming the parental couple. Radhi constantly talks about her love for her grandfather, as against the adopted mother. When therapy started Radhi referred to her adopted mother by her name, but of late has started calling her Mummy. Radhi's biological father was an alcoholic at the time of her birth and had been sent to a rehab facility. There is practically no contact between Radhi and her biological father. When Radhi's mother expired – it is not clear what she died of – there seemed to be no connection between her death and the father's alcoholism. There was some vague reference to "lack of calcium." Radhi's aunt also divorced her husband and returned back home and married again after adopting Radhi. The new husband seems a loving and supportive man. The loss of Radhi's mother has impacted the whole family and Radhi carries this unspoken anxiety of being a burden (actual and emotional) to the family. However the husband's mother would not allow Radhi to live with them, as she feared she might be a bad influence on her own grandchildren. Radhi lives with her maternal grandmother, who is bed ridden with sciatica.

During the course of the therapy I realized that Radhi had already been to 2 schools prior to the current one. It reinforced my feeling of her displacement – from home to home and school to school. An intriguing, as well as interesting, feature was Radhi's preoccupation with the story of the "Mad Dulhan" (mad bride), not only as an internalized phantasy object, but as an attempt to stay sane by placing the split-off part of herself who might have experienced being mad with grief, prior to words, into this character. It was also a romanticized phantasy of her mother who went "mad" with grief, of not being accepted, as she felt unaccepted. When asked where this idea came from, Radhi responded that these words had come to her mind while she had watched a Magic Show in which the Magician made things disappear and then brought them back again. We can see it as not only wanting to regain a live internal mother instead of a dead one, but also to reclaim parts of her lost infant self. In enacting this Mad Dulhan she showed a jump into precocious adolescence – pseudo-adhesive identity with Bollywood female stars as an escape from a confused, bewildered, child unable to cope with reality.

With this picture in mind, one couldn't help but admire her sheer determination to find a place for herself, her asserted confidence (albeit not secure) as a second skin in which she could believe in herself and feel valued. It seemed a strong defense against going "mad" with the sense of "nothingness." It made me wonder whether there had been a special bond between mother and child, that has somehow sustained her and allowed her to insist on her own worth, even as a precocious pseudo-self presented itself as part-child, part-adolescent. There was a manifestation of seductiveness to defend herself against both the longing and rage towards the Mother for leaving her.

First assessment session

In the very first assessment, Radhi communicated her sense of abandonment and the fear of it. I fetched Radhi from the classroom to the counseling room. She was wearing a thick sweater, had a runny nose and no handkerchief to wipe it. It was like she had come to session with a protective thick skin, yet communicated that she did not have the equipment to wipe off her unresolved "runny" grief and had come where she could get it. She sat in front of me but kept looking over her shoulder at the closed door. She seemed scared to be alone with me in a closed room. I told her that the lock on the door would stop other children from bursting in and thus we could maintain our privacy. She seemed satisfied with the answer. I spoke to her about the regular analytic procedure and setting. I asked her if she would like to tell me more about herself. She smiled and said, "What do I say about myself?" It seemed such a wry adult thing to say. I said, "Anything that is on your mind."

She seemed a little more relaxed now, and said, "Can I share a dream I often get? Miss, I often get this dream that Mom, Dad and me are driving through a jungle and then suddenly the car breaks down. Dad and Mom tell me to stay in the car and that they will be back soon, as they go in search for something, I am alone in the car. I get very thirsty and there is no water in the car so I get out of the car to search for my parents. I am scared as it is very dark and I keep calling out their names but nobody replies. I suddenly hear dogs, no not dogs, maybe wolves howling and when I turn I see their eyes shining. I start running but they are running behind me. I am running, running, running and then I wake up, but I am covered in sweat. Then I just lie awake for some time on my bed and then cuddle up tightly and try to go back to sleep." As Radhi was talking she kept rotating the pin that was holding the glass top on the table, round and round, but the fear of what she was saying wasn't reflecting on her face. On the other hand there was a constant smile when she was not talking.

I was aware that Radhi was telling me something that is very important to her but oddly it felt very theatrical. But being the first assessment I only said "Radhi you are telling me that you get some very scary dreams at night."

It seemed that the thick sweater was already her way of showing me the thick 'skin' she used as her protection from breaking out in a COLD sweat. The pasted on smile was like that on a clown's face, with painted tears on the eyes.

Radhi corrected me: "Miss not some, SAME! I get this SAME dream every few days."

ANALYST: "Radhi you were telling me something scares you, especially when you feel you are being left alone." She nodded enthusiastically in agreement

ANALYST: "But there is a smile on your face and I feel you smile every time you are nervous, maybe hoping that the fear will leave you if you keep smiling."

Radhi looked down and then looked up again with an even more dazzling smile. "Miss, I smile all the time. I like to smile. My Fairy Miss tells me smile and the world smiles with you, cry and you cry alone. You know Fairy Miss? I like Fairy Miss a lot. She once in a while even allows me to pull her cheeks. She has got very chubby cheeks. But now she is no longer my teacher. She was my teacher when I was younger."

Yet somehow, I also felt it all a bit rehearsed like she had churned everything she was saying to me a couple of times in her mind, the way she was turning the pin round and round on the desk holding the glass.

When I asked her if she was curious about this room, she replied that she has always been curious about what happens in this room.... had always wanted to come inside. "Today it feels God has finally answered my prayers. When I was younger I would keep walking around it hoping to see what is going on inside. But the windows were always shut so I could never make out. But then one day I stayed behind from school and when there was no one I threw a stone at the glass window." She looked in the direction of the closed window. "The glass broke but I couldn't see inside as the window is quite high from outside. Also the sound was loud so I ran away before anyone could see what I had done." She paused as she looked around and said "Also no one in school saw me but even if they had Fairy Miss would have saved me. That year Fairy Miss was my class teacher. Now I know what this room is." This did seem very Cinderella and Fairy Godmother identified. How much fact and phantasy were mixed up in her mind? Yet so intuitive that she has come to the right place.... hopes that the therapist will do magic and get her mother back again.... inside and secure as an always present internal mother.

When it was time, I told her I would take her back to her classroom, but she sat down tightly in her chair and said she liked it here, always wanted to be here and did not want to leave.

ANALYST: "Radhi it's time now, I have to take you back to class I will see you next Thursday again at 11:30."
RADHI: Her smile disappeared and she shrieked, "No you won't come."

In that moment I panicked a little but slowly reiterated that I would come. I was a bit overwhelmed by the force of it and said, "OK, Radhi, we can leave whenever you are ready to leave." In a few seconds she calmed down and meekly said "OK, Miss, I'll go back to class." I walked Radhi back to the landing of the staircase and waited till she reached the floor of her classroom and she waved indicating she had reached up safely.

Some other clinical vignettes:

Radhi had been selected for the annual day event and she was very excited about it. In the session she announced that she would show me the dance piece that she planned to perform on the stage. She started to hum a Hindi song and danced to it like a swaying snake. It was a provocative, sexual dance. The lyrics of the song translated in English were – the fires can burn,

14

the snakes can bite and the heavens can fall, but what I find unbearable is the pain of my broken heart. At this point we spoke about how she used her physical excitement to ease an indescribable pain.

In another session she sat on the couch and looked at me from below her eyelashes, seductively saying "Why are you so far from me? Come closer to me, come and sit here, right next to me," as she patted the seat next to her. Whilst speaking she kept twirling a strand of her hair with a forefinger. She reminded me of a nautch dancing girl as she enacted these scenes, possibly from Bollywood movies that she had viewed. At this moment she showed me her phantasy world where she was seductive and desirable and could use this charm to get someone to sit by her, in what was for her a painful empty space.

Radhi in one of the sessions informs me, "You know there is a new boy in class and the rumor is that he acts in a TV serial. A horror TV serial, where he plays the ghost. I haven't seen him yet and anyways it's what the students say. I haven't seen him yet so I am not saying it."

In the same session later she sang a song and danced to a Bollywood song.

Raat ke show ki do ticketein hain – (I have two tickets to a night show)
Khol ke purse dikhlaun kya – (Should I open my purse to show you)
Arey chipak ke baithoon sath tere main – (I will stick by your side as we sit closely)
Taxi mein le jaaun ga – (I will take you in a taxi)
Arey samajh na mujhko aisa waisa – (Do not underestimate me)
Mere batuve mein hai paisa – (I have money in my wallet)
Tujhe khilaunga jee bhar ke – (I will fulfill your hunger)
Garam samosa, idli ya dosa – (With samosa, idli or dosa)
Chal hatt tu meri hai Pepsi Cola – (You are my Pepsi Cola)
Main tera hoon Coca Cola – (I am your Coca Cola)

Tan tana tan tan tan tara

Arey chalta hai kya 9 se 12 – (Come with me from 9pm to midnight
for a late night movie)

She would often talk of having Bollywood personalities as her friends. Her
phantasy was that they would come to her school and choose to be her
friend.

Another story narration was of her and her boyfriend getting lost in the
jungle at night and falling asleep as they approach a river deciding to cross
it in the morning. When they wake up they find themselves tied together
with their backs to each other. The river is full of crocodiles and the jungle
has predatory animals. How and where could she escape?

Radhi also showed me a frightening and dissociated part of her
personality that was controlled by her mother's ghost. She could hear her
mother, who she claimed was in our session and communicates with her.
For everybody else her mother is dead, but for Radhi her mother is within
her. Her voice would change as she spoke to me as her mother, who would
threateningly warn me to look after her daughter and cause her no pain. The
ghost made Radhi do things that Radhi did. The sessions where the mother's
ghost appeared were frightening and difficult to bear.

Radhi often showed me a small coin that she was given to buy her lunch.
This made me realize that there was no one at home to give her a glass of
milk or any breakfast before school. In our sessions Radhi would often come
and touch my cheek, braid my hair, sit on my lap and use my hand to draw.
Often she hugged me at the end of the session. She would sing, dance, recite
poetry and I became the mother that would delight in her child.

Throughout the years of analysis, there was this mix of a precocious
adolescent and a devastated child. Radhi never shed a tear in her analysis
and kept the fragile grieving part untouchable and well defended. Often I

would find myself crying after the session, shedding the tears for her that she couldn't shed.

Her early drawing was of a butterfly and a starfish. The fishes were swimming from here to there or in and out of her life as they moved around managing two households. And I being the new star in her life and hence maybe the starfish. She a butterfly effervescent flying above everyone, away from the family jostling crowd and also feeling excluded. Slowly as she actively and wholeheartedly engaged in the treatment her drawings changed: there now emerged two drawings of her self and me both in human form. She was no longer a butterfly and I a starfish, not dead inanimate things, but living, breathing flesh and blood human.

A significant event happened in the second year of the therapy. I was entering the school lane, when I saw Radhi just ahead of me. I crossed over to the other side, thinking that I should not be encountering her outside of the therapy room. She saw me cross over and was furious. In the session Radhi rocked her chair precariously resulting in her falling down on the floor. I saw it as her desperate attempt to use the physical rocking motion to keep herself together, and also a re-enactment of the dropped baby that she is deep inside.

RADHI: I was waiting for you for so long. I have to go for tuitions and also then if I don't reach there on time then my tuition teacher will scold me.... she proceeded to ignore me.
ANALYST: I wonder if you felt ignored by me, when I didn't greet you outside and are now wanting to give me the same experience.
RADHI: I saw you coming in the lane
ANALYST: Yes, I saw you too, what about it?
RADHI: Shrugging her shoulders, "It felt odd, so I turned away."

She continued looking here and there, so I tried again.

ANALYST: Maybe you were already irritated at having to wait for me for an hour and then when you saw me out there on the street, I became someone else, someone who disappointed you by not being there when you wanted me.

She heard me out and repeated that I had made her wait an hour. She tossed her head from side to side, along with rocking the chair she was sitting on. She rocked harder and then lost her balance and the chair toppled and she fell. It wasn't much of a fall, but she felt very embarrassed and disconcerted. I extended my hand, asking whether she would like me to help her up. She did not take it, got up and patted her uniform and said, "You dropped me, it was your fault that I fell." She continued standing and said, "You pulled the desk from me, that's why I fell. It wasn't my fault. Had you not pulled the desk then I wouldn't have fallen. It is all your fault."

Even as she spoke, she realized that I was sitting away and couldn't have done so. But that angered her even more.

RADHI: "I am leaving, I don't want to stay." She continued muttering to herself as she packed her bag. "I shouldn't have waited for you." . . . . "You were laughing at me . . . . I want to leave, I cannot sit."
ANALYST: (Kindly) I think when others fall you enjoy laughing at them and when you fell you probably felt that I too was laughing at you and that felt very difficult to bear.
RADHI: I'm leaving, I don't want to listen your talk.

There were still 15 minutes left for the session and I said I would wait for her.

RADHI: "You keep waiting, I am going" and stormed out. She did not return.

Radhi does not take the hand of the therapist, seeing it more as the hand that has dropped her (the therapist that crosses over to the other side – like her mother crossed over to the other side of life – death – and left her waiting.) She is very clear in her internal world that she has been dropped, by someone moving away from her and leaving a gap-space-void. The humiliation of people distancing themselves from her and the pain it has caused her, deep inside and the helplessness of her not being the "Master of her Fate." Yet there is something quite positive if one hears beyond just the spoken word.... the fact that she has been waiting. She has not given up on the mother. She says "You keep waiting, I am going." While it can be seen as reversing the trauma and placing it in the therapist, both of them know that she WILL BE BACK. In this way she has never let go of the mother. Despite the Ghost mother, the Mad Dulhan, she has an internal good mother that she holds onto with faith and affection. This is my hope for her, a good life and good relationships ahead for her.

All the same it enabled an angry, fierce side of her personality to emerge. Hated parts of herself now freely flowed into the sessions. She constantly called me "mad." The phantasy object of the Mad Dulhan faded, as the madness now entered into the session and into me. She would often say that the sessions were polluting her. She needed to dip into the Holy River Ganges, to cleanse herself of all the dirt that I was putting into her. I became the abandoning Mother whose ghost she had to get rid of by throwing these angry red hot balls of fiery words. The hatred was often unbearable and I had to remind myself of the transference and the necessary working through. Slowly the hatred subsided and loving feelings emerged. It seemed she had managed to immerse the ghost in the holy Ganges. The mourning process seemed to have begun.

My "maternal" receptiveness seems to have led to a modification of Radhi's persecutory anxieties. As the sessions progressed Radhi started to slowly put the pieces of her family tree together and in that way there was a development of a recognition of relationships. A sense of not being alone but a part of something larger – a leaf in a tree full of so many leaves. Radhi also had gained some sense of my capacity to take in her experience, not fall apart or retaliate.

Thereafter, externally, Radhi started showing progress. At the end of that academic year she did well in her exams and her parents and teachers were happy with her results. She was also making friends at school and trying to participate in the extra-curricular activities of school.

With the outbreak of the COVID pandemic, and the ensuing lockdown, our work came to an abrupt halt. At that point we didn't know how long the lockdown would last. Also we were heading for the school summer break and Radhi's family expressed their desire to resume sessions post the break under the assumption that school would start on time. When the lockdown continued and Radhi had access to a device we resumed our sessions.

The below session is in our fourth year of her analysis and Radhi is now 13 years old.

We got on the call at our usual time in the afternoon. She took a few seconds to get into her room and closed the door behind her. She was carrying a book which she placed on the bed. She then aimed her device camera at her hands which were full of mehndi (Henna). (In India, this is also the decoration on the bride's hands on her wedding day). The picture of her and the boy that she often mentions in our sessions came to my mind. As she showed me the design I noticed there were 2 of everything, 2 paisleys that she had made, 2 flowers and then designs within it. And on her palm she had written her name. Radhi informed me that she had painted this herself. I thought of the two hands. Each painstakingly beautifying the other.
ANALYST: "I notice there are 2 of everything and a lot of design in it."

Radhi responded saying "my sister and me, my brother and me," then looked into the camera, "you and me.... wait I want to show you more."

She flipped through the picture book and asked me to hold on as she adjusted her phone to show me the drawings. As she was flipping the pages for me to see the drawings she was also talking to me where she informed me that she had done these drawings over the weekends.

Radhi flipped through her drawings as she showed me the drawing of a parrot, a kitten, an elephant, a rainbow, Diwali light festoons and then the drawing of a boy. But instead of the head there were these wires sprouting out as thoughts and each one had an object attached to it. At the end of one was the planet Jupiter, on the other was the planet Venus and so on with there being 5 planets (Jupiter, Venus, Mars, Mercury, Pluto).

I said that it was an interesting drawing and asked what comes to her mind when she looks at it.

RADHI: "Boy with lots of planet in his head."

ANALYST: "But it has no head."

RADHI: looked at it again and said "Yes because that is where the planets are there."

I wondered if she was showing me a boy that meant the universe to her. Or that she had a mother in her head watching her from up above in the stars.

ANALYST: "It seems like a drawing of a boy who has so much going on in his head."

RADHI: Smiled secretly "But I don't want to talk about it, right now, maybe I will tell you some other time.... I am going to draw something else today." She then propped the phone up in a way that I could see her draw but I couldn't see the drawing.

Every few seconds she would look up at me and then down and start to draw. I wondered if she was drawing my face.

ANALYST: "It seems I am not to see what you are drawing."

RADHI: "Wait – will show you when I finish."

As I waited, in my mind I went back to our in person sessions where very often she would sit and draw and I would watch over her.

She continued to keep looking at me every few seconds. There were also 2 knocks on the door where she shouted back saying that she is in class and she cannot let anyone in. I felt glad that she was protecting her session.

At some point she also started to hum a song as she continued to draw.

She then stopped drawing and was making a face where she was trying to touch her tongue to her nose. It was difficult and after a few attempts she managed.

ANALYST: "Well that was difficult but you managed it.... It seems you are also showing me how distant you feel we are and yet this is a new reality for both of us."

Radhi shrugged her shoulders and said "I don't mind it."

Some silence as she continued to draw.

She then made a V with her fingers and showed me.

ANALYST: "Are you showing me a 2, again?."

RADHI: "No, you forgot, it's the peace sign, you had taught me in one of our sessions in school."

I didn't remember teaching her but she thought that I had taught her something.

ANALYST: "You are saying that you remember the things that we spoke about in our sessions at school."

RADHI: "Ok finished," as she turned her drawing for me to see. She had drawn a girl with one eye shut, like winking and tongue stuck out in the corner. Just a while back she had been trying to touch her tongue to the tip of her nose. Is she ready to mourn and give up the breast – internalize it – to begin to have a capacity for herself to be this loving, giving breast?

RADHI: "This is me on a Sunday with 2 buns tied on my head. I make these kind of buns with my hair. (Her hair has grown long).

ANALYST: "So a more grown up you, with 2 buns but why only on Sunday?"

RADHI: "The rest of days we have school. I used to switch my video off but now we have to keep it on."

ANALYST: "So on Sunday you wear your hair like your mother's."

RADHI: Grinning: "Mummy gets tired" then looked away. "I help mom with the house work, ... earlier I didn't .... now I feel bad for her sometimes."

RADHI: Changed the topic and diverted my attention to the drawing. "And see I also made matching flowers on the T-shirt and pants." As she gave it her final, finishing touches.

It was time up as I informed her and she nodded and said bye.

It was very touching, to see her journey from when she couldn't accept her 'new' mother and feeling like the one outside the family, to her being able to reclaim her place in the family as a daughter. Her own awareness that she can now (albeit sometimes) think of how her mother feels, the work that she does, the tiredness that she must feel and then reach out to this mother to relieve her and becoming a 'helping hand,' not just a hand that admires its own design or decorates the other part of herself. This is about giving to someone else. There is an acceptance of herself as a third and the parents as a couple. Hopefully this is the 'peace' sign – her feeling that the Mad Dulhan now rests in peace .... that she is at peace with her world. That she is embarking into her adolescence and adolescence with a partner to love and an excitement about her own emerging sexuality. This is also her journey into ultimately becoming a caring and thinking adult.

COMMENTARY 1

This moving and comprehensive account highlights critical aspects of our clinical work with traumatized children and adolescents. It also illustrates how embedding psychological support in the school setting allows psychotherapists to reach students like Radhi, those most in need of and, in the United States as in India, customarily unable to access our services.

Radhi began psychoanalysis at age 9 through a psychotherapy program situated within her school by a local psychoanalytic society. Radhi presented as many troubled students do, with a precipitous decline in academic performance accompanied by unusual, "inappropriate" classroom behavior. Radhi's symptoms alongside her well-documented history of traumatic loss urgently called for psychological intervention. Her analysis with the author made it possible for Radhi to engage in several crucial psychological and developmental tasks:

- Grieving the loss of her mother in infancy (and the subsequent loss of her father to alcoholism).
- Retrieving and maintaining her original psychic connection to her mother.
- Internalizing the person of the analyst.
- Building new psychic structures that facilitated her healing and developmental transition from childhood to early adolescence.

Familiar experiences with traumatized children

Many of Radhi's features and those of the analysis are resonant with what we routinely observe and experience with traumatized children. The analyst describes Radhi as part-child/part-adolescent. She elaborates by describing a "manifestation of seductiveness to defend herself against both the longing and rage toward the mother for leaving her." Here is a quintessential way that children who fear being abandoned by those they most love and need engage in compromise formation, at once protecting themselves by not revealing their underlying authentic parts *and* over-exposing themselves, behaving in a seductive way toward, in Radhi's case, both peers and therapist.

Also familiar in the context of our work with traumatized children, the author comments to Radhi that her affect seems inconsistent with the content of what she is saying. She offers a thoughtful, substantial interpretation in response to hearing Radhi's scary dream: "But there is a smile on your face and I feel you smile every time you are nervous, maybe hoping that the fear will leave you if you keep smiling." Radhi then acknowledges smiling intentionally in order not to alienate people and perhaps in order to minimize the chances that she will be abandoned yet again by others. Similarly, Radhi's precocious, developmentally inappropriate seductiveness serves as a simultaneous survival tactic to draw people in *and* as a defense (against vulnerability) that keeps people out.

Radhi also engages in another common practice among children with histories of traumatic loss: frequent retreats into fantasy through identification. The author describes Radhi's "preoccupation with the story of the "Mad Dulhan" (mad bride), not only as an internalized phantasy object but as an attempt to stay sane by placing the split-off part of herself who might have experienced being mad with grief, prior to words, into this character. It was also a romanticized phantasy of her mother who went "mad" with grief, of not being accepted, as she felt unaccepted."

Radhi's connection to the "Mad Dulhan" reminds me of my experience with another 13-year-old girl, an abuse survivor who also lost her mother at an early age and came to my practice via a special program that provides long-term psychodynamic therapy to children in the American foster care system (https://www.ahomewithin.org) (Heineman et al 2015). Referring to my patient by the pseudonym "Lucy" I recall that she introduced me to a popular Japanese "manga" series, "Naruto" (https://www.netflix.com/title/70205012). The protagonist is an orphaned boy who has a demon fox sealed within him and grows up alone, hated by the villagers around him who believe that he himself *is* the demon fox. Lucy enacted her identification with Naruto by provoking a massive crisis in her relationship with her foster parents. It was only through psychodynamic interpretation *to the foster parents* regarding the defenses that children like Radhi and Lucy use that the situation was ultimately resolved.

Another parallel between Radhi and Lucy is their recurring dreams featuring themes of abandonment. Like Radhi, Lucy had the capacity not only to recall the dreams but to share them with me. Though traditional psychoanalysis is out of fashion, at least in the U.S., today's adolescents appreciate the significance of their dreams and can make use of psychodynamic interpretation in therapeutically meaningful ways.

Resilience

As the author introduces Radhi, she notes that "What has saved her is a consistently caring Aunt/mother and a supportive father to form a good parental couple. Most of all it was her ability to adapt to the exigencies of her external circumstances and latch on with full force to whatever good is given to her."

This describes what psychologists call "resilience." What fosters it, in addition to a child's constitution and whatever early "good" attachments a traumatized child may have had, is a caring connection with at least one trusted adult. Radhi's story illustrates the coping capacities and potential for resilience in children with major trauma and loss; *and* demonstrates that psychotherapy is likely needed to propel a child like Radhi into what the author describes in the conclusion as "her journey into ultimately becoming a caring and thinking adult."

The "crunch"

An impressive element of Radhi's work with the author is Radhi's ability to bring her conflicts and struggles right into the room. Radhi's difficulty leaving at the end of each session makes perfect sense given her life history. She's finally found someone who can understand and hold her; naturally it's extremely difficult for her to let go. Radhi brings her sexuality and her seductiveness into the session when she performs a Bollywood song for her therapist, and Radhi's therapist becomes deeply and intimately engaged with her. She learns about not just Radhi's historic drama but her real-world, immediate problems; for example, not having access to breakfast before school. (Another piece of rationale for school-based therapy.) A compelling aspect of the countertransference is the author's own tears following the sessions in which Radhi never cries.

It therefore surprised me when she decided to cross to the other side of the street when she encountered Radhi outside of school! Radhi's reaction reflects her acute sense of rejection and abandonment in this spontaneous encounter. I wonder if the author's choice reflects less of a difference between American and Indian culture than a difference between traditional psychoanalytic culture and school culture. In American schools, teachers are generally accessible and "friendly." While seeing one's teacher at the grocery store or ice cream shop is at once exciting and jarring, as children tend to assume teachers exist only within school walls, it's hard to imagine a teacher deliberately avoiding contact upon running into a student in the world. The beauty of the school-based psychoanalytic office is the integration of emotional care into the child's natural daily habitat. When in the author's position, I choose a small friendly wave and a smile to feel out whether the child might like to wave back, or perhaps stop for a chat. That said, Radhi's sense of abandonment and loss in this encounter brings out a whole other side of her psyche. She is subsequently able to partner with her therapist to proceed in genuinely grieving the actual loss of her mother. Perhaps this "empathic failure" represented an important enactment. In any case, as we say in the U.S., "all's well that ends well."

Parent guidance

Concurrent, biweekly parent guidance/therapy allowed Radhi's new parents to understand and support Radhi (and presumably to manage their own reactions to her complexities). Parent work always offers parents an outlet, a sense of perspective, a source of practical recommendations. It can also prove crucial to mitigating the "secondary trauma" that relatives, foster parents or other caregivers may experience with a child or adolescent who has a significant history of trauma and loss.

The value of school-based psychological care

Radhi's is a classic case of a child with a trauma history that is clearly defined and documented. It's also a typical school referral in that the symptoms of children so frequently arise in their classrooms, i.e., her grades had fallen "miserably," a common and predictable symptom of childhood distress. How efficient and useful that Radhi's teacher could make a referral directly to a school-based psychotherapist. And how amazingly fortunate that the therapist was able to respond to Radhi's "eagerness" (urgency?)

by offering her four sessions per week, surely the appropriate frequency of treatment for a child with her distinctly tragic history. Of course, Radhi's developmental journey also offers lessons and clinical wisdom for our work with other, more fortunate children navigating less acute or extreme trauma, loss, and/or complex familial relationships alongside their developmental unfolding into adolescence.

It is extremely useful to consider the case of a child who has had access to psychoanalysis who is not, like most American child psychoanalytic patients, from a privileged family with substantial financial means and cultural capital. From the author's description, Radhi sounds like one of many American children who live in much more modest environments and may have had – in ways that are independent from or related to these circumstances – significant disruption and loss in their lives. As American schools begin to adopt "trauma-informed" or "trauma-responsive" approaches to student well-being, I hope that we too will be able to provide more extensive psychological support to children like Radhi. A "former storeroom facility" is a fine "office" in which to start. Creating the space is what's important.

I finished reading about Radhi exactly where I started – in my home, sheltering from the COVID-19 pandemic as well as the cold winter weather of the Northeast United States. I chuckled at the author's final description of Radhi at 13, engaging her in playful, adolescent ways during their remote video session. This phase of their relationship illustrates how child psychotherapy continues robustly despite the social distance measures taken by India, the U.S., and countries around the world in response to the global public health crisis. I'm reassured, somehow, to imagine Radhi and the author in India, like my own teenage patients and myself in the US, continuing to learn and grow together. Perhaps none of us are as far from each other as we might have imagined.

COMMENTARY 2

In the case of Radhi, a young girl was referred for therapy at nine years of age due to fallen grades and acting out behavior. The material presented throughout the treatment is quite heightened and very overwhelming for both patient and analyst.

Radhi's history reveals that she experienced early childhood trauma, loss, and abandonment at eight months of age when her mother died. Following the loss, she was adopted by her maternal grandfather and her maternal aunt (her mother's sister), who is referred to in the case as the "Father/Mother" and "parental couple." Early in the treatment, Radhi reveals that she feels close to her grandfather, but distant from her aunt, who adopted her.

What I find interesting from a psychoanalytic point of view is the symbolic parallel between Radhi's feelings about her aunt and what initially transpires between Radhi and the therapist. The parallel begins early in the treatment when Radhi reveals that she loves her grandfather, but does not feel as close to her aunt. She calls her aunt by her first name rather than "Mummy."

In the initial session of treatment, Radhi asks what she should talk about and the therapist responds, "Anything that is on your mind." This encourages Radhi to share a recurring dream, and asks, "Can I share a dream I often get?" and begins telling that she is with her Mom and Dad, then abandoned, and as dogs chase her, the dogs turn into scary wolves. At the conclusion of the dream, the therapist says, "Radhi, you are telling me that you get some very scary dreams at night." Radhi replies, "Miss, not some, SAME! I get this same dream every few days." As the treatment progresses, Radhi continues to discuss her dreams in her sessions and reveals a dead, abandoning, ghostlike introject, which is common in children who have experienced early childhood trauma.

In this moment, when Radhi emphatically corrects the therapist stating "SAME" instead of "some", she communicates her deep longing for her mother, while also exhibiting fear of attachment and the anger she feels about the loss. We do not know what Radhi's attachment was like before her mother died. Were they securely attached? At the early age Radhi experienced the loss, she and her mom were not separate: they were one together, the *SAME*. Was she stuck in a state of "nothingness" from her early loss and trying desperately to release her pre-verbal feelings that she has no words for?

These early mismatches with her therapist, coupled with expressing the strong feelings that continued to overwhelm her, allowed her to work through her pre-feelings with the therapist regarding the loss of her mother and work through her feelings to have a positive attachment to her aunt, as she entered adolescence. With therapy, Radhi eventually calls her aunt "Mummy."

EDITORIAL REFLECTION

This chapter presents us with numerous themes significant to thinking about adolescence. We are helped to engage with the nature of development, looking at what will constitute real adolescent experience, in contrast to defensive pseudo-maturity. The role of trauma in disrupting development and functioning, and derailing the passage into adolescence, is clearly recognized. The critical importance of availability of therapeutic intervention is manifest, and psychoanalysis as the effective treatment of choice for severely traumatized young people is validated. We are reminded of the enormous human and economic potential in school-based psychotherapy services to meet children where they are and to meet the needs of underserved populations who might otherwise have no access to psychoanalytic treatment.

There are also interesting technical questions examined. The contributors all acknowledged the importance of the analyst's persistence and willingness to be open to all the intense emotions of the history and present situation. There was courage in grappling with the fallout from moments of friction, misunderstanding, dysynchrony. This chapter illustrates a point we have articulated about the emotional muscles therapists need; perhaps treating adolescents calls upon the reserves of emotional muscle that therapists develop in the course of their work (Novick, J. and Novick, K.K. 2012).

Another dimension vivid in the chapter is the similarity across cultures of the impact of early trauma. Content and symbols may be different, but the course of treatment is familiar to therapists from different countries. This chapter allows us to raise the question of whether the tasks of adolescence are similar or different in different cultures. Certainly this child in India had to come to terms with her history, her aggression, and her sexuality. These challenges are the same in any country, but perhaps we can usefully consider the effects of different meanings, expectations, and modes of validation for the adolescent. How will these affect Radhi as she grows into middle and later adolescence and the confusion of separation and separateness and their impact on individuation becomes central and is often influenced by culture (DeVito et al 2000)?

CHAPTER 2

KEVIN – age 10

"Pen-15"

Kevin entered analysis at age 10 ½, at the start of fifth grade. He had been an easygoing baby but had developed allergies and asthma during his third year when his mother was pregnant. After Alex (the younger brother) was born, Kevin's relationship with his mother became mutually ambivalent and Kevin and his father turned to one another in a way that left the family with two "couples" – Mother and brother and Father and Kevin. This pattern contributed to an overly intense relationship with his father and negative oedipal conflicts for Kevin. By first grade, teachers noted impulsivity and poor self-control. Kevin was not reading and was falling behind academically. Aggression and teasing between the brothers permeated family life. For the next few years, Kevin progressed through elementary school with consistent support from an array of tutors, without whom his compulsion to procrastinate led to academic underperformance. By the end of fourth grade, he was socially and emotionally immature at school. At home his regressed and provocative behavior controlled his frustrated parents. Mindful of the approach of middle school, they contacted me for an evaluation which helped them recognize and accept a recommendation for analysis.

Though bright and verbal, Kevin was an anxious boy with internal and internalized conflicts. He viewed his brother as a rival for Mother's attention and ambivalent feelings and active-passive conflicts were evident. He was defensively placating and solicitous and used "passive into active," "denial in fantasy," and immature, magical thinking to avoid painful affect and narcissistic injury. Fixations were noted at all pre-oedipal levels and his harsh conscience indicated poor oedipal phase resolution. A symptom of bedwetting was revealed and active-passive conflicts and persisting anxiety continued to compromise his school performance.

During the early weeks of analysis Kevin settled into games of Uno and War, that quickly gave way to blackjack and rummy. He struggled with a temptation to cheat, sneaking peeks at the cards and trying to "stack the deck" in his favor. It was hard for him to tolerate losing. When I noticed him giving me sidelong glances, I thought he was wondering if I would notice his cheating and, if so, how I would respond. At the same time, I was also struck by the difficulty he had handling the cards. I thought it odd that a 5th grader who was also an accomplished pianist would have such poor hand and finger coordination.

I began to share these observations and thoughts with Kevin, and we noticed a pattern. After doing well, he would do poorly; any success was quickly followed by misdeals, dropped cards, and poor play. Bragging was followed by mistakes and failure. When I asked what he thought I would think or feel should he beat me, he admitted that he thought I'd get angry. His smile when I asked this question led us to begin to wonder about the excitement he seemed to feel in anticipation of what might occur.

One morning, after coming late, Kevin struggled as he tried to shuffle the cards. As I noticed this and wondered about its meaning he observed – something he was more and more taking the initiative to do – that he was avoiding telling me how his parents had gotten into an argument the night before. Kevin had read about a heightened terrorist alert and had told his mother he was worried. She was sympathetic but Father had asserted that it was unreasonable to be worried. I asked Kevin why he thought he'd been reluctant to tell about this and why he'd been late and been having trouble handling the cards or playing well? Though he said he could not think of any reasons, he associated to our discussion about feeling excited by thoughts of others getting upset or angry.

Kevin's compensatory use of exaggeration to ward off narcissistic hurt came more into the work. When he slipped on the walk leading to my office, he seemed embarrassed but responded defensively. He bragged that he would beat me at cards and throughout the session was preoccupied with the "fanciness" of his shuffling technique. He bragged that as a soccer goalie he had played "400 games in the past year" and had allowed "only 51 goals." When I wondered about the possible truthfulness of what he was claiming, he said it was his father who had given him those statistics. It seemed he wished his dad were there to vouch for him. I was sympathetic and said it seemed he was feeling poorly about something. He continued to insist his story was true but as he did, he committed a misdeal, dropped more cards, and eventually dropped the entire deck. Finally, he could admit he was telling a story, but couldn't say why he felt such a need to do so. What seemed noteworthy was the simultaneous presence of excitement and guilt.

One Monday morning when Kevin brought his unfinished breakfast, he explained he'd overslept. He'd been unable to fall asleep after spending the night before at a friend's home. He bragged that he'd driven his friend's tractor to plow snow but then admitted that he'd only steered a bit while his friend did the plowing. As we began to play rummy, he continued his bragging, claiming he had an "excellent" hand and showing how he'd been dealt all four aces. Nevertheless, he lost that game and the three that followed. We were again able to notice together the two sides of his conflict. When he felt jealous or inferior, he compensated with bragging and showing off. When he really was doing well, he faltered and did poorly. As Kevin recognized this pattern, he began to wonder how these two ways of feeling and behaving could co-exist.

Somatic tendencies came into the work when Kevin complained of a migraine. After winning the first rummy game he said he thought he'd concentrated better because he was aware of how his head felt and he'd tried to reduce the pain by thinking slowly and deliberately. I asked if he was giving us a clue and wondered if, to succeed, he needed to suffer or feel he was being punished. Kevin seemed thoughtful.

From his parents, with whom I met fortnightly, I'd learned of increased episodes of bedwetting. Shortly after, Kevin brought this to his analysis when, in explaining his occasional lateness for his sessions he complained that there were "problems at home with the laundry." Either it had not been done so he had no clean shirts to wear or "someone" had used too much detergent. When I wondered how this could keep occurring, he admitted that he had not been responsible about laundering his sheets. He acknowledged his embarrassment. We discussed that it would be hard to master a trouble if he felt he could not talk about it in his analysis.

Kevin's struggle with feeling guilty came into the work in another way as he anticipated going to Florida with his family for spring break. His teacher would be staying home over the vacation. He worked diligently over a couple of sessions on a picture for her. It featured a large sun with the words "Florida Sunshine." He carefully filled in the large block letters with metallic colored pencils. He imagined as he colored that she would like it so much that she would hang in on the classroom door for all to see. As he drew and talked, I noticed that he spoke with the voice of a younger child. I found myself thinking that displaced onto his relationship with his teacher, and at times onto me in the transference, were feelings from his early relationship with his mother. He'd felt rejected and abandoned by her when Alex was born but then felt guilty over his anger. Now he felt guilty to be the one that was leaving, as though he were abandoning his teacher. Even as he felt this way, he yearned to be remembered and favored by her.

After coming late one morning, Kevin complained it was his father's fault as he'd been unable to find his necktie. But as we noticed together how he banged his head on the wall while hanging up his coat and dropped several cards while trying to shuffle, I asked if his conscience was letting us know there was more to the story. He sheepishly admitted that the real reason he was late was that he'd been unable to find his homework. He'd worked hard on it the night before but had not put it away in his backpack. He agreed it seemed important that he would need to punish himself in this way.

The elusive homework was for an oral book report he was to give on a book about George Washington. On the day of the report Kevin said his father would be going with him to school to hear it. In a boastful way he described how he'd added material that wasn't in the book as he planned to tell his class that his father's "great, great, great, uncle," a "Captain in the Revolutionary War," had been Washington's "right-hand man." As the session progressed, I asked Kevin his thoughts about how he was acting and, while he was at first defensive, he was able to recognize his excitement and boastful attitude. When I asked his thoughts about this, he became reflective and admitted that he'd not remembered that it was the day for the report until his mother had reminded him. Again, we noted his wish to be fancy and the guilt that seemed to accompany it.

This discussion coincided with the further development in the work of negative oedipal material, conflicts about masturbating, and elaboration of active-passive conflicts. When Kevin went on a field trip with his class, he got into an excited tag game and, while trying to jump through the split branches of a tree, his knee became painfully stuck. Afterward, he limped so severely that his teacher called his mother who took him for x-rays that were negative. After arriving several minutes late, the next morning he described how he'd kept "rolling around in bed," waiting for his parents to finally call him. I asked if we might take it to mean that he'd spent part of his analysis in bed. What could we understand from that? Though he resisted this idea at first, Kevin became thoughtful as he noted his clumsiness as he tried to shuffle cards, dropping several on the floor. When he commented, "I always seem to have to be doing something with my hands," I wondered if that connected to the idea of bringing something from bed. In response, though he at first denied this, he smiled and became somewhat silly saying, "Well, sometimes I touch my arm, or my shoulder, or my back...."

As we continued with this material, Kevin brought more evidence of his defensive use of exaggeration to ward off feelings of inferiority. As I tried to wonder about this with him, he complained I was being critical of him and retreated into drawing pictures, taking pains to make sure I couldn't see what he was drawing. This went on for a few days and at the end of each session he would resist my reminders about the time and ignore my comments about how it seemed hard for him to stop these projects that he seemed to want to keep private. As he drew I observed and asked Kevin if he could notice that he was tugging at his lips, cheeks, and eyebrows while he was working.

One morning, abandoning his drawing, he talked about participating in a horseshow. He boasted that he'd received an overall achievement award. As he talked about this I asked if he could notice that while he seemed proud, he was covering his mouth with his hand so that his words were hard to hear. He then admitted that while he'd received the award, he'd also finished in fifth place in each of three the events. He could then notice that he was trying to make it all seem more "fancy" than it really was.

When he came late another morning, he was preoccupied with a stain on his shirt. At first, he said he'd spilled some of his breakfast but then, feeling guilty, admitted he was lying. In fact, he'd overslept and had no breakfast. As he talked, we noticed that he was again tugging on his face and pulling at his fingers. I commented that since he'd again spent part of his session in bed, was there something he wanted to bring from there? He smiled and with embarrassment asked if I was referring to his "tentacles." I was struck by this word choice. He had obviously meant to say "testicles." By saying "tentacles" it seemed he was alluding to conflict he felt about touching this growing and changing part of himself. I asked if he noticed that he had used the wrong word and wondered if there was something he was finding hard

38

to talk about. He smiled and asked if I meant "Pen 15," explaining this was his "code word" for it. This confusion of words and defensive use of a code illustrated how discombobulated Kevin felt about the bodily changes he was experiencing and trying to understand. While his code word focused on what was on the outside, his slip of the tongue – "tentacles" for "testicles" – revealed awareness of his inner genital sensations and his burgeoning desire to touch himself.

During the sessions that followed Kevin used the dictionary to look up words he had questions about, including "penis, vagina, uterus, womb, testicles, etc." As he conducted this "research," as we came to call it, he struggled with excitement. He could not bring himself to say the word "sex" and shared the idea that a man "peed" into a woman. As he focused on drawing faces of cartoon characters, I was led to comment that it seemed he was avoiding everything below the neck. He confessed that the evening before he had spent a long time in the bathroom using gel to make his hair stand up. I asked if there was a connection between wanting his hair to stand up and his thoughts about "Pen 15." Smiling, he agreed and said a friend claimed to have fallen on his penis when it was stiff and had broken it. I said that hearing such a claim could make a guy feel worried. He said it felt like his penis "hurt" sometimes when it got "stiff."

After this apparent focus on his external genitalia, Kevin again turned inward as he began to bring more about his bodily worries and symptoms. I began to appreciate the degree to which the growth and changes he was experiencing in his testicles brought to the foreground his old prelatency worries and excited fantasies.

Over several sessions we noted how he breathed in a noisy way, claiming it was a symptom of his asthma. We also noted how he was compelled to clear his throat, cough, and blow his nose. He insisted these symptoms only occurred in his sessions. Afterward, he was untroubled by them. As he kept himself active with card games, he added concerns about food to his bodily worries. He said he only ate salad most days at school. The thought of eating cafeteria food left him with a gagging feeling. As he became more invested in noticing himself, he brought more symptoms. He had become sick during a soccer game when thinking about a burrito he had eaten and when he wondered why this would cause him to feel sick, I asked if the shape had anything to do with it? He responded with a grin and said, "Oh, 'Pen-15' again!" He admitted he could never eat hot dogs unless they were grilled and charred. As he tried to explain he associated to how boiled hot dogs were pink and actually looked like "Pen 15s."

When I asked Kevin how he might have come to have such thoughts and worries about hot dogs, at first, he couldn't say. I wondered if there might have been times when he was little when he was surprised to see someone's penis. He responded by recalling how, as a small boy he'd often showered with his father. He thought this had gone on until he was five or six. He also recalled bathing with his brother.

As the school year came to an end, Kevin anticipated going to camp for part of the summer. We noted that he'd miss a few weeks of analysis. He avoided his missing feelings by retreating again into drawing. He made several versions of the emblem of his camp and then drew scenes from a cottage where he'd be reunited with his family when his camp was finally over. During these sessions that preceded our first extended time apart, we were able to work productively on Kevin noticing his defenses. His tendency to be grandiose and exhibitionistic as a defense against feeling small, lonely, or having missing feelings was frequently observed and acknowledged.

During the vacation I received a letter from Kevin. He reported with pride that he'd avoided visits to the camp nurse (something that had happened several times the summer before). When he returned in the fall, though, he recalled somewhat sheepishly that after mailing the letter to me he'd gone to the nurse with the worry that he'd eaten nuts in a cookie and that they would make him throw up. It was in this way that Kevin began to bring more about his bodily worries and symptoms into his analysis.

After returning from the summer vacation and with the start of sixth grade, Kevin's negative oedipal conflicts and pregnancy fantasies and fears came more to the fore. He brought examples of courting his father's attention (often at the expense of any attention his brother or mother might receive from Dad). He had excited ideas about projects that he and Dad would work on ranging from creating a "special workshop" for Kevin in the basement, to plans for building models and boats together. He brought catalogues of models and tools that he imagined his father would buy for him and bragged that his father had given him his own "belt sander." He boasted his father had said that Kevin could design a pergola for the family garden and once the design met with father's approval, they would build and install it together. As these ideas poured from him, I asked Kevin if he could notice the "fancy" sound of all that he was saying. While he mostly dismissed my questions, he eventually admitted that the projects were ones for which he felt both unprepared and incapable. He began to acknowledge how important it felt for him to have his dad want to make these things just with him.

Over several sessions Kevin brought this "courting" behavior to the transference. He drew pictures of flowerbeds that I might plant outside my window using his designs and selection of flowers. Sensing that I was less responsive to this approach than his father, he spent sessions reading to me from biographies of sports heroes. It was clear that he was not much interested in the content of the books and his goal was not to show me what he was learning. Rather, as he kept stopping to ask me questions, it became evident that he wanted me to show off to him; to be the one to tell him what I knew of these men and their accomplishments. I told Kevin that it seemed he was behaving with me as he behaved with his father, but he ignored my words and redoubled his efforts.

I then cautioned that I had a thought to share that might be hard to listen to. After receiving permission to proceed, I said it seemed as though he was courting me, as a woman might court a man. This led to discussions of this word, "court," which he looked up in the dictionary, and of his observations of his mother and his father. We recalled then how, in his descriptions of his interactions with his dad, it seemed he wanted to be the one to whom his father was most attracted. I wondered if it seemed to him that he wanted to take his mother's place with his dad.

With contempt he asked, "You mean you think I want to be my dad's wife?" I said it was complicated but that, in a way that was what I meant. I wondered if he could see that he'd been acting that same way with me. Even as he asserted that the idea was "disgusting," a smile came to his face and he asked, "What kind of coffee do you like?" When I asked why he wanted to know, he said he'd just had a thought of buying me coffee and surprising me with it. I said the idea of surprising me with a gift like that was the kind of thing a wife might do for her husband. It seemed a confirmation of what we had been talking about. After a thoughtful pause he associated to Christmas when he had not even noticed what his mother had given his father as a gift. He realized he had not wanted to think about it or their relationship. He agreed that it seemed he could not let himself know what the "competition" was doing. While I said that I thought there was much more for us to understand about all of this, my thought was of how painful it had been for Kevin to feel the loss of his mother's attention when his brother was born, and of how he had perhaps subsequently turned increasingly to his father.

By the end of sixth grade, Kevin remained passive and provocative in sessions. He started sentences without finishing them; asked questions to which he already knew the answer; and resisted opening the door when he arrived, waiting for me to open and hold it for him. I continued to interpret his passivity and wish for me to be the active one. When he connected to how his father always held the door for his mother, I noted that it again seemed he wanted to be like a woman with me so that I would be the man. Though he acted as though he ignored this interpretation, he began to talk of other men, like his great uncle and an elderly neighbor near his cottage, recalling how they would invite Kevin to work on projects with them in their workshops whenever he would visit them.

An important breakthrough came when Kevin angrily described a Saturday morning outing with Father. Mother had gone to the market with his brother and Kevin was to run errands with Dad. Perhaps partly in response to conflict that had been growing as a result of our work, Kevin had resisted the request that he accompany his father to the downtown library. He had balked at his father's suggestion that he wear boots and gloves. Then, when they had parked at some distance from the library, Kevin had erupted in angry tears and told his father he would not get out of the car unless his father promised to hold his hand all the way to the library. As Kevin and I worked on this material I was able to explore with him the seductive, passive, and feminine aspects of his behavior. He was initially defensive and resistant but was sobered when I asked what he would have done if, while walking to the library, hand in hand with his father, he had encountered a school friend on the sidewalk. He was stunned to think of this and admitted he would have jerked his hand away from his father and would have felt embarrassed to have the friend see him that way. It was through this lens of comparison that Kevin could begin to feel conflict about the way he had been behaving with his dad.

When Kevin and his brother were left with a sitter who made cookies with them, Kevin got excited and began eating the uncooked dough. When he would not stop, he was sent to his room where guilt and worry overcame him. He felt sick and imagined that he would vomit. When I asked why he'd been so unable to control himself, he remembered thinking that the dough would expand, and his stomach would explode. When I asked what that made him think of, he associated to when his mother had been pregnant. I asked if he'd thought she'd gotten pregnant from something she had eaten. He laughed but said that probably had been what he'd imagined when he was little.

Another evening with a sitter, Kevin teased and excited his brother by drinking large gulps of soda and belching. After saying this, he stopped talking and said he did not want to tell me the next part. I asked if not telling was connected to not wanting to give up an excitement that he wanted to keep. After a pause he agreed but then proceeded. His brother had laughed so hard that he'd wet and soiled his pants. As Kevin told how he got sent to his room, I noted that he pulled his fingers and twisted and rubbed his hands on the desk and on his arms and said it seemed he was showing us there was something more to understand. He said that he had asked the sitter if she would tell his parents about how he'd behaved and was thoughtful when I said this seemed an indication of a wish to get punished. He recalled how he had spent the rest of the evening bringing to his room from his basement workshop all the models that he and his father had made. His idea had been to create a "display" of them. I said it seemed that he thought of the models as their prized creations and asked if he could see a connection between the models and the pregnancy and baby ideas we had been discussing. It seemed he thought of them as "babies" that he and Dad had made together.

He thought of his mother's ongoing struggles with weight and said he'd "caught" her "sneaking" ice cream from the carton in the kitchen. She'd been embarrassed. He became angry and complained that she shouldn't be so critical of what he eats. He described how concerned she is about the family's food, buying only organic products and refusing to let the boys eat anything containing sugar or butter.

I noted with Kevin that he'd stressed that his mother had been "sneaking" the ice cream and asked if that made him think of anything. He remembered, from our previous talks about his "research," that he'd told me that, when he was little, he used to "sneak" out of his room to go to the door of his parents' room. He'd described in detail how he'd become adept at turning off the baby monitor in his room so they wouldn't hear him. He'd been curious to know what his parents were doing in their bedroom. He thought this had occurred when his mother had been pregnant with Alex.

A thoughtful look came over his face. After a pause I said there was something I thought we still needed to understand. Why had he felt so compelled to get his brother excited? And why did this keep happening when they were left with a sitter? Kevin then associated to a sitter he'd had in preschool. She'd had a boyfriend. I asked if he had ever come to the house, but Kevin said he didn't think so. What he did remember was the sitter talking on the phone with her boyfriend and getting into excited arguments. Once she'd gotten Kevin into it by handing him the phone without the boyfriend knowing. Kevin said he'd never told anyone the words the boyfriend had used and described how he'd yelled obscenities into the phone. I interpreted that it seemed that, just as the boyfriend had "stuck" excited, scary words into Kevin, he was repeating that now with Alex. He recalled that the next time the sitter had come he'd felt angry and wanted nothing to do with her. He agreed when I said it seemed he felt jilted by her. I asked if this was how he must have felt about his mom when his brother was born. Now, every time there was a sitter, a "little boy" part of him wanted to recreate those old experiences and feelings; only now he wanted to be the one to cause the upset. Kevin became quiet and thoughtful. He said how angry he felt over all the old experiences – with Mom and his brother, with the sitter and her boyfriend. They kept "messing up" his life.

In the weeks that followed I began to be aware of a gradual change occurring in Kevin. He seemed calmer and more inwardly directed. In the transference, I felt less of a sense of preoccupation with me and my thoughts or feelings about him. Oftentimes he would sit in silence, something he had almost never done before. When he spoke, he shared not just the events of his school day or time spent with friends or family, but ideas about what motivated his thoughts and behavior as well as the behaviors of others.

During this time the family learned they would be getting the puppy that Father had long wanted. Kevin found himself thinking not of the new puppy but of the death of their old dog, which had occurred when Kevin was seven. There'd been no preparation. When he was picked up after a sports practice, Kevin was told of the death (by euthanasia) and had sobbed all the way home. He'd been unable to catch his breath. As he tried to talk about this and the "funeral" that followed, we noticed that he struggled to suppress a smile, even as there were tears in his eyes. He agreed when I said the smile seemed an effort to keep the tears away. Finally, he was able to cry and realize how it had hurt to have not been told about what would happen until it had occurred. After gaining his permission to offer a thought, I said I thought he'd felt the same way when Alex had been born. He'd never really understood what was happening until it was over. His brother was there; he felt replaced and left out. He agreed this was so.

Further work on this material continued through the duration of the spring and early summer. As Kevin strove for mastery and maturity, he decided to transport himself to his summer sessions by riding his bicycle each morning. While there were increasing signs of independence and a turning away from his family toward activity with peers, the return to analysis and to seventh grade in the fall brought with it a return to work on his anger with Alex and corresponding conflicted feelings of oral greed.

One morning Kevin came in wheezing and having trouble breathing. This had been happening in his sessions with some frequency and while he dismissed it as a symptom of his asthma, when he admitted that the wheezing had only begun after he'd entered my office, he became less defensive and was thoughtful. He then told of how he'd attended a church picnic the day before, which happened to be Alex's birthday. He'd eaten some casserole and thought he tasted nuts in it. He'd panicked and gulped water to dilute their

46

impact. He'd worried he'd made himself ill. He then thought of feeling angry with Alex later in the afternoon when he'd interrupted Kevin and his visiting grandmother while they were watching TV. He thought of his grandmother's failing health and admitted he was wondering what of her possessions would come to his family should she die. After these comments we noted that the wheezing had abated.

When I met with his parents later that day, I learned more of the story. On the weekend Dad had interrupted several excited fights between Kevin and Alex. At the picnic, when they were playing touch football, he'd had to intervene to stop Kevin who was wrestling Alex to the ground. It was after that occurred that Kevin ate the casserole and became worried that he'd vomit. I later shared this version of the story with Kevin. At first he was defensive and denying but as he shed angry tears and noticed that the wheezing had again abated he was able to reflect further upon his old and deep feelings of anger about Alex's arrival and how he'd replaced Kevin as his mother's baby.

Much effort to address and work through this anger followed. Alex started an analysis and began to tell his parents that, when he was younger, Kevin had tormented him by pinching his penis. I learned of this through the parents. When Kevin admitted that he'd gotten into another wrestling match with Alex, during which he'd kneed him in the groin, I gained permission to share with him what I'd learned. Kevin's response was to struggle with tears and a combination of anger, shame, and excitement. We noticed that his breathing again became labored and wheezing. Though he continued to deny any memory of pinching his brother's penis he admitted to patting him on the backside, "You know, like a football coach does with his players." After saying this, Kevin complained of times when his father had not been private, especially on family trips when Alex's regressed behavior had either resulted in Alex sharing a room with Mother and Kevin with Father or Dad sharing a room with both boys. Kevin complained that his dad left open the bathroom door and exposed himself to his sons. After he spoke of this, Kevin and I recalled his early history of showering with his father. During sessions that followed, as he tried to remember more from his early childhood, we both noticed how little he was able to remember about his brother until Alex was four or five. Kevin agreed that much remained repressed regarding his early interactions with Alex.

An apparent screen memory was then recovered. Kevin recalled how his parents would dress up and take Kevin to parties. When he was seven, he'd gone "trick-or-treating" with an aunt and cousin while his parents stayed with Alex. He remembered coming upon a mother with her little girl of about four, Alex's age at the time. She was dressed as an angel. Kevin was in an elaborate skeleton costume with a bulb he could squeeze to make it look like blood was dripping from his bones. He thought he remembered making the girl become frightened by the bloody display but later acknowledged that what really had happened was that the girl wasn't really frightened. She'd taken her mother's hand and turned to her for reassurance. Kevin remembered feeling jealous that she had her mom while he was with his aunt.

Subsequent material involved further work on Kevin's passivity, and particularly how it seemed to contribute to his ongoing compulsion to procrastinate. Again, I observed that frequently Kevin failed to finish sentences. As he thought of this, he associated to how he'd had to call his mother from the car that morning to ask her to bring his band instrument when she picked him up for school after his hour. He'd not remembered it until his father had asked him about it. Kevin admitted that his band teacher had become so frustrated by Kevin's repeated failure to have his instrument on band days that he'd called the parents to ask them to take responsibility for it.

In the aftermath of this we worked over several weeks on Kevin's struggle with procrastination. Further examples of this it made apparent the pleasure that came when his passivity would get his parents involved in his life. He got his mother to be attentive when he avoided playing and practicing the piano. Having to attend to him in this way took her attention away from Alex. While I agreed that this occurred, I reflected how sad it was that he cheated himself out of being able to take pleasure in his hard work, something he ultimately engaged in when forced to meet a deadline.

In the midst of this work, Kevin came in one Monday morning to say he'd watched a movie over the weekend that had helped him to understand what I'd been talking to him about. It was "The Pursuit of Happiness." Will Smith played the role of a single-parent father desperately trying to get a new job to save him and his son from homelessness. After much effort at this throughout the movie, he succeeded, and felt very happy and relieved. But then, at the end, as he was sitting at his desk at his new job, he seemed distracted, even bored, and didn't know next what to do. Kevin sat quietly for a bit, lost in thought. Finally, a broad smile came to his face and he said, "You know, that movie has the wrong name, it should be called, "The Pursuit IS Happiness!"

By the end of seventh grade, while some episodes of conflict with his brother continued, Kevin focused more on peer relations. Following the summer break and his return in the fall, corresponding with his entry into eighth grade, Kevin seemed more focused on relationships with girls, in particular. Each morning he would enter the office, put down his backpack, hang up his coat, smooth down his hair, adjust his shirtsleeves and sit in the chair at the desk where he'd remain for the duration of the hour. There was no longer any card playing or drawing. In many ways, except for the fact that he was sitting in the chair across from me, it began to feel that I was working with a patient on the couch. Material from a session during this time illustrates this.

Kevin arrived a few minutes late and said, "You probably think it's my fault." I said, "I can't know what to think but it does seem you're feeling you'll get criticized for something." He became reflective and said he hadn't noticed the time. After a pause he asked what we had been talking about at the end of the last session and I asked if he thought it should be my job to do that remembering. He sat quietly then recalled that we had talked of a swimming party he had attended. It made him think of a swim meet that he would be in at school that day. He wanted to show me the swimming trunks he would wear and as he got up to retrieve them from his backpack, he tripped over the chair leg. He smiled and gave the chair a wide berth as he circled back to sit down. I said he was acting like the chair had tripped him. He chuckled and said, "I realized yesterday that the pants that I wore to the swimming party were the ones with the broken zipper. I'm glad it decided to stay in place during the party." I said, "It seems you think of the zipper on your pants in the same way as the chair leg; things that can act on their own without you expecting or having control." After another pause, he started to tell of an event from the day before at school. "I was in Lauren's homeroom for English class when I found a pencil…Oh, never mind. I don't know what I was trying to say." When I observed that this seemed puzzling, he said, "You know it's like everything in my mind gets 'conjambled' sometimes." I said I was not familiar with that word. He laughed and looked it up in the dictionary. When it was not there, I said that even if it wasn't a word, it had conveyed to me what he felt – a combination of "confused" and "scrambled." After he agreed I noted that he had stopped short of saying what the confused and scrambled feelings were. He laughed nervously and I wondered if this was a time when he wanted to keep thoughts private so that he could keep them to himself. After a pause he said, "Oh, all right, I'll tell you."

He then described how he had found a pencil that he knew belonged to a girl that he liked. He had decided to return it to her after class when he would see her in the hall. She had thanked him and seemed appreciative. He smiled at the thought of this. He continued, "I was remembering the old way we used to flirt. You know, teasing a girl, or tripping her when she walked by." "Like the chair leg?" I questioned. He smiled. "Anyway, I was remembering how I didn't want to tease her that way on Sunday. And last year when we were working on a class project together, I spent three weeks convincing her that I wasn't that kind of guy and it paid off when she offered to let me use her markers." He then thought of how he knew that 9th grade boys acted more mature and he wanted to be like them. On the school bus he had heard some girls talking about how they liked a guy that behaved that way. As the hour drew to a close, I took the opportunity to notice what he had been bringing. He'd called himself "conjambled," but it seemed he was letting us know about a private place inside his mind where he liked to collect and organize his thoughts and observations. Kevin agreed this was so.

This work foreshadowed Kevin's termination. Throughout eighth grade he grew in poise, calmness, and increased confidence. He looked forward to the transition to high school and, as he'd spent the year achieving quite a growth spurt, he talked of plans for going out for football in the fall. Gone was the old defensive fantasizing as he and Alex spent hours playing catch with a football in their yard. By spring he was pleased to report grades of "all A's" and broached the topic of finishing our work. While he rationalized that he'd be busy with summer football practice and then with "heavy load" of practice and homework in the fall, I responded by saying that I thought his thinking was quite sound and sensible. I agreed that he'd worked hard throughout his eighth-grade year.

He set a "finishing" date for the end of June. He sat thoughtfully on that last day at the desk chair where he's spent so many early morning hours. He went through an old basket that had long been the storage repository of many of his drawings and enjoyed remembering them. At hour's end he stood, now a few inches taller than me, and shyly but also proudly, extended his hand. We shook and, making good eye contact, he thanked me and we said good-bye.

COMMENTARY 1

I have been reflecting on this interesting case vignette and wondering how this sensitive analyst understood the presenting problems of this bright and verbal latency boy being anxious with internal and internalized conflicts, when he was first presented with them. He states that Kevin viewed his younger brother as a rival for mother's attention and that ambivalent and active-passive conflicts were evident. Kevin was defensively using placating and solicitous ways, which the analyst understood as turning "passive into active," "denial in fantasy," and immature magical thinking to avoid painful affect and narcissistic injury. Fixations were noted at all pre-oedipal levels and his harsh conscience indicated poor oedipal phase resolution. He had a symptom of bedwetting and persisting anxiety which continued to compromise his school performance.

As I read the history and the issues Kevin was struggling with, I found myself thinking about his early attachment to his primary caregiver, his mother. He was described as an easygoing baby, which might suggest a secure attachment, however when he developed allergies and asthma in his third year when his mother was pregnant, I began to wonder if his attachment was more insecure as he seemed to experience the loss of his mother during her pregnancy. I began to wonder if he then was more anxiously attached to his mother during the first two years of his life. His symptom picture suggested to me he became a difficult child for his parents to have empathy with, due to his anxiety and how this manifested itself.

As I continued to read about the beginning of Kevin's analysis and how he presented himself as a player of games and revealed his need to win, as well as his concern that his analyst would notice his cheating, I thought more about how insecurely attached he has been to his primary caregiver. The analyst began to notice his difficulty handling the cards and knowing he was an accomplished pianist he began to wonder what was going on within him.

I was pleased the analyst began to share these observations with Kevin and he was able to reflect on his feelings and say he thought his analyst would be angry with him. His smile at this point led both of them to wonder together about the excitement he felt at what might be his reaction. Kevin seemed open to discovering what might be behind his worries, indicating to me that Kevin and his analyst were developing a good therapeutic alliance. It seemed clear they liked each other and that the analyst had created a secure space for beginning to explore his issues.

How much trust was in their relationship was apparent early on, as Kevin was able to share his upset by the argument between his parents and how this had affected him. Kevin acknowledged again that he became excited at the thoughts of others getting angry or upset.

What followed was Kevin's desire to have his father interested in him through the analyst's astute attention to him and his behavior. Kevin then was able to admit he was telling a story, he felt safe enough with his analyst to now tell him the truth, he had found a secure base.

The session that followed gives even more evidence of the safety Kevin feels in the presence of his analyst, when once again he tells a story but with the analyst's help is able to be curious about himself and how he can have two sides of the same conflict and was able to accept this was a pattern within him. The analytic work continues to deepen. Somatic tendencies came into the work, reminding me of the somatic complaints Kevin developed when his mother was pregnant with her second child, maybe felt to him as a replacement child, so his symptoms created interest in him and concern from his mother. The analyst's interpretation seemed to make Kevin thoughtful, as he considered the idea: to succeed he needed to suffer or feel he was being punished. Both of these feelings could be what he experienced at the time of his mother's pregnancy when he felt her loss of interest in him, her turning inward, away from him.

Interestingly, at this time the parents reported his bedwetting, a behavior often found in earlier stages of development. The question in my mind was this secure base with the analyst enabling Kevin to regress to an earlier time when his symptoms first began? Kevin was embarrassed to talk about this and wanted to blame others for his lateness to his sessions, but then the analyst wondered how they could master his problem if he did not talk about it. Again, I was struck by how the analyst brought himself into the problem as someone who was there to help and understood the shame Kevin felt.

This connectedness with Kevin seemed to allow him to go even deeper in his analytic work as he was able to reveal his preoccupation with creating a picture for his teacher as he left her, and his analyst, for a trip with his family to Florida. I totally agree with the analyst that Kevin was displacing onto his teacher and to his analyst, the reactivated feelings he had from an earlier time when he felt the loss of mother with the birth of his brother and his feeling guilty over his anger and shame for having these feelings. Kevin felt he was abandoning both his teacher and his analyst.

Following, Kevin was able to bring more of his maladaptive behavior into the sessions, his boasting ways to cover up his forgetfulness for his school assignments. And he also brought in hints about his developing body and his sexuality. I was impressed the way his analyst was able to link his dropping the cards and being late for his sessions because he was rolling around in his bed, by saying to him he had spent some of his session in his bed! This seemed to make it possible for Kevin to acknowledge his sexuality as his analyst was so attuned to him.

With the deepening of the transference, Kevin was able to bring his hidden, negative behavior into the sessions. He showed this negativity when there was a return to his earlier boasting, storytelling behavior. A question I wonder about when negativity returns and is in the session towards the analyst, how does the analyst deal with countertransference feelings and reactions. Does the analyst understand this negativity as an attempt to project unwanted feelings within the self onto the analyst? Does the analyst use this to inform himself of how to understand the projection?

It seems this analyst tolerated this acting out in the sessions and understood it as a defensive measure to avoid thinking and talking about what was making him late. His behavior in the sessions of pulling at his face and fingers and hiding his drawings from his analyst, gave the clue to the issue being avoided, masturbation. The use of Kevin's word "tentacles" instead of "testicles" was understood by the analyst as his conflict of touching himself in bed. Kevin's confusion of words allowed him to share his code word for his penis, "Pen15." This revelation led to an opening up of his curiosity about private body parts and he began to do his "research" and, struggling with his excitement, he shared his habits of putting gel on his hair to make it stand up, and revealed that sometimes his penis "hurt" when it got "stiff."

Once again, we see this analyst's sensitive attunement to him made it possible for Kevin to confront more of his early symptoms of asthma, which were understood together and then disappeared. However, Kevin's concern about his changing body and his interest in it was projected onto his concern about what he was eating. We often see bodily concern with pre-adolescent development in both boys and girls, when the therapeutic alliance is a secure base from which to explore thoughts, feelings and fantasies.

Kevin was able to go off to camp easily and when he returned from the summer break, he was able to explore more thoughts and admit to wanting his father to be interested in him. He wanted to spend time alone with father. However, he felt he was in over his head with what his father expected him to accomplish. His "courting" behavior appeared in the transference. The analyst was sensitive to Kevin and asked his permission to say what he thought Kevin was displaying to his analyst. When he received Kevin's permission to proceed this represented an important moment in the analytic process, and the work deepens and Kevin was able to hear his analyst's interpretation of his oedipal desire with his mother. Although he denied this and was angry at the analyst for saying such a thing, he proceeded to give material which enabled the analyst to know he was right.

What followed was an expression of passive anger at the analyst, which the analyst tolerated as he seemed to know it was Kevin's attempt to push him away and try to enact the early loss of his mother in the analytic process. Kevin was now ready to confront the multitude of mixed feelings he had towards his analyst, his father, his mother and his brother. Kevin was able to bring more incidents to discuss of what he was doing at home, both present and past, as well his curiosity with the primal scene. Once all of this was revealed in the sessions, his analyst began to observe a change in the process of their sessions. Kevin became calmer and more reflective and less concerned about his analyst's thoughts and feelings about him.

The analyst was always mindful of Kevin's sensitivity and was careful to ask his permission before he made an interpretation he was able to share, based on his understanding of the material within the session. Kevin revealed his upset when he was not told about the death of his dog when he was seven, which allowed him to be in touch with his sad feelings. His analyst could make the link to how he felt upset when his brother was born, as he felt replaced and left out. Kevin agreed it was so. Kevin then seemed freed up to enact his angry and rivalrous feelings against his brother. This at first was met with denial by Kevin and as his asthma returned this confrontation about his angry feelings actually abated the wheezing.

The rivalrous relationship between the two boys continued and the parents decided that Alex needed to be in analysis. Kevin began to recall repressed memories of how his father had not been private with him on trips, which had left him with confused longings to be with his mother and angry at his brother for taking her away from him. He began to understand his procrastination with his school work as a way of getting his parents' attention, although it was negative.

As the analytic process continued Kevin was able to let his analyst know he was beginning to become interested in girls. Here we see another example of Kevin's use of words which reveal his conflict. His creation of the word "conjambled," which the analyst noted not being familiar with, enabled Kevin to admit he was "confused" and "scrambled" by some feelings he was having. When his analyst said he wanted to keep these feelings private, Kevin decided he would tell him. Once again, we see the sensitivity of the analyst, being able to relate to and understand that having feelings for girls might be something Kevin would want to be kept private and as the analyst understood this, Kevin felt understood and was able to share these feelings. Later the analyst was able to say he knew Kevin had a private place in his mind where he could collect and organize his thoughts and feelings. The analyst was referring to reflection which was a gift to Kevin, it gave him permission to think his own thoughts and work within himself with his thoughts and feelings.

The analyst had become aware that Kevin had given evidence that he had internalized the process of working together, to understand the conflicting feelings that he had struggled with throughout his growing up years. Kevin's marks had improved at school. Termination was in the air and they set a date for the end of the school year. Kevin reflected on the material that he reviewed that was in his box. He enjoyed remembering. This is a most helpful when terminating an analysis or a therapy. Youngsters feel accepted and appreciated for all they have shown, and eventually understood with the help of the other. Shaking hands, looking in the eyes of each other and saying thank you, is the acknowledgement of the help the process has been to both. How did the analyst feel at this ending? It is my hope that the analyst felt proud of all the work he had done to enable this boy to get onto the path of healthy emotional development.

COMMENTARY 2

The account of Kevin's treatment brings our attention to that delicate passage in time from pre-pubescence to early adolescence, often a confusing transition. Once puberty starts, there is no going back to childhood. Here, we see the analyst ushering Kevin through this vulnerable period, made more complex by an early history of asthma and allergies beginning when he was 3, when his brother was born, a time when Kevin's mother was preoccupied and unavailable to tend to his bodily needs, a time, in the phallic stage of development, where he felt the push into being a "big boy." A symptom at the time of referral was bedwetting.

One challenge of current psychoanalysis is that often there is more focus on representation and fantasy, while the grounded reality of what's going on in the body may not get as much attention. So, it is refreshing to read about a treatment where the analyst was deeply attentive and curious about what was going on in Kevin's body. Kevin brings to the analyst his experiences of growing bigger, feeling smaller, fears of bodily injury, a preoccupation with his testicles, penis, hands, guilt and masturbation conflicts.

As they play Uno and War, the analyst notices that it is "odd that a 5th grader who was also an accomplished pianist would have such poor hand and finger coordination." Why is that happening with a bright child who plays piano beautifully? The analyst notices a pattern. After doing well, any success is quickly "followed by misdeals, dropped cards." The analyst and Kevin notice when he feels vulnerable, Kevin may compensate by showing off. When he claims he's doing well, he then loses the next few games. Together, they wonder about the underlying causes and meanings of his conflicts.

I admired how the analyst and Kevin were able to playfully talk about his body changes. Kevin is late for a session and says he overslept. The analyst mentions since he spent some of the session in bed, was there something he wanted to bring from there? Kevin smiles and says, "You mean my "tentacles?" When the analyst wonders if he meant testicles, Kevin smiles and says, "You mean "Pen-15?" A series of sessions follow where they moved through initial confusion about the bodily changes Kevin was experiencing, his "discombobulation" and sense of physical vulnerability. Anita Bell (1965) wrote about anxieties associated with the prepuberty changes in the testes, how this is an area often not discussed and how some of the anxiety is displaced to the phallus.

As the analysis deepens, Kevin brings in more of his bodily worries and symptoms related to the asthma and allergies. He tells the analyst about how "he breathed in a noisy way, how he was compelled to clear his throat, cough and blow his nose." He added concerns about gagging and food fears to his bodily worries. He associates to hot dogs and says he would only eat them if they were grilled or charred, not pink. He associates to "Pen-15." When the analyst asks about how he might have come to have these worries, he thinks about when he was small and taking showers with his father for a few years.

Through their discussions, Kevin integrates his new body, its sensations and its functions into a new self-image, psychic organization and sense of self, an essential part of the adolescent identity formation process. As Kevin moves into early adolescence, we see the unfolding of the salience of sexuality by virtue of his changing body. He is preoccupied with all the ways he is getting bigger and more independent. He rides his bike to the sessions now. He is more interested in spending time with his friends and "he seems more focused on his relationships with girls." We see he's on the path to coming to terms with his sexuality.

I am not sure when this case is written, or what the Zeitgeist of psychoanalytic theory was at the time. But reading the analyst's account now, I found myself aware of an additional way of framing Kevin's development of the oedipal constellation. Marsha Levy-Warren (2008) writes about how the oedipal constellation derives from early childhood, but changes as one moves through childhood and stages of adolescence, reflecting the ways in which self and object representations change over time. Moving from latency into adolescence, there is a transition between binary ways of thinking to more complex ways of thinking about sexuality and gender. Reading this account invites us to listen for other factors that affect the oedipal constellation such as changing relationships to parents and identifications with those parents.

I was struck by some of the bold language the analyst used, and I had my own reactions when reading. It made me wonder what the analyst was feeling and thinking at certain moments. I reread and reread the account and thought about the interpretations in the context of this analytic pair. I suspect it was the strength of the therapeutic alliance that allowed the aim of the interpretations to reach Kevin in a way that opened his capacity to move forward in development. I think of Aulagnier's writing in "The Violence of Interpretation," in that the 'violence' of contact with Kevin's mind may well have been the kind of analytic work he needed. The analyst knew his/her patient well. Exchanges like the following give me a flavor of their warm, close relationship:

Upon hearing one of the analyst's interpretations, Kevin replies: "You think I want a date with my father?" Kevin is ironic and funny and clearly enjoys challenging his analyst.

The analyst focused on Kevin's close relationship with his father after his mother gave birth to his brother and was preoccupied. We are reminded about Erna Furman's writing about the protective function that the father filled for an older child, when the mother had another baby. We hear about the many positive identifications Kevin has with his father throughout the treatment. He tells the analyst that he benefits from doing projects with his father and other men; how lending their expertise and companionship helps him feel skilled and confident. Kevin yearns for more of this "doing together." As I read, thinking about a changing oedipal constellation, I wondered how Kevin would navigate reaching the threshold of early adolescence and leave behind his "childhood version of the self" (Levy-Warren, 2016).

The reader hears how his mother can be protective and attuned to his worries, that much we are told. Erna Furman, in "Toddlers and their Mothers," wrote about steps towards independence, how a parent first does for the child, then does with the child. Then the child shows the parents what he/she can do, and the parent acknowledges the achievements, and finally the child internalizes a sense of mastery independent of parents. I sense that between Kevin's parents and the analyst, this developmental progression evolved.

There are certain turning points in the treatment where the analyst, listening to pre-oedipal themes, awakens in Kevin long-held embodied feelings, linking them to multiple losses. When the family learns they will get a puppy, and Kevin finds himself thinking about the loss of his dog when he was 7, the analyst is sensitive to Kevin's vulnerability and writes: "We noticed that he struggled to suppress a smile, even as there were tears in his eyes. He agreed when I said the smile seemed an effort to keep the tears away." The analyst is with Kevin on this painful journey. They share a transitional space where reflection occurs that occurs nowhere else, in no other way and no other time. As Kevin tearfully talks about the sudden death of his dog and remembers no one prepared him for the death, the analyst wonders if he felt the same way when his brother was born.

Another turning point is when the analyst made a choice to think prospectively, into Kevin's future, so he could do the same. Throughout the treatment, the analyst notes Kevin's struggles with passivity and procrastination over early wishes to be cared for by his mother. Kevin tells the analyst how he frequently forgets his band instrument and his mother must bring it to school and how she must remind him to practice piano. The analyst says, "that it was sad that he cheated himself out of being able to take pleasure in his hard work, something he ultimately engaged in when forced to meet a deadline." Here, the analyst supports Kevin's capacities and his more mature ego functioning.

A few days later, Kevin says he watched a film that helped him to understand what the analyst meant. It was called "The Pursuit of Happiness." With a broad smile, he says. "You know that movie has the wrong name, it should be called, "The Pursuit IS happiness", a beautiful commentary about his experience in analysis.

This exchange and others highlight how the analyst provided certain developmental assists, and uncovered Kevin's identifications with good enough, loving parents. There is a shift in Kevin's self-awareness and internalization of certain parental functions; affirmation, validation for his hard work, and standards to set for himself going forward.

Like the necessary passage that parents must take as their child moves into early adolescence, so the analyst moved with Kevin. Fred Pine (1990) wrote that the structure of the analytic process itself can be seen as a mirror for the structure of the developmental process. Here, the analyst created a holding environment where Kevin could experience this transition into a new developmental phase. In this good enough holding environment, a path was created towards increasing autonomy.

In this case, Kevin's parents appear as reporters of family information. I wondered about the possibility of the analyst creating a holding environment for both parents and adolescent to make that shift together. We hear about Kevin's parents throughout the treatment and the analyst introduces the issue of how we use what we learn from parents, with whom we meet periodically, but who are not part of the formal structure of the treatment. At times, the analyst introduces information that came from the parents, but probably would not have been offered by Kevin. ("From his parents, I'd learned of increased episodes of bedwetting. Around this time, Kevin was late for a few sessions and noted there were problems with laundry. We discussed that it would be hard to master a trouble if he felt he could not talk about it in his analysis.") The analyst rises to the challenge of sharing this information with grace and tact. But there are other instances when the analyst shares with

Kevin stories from his parents about mistreatment of his younger brother, information that is upsetting for Kevin to hear as the rivalry with his brother is a well-known source of pain.

One of the things this case evoked for me was the gentle vulnerability of this boy and I wondered about ways of developing the existing bridge with his parents. I think the Novicks bring to their work an intuitive appreciation of the need for safety for all. They have created a sophisticated model for including parents in the formal structure of a child or adolescent's treatment (Novick, J. and Novick, K.K. 2016). The way treatment is framed at the beginning safeguards and lays the foundation for multiple therapeutic alliances. The analyst stays equidistant from the parents and the adolescent's needs. Unlike family therapy, it makes explicit the parent/adolescent relationship, rather than just the adolescent, as well as parenthood as a developmental phase. A measure of the work's effectiveness is in the increased synchronicity.

With this work, an otherwise awkward, confusing time for young adolescents and their parents can become a "holding space" (Winnicott, 1965) for everyone to experience how the shift into puberty affects them. Instead of parents in the role of reporters, a framework is constructed where parents experience themselves, enlisted in the service of their child's needs. And for parents, a helpful concept to internalize is that any breakdown in understanding can result in everyone surviving and the building of increased ego capacity.

I was deeply moved by the last segment of the analysis where the analyst was attuned to this phase of life where the attainment of the capacity and need for privacy and autonomy is important. The analyst tells Kevin "he was letting us know about a private place inside his mind where he liked to collect and organize his thoughts and observations." Perhaps the analyst was seduced by this charming boy's earnestness. Through it all, with their humor and moments of anguish, we are left remembering that these two shook hands at the end, a veritable "analytic hug."

EDITORIAL REFLECTIONS

This chapter reminds us of the profound changes that come with the passage into puberty and of the importance of managing this momentous transition in a way that allows for growth and change. Creating conditions for creative, pleasurable engagement with the new real possibilities of adolescence combats the slowing or halting of development that results from defensive symptomatic functioning. Psychoanalysis offers a space for realizing that aim.

Psychoanalysis also provides a space roomy enough for learning about the details of the transformations of puberty. All the contributors to this chapter direct us to the action of a developmental process, stalled in Kevin's life, and facilitated, indeed liberated, by the therapeutic work. Kevin does not leave his childhood behind; his treatment helps him to integrate his earlier experiences of himself into his new teenage identity and we have the impression that he has internalized aspects of the therapeutic relationship and alliance that will support him in continuing the process of transformation of his relationship to his body, mind, and self, along with his relationships to important people in his life, both adults and peers.

Currently there is much criticism of the traditional use of a linear developmental focus; non-linear development is now viewed as the more accurate model (Galatzer-Levy 2004, Knight 2022). We have noted that, in contrast to progressive development, pathological development (often linked to trauma) seems more linear, as many of the same early defenses and responses to trauma remain basically unchanged through the phases (Novick, J. and Novick, K.K. 2013). This chapter illustrates such a case where trauma at age three led to closed-system responses (asthma, allergies, passivity, and exclusive tie to father) that remained unchanged (with the addition of enuresis) until he started analysis at age ten.

The treatment began in prepuberty and the hypersensitivity of this phase intensified Kevin's passive relationship with his father and perhaps a negative identification with the mother who was the source of the trauma. The chapter also raises the question of what can be defined as trauma. His reaction to the birth of a sibling at age three overwhelmed his ego and neither his parents nor his available ego capacities provided a protective shield. It is the helplessness of the ego and not the external event which defines a trauma.

Adolescent breakdown is often attributed to the massive neurobiological changes of this phase; but here we see pathology at least as far back as age three and one commentator suggests an insecure attachment as the infantile underlay of his later traumatic reaction to the birth of a sibling. Analysis at this pubertal stage is often considered impossible because of the hypersensitivity of the patient and the extreme defenses against humiliation. We see examples of his hypersensitivity, for instance, in his lying, cheating, keeping important material, like his sadistic attacks on brother and his bed wetting, a secret.

At the same time we see the therapist serving multiple functions and becoming a loved and important person in the child's life. We are reminded that the goal is not only conflict resolution, but that analysis is also a profound developmental experience in which the therapist is also a developmental object who responds to the young adolescent with respect, tact, and playfulness (Hurry 1998, Tahka 1993). Kevin's self-defeating behavior (sadomasochism) was interpreted via the transference in combination with thoroughgoing defense analysis. We could consider that offering an adolescent ownership through understanding of his defenses can contribute importantly to identity formation during this phase, as he comes to know his own mental functioning. The pubertal sexual changes (masturbation, scrotum anxieties, misinformation, infantile theories) were dealt with in a straightforward fashion by the analyst as a developmental object <u>and</u> in the transference. A strong and positive therapeutic alliance allowed for this.

From this vignette we see that for this analyst the therapeutic alliance is central, something the analyst does not take for granted but works to establish and maintain. When the moment seems right for an interpretation the analyst asks the patient's permission to do so. "I then cautioned that I had a thought to share that might be hard to listen to. After receiving permission to proceed, I..." and the analyst goes on to interpret the homosexual transference. This technical approach was noted by the commentators as an important contributor to the success of this treatment; this chapter illustrates the utility of devising and adopting techniques that address sensitivities particular to the age and stage of the patient's development, rather than characterizing such patients as unanalyzable because of their prickliness, or proneness to humiliation, or defensive externalization of responsibility, and other descriptors of younger adolescents.

The birth of a younger sibling and the subsequent "sadistic" nature of the patient's relationship with his brother was a secret he withheld but eventually became central to the work. Many analysts have ostensibly abandoned the topographical point of view, Freud's first division of the mental apparatus. The distinction among conscious, preconscious and unconscious was absorbed and subsumed by the structural model of id, ego and superego. But this case illustrates how much is kept secret, especially by young adolescents who find it painful to admit to certain behaviors, such as sadistic ones. The parents told the therapist that Kevin would pinch his younger brother's penis or get him so excited that he would lose bowel and bladder control. The chapter illustrates the importance of a topographical point of view, and of exploring the sibling relationship as a powerful positive or negative force in its own right, not something to be ignored or relegated to a mere displacement from the parents.

The termination of this treatment is a mutually agreed event, truly a good goodbye. We have suggested that the major developmental task for adolescents is to set aside closed-system omnipotent defenses, such as sadomasochism, and choose instead open-system love, cooperation, and creative joy in the process. At the end of his three-year analysis Kevin was ready for high school, looking forward to the future, in the midst of his growth spurt, was taller than his analyst, enjoyed his body, planned to go out for the football team. He and his brother now spent hours playing catch with the football. Kevin had seen a film about a single father titled, "The Pursuit of Happiness." He decided that the film should be called "The Pursuit IS Happiness."

Finally, this chapter reminds us of the efficacy of reconstruction in work with pubescent adolescents and reaffirms the value of that essential technique in the successful work with an age group that is so often dismissed as unanalyzable.

CHAPTER 3

CLAIRE – age 12

The slight, short-haired twelve-year-old girl who came into my office in jeans and a t-shirt looked frightened. Her mother had called to say that her daughter would not go to school. This was a first. School was always "a happy place" for Claire. Her mother was puzzled about why it was suddenly so upsetting for her.

"Hi, Claire. "

"Hi." (Claire looked down as she spoke).

"I help kids your age when they feel unhappy or worried, and your mom says that you have been feeling really unhappy about going to school."

Claire nodded, still looking down.

"Did something distressing happen at school?"

"Not really."

"So, something inside just doesn't feel right?"

Claire looked up for the first time. Her eyes were very round, and a bit wet – "I can't go there anymore. It's too hard. It gives me a stomachache."

Claire was in seventh grade. She said she had always enjoyed school. She didn't really understand why she now felt such dread. She had friends, enjoyed learning, and was involved in a number of satisfying extra-curricular activities. The feeling of dread had begun right after her summer break. It was now the end of September. Her mother had told me that the discomfort seemed to begin after the first week of school. I decided that I needed to do some investigating.

"What did you do last summer?"

"Camp."

"What kind of camp do you go to?"

"An all-girls sleep-away camp."

"Did you have a good summer there?"

"It was okay."

"Had you been there before?"

"Yes."

"Were things any different this summer from other summers?"

Claire seemed uneasy. She was looking down as she spoke, pulling at her fingers – one by one – and kept crossing and re-crossing her legs.

"The girls were different. Camp was the same." Claire fell silent.

"Can you describe how the girls were different this summer?" I saw that Claire was very uncomfortable, but sensed that something had happened at camp that had set the stage for her discomfort coming back to school. I was hoping to at least begin a conversation about it.

Claire shook her head in the negative.

"Hard to talk about?"

She nodded (in the affirmative).

"Let's talk about something else, then."

"Yes, please."

I continued to ask Claire questions, but shifted to inquiring about her friends, family, and extra-curricular activities. She was more responsive, though still contained, seemingly shy, and definitely anxious. She appeared a bit younger than her twelve years.

Claire noted in our conversation that she had a best friend, Naomi, with whom she had been close since kindergarten. She seemed detached when she spoke about her:

"I have known Naomi since we were little. We met the first day of school."

"So…you liked her right away?"

"Yes. We had the same backpack."

"And you are still close?"

Claire looked as uncomfortable as she had earlier. She looked around the room, began pulling at her fingers.

"I think this is making you feel uncomfortable again. Would you prefer to talk about something else? Or should we do something together, other than talking?"

Claire looked up.

"Like what?"

"Sometimes, it's more comfortable to get to know each other by doing something fun together. I have a good game I can show you – let me go get some paper, a marker, and a pencil."

I decided that it might make Claire less apprehensive if we played the Squiggle game. Though I usually use this game with younger children, I felt that Claire's physical expressions of tension were so frequent and her difficulty speaking about hard things so palpable, that it might be easier for her to use her hands and imagination more and her words less.

I retrieved the supplies, explained the game, and asked Claire to make some squiggles on our first sheet of paper with a marker. I then converted her squiggles into some pictures, and we talked about what we each saw in the drawings.

Claire's squiggles were very contained, drawn slowly and carefully, and tended to form bounded even shapes. I converted each of them into cartoonish, smiling figures. I wanted to allow for some foolishness in our interaction, to get a sense of how bounded up she felt.

"You're being silly!" she exclaimed.

"Sometimes it's fun to be silly, right!?"

Claire became pensive.

"I don't know."

Though her face was impassive, I felt the pain in her response.

"Maybe we can remember together what it's like."

Claire is the youngest of three children. She has a 15-year old sister and an 18-year old brother. She comes from a financially secure family, one that her parents denote as "upper middle class." Her mother works as a public relations executive, her father is an officer in a bank. Claire attends a private college preparatory school. She has always been a strong student, and someone who bounded off to school in the morning with enthusiasm.

She is close to her siblings, but neither her brother nor her sister knew what was upsetting Claire. The whole family was perplexed.

I decided that it would make most sense to meet three times/week. Claire was clearly in need of as much help as she could get, as quickly as she could get it. She was sad, constrained, and anxious. I felt that meeting with regularity would facilitate her trusting me and the therapeutic process. Her parents supported the treatment plan with Claire. I also arranged to meet with them on a regular basis, though we did not specify the frequency for the parent meetings right away. I wanted to see how the work with Claire proceeded first.

Our first few weeks of treatment yielded squiggles that illustrated a strong need on Claire's part to keep her feelings and impulses in check. Her "squiggles" were not squiggly: they continued to be contained, bounded shapes, just as in our first exchange. I noted with Claire that she seemed to like order:

"You draw so neatly and carefully!"

"I like things to be clear. I don't like messes."

My more uncontained squiggles (in contrast to Claire's), were most often made very carefully into animals and flowers. She worked slowly, with repeated erasures. The representations were quite realistic.

There was a notable absence of people in what she drew or spoke about in response to the drawings. When I mentioned this, Claire was again very uneasy.

"You seem to like animals and flowers more than people!"

"They are just easier to draw."

"Hmm.... I guess in the world of people, there also are a lot of complicated feelings that are hard to show."

"Um-hmm."

Claire, characteristically for this time in treatment, became quiet and withdrawn. It was clear that the social world was one that felt problematic for her. I had the sense that trying to broach the subject of her relationships with her contemporaries directly would not be effective right now. We went on to talk about her favorite flowers (very bright colorful ones) and the kinds of animals she liked (cuddly ones). She told me that she had a bedful of stuffed animals and that she surrounded herself with them each night. She put them in a particular order around her so that she could feel "cozy and safe." If they were out of the "correct" order, she had to start all over again.

It was clear that she was trying very hard to create order in her outer world as her inner world became more chaotic. It was reminiscent of a lot of latency age/pre-pubescent kids who struggle with their upcoming transformations. I wondered what was precipitating this concern for her, since she was not yet pubertal herself.

Over the course of the next few weeks, she was able to describe her very elaborate fantasy play with these stuffed animals. She played with them every day after school. The stories were replete with kingdoms, rivalries, men going off to war, and girls falling in love. She was willing to tell me the stories, which we talked about in detail – who went off with whom, who was battling with whom, who fell in love with whom.

She dictated, I wrote. We created a book. We called it <u>Claire's Concoctions</u>. I wondered whether the fantasy play had ever been shared.

"Do your friends ever play with you?"

"They used to. So did my sister."

"Hmm ... used to ... so, not any more?"

Claire looked sad.

"Too baby-ish."

Claire felt left behind. We talked about what that was like for her, and she was able to articulate that she felt sad, betrayed, and angry with her friends. And then there were her siblings.

Several weeks later, after a session in which Claire said that she didn't feel like going home that day, I asked in our following meeting:

"So, what's it like at home these days?"

"Ok, I guess."

"That doesn't sound so enthusiastic. What's going on?" We had come far enough in our work together that Claire generally was able to speak more spontaneously. Her laconic response to this question was now uncharacteristic.

"Can you ask me questions?"

"You mentioned that Brian [her brother] is busy working on college applications these days. Does he have ideas about where he might want to go next year?"

Claire looked stricken.

"Maybe Stanford. That's the one in California, right?" She spoke very quietly.

"Yes, it is ... pretty far away..."

Claire softly began to weep.

"Hard to think of him being so far away?"

Claire nodded.

"Big change."

"Not the only one." Claire seemed to be gathering her forces, trying to muster up the oomph to say more. I sat quietly, waiting to see if she could speak.

"Rosie [her sister] is totally into her friends. And her **boyfriend**. [said with a very unusual tone of sarcasm]. She is barely home. I don't get to see her much anymore, either. She might as well already be in California. Or on the moon. Or wherever."

It was a relief to hear Claire expressing such strong affect. It had now been three months of treatment, and it was the first time she had been able to be so clear about her feelings.

"Wow. A double whammy...so both your brother and your sister are preoccupied. That IS a lot of change."

Claire had always been close to both of her siblings, She said that it was as though they had their own family within the family. Her parents both worked hard and had long hours; her brother and sister were often the ones with whom she played and the ones she went to with problems and questions about life.

Over several weeks of talking about this, always in dribs and drabs, it became clear that the change at home had begun at the end of the last school year. Brian was making college visits, and talking a great deal with his parents and friends about where he might want to go to school. Rosie had begun going out much more over weekends, and spent hours on the computer and phone interacting with friends. She had her first boyfriend, and was consumed with that relationship. Claire felt that neither one of them had nearly as much time for her as they had in the past.

"Sounds like you miss your brother and sister these days."

Claire nodded.

"This reminds me of when we talked awhile ago about how you like to draw animals and flowers more than people, and play with stuffed animals

more than your old friends – remember that? Sounds like there were quite a few people that you didn't want to think about – both at home and elsewhere."

"When I play, it's just me and my characters. I like that. I don't have to think about what is going on with everybody else. I'm in charge."

"Less pain caused by what the other people are doing, I guess."

Claire was increasingly able to speak of her sadness about how everyone around her was changing, how much she did not want things to change, and how it was all happening too quickly. Simultaneously, her comings and goings from my office were becoming increasingly charged. She often arrived at my office early and played with a stuffed unicorn in the waiting room until I came out. When it was time for our now all-talking sessions to end, she would dally.

"Can't we just talk a little more? There's something I forgot to tell you."

At times, she literally stood in front of the door in a way that made it difficult for me to open it.

"I'm the sentry. You can't get past me."

I sensed the challenge in this. The shy, compliant, good girl Claire was evolving into someone who was a bit more defiant. I knew that this was a sign of differentiation, of progress, but also that it foretold a different chapter in our treatment.

Over the first few months, I met with Claire's parents at least twice a month. We spoke about the various changes in Claire's life and how they might best attend to her – especially given the changing dynamics with her siblings at home. I encouraged them to spend time alone with Claire. I felt she needed to form a closer relationship with each of her parents to aid her in moving forward.

I also asked them about their own families of origin and their development. They were open to talking. Both had experiences in adolescence that were relevant to Claire's current struggles. Speaking as three adults deeply involved in Claire's life created an alliance that ultimately aided Claire in feeling more held by the adult world.

At this time in our meetings, her parents were speaking about Claire's increased obstinacy, particularly her refusal to stop her fantasy play and get ready for bed. She would insist on lining up her stuffed animals in a particular order and would take a long time to set them up. They were feeling increasing frustration with her.

They were pleased that her discomfort with going to school had decreased and that her spirits were much improved, but not so happy with her increased moodiness and recalcitrance. I tried to put it in context – she might not look that pubescent physically, but she was surrounded by peers who <u>were</u> pubertal – and she was in a world at school in which kids were surely acting in ways that were markedly different from how they had been before their bodies had begun to change. Claire was trying to catch up.

Six months into treatment, it became clear that the sadness she had felt at home the previous Spring set the stage for what turned out to be a difficult time at camp. I had sensed that there had been such a difficult time in our very first appointment, but it was not until now that Claire was able to begin to speak directly about it all.

Last Spring, she was alone in her "family within a family." The stories in the book we had made together in our early weeks, <u>Claire's Concoctions,</u> were very much about comings and goings, people leaving, people going off to do wonderful things and leaving others behind, people hurting each other. These were the themes in her life at the time.

She had felt that the circle of siblings was a like protective wall against anything frightening in the world. Now it was gone. Then, Brian preparing to leave home and Rosie becoming most concerned with her boyfriend and friends "left her in the dust." So, she was alone and without protection. Everything was happening too fast.

Especially because of this, she very much looked forward to going back to camp. Camp was a familiar place. It had a stable schedule and kids that she had known for a few years. It would be a source of fun and a source of comfort. She always liked the sameness.

But last summer was not like the others. As she put it when we first met, the girls were different – camp was the same.

When Claire arrived at camp last summer, she felt like the youngest girl in her bunk. She knew this was not true chronologically, but she certainly felt everybody's body had changed except hers.

"It wasn't bad enough that they looked bigger than me, they also acted really differently. They were fresh to the counselors, they talked about sex – who they were attracted to, whether they were attracted to each other…." she trailed off. The now (much) more talkative Claire retreated into the old, withdrawn, silent version of herself.

"Where'd you go, Claire? You feeling ok?"

Claire was quiet for several minutes. I felt that I should allow her this time – but I knew it was a calculation of some kind: I did not want her to feel alone, but I wanted her to feel she could transport herself back to that time as slowly as she needed to go. I was trying to balance her effort at self-regulation with my concern that she not feel abandoned (again).

"They said I looked trans." She said this in a monotonic voice, staring at the wall.

We waited. I felt uneasy. Claire had the old look – drawn face, fingers pulling at each other, leg going up and down. It was not as intense as it had been, but there it was.

"They said I didn't really dress like a girl, I didn't much look like one, I didn't seem interested in 'girl talk.'" As Claire spoke, she stopped pulling on her fingers, and stopped pumping her leg. Her voice shook.

"I didn't know what to think. They were kind of matter-of-fact about it. I couldn't say anything at the time. I was completely confused. Trans? I was a girl. I never felt like I was anything but a girl. But did they see something I didn't see? I didn't know. I really wanted to talk to Rosie. I knew she could have helped me." Claire started to sob. I had never seen her this filled with emotion.

*"It was a lot to deal with. It **is** a lot to deal with . . . but we will figure this out together. I am glad you could tell us about it this way."*

For the next couple of months, we spent most of our time talking about what happened that summer. It was painful for Claire to bring it all back, but she was stalwart in her efforts. She felt that her old camp-mates were very different from who they had always been, and she was the same. She was not at all sure that she wanted to be any different.

"Maybe I just like who I am. Why do I have to be different?"

"Who says you have to be different?"

Claire was contemplative.

"I guess I feel like now I am supposed to be different. You know, Brian is leaving. Rosie is off with Billy [boyfriend] and her friends. The girls at camp are acting older than me. And then there are the kids at school . . ." (Claire trails off).

Her best friend, Naomi, also had grown a good deal over the summer. She, too, looked older than Claire. She had begun menstruating over the summer.

It felt like too much. In September, Claire did not think she could face another tidal wave of feeling different from other kids. That is where she was when we began our work together. What emerged in our meetings was that the "stomachaches" she described when we first began, those that had kept her home from school, represented a very conflicted wish to be like Naomi and her pubertal camp friends, i.e., to have the cramps associated with menstruation.

"Why **am I** so slow to develop? What's wrong with me," alternated with "I don't want to get my period. It seems gross."

The next several months of treatment were about sameness and difference in a number of different contexts, about her sense that time was marching forward (whether she wanted it to or not), and her feeling that she had to safeguard her childhood. We coined this her "sentry" Self. She showed this at my door when she wouldn't (or couldn't) leave, by not going to school, and by entering the world of make believe with her stuffed animals.

At the end of the academic year, Claire again went away for the summer. This time, however, she went to an adventure program. Over the course of the summer, she grew taller and began to develop. We continued to work together for most of her eighth grade, but the work shifted. She joined the soccer team at school, which met most afternoons after school, so she came once a week. Meeting less frequently was a necessity, but Claire was also in a very different place from where she had been. I did not feel concerned about our changed schedule.

In this second year, our focus was more on her parents and her friends. It became clear that the siblings formed their inner circle to protect themselves from shared disappointment. They felt provided for, but not always emotionally nourished by their parents. They looked after each other.

"I always had Brian and Rosie, even when Mom and Dad were working. They worked a lot, but Brian and Rosie were always around."

"I can see why not having Brian and Rosie around last Spring was rough for you."

"It is going to be really hard when Brian leaves next year." Claire looked sad and began to tear up. She became quiet and stared off.

"You look lost in thought. Feel like talking about what you are thinking?"

"Oh, sorry...I was thinking about how excited he is that he will be going away. I don't think he knows how sad it makes me and I don't want to tell him."

"We can always talk about it here."

Claire gave me a quick smile.

"We always do, whether I like it or not."

It was a treat to see Claire able to bring some levity into our relationship!

Joining the soccer team was a very significant change for Claire. It helped her to find a new group of friends with whom she felt compatible. They were a bit less socially sophisticated, more focused on sports and academic achievement, and generally highly regarded at school.

"I love these kids. They're just like me. I don't feel like they are ahead of me or anything."

Claire seemed settled in.

Talking about her parents and placing herself more squarely in her peer group took away the need for Claire as Sentry. She was able to stare at the future with more hope and leave childhood behind. At the point of ending our work together, Claire was heading off to a soccer camp, having started very much to look and act like the 13 year-old she had come to be.

She saluted. "No more sentry needed! I am leaving her here, if that's ok with you."

COMMENTARY 1

Introduction

It was a pleasure to read the engaging case of twelve year old Claire, brought to treatment by her parents after she became unaccountably miserable about returning to school from summer vacation. The case showcases the strengths of intensive psychoanalytic treatment – responsive and adaptive to the patient's acute needs and smoothly integrating ideas of developmental and family systems as multiple facets of Claire's difficulties come into focus.

Course of treatment

When Claire arrived for treatment, the author set out to investigate the origins of her distress, but Claire immediately retreated under the pressure of being questioned. Thoughtfully and empathically, the therapist changed direction and offered Claire an alternative: drawing, and playing the game of "Squiggle."

How fortuitous for Claire that she had come to the office of an analyst with child training, who brought her knowledge of childhood, development and child treatment to their fledgling relationship. And, how helpful that the analyst's comfort and familiarity with Squiggle allowed her to shift gears fluidly and, further, to draw diagnostic information about Claire's emotional style from her careful and precise drawings.

Claire and her analyst made a good connection, the parents were amenable to intensive treatment, and the work proceeded. The analyst continued to navigate smoothly moments that might have been challenging or even impossible for a less-experienced clinician. At one point, Claire blocked the office door at the end of an hour. Rather than restate the frame or set limits, the author drew Claire into a process of reflection and analysis. Together, they came up with the language of "the Sentry," a guardian of Claire's childhood.

Observing Claire's early adolescent development within a social and relational context, the author notes that Claire seemed to have been on a slightly slower developmental path than her closest friends. She also notices that Claire's parents, while loving and responsible, were in some ways disengaged and more focused on their professional lives than on Claire. Claire's older brother and sister had become her primary caretakers, even substitute parents.

A year of three times weekly meetings helped Claire mourn the disappointments of the previous year and resume developing. A further year of weekly sessions helped her consolidate the gains she had made and launch into adolescence.

A developmental perspective

I admire the analyst's use of developmental thinking to frame the case. More than simply understanding development in an abstract way, the analyst appreciated the challenge and difficulties of psychological development from a child's point of view. For Claire, the transition from middle childhood to adolescence had arrived without warning, presenting her with an overwhelming loss of connection and familiarity. Her friends from camp and school had suddenly become different. No one wanted to play fantasy games any longer. And, right at the time a girl might turn to her mother or father for support, her brother and sister were taken with developments in their own lives – college and a new boyfriend. Claire felt unprepared, then lost.

The analyst learned that Claire's developmental difficulty was situated within a developmental shift impacting the entire family: some years previously, to facilitate their dual careers, the parents had disengaged from parenting Claire and passed many responsibilities – and opportunities – to Claire's older brother and sister. But, now, changes were afoot: each was moving on to new things. To whom would Claire turn? Maybe this sheds some light on the parents' easy acceptance of intensive treatment? Perhaps they were hoping the analyst would now parent Claire.

Claire's analyst knew how unsettling development can feel. She read Claire's obsessions and compulsions as efforts to "create order in her outer world as her inner world became more chaotic." The analyst doesn't offer specific or concrete evidence that Claire's inner world was truly "chaotic," but Claire did become estranged from friends and consumed with time-consuming rituals around bedtime. And she had begun pushing back in new and vigorous ways against her parents' wishes.

Further considerations

There are several elements of the treatment, frequently challenging for clinicians seeing adolescents intensively, that I would like to know more about: the initial recommendation for three times weekly treatment; the parent work; and psychopharmacology consultation. I am also curious about whether the author thought of Claire's presenting problem as one of thoughts and feelings unspoken or unknown.

Parent work

The work with Claire's parents seems to have been quite successful, and I'd like to know a good deal more about it. Meetings with the parents were only intermittent at the outset of Claire's treatment but became more regular at a later point. The analyst reveals that both parents had experiences in adolescence "relevant to Claire's current struggles," but the details go undiscussed and Claire's parents don't emerge as people. Aside from Claire's reluctance to go to school, what of their daughter's distress have the parents noticed? How have they made sense and tried to address it? How have their "relevant" experiences conditioned their capacities to be close with Claire? The analyst's experience working with the parents can yield vital information for the child treatment. The analyst recommended that they spend more time alone with Claire and each develop a close relationship with her. How able were they to put these ideas into practice? What obstacles did they encounter? Did they seek the analyst's help? How did that go?

Claire's initial presentation sounds familiar: affluent parents needing children to behave autonomously enough and free the parents of obligations. But we also know that when researchers try to understand the notably elevated levels of psychological distress and disturbed behavior among children of affluent families, "isolation from parents" emerges as an important contributor.

Recommendation of child analysis

In contemporary practice, it is unusual that parents would accept a recommendation for intensive treatment absent significant preparatory parent work or worrisome acuity in the patient. The parents' objections may be highly personal but, frequently, are justified with reference to money and time. I'm very curious to know more about how Claire's analyst secured agreement from Claire and her parents around her recommendation of three times weekly treatment.

Psychopharmacology?

How one responds to a request for psychopharmacology evaluation is a familiar challenge for analysts of adolescents. The author doesn't mention whether the idea of a psychopharmacology consultation was ever introduced. There are good reasons a clinician might hesitate to recommend or endorse one. A young person like Claire may do very well without medication. Further, a twelve-year-old stands in the doorway to puberty. Her treaters might well wish to avoid introducing a medicine that would alter her experience of her body. But, responding to a request for a psychopharm consult is a familiar feature of contemporary adolescent practice, whether from parents, the pediatrician, or the patient herself. It is useful to learn how our colleagues respond in the context of different kinds of cases. [2]

---

2 The editors note that one commentator for this case raised the question of whether a psychopharmacology consultation had been considered. Medication is discussed more extensively in several other chapters, notably Karl and Claude.

Unspoken or unknown

The analyst appears to have had mixed thoughts about whether Claire's was a story withheld or a story unsymbolized and inaccessible even to Claire herself. Indeed, in practice, "unwillingness" and "lack of capacity" frequently condition each other and become intertwined. But the distinction retains significant implications for technique: do we address patients as if they are keeping troubling and complex feelings out of mind? Or do we speak as if they're needing new capacities to feel and to know? Are we working to analyze defense or to help development?

Conclusion of treatment

It is familiar that the treatment plan was sharply revised by Claire and/ or her parents at the outset of the second school year. School years are often used as substitutes for markers of progress in treatment, especially if the analyst hasn't offered alternatives.

New school schedules impersonally demand new treatment plans. Claire's mood was brighter. She had begun to re-engage with the social world, joined the soccer team, and made new friends. The acute phase of her illness seemed to have passed. Was there a case for continuing to meet intensively? We can only speculate. The analyst remarked that at termination, Claire was ready to "leave childhood behind." Is that a turn of phrase or was there a way of integrating "childhood" more deeply and on her own terms?

COMMENTARY 2

Claire's case presentation made us silent witnesses of the processes that occur in the psychoanalytic intervention of a young 12-year-old girl. Her parents became aware of the sudden changes in Claire, who started behaving differently to how she had normally been. Neither her siblings nor parents were aware of what was going on, as the only sign had been showing distress on attending school, which up to then had been a good experience.

As readers, we became aware of the analyst's high sensitivity to perceive the moments where Claire struggled to verbalise what was perturbing her and how skilfully the analyst managed to prevent this from becoming a bigger hurdle. The analyst perceived anxiety in Claire, but reacted with ease, probably having to do with the experiential knowledge that psychoanalysis embarks on a gradual slow opening that will not rush to get to know someone like Claire.

When Claire struggled with talking, the analyst allowed her to shift her attention to other topics, and even invited Claire to do other things that may not be talking, which clearly appeared to be welcomed by Claire. It felt sensible not to challenge Claire's fear of having to talk about something that as yet did not appear to be ripe enough for talking. The analyst correctly understood that Claire was not as yet ready to speak. Her analyst offered space and time for such issues to emerge when they would be ready to be spoken, whilst building between them the landscape of a new relationship.

The psychoanalytic perspective tends to dissonate with how other clinicians are traditionally taught to perceive symptoms in the mind. We have in this case presentation someone who was seen three times a week for somewhat less than a year. But this treatment did not have as its aim to reach a diagnosis or to put a psychological or psychiatric label on Claire, but to accompany her in this difficult patch of her life, adding the presence of another mind, of an alter ego who was not frightened to make sense about what was going on in Claire's life. It took six months of calm work for the material that so distressed Claire to come out, probably having to do with the gain in self-esteem necessary that was probably gained via the regular meetings with the analyst.

We learnt that Claire had created with her siblings "a family within a family," as her loving but hard-working parents were more absent than present, to the point that siblings had created some kind of shield by which they gave company to each other. We became aware that both of the older siblings (by 3 and 6 years) were starting new stages in their life, leaving Claire at home to her own devices. One sibling's attention looking for the university he'd go to, and sister's attention encapsulated with her first boyfriend. Claire's protective shield failed and left her vulnerable at a time where her school peers were a bit further ahead than her with the changes of puberty. Unfortunately for Claire that summer before the crisis, when going to the summer camp, those who "used to be her good friends" grouped together speaking of topics she was not as yet ready for, about boys and flirting, which made Claire feel even more alienated from them, and to top it off, these friends suggested to her that she was "Trans," as Claire had not joined them in their new sexualized environment.

This appeared to be the straw that broke the camel's back. Claire felt she was being thought of as someone she was not but had no one to talk about this with. Her world outside was collapsing, something in her tried to compensate for it by exercising increased control of her internalised world, which was exemplified when she communicated her tendency to obsessively organise every evening her collection of stuffed animals before going to sleep. Trying to have some control in what had become a chaotic world. All this information came accompanied by its appropriate emotional discharge at the sessions, when she appeared anxious of leaving the analyst probably having to do with not wanting to feel trusting of someone and then being left on her own again.

The way in which the analyst related to what appeared to be clear signs of transference is worth highlighting. After some months of treatment, when Claire started arriving early to sessions and not wanting the sessions to end, it was clear that Claire had transferred on to the analyst various aspects of her own internal world, exemplified in becoming the door's sentry trying to prevent the analyst from opening her door, hence not ending the sessions. The analyst clocked this but continued to unveil and accompany Claire's fragile narrative. Her analyst did not focus on trying to make of these distinct manifestations of transference the center of the analysis, despite, I suspect, clearly recognising such manifestations as transference.

What appeared to be at the center of the analyst's attention was Claire's world, and how difficult it had been for Claire when falling in this void where the world that contained her, at home and at school, collapsed. It was as if these sessions and treatment provided Claire with a lifeline that bridged the gap that started earlier the previous year, with the distance that both of her older siblings created, followed up by her peers at school. The analyst became a transitional object that contained her and helped her to catch up with the new situation with her family, with her peers as well as with her body. The analyst immensely reduced the risk of some kind of breakdown that could have occurred had Claire not had a safe space to think about her loneliness, her siblings, her gender, her sexuality and her friends. Claire was fortunate to have this analysis and it is no surprise how it was during this analytic period where Claire also appeared to "allow" her pubertal self the green light, signalling a recovery and the energy to continue her path of life.

EDITORIAL REFLECTION

This case seems a beautiful example of Anna Freud's conceptualization of analytic treatment providing restoration to the path of progressive development at any stage (1965). Despite the fact that Claire was not yet actually an adolescent at the beginning of her treatment, adolescence is present from the very beginning in the minds of the analyst and commentators, emphasizing the utility of always staying aware of development. The disparity between Claire's age and emotional maturity directs us to think about developmental transitions, what the move into adolescence entails, and also about the impact on individual and family dynamics when there is harmony among phases in all family members in contrast to times when there is dysynchrony.

We learned that Claire's passage into adolescence included an increased capacity for assertion, in contrast to aggressive interactions with her parents, although they needed help to acknowledge and appreciate the difference. This is an interesting dimension to track at the beginning of adolescence, just as we look for certain markers of the transition between adolescence and emerging adulthood. The question of whether consolidation in adolescence involves "leaving childhood behind" or integrating it speaks to how we conceptualize adolescence in general terms – do we emphasize an epigenetic view or retain a linear conceptualization of adolescence? This case seems to us to exemplify a process in which each phase influences and is influenced by each other phase, forward and backward in time. We might also note the sense of this treatment as a preventive intervention, likely to change the course of Claire's teenage years and her adulthood beyond.

Another dimension illustrated in this chapter is the extra power of peer relationships when a young person lacks support from parents, other adults, or siblings. Conventional descriptions of adolescence stress the importance of peer relations for good or ill, but we learn here that availability of influences from multiple sources makes for an optimal result. When the analyst could offer themselves as a transitional object to bridge the gap in Claire's relationships at this transitional time, it gave Claire room to catch up developmentally.

This chapter also reminds us of how powerful and efficient intensive treatment can be as an instrument of change, and how it can work to integrate individual developmental and family systems at new levels, sometimes relatively quickly. Authentic change over a relatively short period of time depends on multiple factors falling into place, notably the analyst's skill, sensitivity, tact, and flexibility. Some specific aspects of technique are highlighted by both the author and the commentators as contributing to a good outcome.

The analyst's choice to meet the patient where she was, respecting her defenses and not pushing her faster than she could manage, suggests that constructive analytic technique with adolescents most usefully keys into developmental level, regardless of the patient's age or grade. Gentle and gradual work to form a therapeutic alliance generated in this case a sturdy and internalizable set of new and enhanced ego capacities.

CHAPTER 4

JOHN – age 12

After a brief twice-weekly psychotherapy, twelve-year-old John started to see me four times a week in analysis. His analysis lasted for over two years. I also worked with his mother for parent work.

John was a bright, articulate youngster, who told me loud and clear in his first visit the story of his birth, "I was born only two minutes after my brother was born!" John, a fraternal twin, was first referred at eleven because of his difficulty controlling his compulsive hair pulling; when I met him, he was completely bald, hiding his head in baseball caps and do-rags. He denied having any pain when he pulled his eyelashes or hair. Evident in meeting him was his repressed anger with underlying depression. But his troubles had started much earlier, with head banging and hair pulling from around the age of five. This coincided with his parents' marital discord. John's problem with trichotillomania and his self-harming behavior escalated more around the time their divorce was finalizing.

When his parents divorced, his father stayed back in the city where they were raised, while John's mother made a unilateral decision to move to the other side of the country, with her sons and their nanny, despite father's protestation. The judge granted physical custody to the mother, with joint legal custody and visitation rights to the father.

There was a long history of parental friction. Early in their marriage, despite her ambivalence about pregnancy and motherhood, John's mother tried for several years to become pregnant, and eventually attempted several rounds of IVF. At last, when she was in her early forties, they eventually succeeded, and the twins were born. It was difficult for this mother to bond with her children, as she vacillated between emotional over-reaction and withdrawal from the boys. She seemed unable consistently to read emotional cues or be available. She delegated maternal functioning to the live-in nanny, hired when the babies were 6 months old.

I gathered from John that his nanny was generally nurturing and warm towards the boys. However, whenever the mother lost her temper with John, the nanny would not interfere to protect him. When heated arguments arose between John and his mother, the nanny was afraid to stand up for him for fear of losing her job. From John's perspective, the nanny was ineffectual in providing him the comfort, safety and reassurance that he needed when his mother lost her temper. On those occasions, John said, "She would put a blank face on."

The father was an educated man in his own field, who suffered from long-standing depression. He seemed warm and nurturing when I spoke with him but was also rather passive in relation to his ex-wife. This impacted his support for John's treatment, as the mother was often very ambivalent. It was striking that John's capacity and motivation for self-reflection helped him to stay engaged effectively in his analysis with me, ensuring that it continued long enough for real change. His wonderment about his own mind, his desire to make deep and empathic connection with people, especially maternal figures such as teachers and me, was remarkable. Additionally, his high intelligence along with his obsessive character structure made his analysis efficient and successful.

His central issue was his trouble in identifying his intense anger and being able to regulate himself when he lost control. He was struggling about not wanting to get in touch with his anger and rageful feelings. He often denied having been angry with his mother. Acknowledging his rage was a terrifying idea and he feared he would lose control as his mother did. Gradually, in the course of our work, he learned to own his angry feelings and was able to use his anxiety over his anger as a signal to stop his self-destructive thoughts and behavior. Initially, he became quite good at being able to tell what was going on with him at the sight of his mother's angry outbursts. He then was able to articulate in his own words his anxious feelings and thoughts. He thought he got better at anticipating such frequent episodes and he soon felt he was getting to be ahead of the game in anticipating it. He could beat his mother in catching the signal of anger in her early enough not to let himself to be targeted by her to be verbally criticized.

He told me how he got so good anticipating his mother's growing anger culminating in an outburst. He was aware that he had to learn early on how to read his mother's negative emotions, primarily *anger*. For example, he was vigilant when he heard his mother come home after a full day of work; she would complain about her co-workers at her workplace by relating to the children that she had a terrible day having to deal with frustrating people. John was afraid she would take out her anger on him. He made sure to stay in his room and stay quiet. He learned to wait until her angry storm passed. He also would hesitate to tell his mother about his day at school for fear of mother's lack of tolerance in listening to his account of his day.

John wanted to be heard for his own autonomous self and not just as part of a pair, what he called "the we-self-unit" with his fraternal twin brother. Well into his treatment, he held on to the belief that his brother was his mother's favorite son. He constantly compared himself with him and at the end he knew that he fell short academically while his brother made high grades. This was a sore point for him. Both boys facially looked more like their father. John was pudgy and his brother was taller and lean in his physique. His brother apparently was more popular than him among his school friends and girls. John loved to play sports and hoped to become a star athlete in football and golf. His brother was not interested in sports at all. Addressing and coming to terms with these actual differences contributed to his steady consolidation of his sense of self and autonomous identity, searching to build his sense of independence, as we continued working on his growing self-concept.

His articulateness and intelligence were positive protective factors that helped and motivated him to want to be heard, especially a strong desire to want to be understood by me in the transference. Through the use of my empathic and interpretive work and the use of words to name his feelings, I was able to help him to contain his anxiety and help him with his affect regulation. As I was able to interpret his conflicts consistently, his anxiety lessened. John developed a good working alliance with me. When he started to see me, everyone, especially John, was struggling to find an anchor of stability and a holding environment. We were a good fit and he liked seeing me every day in my office. I was his wished-for mother in the transference, as well as a stable and containing presence in a disruptive and disrupted world for John.

One day he walked into my consultation room looking serious.

J: Just for you to know I got A plus in history, in science I got C plus. I need to get my math grade up. English is my strong subject. See, I got my thesis done on one of William Stafford's poems. You must know his poetry and who he is. He got the United States Poet Laureate. I like his poems.

Analyst: *You want to be sure that I know him well and this way I understand you completely when you talk about him with such enthusiasm.*

J: He is a pacifist, you know? I am going to work harder on my essay. I know I can get my grades up. I guess my brother's grades are better than mine.

A: *You seem to think that your grades are not exactly at his level and you have certain feelings about it which makes you want to prove and show that you have superior ability and are a better student than him.*

J: Yes, I *can* show I *can* do well too and even better than him in the next quarter. My mom does not want me to go see the movie "Godfather." I like to see it. She saw part of it with us, but she left the room, and we did not know why. What's wrong with seeing the movie in the middle of the week? Besides we had a short day at school, and it was not a regular day. I think you would let me see it if you were my mom. Wouldn't you? I know you understand why I like to see the "Godfather." My father's family belonged to the Mafia, and my Italian American background is my reason for wanting to see it. Mom does not understand how important it is to me. This is a special occasion and she does not understand it. I am mad at her. She says the sky is blue and then says, "John you said the sky is yellow." My brother thinks she has a memory problem. Is it really a memory problem or she can't help lying? She lied to us and our father! She does not believe us. She accuses me of lying. I just repeat myself to make sure she will hear me out. She thinks I changed my position, but in reality, she is the one who says one thing and then claims that she had never said it.

A: *You sound frustrated with your mom and are finding it hard to trust what she says. Now that you are leaving to spend three weeks with your father, it makes it easier to tell me more about what you do not like about your mom.*

He nodded and said "Now I am hungry and tired. Do you have a granola bar or fig bar?" (I handed him the snack. He often comes to his sessions hungry because he does not have enough food in his lunch box on a daily basis.)

A: *Talking about your big intense feelings makes you hungry and tired especially when you are getting ready to leave for your holiday. You will also miss seeing me since you will not see me for three weeks.*

(I think his request for food was his way of assuring himself that he continues getting nurturance and warmth from me and that I would not stop caring for him. This is the way he can remember me when he goes away on his trip.)

J: "I do not know, but I have been having a stomachache the last two days.I think you are right about not seeing you for three weeks. Maybe my stomachache is telling me something about how I feel inside, just like now, I know pulling my hair out had to do with me getting rid of my internal bad feelings. See, for some reason this holiday, it feels longer than other times. I won't be seeing you for three weeks! Can I call you if I need to talk? I know you'll say yes." This was the end of our time and he said, "Goodbye for now. See you later!"

My most challenging concern and effort went into working with his mother in parent work. His parents' marriage had ended in a sea of turbulence, chaos and bitterness. John had learned to isolate his own feelings when he witnessed parental dispute and disharmony. He distracted himself in order not to feel his own feelings. He struggled with his much earlier conflicts and needs for a stable, predictable and genuine maternal figure. He was born into a world of ambivalence with a mother who had significant inner conflicts. His attachment to his mother was insecure and ambivalent, and she seemed to lack desire for emotional attunement with her sons. In addition, there was the burden of a secret in this family, as John's mother had concealed her extramarital affair and did not want to tell her sons the truth and the real reason for her move across the country.

Unfortunately, John's nanny did not seem to offer much compensatory engagement and involvement with him. She gave me the impression of a nanny with an almost robotic nanny duty by escorting John to his appointments without showing any emotional expressiveness, never smiling or greeting me or even conversing with him in the waiting room. His nanny rarely waited for him in the waiting room, but more often waited in her car in the parking lot of the building. When I first met him, John never called his nanny by her name, referring to her only as "my nanny!" As his analysis progressed and he allowed himself more access to his adolescent inner turmoil and his positive transference feelings for me, he spontaneously began to call her by her first name.

Near the end of the first year of treatment, John's mother asked his nanny to stop her nanny job and instead she was to become her tenant. That meant the nanny was supposed to give her rent money for her room in their house. This was rationalized by his mother as a need to make extra money, despite the fact that she was receiving sizable monthly child support. She also showed her ambivalence about the length of John's treatment, and probably about his full engagement in his analysis, by using financial hardship as a reason to change the frequency of his sessions. The mother also tried to save money by not buying nutritious meals for her children. To me this reached close to the level of actual neglect. Her insistence on limiting their food quantity and poor food quality by using frequent fast-food meals was an expression of her mixed feelings about her children.

During this period, I struggled with my feelings about John's mother and worried about the impact of an interruption of our work on his growing psychic stability and internal ego consolidation as an adolescent. My feeling about his mother's superego issues evoked a sense of wanting to help John even further. His mother lied to me on many occasions, which also gave rise to my concerns about John's superego development.

John was aware of his mother's dishonesty as well as her other shortcomings. With his newly formed reflective capacity, he became more able to anticipate his mother's volatile emotional states of feelings. When his nanny was fired, I did not initially realize that I was also the next in line to be demoted if not fired. Because he lost his nanny's presence in his life, John no longer could come to see me four times a week. His mother kept promising that she was going to rehire the nanny soon. Eventually, after a long wait through the summer, the nanny was rehired and she could bring John to his sessions, and he resumed his analytical frequency.

When he returned to see me after his nanny was rehired, that day he showed his delight when he saw me in my waiting room. His nanny was sitting on the chair next to him.

J: See, here she is! From now on my nanny will bring me to see you for my appointments like we did in the past.

When we entered in the consultation room, he walked around the room and checked everything on the shelves and toy boxes.

J: Have you kept my drawings in my folder?

A: *You know I would, and you remember where you can find it. Perhaps, you are thinking about drawing today?*

J: Yeah, I wanted to check to see if you lost or threw them out?

A: *Not having been able to see me regularly made you feel unsettled and brought doubts to your mind. You wondered if I kept your art works in a safe place for you or I just got rid of them.*

J: Yeah, when we moved, my mom did not want me to take my story books or even my own drawings with me!! See she got rid of my nanny just like that. I am so mad at her. She just does not want to know how I must be feeling. Now, I am really happy my nanny is back, and you are here too! I showed him where I kept his folder (He seemed to forget that I showed him in the past). When he saw it, he sighed a big sigh of relief!

J: (with an excitement in his voice) "Thank you Dr. X for keeping it for me!"

John's cats were important attachment figures for him, as well as useful displacement figures. For a time, their symbolic presence in the material that represented his inner life was rather noteworthy. He was attuned to his cats' affective states – he noted their capacity for closeness and their capacity for independence; he gleefully made jokes about his cat's similar emotional state and that of his own. He identified with his cats especially with the female one. She was his and the male cat was his brother's.

My first name and his cat's name rhymed, and I interpreted that perhaps she replaced me when he was not in my office. He pondered about it and smiled. It was intriguing to him; he had not thought about it until that moment. This increasing openness to ideas and his own experience represented a significant shift in John's defensiveness. He was quite eager to see me and he was proud to discuss his wide range of interests in political, social, cultural matters, sports, and literature with me. I interpreted his desire to be admired by me as his wish for a perfect mother whom he could love and would be loved by, in return. His vulnerability to wanting to be loved came alive in the room with me, often through his questions about my other patients who were leaving my office before him. He developed a quick positive transference. His verbal ability and his storytelling talent often seduced me into a position of passive admiration, while John controlled all the action.

He would tell me stories about his father's ancestors that he heard from his aunt, and the way in which they operated in their day-to-day life. They were suspected of having had shady business deals with bad guys and had broken laws.

He passionately would narrate a scene of bank robbery or a suspicious business transaction between two groups of gangsters, as if it truly had happened, and, as I was listening to him, I wondered if there was a shred of truth in what he was telling me. What if there was a historical truth about these narrations in his father's side of family. What if he did exaggerate and made it into more of a drama to impress me?

He wondered about his father's image on his mind, since he could not detect anything being wrong with him or him being untruthful. He wondered if his father would ever become like his great-grandfather or grandfather.

He asked me one day if that was possible? I said that he is also curious wanting to know how he will turn out when he grows older. He agreed that he does think about these ideas. He said how would he find out if it was in his father's genes and his father gave him his gene. I told him he has hard questions and wants to know if genes are all responsible for who a person becomes or is it their environment and upbringing. We continued the discussion for several sessions.

John had a strong desire to share his interest in computer games with me. Specific identity questions and the theme of who he thought he was becoming had emerged in his play. We were able to connect his conflicts over his anger with his concerns about what kind of person he was and wanted to be. John also displayed a touching wonderment about his own changing body and self in the form of direct questions about his budding sexuality and sexual identity.

He asked me one day if I think girls are going to like him for who he is.

I asked him to elaborate. He said, he feels his body is plump and not like a teenage boy who is slender like his brother. In reality, he looked chubby and even though he was an active football player, he had not lost weight in some areas of his body like his upper chest.

One day, he lifted up his shirt and asked "See, can you see? Do you think I will lose these fatty tissues in my breast area? I thought I would show it to you because you are my doctor." (I was taken aback with his quick action of showing me his bare chest. It was true he had still some baby-like fat especially in his breast area. I thought maybe he worried he has some feminine signs of breast budding like girls his age.)

J: Does my chest look like girls my age who are growing breasts?
A: *Everyone grows differently and at a different rate and speed. It looks like you are comparing yourself with your brother's body. You are wishing to have his body type. You sure have a lot of questions about how fast your body is changing*
J: yeah, I do. He seems to attract more girls. There is one who is very crazy about him.
I thought to myself that he is a very young adolescent, and his body will be in process of changing for some time as his puberty continues to blossom. His brother's body type is quite opposite.

John expressed emerging erotic feelings towards girls when he spoke about his classmates. He admired girls with good minds who excelled scholastically. He felt identified with his father; and saw his mother as a rejecting figure. He developed a theory that girls were going to reject him as well. His self- esteem was fragile, as he compared himself to his brother who was tall and slender.

John read a lot and usually brought articles and books to his sessions, especially Stephen King novels. Then he asked me if I had read them. It seemed his interest in these books was both counterphobic and an enacted effort to see if I would find these books disgusting as his mother said she did.

With John's intellect and perceptiveness, he was able to identify with his teachers, coaches, and his father as role models. He also sometimes used his charm to his advantage in a particular way to seduce his mother and friends and at times behaved in a secretive deceptive way. This was an important theme that came up frequently especially before his mother's secretiveness about her infidelity was revealed, acknowledged or talked about. Secrets were a recurring theme in his play and game interests. John knew through his father that the extra-marital affair was the cause of the divorce, but his mother had never admitted or talked to the boys about it.

He talked in defense of his father and was very angry with the man who stole his mother from his father and him. He said once "he *robbed* me from my childhood happiness." One important issue in the parent work had to do with the secrecy around his mother's affair. I encouraged his mother to disclose her affair with her sons; she agreed to have a family session and to explain what had happened that she divorced his father. John was relieved when his mother said it with her own words that she fell in love with another man and that was her reason for uprooting the family. He became less defensive in general when his mother decided to discuss it with them, rather than having to deny it persistently with her as it had been in the past. John explicitly said on multiple occasions in his treatment that he knew she had an affair, and he identified with his father's pain and sense of betrayal.

John's superego became less harsh or punitive in the second year of his analysis after his mother decided to disclose her affair. The revenge fantasies about the man who "ruined his father's and his life" subsided gradually. He was scared to imagine that his anger could be so potent that he would lose control of his mind. At the same time, the idea of revenge and murder phantasy was ambivalently satisfying to him. Sometimes it made him feel scared because he knew he is just a child. It also was scary to him that nobody cared about him, and he was *alone*. He was mostly relieved that I was there for him to contain his anxiety.

He often arrived early to see me in the waiting room but pretended that he forgot to turn on the light signal and took delight when I had to come and take him to the consultation room. I interpreted that when I found him in the waiting room, he pretended that he was indifferent, but his presence had to be acknowledged, since I actively would go there to get him. However, deep inside he was happy to see me despite his indifferent facial expression. He knew I cared about him and did not forget him. He responded, "I just forgot to turn the light on!" I said, "This is the way that you make sure that you're loved by me." He was quiet when he heard what I said.

After a brief pause, John said, "Today, I wanted to know if you were coming out of your office and looking for me. I know it is silly of me to think this way. You know, my mom does not even know if I am in my room or not. I might as well sneak out of the room and go to the park. I did it once. She never noticed it." He then told me that sometimes he felt guilty for pretending that he was sleeping in his bed, when he had actually gone out by climbing down from his window and going to the nearby park on a few occasions. He felt badly when he talked about these manipulations, lies, and cheating.

He reported that he got a stomachache when he tried out for the football team. In his football team, he played offense and he had to win. He had difficulty sleeping because of these worries. He got a stomachache each time he had a try-out for a sports team. The same thing happened when he invited a girl to his school winter formal. He also worried unrealistically that he would be kicked out of the gifted program. It was an expression of his underlying insecurity and dread that he would not be considered reliable. His perfectionism was a defense against the pain of his fear of rejection and of many times in his past that he had felt let down and rejected. His focus on detail was an aspect of his obsessive character that helped him to ward off his feeling of insecurity.

After many months of playing out his violent fantasies in the form of drawings or board games, he could more directly express his feelings toward his twin brother. He verbalized his hurt, disappointment, hatred and anger toward him. Although he had made some reference to his brother in the earlier phase of his analysis, I noted that he had seemed afraid that if he had angry thoughts about his brother it would hurt his brother for good, and that he would end up feeling hurt as well. He nodded and said, "I am happy for him that he now sees a therapist too." He told me that his brother only saw his therapist once a week. "I see you four days a week!" He had a big smile on his face.

John's exceptionally high intellect and analytical ability made him feel different from other kids and made it more difficult to make friends compared to his brother. He reflected that his other classmates did not think about social/political issues. He recognized that his intellectual and analytical abilities cause him to feel somewhat different from his friends, and we wondered if, in some ways, his feelings of difference and lack of self-esteem had made it more difficult for him to develop friends as his brother had done.

Presently, John is able to keep the friends he made through his involvement in several sport teams. He plays football, baseball, hockey and golf. He no longer worries about not having friends. He made several close friends and does not feel inferior to his brother who is popular both with girls and boys. He no longer wears a do-rag or baseball cap to cover his baldness. He has a head full of hair. Although it is still easier for him to relate to adults, he is also very aware of the importance of his peers' presence in his life. John is further along in his individuation process and has made progress toward an autonomous sense of self.

John has been less rigid in trying out identifications with each of his parents. He comes in frequently in his football outfits or with his golf clubs, showing me how he feels closely identified with his father's sportsmanship. He is intent on wanting to get a football scholarship and go to the best University that is known for their prestigious team. There was a time that he showed off his musician tee and heavy metal chains to see how I reacted to his new look. He is eager to try out life without analysis and see what happens and so is bringing his analysis to a close.

With all of these aforementioned gains, John still struggles with ambivalent feelings about his future and uncertainty about his own impulses. I wonder, given his long history of eczema, head-banging and hair-pulling, about the strength of his capacity to resist self-injurious solutions in his effort to curtail aggressive and violent impulses. He is well aware of an intergenerational family propensity to physical violence.

On the other hand, John is able to identify his angry feelings more effectively, especially toward his mother. He allows himself to speak assertively to her and not avoid the subject at hand. Likewise, he is comfortably able to negotiate about the hours he is supposed to see me when they present conflicts with his sports practice commitments. He is very interested to become a criminologist, which is in some way rather similar to my work with him as an analyst, so perhaps his burgeoning adolescent self will include an identification with his analyst.

My parent work and John's analysis for the last two and a half years taught me a great deal about the importance of the role of my capacity to contain the mother's anxiety, along with John's. Meanwhile I believe ego structure-building, affect development and formation of increased capacity for mentalization have been in progress. His analysis has been complex, but lively. Whether he will return for additional analytical work in the future remains to be seen.

COMMENTARY 1

My hat goes off to John's analyst. I am so impressed with how much she was able to help him and his family. John began the analysis afraid that his anger at the people he loved and depended on most would hurt them. John was angry at his mother for betraying his father, for moving the family away from his father, for lying, and for keeping secrets. John was angry at his father for being untrustworthy and for letting John go. John was angry at his fraternal brother for beating him to first born status by two minutes and for being more successful and popular than John. John defended against his anger at his loved ones by taking his anger out on himself. He had stomach aches, banged his head, and compulsively pulled out his own hair. John's analysis helped him understand and accept himself and stop his self-injurious symptoms.

As impressed as I am with the work John's analyst did with John, I am even more impressed with the work John's analyst did with John's mother. Many excellent child analysts and therapists fail because they can't find an empathic way to work with their patients' parents. The parents are never our patients and so we are limited in how we can work with them. They hire us as allies to help their children, but as the transference develops, they can come to see us as adversaries. They may be jealous of our connection to their children and resentful of our power in the family. Parent work with adolescents can be particularly challenging since we tend to work less with them and thus have less of an alliance with them than we do with parents of younger kids. Many parents don't tell their children's analysts everything because of their shame and fear of the analyst's judgment. However, John's mother actively lied to and fired John's analyst. Given these provocations, it is even more remarkable that John's analyst was able to form an empathic alliance with John's mother and help her to acknowledge the big secret in the family. John's mother told John and his brother that she divorced John's father and moved the family away because she fell in love with another man.

John's analysis makes me wonder about some of our beliefs. We tend to believe that for a child or adolescent analysis to work we need the support of at least one parent. It didn't seem to me that either parent was very supportive of John's analysis. Yet John was actively engaged in the analysis and clearly benefitted immensely from the analysis.

Another belief I think many of us have is that a child's sense of right and wrong is greatly influenced by their parents' honesty. In some combination of reality and fantasy, John experienced his mother as a cheater and a liar who didn't even give him enough to eat and his father as a member of the mafia. Based on this, one might expect John to either be utterly immoral or someone who defended against those wishes by never once doing anything wrong. However, John comes across as a relatively honest young man who occasionally lies and sneaks out on his mother. He clearly has a sense of right and wrong and experiences guilt when he does something that he believes is wrong. However, he's also not so terrified of his desires that he never does what he wants.

How did all of this happen? John's analyst seems to have been able to allow John to form a very positive transference in which he was able to feel secure and give voice to his aggressive and sexual wishes. As he experienced his analyst's ability to stand up to his mother without rejecting either John or his mother and experienced his analyst's acceptance of his wishes and fears he became able to stop hurting himself and to explore more of his world.

Reading the report, I'm unsure if John's analysis could have explored more of his negative transference and some of his sexual wishes or if it's merely that the write up didn't cover that work. For instance, I wondered if John might have felt betrayed by his analyst (in the transference) when they stopped meeting because John's mother fired the nanny. I would have expected John to be angry at his analyst for not making his mother arrange transportation for John to continue his analysis. Was John trying to express this when in his first session back he asked his analyst if she kept his drawings? I wondered if this might have been an opportunity to make a transferential interpretation about his fears that the analyst got rid of his drawings and maybe even him, just as he felt his mother got rid of his father, his nanny, his analyst, and maybe even him. It might be that this was repeated in the eventual termination. Did John want his analyst to say he wasn't ready to stop and fight for him to stay? Did John feel rejected by the analyst agreeing to end the analysis? I also wonder if when John lifted his shirt and showed his analyst his chest it was an attempted seduction. Was this an opportunity to explore John's sexual wishes towards his analyst? Of course, none of this takes away from the very rich and successful analysis John had.

It is truly remarkable that in this short analysis, John went from being completely bald to having a full head of hair. Even more important, he learned that he was expressing his feelings with his body. Instead of knowing his feelings he banged his head, had stomach aches, and pulled out all of his hair. John went from defensively avoiding his anger to being aware of his angry thoughts and feelings about his mother, father, and brother. Giving voice to his angry wishes and fears allowed him to stop taking them out on his body. Being less afraid that his anger would destroy those he loved, he was able to assertively enjoy thinking, talking, sports, and girls. John and his family were extremely fortunate to have had such a gifted analyst!

COMMENTARY 2

I would like to begin my comments by thanking the analyst who has presented this precious material about a pubescent boy. It is precious because it provides evidence of the value of child and adolescent analysis carried out in an intense way with a high frequency of sessions. We child analysts have the emotional task of accompanying our young patients in their growth process through the internal work of facing pain and the possibility of developing emotional thoughts.

My paper will focus on the transferential processes, which I consider to be richly expressed in the clinical material. It is through these processes that we can research – in my view one of the most important forms of research in psychoanalysis – the work we do with our patients. I am interested in what the analyst perceives and describes about a valuable inner quality of John's : *"especially a strong desire to be understood by me in the transference."* I consider that in this sense a good prognostic possibility opens up for John, as the analyst discovers this quality and uses it in analysis. By means of my comments, inspired undoubtedly by John's analysis, I would also like to include some ideas about how I conceive the psychoanalytic task in our times. They will be very brief appreciations, with no intention of distancing myself from the case, quite the opposite.

Regarding John's symptoms, I would like to start by thinking about what a young child can do to live when his mother uses him as a receptacle for the projections of her own anxieties and hostility? One possibility is to develop second skin phenomena (Esther Bick, 1968) as a defense, where the mind seeks support and integration through intense bodily sensations, for example compulsive hair and eyelash pulling. *"He denied having any pain when he pulled his eyelashes or hair."* Self-destructive tendencies were predominant in him from a very early age, as well as a long history of eczema. Maybe it was a way of "feeling," of "existing," through extreme skin and bodily sensations. This type of psychopathological phenomena is produced by the lack of an internal containing and integrating object. Within this idea, I would add that hair pulling is a way of freeing himself from his own pain and from the mother's intrusive projections in his mind-head. Freeing himself from an internal object that, instead of containing the intense anxieties expected in a young child, leaves him standing alone, and on the other hand uses him as a receptacle for her own anxieties and hostility. We would also have to consider that John is a twin, a condition that already implies vulnerability in the bond and demands a greater containing effort from the parents. In this case there is the added difficulty of parents with a very conflicting divorce enveloped in deceit.

I find John's evolution during his treatment interesting. I will focus particularly on the development of his capacity to appreciate beauty (Meltzer,1988), most probably as a result of the transferential relationship with his analyst. He begins to be moved by poetry, its beauty; his own body follows a different aesthetic path. This will become evident through his awakened interest in Literature and other "knowledge" (Science, History, English…) which he wants to share with his analyst. I am under the impression that it is an introjective process with a loving quality in the relationship with the object, very different from the defensive second skin processes in which he pulled out his hair. His head seems to be in another mental state, not only because his hair has grown back.

John tells his analyst, "William Stafford, the poet, is a pacifist, you know." It is like he is saying: do not be afraid of me, I prefer love to hatred. I would add, I just need to count with an object internally which is equipped in such a way that it is able to inspire me and, from creativity and knowledge, enables me to think emotionally rather than pulling out my hair. That's a possible interpretation of John's internal world. John is supported by the beauty of poetry, by what it evokes in the analyst, I therefore do not believe that the transferential process is only about counting with the *"Mother that I wish I had had;"* the change that has occurred in his internal world is deeper. The value of knowledge, the symbolic development through the appreciation of poetry, is exposed by the analysis and reveals a different mental state in John, in which introjective processes are predominant; the quality of the relationship with the object, both internal and external, has changed. A mind that is capable of finding itself internally in this type of relationships with the object, in this kind of aesthetic experience, we could say, has had to accept its dependence on a loving object.

"Now I am hungry and tired. Do you have a granola bar or fig bar?" John asks before a holiday break, and adds, *"for some reason this holiday, it feels longer than other times. I won't be seeing you for three weeks!"* In a

psychoanalytic perspective the focus is put on the emotions and on the internal experience that each person has related to these, which enables the development of thoughts and supports us in the desire to know. This type of process involves knowledge which is not comfortable, that is to say, it is not certain, which is invariably linked to a lack of knowledge, and therefore includes pain as part of the transition through this quality of experience. The inclusion of this aesthetic perspective in the psychoanalytic clinic contributed by Meltzer (1988), undoubtedly expands Bion's valuable ideas on the mind of the patient and the analyst, and the internal dialogue between them.

The construction of well-equipped internal objects on which the child's Self can be inspired by means of introjective identifications is part of our clinical work, and I believe that John's analysis is proof of that. John is working in order to "know" more, face the "truth," especially about his internal couple, his parents. The oedipal configuration starts taking emotional shape in the treatment.

In his associations about the film "The Godfather," his own "mafia-related" contents could be about rivalry with his twin brother. Beyond his father 's "legacy," natural and necessary identification with him, John would like to "see them," that is to say, face his own mafia-related contents. I must say that the identification through the film "The Godfather" has something of the epic that the oedipal configuration requires and which his mother wants nothing to do with. The analyst tells us: "*He would tell me stories about his father's ancestors that he heard from his aunt, and the way in which they operated in their day-to-day life. They were suspected of having had shady business deals with bad guys and had broken laws.*" I am under the impression that his unconscious infantile aspects trust the analyst to allow him to face these mafia-related aspects, not avoid them, but "see them."

As parallel tracks: the oedipal legacy, that excites and vitalizes him, but which can also turn him into a thief or a murderer. "*He passionately would narrate a scene of bank robbery or a suspicious business transaction between two groups of gangsters, as if it truly had happened and, as I was listening to him, I wondered if there was a shred of truth in what he was telling me. What if there was a historical truth about these narrations in his father's side of family?"* I think that what is interesting about this narrative of John's is that it was about the truth of his internal world. Something about potency and masculinity is at stake in his fascination for these stories, gangsters can be very "seductive." Later that gives rise to the issue of the value of truth in the sessions. The violent aspect of lies and secrets, as a form of intrusion exerted by the mother, is a form of intrusion that is more subtle than explicit aggressivity, and that turns out to be very destructive for the infantile Self, as we could see in John's disturbing symptoms.

As the analysis progresses, sexuality and its conflicts are manifested, just as expected in any adolescent analysis process. John becomes seductive, not only with girls, but also with certain adults such as his teachers, and this will have an effect on the transference. At times being "seductive" can turn out to be a bit deceiving, it might hide other unconscious infantile aspects: a vengeful murderer with his twin brother or with his mother's new partner; at other times the one who escapes through the window without his mother knowing. This period is accompanied by reading Stephen King's novels. What better symbolic resource to transmit an internal world full of passion and revenge? Stephen King's literature shows us our worst fears: what human beings are capable of doing, moved by envy, jealousy, revenge, greed. . . . Thanks to his internal changes, John is willing to offload this fear of his worst side in the transference in the hope that his analyst will not be scared of him, and will contain and understand him. He will start to find out what his world of internal relationships is about. The analytic experience has made him realize this, and he values it. He values the analytic method, that is why his pains have started to cure.

In my experience as an analyst I have been surprised by the capacity of young children and adolescents to value the analytic method, appreciate its beauty, as Meltzer described (1967), when the analysis has gone well. John tells his analyst that his brother has started therapy: *"I am happy for him that he now sees a therapist too." He told me that his brother only saw his therapist once a week. 'I see you four days a week!' He had a big smile on his face."*

Money-Kyrle helped us understand the patients' attempts to let the analyst know about their "upset and perturbation" in different ways. It is necessary for the analyst to feel that perturbation and feel perturbed. In my opinion, this is an interesting idea of analytic receptivity: observation and work on the mechanisms on which the projections of the patients and the introjection of the analyst are based. This idea was later taken up by Bion. It is the analyst's disposition towards introjection, being able to receive the projective identification and its pain, and above all their "sincere desire to understand," Meltzer would add. Undoubtedly some of this took place during John's treatment.

EDITORIAL REFLECTIONS

Freud formulated his ideas on transference in work with the adolescent Dora (1905b). In this chapter 12-year-old John and his mother and his analyst take us beyond transference so we can begin to explore additional curative forces. John is a very successful case. In a relatively short time John seemed restored to the path of progressive development or, more precisely, the "growth force" was recognized, validated, and encouraged by the analyst. In our most recent work we have added the "growth principle" to our understanding of the action of the reality and pleasure principles (Young-Bruehl and Bethelard 1999; Novick, J. and Novick, K.K. 2022). We now say that a major task of adolescence is to integrate the three principles so that they work in harmony.

In this chapter, as well as in the others addressing work with very young adolescents, we see the unfolding through puberty of John's relationship to his changing body. A major early adolescent task is coming to terms with having a sexual body, which entails transforming one's relationship to body and self. Transformation will be ongoing throughout adolescence, as the young people adapt to real changes within and in their perceptions of others. Owning one's own body, taking responsibility for being a separate self, entails a new correlation between the reality and pleasure principles, as the growth principle impels integration of change. Rather than conceptualizing this process as 'separation,' we look at transformation throughout.

John started his analysis guided only by closed-system pleasure, avoiding reality to avoid pain, but his growth had stopped. He was in a rage, mostly directed at himself, which he used as a hidden attack on his mother. The analyst talked of working in the transference, using the term transference in its current generalized form, meaning any and all feelings or impulses that the patient brings into the treatment relationship. Anna Freud differentiated externalization and transference and warned that confusing the two can interfere with progress (1965). This distinction feels especially relevant to working with adolescents, who struggle with integrating all the many different aspects of themselves and experience conflict over how they appear and may be judged. Adolescent externalization may appear in the form of an externalizing transference, particularly at the beginning of a treatment (Novick, J. 1982). From the writeup we perceive that the initial work focused on John's externalizing defense, his way of being, which attributed the rage to another, then directing it back at himself. Through this work he could begin to feel safe enough to admit his longstanding rage at his mother to his analyst and himself. At this point the mother managed to manipulate the home situation so that John's sessions were effectively reduced from four to once per week to none for a period of time.

It was clear to all that a major obstacle was the mother's ambivalence toward John and probably her active preference for the "older" twin boy. The analyst worked regularly with this mother, creating a relationship within which she could eventually directly confront her, enabling the mother to allow the resumption of John's analysis. The mother also had lied to the children and here we see the analyst's willingness to engage the mother in basic issues, as, through the work, the mother could tell the children that the reason for the divorce was that she had been having an affair. We can see in this chapter the important role of secrets, not only those of the parents' marriage, but also the IVF conception and the family history. With the adolescent push to engage with reality, secrets have to be canvassed. The analyst is demonstrating not only the importance of concurrent parent work but that the work is not superficial – it gets to central issues in the parents, such as lying and being ambivalent. All this is *dynamic* concurrent work with the parent of an adolescent, which is still avoided by many.

John was aware of the analyst's impact on the mother and this probably helped make her feel to him like a safe and protective object. In fact, we infer that, simultaneously with working with John on his self-destructive defenses, the analyst worked with John as a new developmental object. The analyst became a mentor, a supporter of John's explorations, a new superego model. The analyst became a model for growth, reality possibilities, and open-system pleasures, all working in harmony. This chapter teaches us that what the patient sees and can identify with in the analyst is critical to outcome. The analyst's courage to confront the mother and father and the analyst's appreciation for art and literature gave John alternatives that fruitfully brought him into the analytic work. He came to the work equipped only with closed-system magical omnipotent defenses, primarily repressing his rage at his mother and secretly attacking her by destroying his body, thereby destroying her creation. The analysis allowed for the emergence of an alternative solution in identifying with the analyst's creativity and finding pleasure in reality, truth, and growth.

II

EARLY ADOLESCENCE

CHAPTER 5

KAITLYN – age 12

Kaitlyn, a 12-year-old, came for treatment due to her obsessional thinking, inability to make decisions and endless doubting. She tormented herself and her parents in the process of making most decisions. Big or small decisions, it was always the same and they were all worn out from it. The problem seemed to only be getting worse, rather than better, as Kaitlyn was getting older.

Kaitlyn looked her age, with long, dark hair and bright blue eyes. She related in a warm, anxious manner. Kaitlyn was involved in many activities, participated in sports and had many friends. It was when it came to making choices that she became despairing and anxious. She explained that it had been easier when she was younger, when her parents made all the arrangements, bought whatever she needed, decided on her activities, when mom and dad took care of everything. She claimed that she was always happy with whatever they chose for her. She wished her parents could continue to be involved in all her activities. She still longed for Mommy and Me classes, parents at birthday parties, parents involved and knowing everything about you, your friends and what you were doing. While she had many friends, she was feeling increasingly out of step, as she was aware of her friend's enjoyment of their increasing autonomy. She was reluctant and embarrassed to reveal her anxiety and uneasiness about going places and doing things without parental involvement, although her closest friends were well aware of it.

Most outstanding was Kaitlyn's longing to return to an earlier way of living, her explicitly stated wish "not to grow up" and her conviction that she was more lovable to her parents as a little girl. While Kaitlyn enjoyed the companionship of her peers and a sense of belonging, there was little evidence of a gradual process of increasing autonomy and diminished idealization of the parents. She expressed no urge to establish autonomy from parents or teachers, or anybody for that matter. Just the opposite. Entering adolescence, the pressures from reality, both internal and external, for a fundamental shift in relationship to family and peers had become disruptive and disorienting and were destabilizing her previous adaptation.

She did well academically despite her procrastination and intense worry about every exam. Although she always participated and enjoyed herself on school trips and summer teen programs, the anticipation and lead up was agonizing. Until the day came that the activity would begin, she would endlessly worry that she had made the wrong choice, whether it was a haircut style, a school club, a camp program, or a summer destination. She was terrified each time that she "would not be able to do it." She seemed unable to view herself as someone who could do it, despite the fact that she was doing it. Kaitlyn's increasing social and cognitive capacities could not be woven into her sense of self, the self-representation of the loved and loving girl who continued to idealize her parents.

Kaitlyn was close with both of her parents, both academics, and both overly involved in different aspects of her life. Both Kaitlyn and her parents described how happy the three of them had always been together throughout her childhood. She had a sister, 6 years older and a brother 4 years older. There had been miscarriages prior to Kaitlyn's birth.

Kaitlyn's parents were disappointed, distressed and truly baffled as to why their daughter seemed unable to take advantage of all they had offered her. They could not understand how she was not thriving and moving on developmentally and becoming more autonomous in her overall functioning. While each parent felt they had reached their limit of what they could offer to relieve Kaitlyn, they found it very difficult to ask for outside help. They were especially frustrated that they could not solve this themselves. It was clear that both Kaitlyn and her parents were suffering.

My treatment recommendation was three individual sessions per week along with regular parent sessions. Kaitlyn was seen primarily at this frequency with intermittent reduction to 2 weekly sessions at the parent's insistence due to school and extracurricular activities. During college and post college, the frequency varied between one and three sessions per week.

Beginning treatment

Kaitlyn was eager for my help, quickly came to depend on me, and formed a positive maternal, often idealizing transference. She described her various worries and shared the details of her daily life. As she felt increasingly dependent upon me, she worried that she was betraying her parents, especially her mother.

Kaitlyn's creative, flexible thinking would easily become inhibited and rigid, or go in endless obsessive circles of doubting. When she had her own thoughts, she could not own them for very long. She would seek out what others thought, quickly losing any sense that she had an opinion of her own. She seemed afraid to have a mind of her own.

She was mostly terrified that any decision she would make for herself would be wrong. Just as she was about to follow through on a decision, she would reverse herself, argue for the alternative and become paralyzed. We explored what might happen, what did she imagine, why was there such a sense of disaster looming.

Kaitlyn gradually became more able to hold on to her likes and dislikes and voice them. She also began to talk about how confusing it was that her mother encouraged her to make her own decisions, yet when her preference did not match her mother's choice, her mother would try to convince her that mother's choice was better. For example, using a binder or spiral notebooks. It seemed she was to make her own choice, but it was to be the same choice as her mother would make. When this happened, Kaitlyn would quickly retreat through the week, no longer caring one way or the other about the matter.

As the treatment moved further along, Kaitlyn expressed not enjoying an activity that her mother had arranged. She felt frightened by her mother's angry response. Kaitlyn's mother screamed at her, calling her unappreciative and ungrateful. Kaitlyn became desperate, explaining that she could not bear for her parents to think she did not love them. She felt confused about herself, was she really a mean, unappreciative, ungrateful daughter as her mother insisted. Neither mother nor daughter seemed able to maintain a differentiated view of themselves from what the other thought of them. Kaitlyn would look to me, wanting to know "was this who she was." It took years to distinguish grateful from agreement.

Following angry arguments Kaitlyn would go to her room, procrastinate, and not get any homework done. She punished both herself and her parents and drew her parents in to rescue her. Both Kaitlyn and her parents insisted she needed a parent with her to study and overcome her procrastination. A new cycle of being grateful and feeling that she could not manage without her parents ensued. Kaitlyn again felt like a needy, dependent little girl who was compliant and grateful for the help she received, and this drove her anger underground.

Kaitlyn's mother was deeply invested in maintaining close control and a close tie, as if Kaitlyn having a mind of her own would threaten the mother in some way. Yet this was only part of the equation.

High school

We mapped the landscape toward recognizing and understanding how autonomy had become equated with aggression. We analyzed many instances of desperate anxiousness. The desperation derived both from a belief that making an independent choice would destroy the object as well the belief that there was no pathway to individuation. By taking comfort in the feeling that all would be good and perfect in the world under the care and tutelage of her parents, Kaitlyn had made it easier to inhibit her own thinking. She doubted incessantly until she could feel she was complying with what her object wanted. Autonomy threatened attachment.

As the central dynamics were mapped out and put into words, Kaitlyn's unreflective reliance on her parent's guidance diminished somewhat. Kaitlyn slowly began to make more choices for herself and they no longer felt as gravely consequential. She enjoyed her newfound freedom and flexibility to try out and also drop out of various clubs and activities. There was more excitement and adventure in high school.

Academic decisions and college prep work remained very conflictual and difficult, but she was able to move forward. Kaitlyn's conviction that growing up would make her less lovable and threaten her attachments ran deep and made anything associated with readying herself to leave for college especially challenging.

Kaitlyn graduated high school and went off to an excellent college. She continued her treatment through the summer. She went off to college knowing that she could reach out to me if she wished. She had the nagging feeling that she was now too old for me to want to continue to work with her.

Late adolescence

Adjustment to college was easier than Kaitlyn had expected. She made friends, enjoyed her classes and became more active sexually. She contacted me, wanting to resume her treatment, due to the dilemmas she found herself facing in her relationships.

The continuing trend in her object relationships was Kaitlyn's worry that she was disappointing and/or hurting her objects. This was familiar territory but by now Kaitlyn was more aware of having an internal world and that it was coloring her experience. Kaitlyn was more aware of the extent of the harm, the hurt, the damage, she feared she would inflict on her object. Her fantasies were more organized and elaborated. It was easier for Kaitlyn to recognize the irrational nature of the damage she feared she would cause with her peers than it had been with her mother. With her mother the fears had still often been justified on the basis of her mother's vulnerabilities.

Kaitlyn described very long conversations, imploring her friends to advise her when she needed to make a decision. At other times, knowing her friends were tired of being asked, she developed strategies which she hoped would allow her to discern their preference without an explicit request. The decision might be about choosing a study group, an a cappella group, a boy or a roommate. The torment that she put herself and her friends through eventually felt the same regardless of the details. She spent hours listening, wanting to again hear what they thought and what she should choose. She would waver back and forth in her decision for days, preoccupied to the point that other important activities would be eclipsed. Initially it seemed she genuinely needed to think the matter through with a friend. Over time, it became clear that what she needed was to believe, to be convinced, that the friend and the relationship with the friend would not suffer if she went a different way, chose a different option.

Kaitlyn had signed up to work on a different research project than her friend. Kaitlyn came to her session explaining that she was exhausted, having stayed up most of the night, for a few nights, needing to explain again and again to her friend what went into the decision she had made. She was afraid that her friend would become depressed as a result of thinking and feeling that Kaitlyn's decision was due to her not wanting to be with her friend. She desperately tried to find evidence that her friend was not devastated. Within days, Kaitlyn felt resentful and burdened, complaining that she had to do this in order that her friend "wouldn't think I didn't want to be with her."

I understood and interpreted that Kaitlyn could not stand for her friend or for herself to not want to be with with the other, and even worse that something else took priority. Kaitlyn could not go to sleep thinking of her friend feeling that Kaitlyn preferred doing something without her. And in this way, the two stayed together late into the night. Later she felt resentful that she wasn't able to get enough sleep.

We had opportunity for further work in this area on an occasion when Kaitlyn was coordinating travel plans with her parents. She had looked forward to one parent spending a few days visiting with her at college and then driving on together to a family gathering. She was furious and outraged when her parents changed the plan and expected Kaitlyn to take a train to meet them. It was a shocking outrage that they were not putting her wishes and convenience first, expected her to navigate the train on her own, and chose to spend more time with each other rather than with her.

She was clearly gratified by the intensity of her self-righteous indignation and outrage, as she continued to insist that she could not and should not have to bear such a disappointment. The more outraged she remained, the more ill equipped she continued to feel to handle and bear the disappointment. The analysis of the transferential experience revealed that she did not feel that I would help her bear the disappointment. She worried I would view her as a spoiled brat, be very critical and reject her, refuse to continue to work with her. She was certain that I would not help her bear the awful disappointment she felt at not being the only one or having to bear the object choosing to be with someone else.

This work allowed us to further analyze the frequent conundrum she experienced in regard to her intimate relationships. Until now, Kaitlyn was typically worried about hurting her objects. We saw this a bit in high school, with her early experimentation with boys. She worried about showing any interest in response to a boy's interest in her, because she expected her level of interest would never match his for her, and she didn't want to hurt him, so better not to start anything.

In college she also worried about the guy's feelings, that he would be hurt if, after a hookup, she didn't want to spend additional time with him. What began as something she wanted and desired turned into a trap. She worried she would spend more time with him than she wanted to in order not to hurt him. All desire, hurt, and disappointment reverted to the object. At this point in the treatment, she began to be able to notice and report that the boy seemed to have survived just fine, she would see him at another party, and he was clearly involved with another girl and enjoying himself. Kaitlyn essentially interpreted her defenses for herself, her own use of projection and projective identification. She began to recognize her own hurt and outrage. She began to recognize herself as the smothering object who wanted exclusivity, wanted the object to always be there for her and remain forever available to her.

Emerging adulthood

Feeling smothered and having to foreclose on a part of herself was further worked through as she attempted decisions regarding advanced study. Any one choice foreclosed on another. What initially felt like an opportunity, entered into with enthusiasm, then became a trap. The decision felt stifling, closing off all other opportunities for a satisfying life, what she wanted for herself.

Kaitlyn gained deeper insight into her central dynamics as we analyzed how they transformed and reemerged as she negotiated the many developmental tasks of late adolescence. We gained access to additional meanings and unconscious fantasies through analysis in the transference and countertransference as she moved toward adulthood.

Kaitlyn progressed to the level of internship. Everything was in place for Kaitlyn to begin her internship, she only needed to make the final commitment. She described how she "was making herself crazy," panicked, not knowing whether to go ahead with it or not. She was calling, texting, emailing her friends. She very effectively led each friend to tell her what she wanted to hear, and she saw herself doing it. She knew that she "was making herself crazy doing this." I interpreted that it was as if she gave her mind away, and then she felt crazy, without a mind, and would put her life on hold again. I had seen her do this numerous times, essentially become mindless and then feel like she needed the mind of the other.

This resonated deeply with Kaitlyn and she remembered many other times where she had done something similar, effectively estranging herself from an important aspect of her mental functioning. Analysis of the multiple meanings of the phrases "driven crazy" and "crazy mad" yielded further understanding of both the transference and countertransference. She was trying to undo what she was coming to me for. She could thwart me, subtly oppose me and the analytic work we were doing. How could I possibly get mad with her, I couldn't blame her, as she was suffering so terribly.

I have focused on the nature and quality of Kaitlyn's object relationships, how they evolved and transformed over the course of the treatment. This is only one of many aspects of the treatment. The focus captures my understanding of the analytic work that was most paramount for Kaitlyn's growth and the relief of her symptoms.

COMMENTARY 1

This case impressively demonstrates the lasting importance and changing uses of the therapeutic alliance over time. Kaitlyn's difficulties speak to the subversive persistence and shifts in the presentation of core conflicts across developmental phases, and the ways that the analyst adapted to the shifting symptomatic picture. Kaitlyn and her mother's troubles conceptualizing and celebrating their minds as separate speaks to early attachment difficulties that later crystallized into a problematic relational style extended to those outside the family. Early on, Kaitlyn appeared to be a "happy" and asymptomatic child, though it is likely that all along, she was falling behind in the tasks of separation-individuation and identity development that later emerged as preadolescent "symptoms." During her early life and latency, Kaitlyn adapted to others' needs, remaining in a merged state in order to maintain parental love.

A fuller developmental picture would have required survival of everyday frustrations (Winnicott, 1971) during which parent and child would tolerate small and bearable differences. Parental support in such moments across development supports the gradual emergence, bit by bit, of a sense of self, flexibility, creativity, and masterful problem solving. When pulled by the developmental thrust of adolescence towards more independence, these bits of self cohere into a firmer, more grown-up sense of autonomy and individuality. Instead, at the onset of Kaitlyn's adolescence, "new" symptoms shed light on previous developmental lags which had been brewing all along. Kaitlyn first became dependent on her analyst, using the relationship in the ways most familiar to her. She eventually used analysis to try to understand moments of disconnection from mother, and as a late adolescent observed how the same dynamic emerged with her peers. In emerging adulthood, she returns, turning inward for the first time to explore her own identification as "the smothering object who wanted exclusivity," needing the mind of another for a sense of stability. There is a feeling that Kaitlyn is still suffering from the same intolerance of separation that brought her in, now in the transference (the analyst thinks, "how could I possibly get mad at her … she was suffering so terribly"), although in a more grown-up and far less destructive way. It is possible that more analysis will continue to assist Kaitlyn, now a young adult, to continue to work towards a more confident and secure sense of herself.

The vignette does not give us a full picture of working with the parents. For the sake of this writeup, my commentary assumes they did not fully engage. This may not be the case, but given the frequency with which parents bring teens to therapy without fully engaging, it is a topic worth discussing. The alliance with this family is impressive; not many families are able to bear the logistical details and emotional toll of maintaining analytic work over more than a decade. I find myself wondering whether these parents, clearly invested, ever fully engaged in their side of the treatment. Were they truly able to fully support (in their own hearts and minds) their daughter's growth into a separate, adult self? My commentary will focus on parent troubles in this treatment, many of which are untouchable in analytic work with children or adolescents without committed concurrent work with parents in which the goal is for the parents to overcome their own obstacles to the child's development.

Given that there are two elder siblings in this family, one is left to wonder why Kaitlyn was so profoundly troubled. Did her siblings experience similar relational problems without "symptoms," or was something different for Kaitlyn? Noted briefly are multiple miscarriages prior to Kaitlyn's birth, which cause me to wonder about mother's experiences of potentially unrecognized/unconscious loss and subsequent melancholia, so often overlooked in our culture and even by parents themselves. Is it possible that mother, in an attempt to hold onto her youngest living baby after the loss of other pregnancies, entered an unconscious coercion with Kaitlyn to keep her close and avoid another loss/death/separation? The intensity of

Kaitlyn's insistence that she will lose her parents and will even be unwanted by the analyst when she grows up suggests that separation and the "creative, flexible thinking" characteristic of healthy adolescent development equals not only threatened attachment but (psychic) death and parental loss. It is possible that, unconsciously, mother feared the same psychic death and loss of her youngest baby, resulting in an unwanted union neither could imagine living with or without. It is also possible that mother (or father) struggled with unprocessed conflicts in their own early experiences that led to the unconscious family mythology that parents and children cannot remain close when children grow up.

Virtually no parent consciously wishes to grow apart from their child as they mature, nor do they wish to stand in the way of development. Yet, parental trauma and loss (either in adulthood or their own childhood) can be passed across generations and often shows up in the consulting room. Assisting the parents with derailed parental functioning in this case would be a hefty (though potentially invaluable) endeavor, and would require significant parental investment along with the analyst's flexibility, creativity, discretion, and capacity to hold the sometimes conflicting desires of parents and adolescents. Goals of such work would be to restore the parent-child relationship that will continue to evolve even over their adult lifetimes and that will potentially include and influence parenting and grandparenting in future generations. Though many parents of teens participate enough to get their child settled into therapy, Kaitlyn's parents also needed an understanding of their own (likely unwitting) participation in her difficulties. In concurrent parent work, the goal would be to restore a loving, growing, and expansive (open-system, per the Novicks, 2002) parent-child relationship that could transform and support Kaitlyn and her parents during the regressions, adaptations, and developmental shifts that will inevitably come, even in her adult life.

The technical question that arises is the role of the analyst working with a teen whose parents are inextricably part of the dependence-coercion scenario. This analyst became a new object to Kaitlyn, one who could tolerate and even encourage her autonomy, which gradually emerged in fits and starts over many years. Kaitlyn could depend on her analyst and chose to return after leaving home with some confidence she would not be pulled back into a merged state. In this way, the analyst assisted Kaitlyn in joining the forward thrust of her development and entry into young adult life. On the other hand, there is evidence that the coercive nature of the parent-child relationship persisted for Kaitlyn and her parents across the analysis and even into young adulthood, when her parents seemingly rejected her before she could reject them. When they cancelled a much-desired visit to her campus, they seemed unaware of her need for them to affirm her choice of a life away-from-home, and to see her as a successful college student. Parents of young adults are faced with balancing the child's need for their support with the need for independence; these parents did not seem to use the analyst for support in the parent-child relationship during this crucial transition from adolescent to adult.

While Kaitlyn may benefit from ongoing work with the analyst as a new object (a model often utilized in adult analysis, focusing on reworking her internalized conflicts within the context of the analytic relationship), I can't help but wonder whether more concurrent parent work starting at age 12 might have helped to restore the developmental pathway of the parent-child relationship. The use of additional parent work might offer a chance for Kaitlyn *and* her parents to enjoy a growing sense of closeness as their relationship evolves across a lifetime, and could provide the freedom for the parents to take pleasure in watching Kaitlyn grow up into her own person but not necessarily away from them. Without such work, Kaitlyn could become successfully independent at the cost of holding her parents at arm's length during important transitions in her adult life, rather than leaning on them during the temporary regressions that characterize even adult developmental shifts such as starting a career, a relationship, having children of her own, or coping with loss. Instead, we see evidence of Kaitlyn pushing parents away but recreating the old obsessions with her friends, partners, and analyst. Though it is not possible in every case, I believe Kaitlyn would have been better served by *both* approaches – utilizing the analyst as a new object as well as an environmental intervention intended to restore the parent-child relationship "in real life." Such work is difficult and often rejected by parents and/or therapists, but may offer a model for a transitional kind of work for adolescents who, like children in analysis, still need their parent's involvement, but as emerging adults, also need their own private analytic space.

COMMENTARY 2

In reading this challenging case, I was struck by the role of the mother in fostering the child's pathological dependency on her judgment, thinking and decision-making. This need of the mother's to make almost all decisions for her daughter and her insisting that her judgments were correct and that the girl needed to act – and think – as the mother directed, fostered not only a crippling dependency, but undermined the child's ability to use her own judgment for fear that she would make an error that would prove disastrous.

A mother like this is bound to evoke in the child a good deal of anger, aggression, and negative feelings toward the mother who she also desperately needs. Thus the child's normal aggression and ambivalence toward the mother, as a result of Oedipal rivalry as well as resentment over the mother's controlling behavior, would create enormous fear that the girl's aggression would alienate the mother and cause her to abandon the child.

For a child who cannot trust her judgment and thinking and who feels totally reliant on the mother, the fear engendered by this fantasy of abandonment would be paralyzing. The child would believe that she had to stay in the mother's good graces to stay alive. As mentioned above, the Oedipal situation would be particularly dangerous, as the unconscious hostility toward the mother would be especially strong, and the child's anxiety over favoring one parent over the other would be particularly threatening.

This would contribute to the girl's later fear of making any decision, as the idea of making a choice would be unconsciously related to choosing one parent over the other with the threat of alienating a parent and risking that parent's anger and aggression toward herself.

What does it take on the parents' part for a child to have confidence in her own judgment and decision-making? It takes giving the child increasing freedom to make choices as well as communicating the act of choosing carries no great risk. If the child makes a poor choice, that choice can be corrected. A mistake is not a disaster. Making mistakes is normal, necessary, and a part of healthy growth. But what if a mother – or both parents – fear making mistakes, if they communicate the idea that mistakes are dangerous, that the mistakes they made in life caused them or others great pain or were even life-threatening? This fear will be communicated to the child and increase the child's fear of choosing, which, in her mind, carries great danger.

If a parent always has to be right, this communicates a dread of being wrong in the child and increases her fear that being wrong risks terrible consequences.

In this case, the patient was made to feel safe and cared for when the parents were with her and did her thinking and decision-making for her. Being alone was dangerous, as she could not rely on herself. This increased her fear of separation to a very great extent. In her relations with others, she consistently projected this fear onto them and believed they would feel as threatened and angry as she did when left alone, or when she experienced disapproval. Thus, ongoing processes of projection and projective identification caused her great anxiety in her relationship with others and made those relationships consistently difficult.

The girl also identified a great deal with her mother's way of being in the world. The mother needed to control and dominate and she had to be right. Her choices and decisions had to be adhered to by others. The patient, too, wishes to control and dominate and has to conceal this aspect of herself behind an outer posture of acquiescent and fearful behavior.

She has been afraid that others would react to this concealed wish to control by being as resentful and angry as she unconsciously has been toward her mother. And just as she wished to get away from the dominant and controlling mother, she believed others would want to get away from her. This increased her fear of being abandoned, which in her mind was closely connected with dread feelings of helplessness.

I am sure that her therapist worked with all these dynamic factors over the years of the patient's treatment as they played out both in the transference and in the patient's relation with others.

The therapist also saw the mother quite regularly. She did not report on her work with the mother and whether she undertook to do therapy with her. In this case, I believe such work, either in conjunction with the child's treatment, or carried out by an independent therapist, would be crucial. The pathology in the mother was so powerful a force in retarding the child's growth and movement toward self-reliance that, in my view, it had to be dealt with in an effective way for the child to make the kind of progress both she and her therapist hoped for.

EDITORIAL REFLECTIONS

This chapter presents us with an account of a titanic conflict played out in and around Kaitlyn over a span of more than ten years. On one side are arrayed the formidable forces of the developmental thrust of the adolescent process, allied with the support of the analyst and the analysis, but on the other the full power of her parents' conscious and unconscious commitment to creating a child in a particular mirror image that reflected their own needs at the expense of their child's individuality. This is what we can characterize as "soul blindness," the condition that allows for externalization on to the child, which we view as abusive (Novick, J. and Novick, K.K. 1994, 2005).

An omnipotent shared delusion of a perfect family where no one is angry and no one is different from anyone else was maintained through Kaitlyn's early and school years. She preserved attachment to each parent by compliance with their wishes and decisions, protected herself from their anger and her guilt by defending against anger or resentment, and gained the gratification of their approval by performing well in school, sports and with friends.

When we meet Kaitlyn at 12 this structure is being assailed by the increasingly visible disparity between her and her developing peers and her parents' annoyance at her anxiety over making the slightest choice. They expect her to do as other middle-school kids do, to become better able to take initiative and responsibility, to relieve them of some of the burden of parenting so assiduously. This is a common cultural expectation for American parents, and Kaitlyn's failure to take these steps angered and embarrassed them. But the worm in that apple is that they seem to have expected that those forward steps should follow the path they "know" is right. They wanted Kaitlyn to develop more age-appropriate independence, but along their lines. In other words, it was to be an illusion of autonomy, a false progression that actually maintained and validated the idealized image of the omnipotent and omniscient parents. The parents were externalizing their own needs on to their child all the while claiming that they were doing what they knew was best for her.

Kaitlyn seemed to have known unconsciously that she was in an impossible position and she felt paralyzed in terror of her own aggression and consequent abandonment and rejection, unable to move forward and desperately trying to stop time and stay a little girl in her mother's lap.

This dynamic was played out repeatedly in the transference. It was interpreted and the interventions appeared to be accepted by Kaitlyn, as she would improve and move forward somewhat, only to have the sequence repeated through each subsequent subphase of her adolescence and young adulthood. This was a long analysis, with superb and heroic work by the analyst, in and out of the transference, but there was constant repetition since the parents did not change. Both commentators speak to the need for more parent work, or more intensive parent work, or more dynamic parent work. It is noteworthy that this idea seems taken for granted by the commentators, denoting increased acceptance of the crucial component of parent work. This is in sharp contrast to negative, even prohibitive, attitudes to working with parents of adolescents still prevalent in many places.

It is clear, however, that the analyst persisted in regular efforts to reach these parents on many different levels. The intractable obstacle, the resistance to engagement in a process of change in the parent-child relationship, appears to be the parents' collusion with each other, each supporting the other's "rightness," so that no doubt or questioning ever provided a chink of light to examine other options or consider that Kaitlyn could and should develop her actual own ideas and discover her very own feelings about things. If we think of this phenomenon in terms of the therapeutic alliance tasks of parents at different junctures in their child's treatment, we can see that Kaitlyn's parents did not truly engage in any of the initial tasks of transformation. They were willing to support her analysis for over ten years, but unwilling or unable to seek to transform the parent-child relationship. This chapter faces us with a profound question – how can the child change and grow into and through adolescence if the parents have no sense of their own need to change?

This chapter underscores the continuing need for parental involvement and support if the adolescent process is to be fully realized, as well as the difference (seen here by its absence) it could make to have their participation in a dynamic treatment process. We are left with the uncertainty of whether Kaitlyn will be able to maintain progressive momentum when these parents will not change and will continue to be soul blind and abuse her by externalizing their own wishes on to her rather than listening to her and respecting her own choices. In thinking about the relational aspects of this young woman's history and the predominant defensive array of externalizations we would characterize the parent-child relationship as abusive. This suggests that it's helpful to 'diagnose' the parent-child relationship, as well as thinking about the clinical characteristics of each individual in the family system. Harking back to the parent work tenet of setting dual goals at the outset of any child or adolescent treatment, we think it can bolster the therapist's conviction of the importance of continuing to try to engage parents dynamically. If, as in this case, that proves impossible, we are left with a clearer articulation of the need to work with the young person explicitly on the kind of relationships he or she is forming – do they follow closed-system sadomasochistic patterns or can they become open-system, mutually-enhancing and loving? This takes on particular relevance in adolescence, when lifetime patterns of relating are being consolidated.

Simultaneously, adolescents are establishing their own reality-testing as a major internal resource, growing beyond reliance on parents as the arbiters of what is real and true. This includes more realistic perceptions of self and parents. If, however, parents are consciously or unconsciously hypocritical, and their defensive externalizations sabotage progressive development at every turn, as we see in this chapter, that soul blindness directly assails the adolescent's reality testing, and the adolescent may need the analyst temporarily to function also as an auxiliary ego, providing reality validation of the young person's experience (K.K. Novick et al 2020).

This chapter also speaks to another aspect of reality in adolescence, which relates to recognition of idealized, omnipotent wishes and images of others and the self and the necessity to set those aside if the young person is to progress into a healthy autonomous adulthood. Despite the analyst's heroic efforts and Kaitlyn's intermittent recognition of the real cost of her maintaining an infantile tie to her parents, we are left with doubts about Kaitlyn's future. At what point does an analyst accept the limitations imposed by parental resistances and confront a young adult with the psychological choice between authentic autonomy and continued dependence/submission in the framework of the decision to continue or cease the analysis?

Kaitlyn's analyst speaks of emphasizing in this account the object relations aspect of Kaitlyn's treatment and development. This underscores a more general point about treating adolescents. We saw many examples of times Kaitlyn made powerful transferences to her analyst, but we can also see evidence of different facets of their relationship, with the analyst serving often as auxiliary ego, as a developmental object, as someone who could scaffold reality for Kaitlyn to calm and reassure her, to offer alternatives to consider, and as a real person in the present who credited Kaitlyn's experience and respected her perceptions in their own right.

We see Kaitlyn over time internalizing those qualities and stances, able increasingly to put herself in her friends' shoes, observe herself, and consider change. Kaitlyn's analyst accompanied her on a long journey all the way through adolescence, and there seems to be some hope that Kaitlyn, as a young adult equipped with that companionship, may be able to find her own voice and stand on her own two feet. She may find her own completion of the adolescent process. We also see exemplified another salient aspect of adolescent technique, in that the therapeutic relationship encompassed multiple dimensions and functions, with the analyst moving freely among emphasis and interpretation of one or another, without a narrow or theory-driven effort to elevate any one facet. Adolescents demand and deserve flexibility.

CHAPTER 6

NINA – age 13

I met 13 ½ year-old Nina's mother during the winter of 2018. Attractive, intelligent and concerned, Mother spoke of Nina's struggle with self-regulation beginning at the age of two. In both the developmental history form and the five hours I spent with Mother during the extended evaluation, Mother described Nina as beautiful, creative, extremely bright and hard-working. As a toddler, Nina experienced difficulty separating from Mother, who worked full-time, when going to daycare. Nina would cling to Mother's legs, screaming as Mother left. Teachers would distract Nina to help her stay and cope. At home, Nina melted into loud and wild tantrums that lasted 1 ½ hours; nothing seemed to calm her. Mother talked to Nina and waited for the meltdowns to "take their course." At the time of the evaluation, Nina was anxious when left alone at night. She feared thunderstorms, public performances during sports events and piano recitals and, when younger, the dark. Mother works hard to talk Nina through these anxieties using reason, but the anxiety persists. Mother strives to be patient with Nina, but sometimes loses her temper, blaming Nina for the unrest in the household. Mother spoke of a recent event when she bought clothes Nina said she would wear; when Nina changed her mind, Mother yelled at Nina who responded by withdrawing in her room.

According to Mother, Nina has close friends she socializes with at school and home and feels very competitive with a group of girls who are academically and socially successful. Nina perceives herself as less capable than these girls, which makes Nina very angry. Nina will return from school furious about a girl acting as though she is failing while making the highest grade in the class; Nina rails about how these girls are ungenuine and superficial, yet Nina seems to long for their recognition. Mother is concerned that Nina is limiting herself to socializing with one minority race, a race different from Nina's. Mother is puzzled by this and assumes it is due to Nina's insecurities. Mother is from a different country than the United States; she immigrated to the United States at the age of twenty, while Nina's father was born and raised in the U.S.

Nina has suffered a great deal of loss in her young life. Two years before I met Nina and her mother, Nina's parents, Nina, and her 10 year-old sister, Isla, suffered through an acrimonious divorce. Mother said the marriage to Nina's father was doomed from the beginning. Though Mother thought she was in love with him, her true motive was to remain in the United States after she graduated from college. Father, as described by Mother, is bright, but a chronic underachiever who does not contribute anything financially to the care of his children while Mother works full-time in a highly stressful job. Though Father also works full-time, he has elected to remain in the same low-paying position for years, when he could have elevated his professional status. Father is defensive, rigid and critical in his parenting style, often favoring Isla over Nina. Nina was upset by the divorce and refuses to talk about anything that happens in her father's house. Mother is concerned about this, fearing her daughters are not cared for in the way they deserve when with Father. Within the six months prior to the divorce, Nina also lost her maternal grandfather, with whom she shared a close relationship, and the beloved family dog. Mother feels Nina's anxiety has significantly increased since these losses, resulting in, at times, severe panic attacks.

Mother describes her family of origin as abusive and oppressive. Mother's father regularly physically abused Mother and her sister while her passive mother stood and watched. Nina's Father's family is described as concrete, narrow minded and incapable of verbalizing their feelings. Father is highly competitive with his twin brother who he feels is more successful. Father's parents divorced when Father was in his twenties, because his Father was in trouble with the law, a subject Father cannot bear to talk about. I met Father once; he then did not "find the need" to be involved in Nina's therapy.

In Nina's first meeting she appeared extremely anxious with frozen still face, while perching on the edge of the couch. When I asked if she would prefer taking the lead or for me to ask questions, Nina chose the latter. Upon my asking the first question Nina calmed significantly, leaning back on the couch and smiling. Nina seemed hungry and eager to talk with me about her life; it was Nina who requested her therapy and surprisingly seemed to know exactly what she wanted from it. Once I asked the first question, she took over. Nina described herself as an introvert who loves a clean and organized room. Her best friend is a boy she has known since preschool who is also motivated and bright. They both share similar interests including excelling in school. Nina feels she is a perfectionist and social activist as is her large group of friends. As we continued to meet during the evaluation Nina described, without prompting, her panic attacks that occur often in relation to the situations previously described. Nina said she knows these reactions are beyond what is reasonable to the situations, but she feels she has no choice but to have them. She said they seem like panic attacks because she has heart palpitations, trouble breathing with hyperventilation and sometimes intense agitation with difficulty calming herself. She attempts to breathe deeply and think calming thoughts, but these strategies only provide temporary relief.

Using the information from the developmental history form as well as the extended evaluation, I recommended a four-times-a-week psychoanalysis with Nina and once-a-week concurrent parent work with Mother. After listing Nina's strengths, I spoke of her difficulty finding words and thoughts related to her feelings. It is our words and understanding that help us contain, engage with and navigate through our most difficult experiences. Once we are able to accomplish this, our feelings can guide us through our life, informing us of what we want and need. Without them we are all lost and prone to anxiety or depression, in an attempt to protect us from the feelings we fear. This is not helping Nina. Instead, she fears her feelings because they overwhelm her; she is left without the energy they provide to enliven and direct her life. I said psychoanalysis will provide a safe, consistent and reliable place for Nina to explore her mind and find her words. Mother and Nina, in their separate meetings, enthusiastically accepted my recommendation. Nina expressed excitement while Mother said, "If my daughter was experiencing a physical problem, I would do everything I could to provide her with the most qualified specialist. Why wouldn't I do this for her mental health?"

Emboldened by the enthusiastic acceptance of the recommendation and Nina's excitement, I eased into the defense analysis of the abundant material Nina and her mother provided. Nina began by poignantly describing her terror of thunderstorms and travel and all that they threatened to rob her of. Subsequent to Nina admitting that she knew the thunderstorms would be unlikely to hurt her, we talked about them representing both the unexpected shock of the divorce and the impending loss. Nina felt blind-sided by the divorce and has spent the last 2 years in shock, unable to experience the depth of her feelings. She intellectually knows the divorce had tremendous impact, but she cannot feel it. After this revelation, Nina watched a movie about the premature death of a young teenager with cancer and sobbed uncontrollably. The teenager was supported by a young teenage girl who was strongly impacted by the loss. I spoke of her witnessing the death of her parent's marriage, the death of her grandfather and the death of her beloved dog within months of one another; it made sense the movie would impact her that much.

Nina's anxiety subsided significantly allowing her to speak of the pain she experienced from the criticism inflicted by a coach in a sport she loves. I said, judging from the description, she seems to be taking on way more responsibility than she needs to, in relation to a coach who is acting inappropriately. I wondered if this is displaced from our conversation about the divorce and her feelings of responsibility for it. Nina said if she would have been a much more talented and responsible daughter, perhaps her parents would not have divorced. I said if she would have been more responsible, she would have been considered a forty-year-old woman and not a fourteen-year-old adolescent. Perhaps, like with the coach, she was taking on her parent's responsibility for the divorce. I said, out of her overwhelming helplessness, she is attempting to compensate by taking on all of responsibility for everything; this only results in her feeling toxic guilt and resorting to self-criticism to relieve it. While feeling freer from the responsibility of loss, Nina's mind had the room to re-discover her love of reading. Her mind has been so preoccupied with her torment, she could not take in, let alone enjoy the literature she used to indulge in.

Her mother was thrilled by Nina's newly found ability to grieve. Mother said Nina has never been able to express grief about anything in her life; since this discovery, Nina has appeared much calmer and emotionally accessible to Mother. Nina's delusion of omnipotence was tested when parents attempted to pull Nina into the conflict they were experiencing over Mother confronting Father's girlfriend at a public event. Father wanted Nina to talk about the incident with girlfriend while Mother wanted Nina to report everything Father said. I spoke to Nina about how her parents were unfairly inflicting a loyalty conflict, when it is so unnecessary. Nina's intense anxiety subsided, allowing Nina to sort out what was her responsibility in the situation and what was her parents'. Mother, in our session, wanted me to be open with her about her role in the turmoil. I told Mother she placed Nina in an impossible situation which was not her responsibility. It is Mother's and

Father's responsibility to face their conflicts and leave Nina free of it. I said Nina needs to work through her panic over these unknown and highly tense situations and she needs Mother to absorb and help her verbally sort through it; Nina is currently retraumatized by anything associated with divorce and parental acrimony. Mother thanked me for this information and apologized to Nina, opening up the possibility for them to talk in more depth about the divorce; Nina was not ready.

Nina was then able to speak of fears of planes crashing; these fears originated in nursery school. We decided Nina was associating the plane crashes to the crushing blows without warning she felt when parents violently argued when she was very small. Nina felt this was spot on. Shortly thereafter Nina was ecstatic over her ability to travel by plane on her own to another state and then to her mother's country of origin without experiencing anxiety. Emboldened by her newfound strength, Nina was able to negotiate a heated argument between a foreign customs agent and her grandmother, who could not speak English, without experiencing the slightest bit of anxiety. Nina is bilingual and grandmother is not; the agents were about to release their guard dogs onto Grandmother.

Sadly, as Nina was strengthening, Isla was becoming more symptomatic. Mother and I paired to help Isla with her growing envy of Nina's strength. I coached Mother to explain to Isla that Nina is much older than Isla; as she matures she will be able to reason with more calm as well. I also told Mother to explain to Isla that she is transforming anxiety into anger. With huge eyes Isla wanted to know how I knew this and was worried that I would think she is a bad person; Mother explained to Isla that there is nothing wrong with anger and I already said she was a girl learning how to cope with her feelings. Isla was thrilled.

Nina then confessed that when alone, she feels she is beautiful, but when with peers she is convinced she is ugly. This began a series of conversations about Nina's urge to project her self-criticism and negative images of herself onto others, especially her peers, resulting in heightened anxiety, avoidance of social situations and perfectionism. With further exploration Nina felt the perfectionism comes from the divorce and from the dynamic between Isla, Nina and Father. Nina and I both felt intense pain and overwhelming fatigue when she spoke of Father's powerful urge to favor Isla. When at Father's house, Isla provokes Nina. While Nina is calmly trying to address the provocation with Isla, Isla screams as if she is being tortured. Father then harshly confronts Nina, often inflicting humiliating consequences for a child much younger than Nina. Nina is crushed and devastated with each horrible occurrence. We both thought of the plane crash. In separate sessions with Nina and Mother we unraveled the dynamic further. We decided Father identifies with Nina as the responsible and devalued parts of himself he feels obligated to confront through Nina, while Isla represents an idealized person he envies and wants to be. Isla also represents Father's twin brother he felt was more attractive, out of control and popular than he is. This analysis gave Nina great relief. She does not want to be like Father in any way nor does she admire Isla's out of control tantrums. Her desire is to be like Mother with all of her exotic intelligence.

In sessions with Mother, we decided the perfectionism is a transmitted intergenerational dynamic inflicted by her family of origin. Mother used perfectionism to survive her father's abuse. She compensated for the humiliation and pain by convincing herself she was the most responsible, intelligent and hard-working person in the family. She succeeded, but at a high price. Mother feels her penchant towards perfectionism is an unneeded burden at this stage of her life. She strives to let go but it is a product of her own delusion of omnipotence and she feels unnecessarily ruled by it. In sessions with Nina alone we decided she is trying to be perfect to make Mother feel perfect. She thinks it is ridiculous. With these revelations, both Mother and Nina seemed to feel a little more relaxed with who they are. Nina, to Mother's delight, became and continues to be more of a self-advocate for herself with friends, teachers and Mother. When Mother erupted with anger when Nina appropriately confronted her, Mother was sad that she was acting like her Father who had no tolerance for Mother's own voice and apologized to Nina.

Nina became more comfortable talking about how she feels different about Mother than Father and is puzzled as to why she was uncomfortable talking about it before. She does not feel judgment from me in the least nor does she feel any sense of loyalty conflict. Freedom talking about Father flowed into more freedom in talking about sex. Subsequent to a European trip, Nina was thrilled to find all of the concrete penises in Pompeii. We laughed about how much less threatening sex is when one can find the humor in it. We then faced the intensity of her anticipatory anxiety at school. Nina tends to feel all academic projects are overwhelming. Once we broke them down into steps, she realized they were not nearly as threatening as she thought. She agreed when I said she was projecting all of the feelings of failure from the divorce onto school. She felt such relief. I spoke with her about how her entire family seems to have difficulty using feelings as signals. They all seem to become overwhelmed by them and paralyzed. I spoke of how feelings can be a signal to activate the mind and don't need to overwhelm.

In sessions with Mother, we talked about how Nina is externalizing a general feeling of dissatisfaction about everything onto her body causing her to feel she is fat or bad. I said we need to relocate this in her mind rather than her body. I suggested Mother refrain from making suggestions and say to Nina that she feels her dissatisfaction is coming from her mind and not her body and Mother has confidence Nina will work through it when she is ready. Mother said she suffers from the same inadequacies. During Nina's session, she spoke of the insights I spoke of with Mother and she was intrigued by them. She was curious about how this transmission from mind to body occurs. Nina was fascinated with how she uses the same process during presentations. She projects negative self-representations and critical feelings about herself onto her audience. After weeks of trying to unravel and give Nina relief from this urge to project her negative self-images onto others, I realized another process was superimposed on this first one. I asked Nina if she was familiar with the quote, "the woman doth protest too much!" Nina was. I said Nina was so insistent others felt negatively about her and she was flooded by her envy of them, I was wondering if the opposite might be true. I suggested her insistence she is envious is a defense against her fear that others envy her. I said envy is often accompanied by hostility. Nina fears others will abandon her due to their hostile envy. I said, to protect herself she diminishes her abilities in her eyes hoping others will not notice her accomplishments, resulting in her only seeing their strengths and becoming vulnerable to envy them! This leaves her in conflict with her conscious self so hungry for attention. I noted she also withdraws from the positive perception of her accomplishments to defend against the fear of losing these relationships. Nina was riveted.

We extended this interpretation, when through displacement, Nina was concerned about a friend's envy. I spoke of how her fear of the envy of others, in part, originates from her Father's envy of her. I spoke of how Father is so hard on her because she has already surpassed him intellectually and emotionally. Father is unable to reason through his feelings, leaving him vulnerable to outbursts alienating others. He also acts this out on Nina through his overcontrol of her. I suggested he is also threatened by her budding sexuality. Father cannot see her as the attractive woman she is. Nina was receptive to this analysis and agreed with it. Suddenly Father's behavior made sense to Nina. If Nina acknowledges her talents, she risks threatening Father and losing him or feeling subjected to more of his hostility. When, in a later session, Nina summoned her inner critics that beat her down further, I suggested she is still fearing succeeding and evoking his hostile envy. Stopped in her tracks, Nina agreed. I reminded her that only he can face and confront his envy. It is not her responsibility to address this. She expressed relief and was then able to keep her academic challenges in perspective and face them with humor.

What followed was months of both Mother and Father struggling to contain their feelings coupled with Nina attempting to resist feeling responsible for them. Mother left her therapist saying she felt as though they were socializing with no therapeutic action taking place. Mother reverted and melted into a pool of anxiety, serious depression and misery that she took out on Nina. Father and Grandmother continued to both criticize Nina and idolize Isla. Father's mother fawns over Isla's gorgeous hair, stellar mathematical skills and cries at Isla's cello concerts. This literally makes Nina sick, feeling Isla shows no sign of superb musical ability. I interpreted more actively to keep Nina afloat. Nina vacillated between believing this was all her father's and mother's problem to feeling extreme hurt and rage turned either inward into lacerating self-criticism or flipped into its opposite of "not caring at all," killing her motivation in school.

I followed her every nuanced word and emotional variation and interpreted as efficiently as I could. I reminded Nina that these are her parent's problems and not hers and she cannot feel responsible for them or fix them. I said they are realizing Nina is transforming from an anxious withdrawn teenager into an extremely attractive, intelligent and capable young woman who is emotionally surpassing them. I said Father is still reverting into seeing Isla as the idolized brother and part of him he must merge with to feel good about himself while externalizing everything devalued onto Nina. He insists on this solution to protect himself from the feelings of inadequacy he feels in Nina's presence. Nina could finally consider this interpretation. That night she had a dream where she encountered a peer she was convinced she could not emulate and landed in a jungle of twisted and thick vines. We concluded the dream represents the concern that everyone becoming more successful than her is actually an elaborate defense attempting to protect her from its opposite. Nina in reality is afraid of being envied with all of the accompanying hostility resulting in her abandonment – her worst fear.

Nina agreed with this interpretation, and added that the jungle represented entanglement in defenses that eventually multiply and suffocate her. She smiled in revelation. What surfaced was an awareness of how much she loves Isla and how she fears Isla will never calm down and find relief. Isla finally has found the right therapist, but she does not seem to be improving. She is more hostile, enraged and volatile than ever.

We also spoke of Mother being haunted by her abusive past while Grandmother is visiting. Nina and I then talked in detail about the abuse Mother has endured. Nina found this conversation very helpful. Nina said her heart goes out to Mother, yet she feels relief in knowing Mother's attacks on Nina are nothing to do with Nina, but a replay of the dynamics between Mother and Grandmother. Mother is playing the role of Grandmother with Nina representing Mother. I encouraged Nina and Mother to talk more about this on their own.

Nina then had a dream of coming to my office when the sun was shining. Her sports team was on a grassy knoll in front of my building, painting their sports tennis shoes. Everyone was happy and energetic. The dream quickly altered in tone when she entered my building; everything was dark and foreboding. She encountered me at a desk on the first floor and I ignored her. She went up to the library where a disembodied head glared at her with no words. I was then in my office and continued to turn my head away from her. We both agreed the sunshiny moment represented her growth and how much freer and happier she feels.

Transferentially she fears I will withdraw from her in response to her growing strength and take all of my love and support with me leaving her on her own, like she feels with parents. Nina was relieved to know this was a dream and I am still here and with her. Lately, though, her Mother has been less available emotionally. She condescends to Nina when Nina is feeling in need of reassurance. Mother finally found a new therapist acceptable to her, but then attempted to reduce Nina's time with me. I challenged this both with Mother and Nina reminding them that the progress is due to the consistency, safety and regularity of her times. Both Nina and Mother agreed.

Nina said she is finally feeling more comfortable talking to family, though this has been a long time coming. She said distrust of family came from the divorce. In seventh grade she never spoke to Mother. She said she felt trust before the divorce and then lost it in the midst of the trauma. I said it made sense given the toxic tension in the household beginning when she was very little. I spoke of how the panic around storms represented the storms in her house and her anger about them and she agreed. She said it was in seventh grade when things became more tolerable because she began seeing me. She said it is sad to say, but prior to coming here, especially between third and seventh grade, her life was horrible. It was in eighth grade when she finally had a happy year. We talked about how blind-sided she felt about the parental storms and how dark and disturbing this was. She said she externalizes her whole perception of the divorce on her social life. Though she is strengthening and changing, she still fears people will be furious when she openly expresses herself. She anticipates and expects social relationships to be conflictual, explosive and temporary. I spoke with Mother about how she is externalizing her self-representation of herself as a teenager onto Nina. She was the one who had to take care of everyone and pull herself up by the bootstraps and blames herself for this. She is the unfavored child, so Nina must be this too. Though Mother was uncomfortable with this, she took it in.

Nina then sunk into a temporary depression. She was convinced she was inferior to everyone; she was slipping in school and there was nothing she could do about it. I interpreted this as a protection from all of her recent accomplishments. We have established that she fears success and the envy of others including her family; she is giving into this by convincing herself she is a failure. This is the ultimate protection against envy and potential abandonment. At first she pushed this away, but then seemed curious. I said she was reliving past trauma when she was convinced there was nothing she had to offer. I said she is not that helpless little girl anymore, she is a competent young woman. As if I had stunned her out of a drug- induced stupor, Nina came back to life and realized my interpretation was correct. Mother responded by attempting to make Nina feel responsible for calming Isla. I spoke to Mother about how this is counter to our therapeutic goals. We have talked about how Nina is not responsible for Isla's meltdowns. I said perhaps she is asking Nina to do what she was forced to do growing up. Is she behaving like her mother now or her father? I said it is her job to set limits on Isla. When she fails to do this, Isla's anxiety rises. I again had the experience of making an intervention that seemed to bump the other person out of a stupor; Mother heard me and began setting firm limits on Isla. Isla responded by calming herself down and taking more responsibility for her life. I warned Mother that she must be consistent for Isla to continue to improve.

In the next session with Mother, I confronted her with why she has been projecting her anger onto Nina. Mother laughed sadistically. I wondered why she laughed at something so serious that is hurting her daughter. Mother seemed shocked, but listened and became somewhat calmer with Nina. Nina and Isla have become closer as a result of this work, but that has made Isla's meltdowns more painful for Nina. Recently she came in angrily saying Mother is not setting enough limits on Isla. I said I thought Nina was hoping Mother's interventions would keep Isla from melting down. I said I appreciate this given how much they cause Nina pain. Nina agreed and realized it will take much more time.

Currently Nina has been made aware that during COVID-19 isolation from school, she has surpassed her peers academically and feels more calm and confidence in her accomplishments. She has established a more tolerant and workable relationship with Father and Isla and she has discovered more pleasure and joy in her friendships and talents. Nina's newfound strength has enabled her to engage with and find words for the rage previously obscured by the panic. Will she find pleasure in throttling Isla or will it throw her more deeply into superego conflict? Nina realizes she still has much to do.

COMMENTARY 1

Nina's treatment is an excellent example of how psychoanalysis can be the treatment of choice for adolescents with life-changing effects. The analyst begins by describing an in-depth evaluation process with Nina's mother, obtaining Nina's developmental history. We learn that the parents, and Nina and her sister, lived through an acrimonious divorce. As I read the word "acrimonious," I imagined the turbulent storms, over a period of years that young Nina may have been exposed to, especially because the mother stated that her marriage was doomed from its inception. Equally important, or even more valuable, we learn that mother worked full-time and that separations were extremely difficult for Nina when she was a toddler. The analyst describes how teachers "distracted" Nina so her mother could leave her (sneak out?) at daycare. While this technique may have worked in the short-run, it may have left toddler Nina distrustful of, and angry with, the adults she depended on. We also learn that Nina's tantrums lasted well over one hour. Listening to Nina's early history we come to understand that Nina seemingly became dysregulated when she experienced overwhelming anxiety related to separations. The analyst tells us that mother does her best to calmly help her daughter regulate, however she loses her temper and blames Nina for the family's problems. I speculate that Nina's difficult affects, such as fear, sadness, and anger were not well understood by her parents. It may be that the emphasis was to stop Nina from having difficult feelings instead of helping her metabolize these feelings. It has been my experience that when the parent gives the message that difficult emotions are to be

154

fixed or even eliminated, the child is left to feel that there is something very wrong with her. If her parent does not like these feelings then she may feel she is defective and/or even a bad person. This results in poor self-esteem.

As Nina enters her preteen years, she experiences several losses: her beloved grandfather dies, her parents divorce, and the family dog dies. Father is rigid and harsh and favors Nina's younger sister. Nina's father demonstrates his lack of care (and love?) by stating that he is disinterested in her treatment. Nina's anxiety now shows itself in the form of panic attacks.

I found it extremely interesting that Nina, in her first session, appeared to have a "frozen still-face." My thoughts went to Ed Tronick's (2002) famous Still-Face experiment. Was Nina's mother depressed during her infancy? Was this the image that met her infant gaze? However Nina has much strength. After all it was she who requested therapy. In addition she has many friends and is a good student, often feeling competitive with her girlfriends. It is impressive that the analyst recommended an analysis after the evaluation period. Both mother and daughter were eager to begin.

The analyst's admirable skills are evident in her attuned and well-timed interpretations. Nina was able to take in her analyst's wise words as she connected Nina's current conflicts with past interactions within her family. The parent work with mother, as painful as it may have been, was paramount in changes occurring. We also see just how important parent sessions are when treating adolescents. Even though mother had her own therapy she needed to be reminded of Nina's needs and her responsibility in not putting Nina in the middle of family problems. It was easy to slip back into old patterns. Frequent parent sessions can make the difference between a successful treatment and a failed analysis.

I was most impressed with the analyst's understanding of Nina's poor self-esteem. She could see how Nina was terrified of her friend's envy, therefore she had to make herself into one unworthy of acclaim. In this way she would not risk their envy, which in her unconscious, would result in loss of love and ultimately abandonment – Nina's worst fear.

As I stated at the beginning, Nina's analysis is a wonderful example of how psychoanalysis can be life changing. I imagine that Nina will continue for some time in her analysis as she continues to work through her conflicts as she moves through her adolescent years. I also imagine that this analyst will continue to help the mother learn new ways of being with her daughter.

COMMENTARY 2

The psychoanalytic treatment of 13½ year-old Nina and the parenting work with her mother is an excellent example of the new method in child and adolescent analysis outlined in a series of revolutionary papers by Jack and Kerry Kelly Novick (2001a, 2001b, 2002a, 2002b), Kerry Kelly Novick and Jack Novick (2002a, 2002b, 20013) and Dowling, S., Lament, C., K.K. Novick & J. Novick (2013) and in two books – "*Working with Parents Makes Therapy Work*" by Kerry Kelly Novick and Jack Novick (2005), and in the "*Parent Work Casebook*" edited by Kerry Kelly Novick, Jack Novick, Denia Barrett and Thomas Barrett (2020). See especially their chapter ten, "Reconfiguring parent work: Adolescents," pp. 227 – 239.

The traditional approach has mostly been for the psychoanalyst to work 3-5x/wk with the child or adolescent and to have a meeting with one or both parents or caretakers once-a-month or once every 6 weeks or so. The parent meeting is usually for information gathering by the analyst, to give the parents educational information about normative stages of child development and to provide concrete parent guidance suggestions on homework scheduling, peer group activities, or suggestions on behavioral management problems of acting out or limit setting. What the patient says and is working on in individual treatment is not shared in the parent meetings and any suggestions on improving the environment of the patient are very subordinate to the main goal of treatment, as it is in adult analysis, for the patient to work through internal intrapsychic conflicts and bring about a permanent structural change in the personality.

How then does the Novicks' model differ from this traditional approach?

1. The parent(s) are generally seen more frequently, such as once-a week or more often and
2. The primary focus of the parent meeting is to improve the parent-child relationship.

As Anna Freud (1970) phrased the goal of child analysis to help the child remove the blocks to development, the Novicks add a second goal:

"helping parents achieve the developmental phase of parenthood that is, restoring parents to the path of progressive adult development, in which parenthood is one phase…The aim of child-and-adolescent analysis can be recast as not only the restoration of the child's progressive development but also as the restoration of parent-child relationship that has been disrupted by pathology to its potential as a lifelong positive resource for both" (K.K. and J. Novick, 2013, p. 131).

The Novicks' model of individual adolescent analysis with concurrent parent sessions is even more of a paradigmatic shift from the traditional approach, where many analysts tend to see the parents fairly rarely, if at all. The adolescent may often request that the analyst not meet with the parents and the analyst, family and the adolescent may mistakenly think the goal of treatment is to help the adolescent separate and become independent of the parents. In my own analytic treatment of adolescents, I have found that as much as adolescents may implore the analyst to help them get the parents to leave them alone in their rooms, not to have to eat with the family for meals or to be allowed to make their own decisions, they also may feel isolated and lonely and deeply want to have a more loving relationship with their parents. As several adolescents approach their last year of high school before they leave home to go to college, many express a desire to improve their relationship with their parents, so that they can leave home with a stronger secure feeling of loving attachment with their parents. I have found their desire for separateness and independence almost equal to this desire for loving closeness in most adolescents at this important rite of passage time before going off to college

Hence, it is an honor to discuss this case of Nina in the valuable way that it illustrates how the Novicks' model can be used particularly in the parent sessions on strengthening the parent-child relationship. The purpose of this commentary is to discuss how the analyst worked in the parent meetings to improve the parent-child relationship and to consider some suggestions how the parent work could be approached a little more analytically in a deeper manner in some places to help parents work through their own intrapsychic conflicts in their parenting in order to restore a lifelong healthy parent-child relationship with their child.

Beginning of treatment

At the beginning of treatment, Nina was a 13½ year-old girl, who appeared to have an anxiety disorder or panic attack disorder consisting of severe panic attacks, being anxious when left alone at night, having fears of thunderstorms, planes crashing, travel, public performances during sports events and piano recitals, being perfectionistic and feeling very competitive with many of her classmates and at times perceiving herself as less capable. Her mother described her as beautiful, creative, extremely bright and hard working. However, she had suffered several losses beginning with the birth of her sister, Isla, when she was 3½ years old, the death of her maternal grandfather and her beloved family dog when she was 11 years, and the acrimonious divorce of her parents when she was 11½ years. The father was born and raised in the U.S. and the mother had immigrated to the USA at the age of 20 from another country, where her native language was not English. It appeared that the children had visitation with the father at his home. However, in over the 2 years of treatment reported to date, the father only had one meeting with the analyst. The mother's family of origin was described as abusive and oppressive, where the mother's father regularly physically abused the mother and her sister, while her passive mother stood by and watched. The father's family was described by the mother as concrete, narrow minded and incapable of verbalizing their feelings.

Saturated and unsaturated interpretations

In Nina's first session, the analyst reports that Nina described herself as an introvert, who loves a clean and organized room; spoke about her best friend, a boy who is also motivated and bright and how they both like to excel in school; and how she feels she is a perfectionist and social activist. She then described details of her panic attacks. The analyst recommended 4x/wk psychoanalysis and once-a-week concurrent parent work with her mother. After listing her strengths, the analyst then gave her a very specific description of how psychoanalysis would be helpful to her:

"I spoke of her difficulty finding words and thoughts related to her feelings. It is our words and understanding that help us contain, engage with and navigate through out most difficult experiences. Once we are able to accomplish this, our feelings can guide us through our life, informing us of what we want and need. Without them we are all lost and prone to anxiety or depression, in an attempt to protect us from the feelings we fear. This is not helping Nina.

Instead, she fears her feelings because they overwhelm her, she is left without the energy they provide to enliven and direct her life. I said psychoanalysis will provide a safe, consistent and reliable place for Nina to explore her mind and find her words."

While this would be described as a "*saturated* interpretation" in Ferro's (2006) terms given its rather more full details of the analyst's thinking, it was very stimulating and hopeful for the mother and Nina, who, in their separate meetings, "enthusiastically accepted my recommendation". Nina described her terror of thunderstorms and travel to which the analyst talked about them both representing the unexpected shock of the divorce and the impending loss, which Nina said she intellectually knows the divorce had tremendous impact, but she cannot feel it. This, then, appeared to be a confirmation of the analyst's *saturated* interpretation and an important goal in the treatment. An *unsaturated* interpretation to Ferro (2008) is a more open-ended question, such as after a patient describes a dream, when the analyst may ask, "What does the dream suggest to you?" Ferro feels that *saturated* interpretations should be kept to a minimum to help the patient increasingly lead the way in the work, but that both *saturated* and *unsaturated* interpretations are important, as the analyst's interpretation to Nina above turned out to be.

In a following session, Nina talked about watching a movie about the premature death of a young teenager with cancer, and sobbed uncontrollably. The analyst linked the emotional impact of the movie to her witnessing the death of her parent's marriage, the death of her grandfather and the death of her beloved dog within months of one another, which then allowed her to speak of the pain she experienced from the criticism of her coach and her seeming to take too much responsibility for the problem on herself. She felt that, if she would have been a much more talented and responsible daughter, perhaps her parents would not have divorced. Expressing her interpretation in the hypothetical, the analyst helped her to see that, "Perhaps, like with the coach, she was taking on her parents' responsibility for the divorce" and interpreted Nina's defense of omnipotent control against her feeling of overwhelming helplessness in the divorce by attempting to compensate by taking on all of responsibility for everything. As Nina began to feel freer from the responsibility of loss, the analyst noted that she was able to re-discover her love of reading, which she had previously enjoyed. In her session, the analyst reported that the mother was thrilled by Nina's newly found ability to grieve, which she felt Nina had never been able to express grief about anything in her life, and she now appeared much calmer and emotionally accessible to her mother.

However, there was an incident in which the mother confronted the father's girlfriend at a public event, and the mother wanted Nina to report everything the father said. The father wanted Nina to talk about the incident with the girlfriend. In Nina's session, the analyst spoke to Nina about how her parents were unfairly inflicting a loyalty conflict, when it is so unnecessary, which helped Nina's anxiety to subside. In the mother's session, the mother wanted the analyst to be open with her about her role in the turmoil. The analyst then told the mother she placed Nina in an impossible situation which was not her responsibility. It is mother and father's responsibility to face their own conflicts and leave Nina free of it. The analyst said, "Nina needs to work through her panic over these unknown and highly tense situations and she needs mother to absorb and help her verbally sort through it; Nina is currently re-traumatized by anything associated with divorce and parental acrimony." The mother then thanked the analyst and apologized to Nina, which the analyst felt opened up the possibility for them to talk in more depth about the divorce, even though Nina was not yet ready to do it.

This is an example of the analyst helping the adolescent work through and resolve the adolescent's attempt to defensively take responsibility for the traumatic impact of the parents' divorce upon her and in the parent meeting, then helping the parents not to triangulate Nina between them in a loyalty conflict, and to help the parents place the responsibility for their divorce back on themselves. The analyst's interpretation to the mother here feels more like a *saturated* superego imperative. However, in each of their separate sessions, it is clear to Nina and to the mother that they are each concurrently working on this same issue for Nina not to take responsibility for the divorce upon herself. The analyst's interpretations are mostly phrased as a hypothetical, beginning with the words, "Is it possible that…" or "Perhaps it could be that…," and the analyst characteristically frames the work in a collaborative way by stating that, "We decided Nina was…", "The mother and I paired to help Isla…", or "Nina and I both felt…" Rather than a therapist making direct interpretations of unconscious dynamics by assuming the role of an all knowing self-confident verbal interpreter to the patient of his or her unwitting behavior or thoughts, the therapist collaborates with the patient and may phrase a more *unsaturated* interpretation as, "Can we pause and look at this situation together for a moment? Do you feel that it could be that…" (Sloate, P., personal communication). This takes the analyst out of the position as an authority, communicates the analyst's more open position as unknowing, and invites the collaboration of the patient and the analyst together.

Critique

In the initial intake evaluation, the mother communicated to the analyst that her family of origin was abusive and oppressive and that the mother's father regularly physically abused her and her sister, while their passive mother stood by and watched. This suggests that when the analyst was advising the mother to leave Nina free of any responsibility for the acrimony between the parents in a rather saturated superego imperative sounding interpretation, the mother could have experienced this as a transference re-enactment of the analyst being like her abusive father. It may, then, have been better to work on this issue with the mother in a gentler more *unsaturated* and open manner without a directive in order for the mother to come towards this realization of Nina's need for a clearer boundary between Nina and the discord between the parents. I believe that it is always best to work consistently analytically in both the child's treatment and in the parent work. However, since the mother was in her own individual analytic treatment during the Nina case, she was probably working on this and related issues, so the analyst being more directive with the parents in this instance is certainly appropriate.

Discussion

A major problem in the case of Nina was that the acrimonious parents continued to clash with each other at times, as Nina associated her fear of plane crashes without warning, when the parents violently argued when she was very small. The analyst was only able to do parent work with the mother, as the father only came once to meet with the analyst at the beginning of the treatment. Therefore, the mother had to share the analyst's parenting suggestions with the father, which obviously did not always work out successfully. The case could have worked better with a frame of the parent work being conducted with both parents together or, as is often done with divorced parents, to meet one week with the mother and the next week with the father.

I have found that many misunderstand the Novicks' approach as simply a call to work with the parents more frequently. As we feel that treating a patient more frequently per week becomes "more psychoanalytic" by facilitating a more deepening process, we often define "psychotherapy" as working 1 – 2 times a week, while working 3-5 times a week is defined as "psychoanalysis." Concurrent work in individual child and adolescent analysis has a history going back to the early child analytic pioneers, such as Dorothy Burlingham (1932), whose paper was earlier commented upon by Freud (1933, p.56), who opined that it was no longer a rare situation "…in which a mother and child are simultaneously in analysis." In the next two decades, two former pediatricians from Vienna, each becoming noted child analysts, influenced many child clinicians with two different approaches to concurrent treatment of parent and child. Melitta Sperling (1899-1973) developed a method of "simultaneous analysis of mother and child in which mother and child are treated psychoanalytically in separate sessions (preferably without the child knowing of the mother's analysis) by the same analyst" (1974, p. 243). Margaret Mahler (1897-1985) developed the "tripartite method" of treating younger children with both the patient and the mother in the same room. Mahler criticized Sperling's approach, because she felt that the child always knows the parent is also in analysis with the analyst (Anni Bergman, personal communication), and Sperling criticized Mahler, because she felt that the mother often will compete with the child for the analyst's attention, which will cause the child to compete negatively and show itself at its worst, which she thought "seemed to be the case in most situations described by Mahler" (Sperling, 1974, p. 353-354).

The case of Nina demonstrates that it is possible to work analytically with the adolescent 4x/wk and with the parent 1x/wk in the Novicks' model where the goal of the parenting work is to strengthen the parent-child relationship. Throughout the case, we can see the analyst helping Nina work through a problem, such as her perfectionism, in her individual sessions and helping the mother work through how this issue in the mother interferes with their parent-child relationship. For example, the analyst reported that:

"In sessions with Mother, we decided the perfectionism is a transmitted intergenerational dynamic inflicted by her family of origin. Mother used perfectionism to survive her father's abuse. She compensated for the humiliation and pain by convincing herself she was the most responsible, intelligent and hard-working person in the family… With Nina alone, we decided she is trying to be perfect to make Mother feel perfect… With these revelations, both Mother and Nina seemed to feel a little more relaxed with who they are. Nina, to Mother's delight, became and continues to be more of a self-advocate for herself with friends, teachers and Mother."

In session after session, the analyst illustrates how a similar issue may be worked with in Nina's sessions and in the mother's parenting session, when often parent and child later discuss the issue with each other outside the treatment setting. As the case proceeds, the analyst is no longer giving parent guidance suggestions to the mother, but helping the mother in-depth analytically in the parent sessions and the mother and Nina may be talking the issue through with each other directly. Towards a later point in the treatment, the analyst described this approach very movingly when the analyst spoke of Mother being haunted by her abusive past while Grandmother was visiting:

"Nina and I then talked in detail about the abuse Mother has endured. Nina found this conversation very helpful. Nina said her heart goes out to Mother, yet she feels relief in knowing Mother's attacks on Nina are nothing to do with Nina, but a replay of the dynamics, between Mother and Grandmother. Mother is playing the role of Grandmother with Nina representing Mother. I encouraged Nina and Mother to talk more about this on their own".

At the end of the case report, Nina is able to verbalize her feelings, she is doing better in school and with her peers, and she no longer has panic attacks or crippling anxiety. The parent-child relationship is much improved and the case report ends with these words that, "Nina realizes she has much to do."

EDITORIAL REFLECTIONS

This chapter confronts and contradicts many current assumptions about the treatment of young adolescents. Many clinicians, including psychoanalysts, believe that young adolescents are very difficult, if not impossible, to treat. Few cases are referred for psychoanalysis and medication/chemical restraints have become the primary mode of intervention. Therapists tend to avoid work with this age group and adult patients often repress memories and associations to their adolescent experience. This case should inspire others to try intensive treatment of young teens. The child and mother both accepted the recommendation of four times per week; in fact 13-year-old Nina was eager to work and engaged in her analysis from the beginning. The commentators emphasized that the analysis was "life-saving" and not only was of great benefit to the child but also transformed the parent-child relationship.

Dynamic concurrent work with parents is now generally accepted in treatment plans for younger children, but there is still much resistance to doing this work with parents of adolescents. This case is another in the growing list of publications that demonstrate a successful alternative.[3] In addition this chapter illustrates the range of techniques used and the wide scope of application of dynamic concurrent parent work. In particular this case underscores the importance of parent work to deal with the toxic impact of the transgenerational transmission of pathology. Without the concurrent work with the parent, the analyst would not have known nor have had the leverage to work with the parallels between Nina's and mother's sadomasochistic battles and mother's similar battles with her own mother. The analyst would also not have been able to see and engage with the intense

---

3 See the adolescent cases in "Parent Work Case Book," (2020) Novick, K.K., et al; also Langley, J.(2020), A suicidal adolescent; Novick, J. (2020) The courage to grow: creative transformation in patient and child analyst; Novick, K.K. and Novick, J. (2013).

sibling rivalry between Nina and her sister as a dynamic driven by father's intense rivalry with his own brother. These intergenerational resonances are directly relevant to Nina's adolescent developmental tasks, as she struggles to assert her own individuality. We can see the need to help her set and maintain boundaries, a process which is central to identity formation.

This chapter also conveys the need for analysts to maintain conviction and persistence, to exercise their emotional muscles, in holding on simultaneously to the dynamics of work with both the adolescent and the parent(s). Soul blindness and externalization do not respond easily or in one effort to interpretation. At moments of stress and overwhelming, Nina's mother reverted to her old ways of dealing with her experience of abuse and this transgenerational acting out reverberated in Nina's functioning. Only with repeated experiencing and insight could Nina and her analyst and her mother recalibrate at a new level, allowing Nina to resume growth.

The very concept of concurrent parent work has now been accepted by a sufficient number of child analysts that we can turn to examining specific techniques that have proven useful. In our earlier work we have emphasized the importance of having a long enough "exploratory period" to start a treatment alliance with the parent(s) (Novick, K.K. and Novick, J. 2005). This was done in this case but the analyst also framed the child's difficulties in relation to her adolescent growth and development and the transformation of the parent-child relationship, rather than taking a "medical stance" and talking only of symptoms. In the case of Nina we can see a developmental line of pathological anxiety, starting with infantile difficulty to soothe, moving into childhood anxiety around perfectionism, to adolescent panic attacks. This chapter illustrates how her treatment began to generate a new, alternative set of developmental lines to traverse through her adolescence.

CHAPTER 7

MARIA – age 13

My Analytical Experience With Maria

Patients are made of the same material as our loved ones, and even though our dealings with them are limited by the reservations imposed by the clinical framework, the generosity with which they share such intimate aspects makes it difficult to banish them from our lives. It is within this context of gratitude that I share the experience of the psychoanalysis with Maria. She was referred to me by a colleague who was treating her mother. When Maria's mother asked for an appointment, she told me that Maria – thirteen years old at the time – was depressed, she was getting low grades and was suffering from suicidal ideation as a result of a violent separation between her parents.

So, that's how I met a very thin and tall nice girl, with brown skin. She was fashionably dressed, with all the outward indicators that she belonged to a wealthy family. She was intelligent and sensitive. Her posture and muscle tone, as well as her mood, showed a strong depression and despite her emotional state, Maria had the capacity for introspection. I observed that when suicidal thoughts predominated, the barrier between her anguish and the frustration-generating world was too thin, as if it was unable to contain it. We started a psychoanalytical experience of four sessions per week.

Life story

Maria is the fourth child in a family of six – including her father, mother and three brothers – of which she is the youngest. She defined herself as her father's favorite as a child, and she would recall that her parents were never home. Her father held important positions, and her mother was a full-time housewife. She described the family environment as very violent. The relationship with her parents was ambivalent, since she felt that she had to protect her mother from her father and at the same time, she felt genuine affection towards him; although at times she remarked that the emotional exchanges between them were only 'money for affection'. She described herself as a lonely girl who spent most of her time with the domestic help.

The relationship with her siblings was described as adequate. She felt close to the second brother who suffered from neuro-dermatitis since childhood, something that Maria blamed on the bad relationship that he had with their father. The driver was somebody important to her; he had been working with the family since she was five years old. She once recalled that when she was seven, her mother pulled down the bed sheets to make it seem as if her father had slept at home. She commented that, as of that moment, "I learned that everyone in the house altered reality." If for most adolescents it is difficult to confront, integrate, and elegantly overcome the struggle of the psychological, physical, and emotional changes of that life stage, for this young patient, it was not only a challenge, but an almost impossible task, considering the narcissistic games played within the real family problems.

Treatment history

During the first meetings, Maria cried due to family problems and because her mother would no longer let her sleep in her bed. She had no life project, no desires, a foggy lethargy isolated her, and abundant tears flooded the sessions. Two months into treatment, I suspended our sessions due to a lack of payment. Maria negotiated with her father and resumed her analysis, but a month later, he declared that he would only pay for three sessions, only to later reduce them further to two, and finally to a single session. A few weeks afterwards, Maria suffered from panic attacks, her body became paralyzed, and she had nightmares of persecution, and dreamed that her body would paralyze. Her grades worsened and the likelihood that she would repeat the school year was very high.

After several interviews with her father, he agreed to honor the four-session commitment. He also accepted that at least during her high-school years, Maria would not be sent abroad to study (a desire shared by both parents). In the meantime, her mother would frequently call me to suggest that Maria 'should' take antidepressants (the mother was taking them).

During this initial phase of treatment, Maria navigated through polarized affects ranging from omnipotence to disillusionment. The unbearable severity of the 'ego' did not allow her to process either the typical adolescent mourning, or the (real) separation of her parents. Maria had a conflict regarding her relationship with her parents: to whom should she be loyal? Sometimes the shallowness of her interests (clothes, cars, luxuries) prevented me from making an emotional connection with her. I felt as if I were dealing with someone with no inner life, even though she cried in all sessions. What prevailed the most in that first phase was a permanent state of desolation, as if nothing was of any use. It seemed as if she wanted to convince me that there was no hope.... in this period there was a struggle to keep an alliance with Maria's vital parts, since despair seeped in, session after session, to the extent that I came to question my analytical approach.

The orbit of the primary process governed her life, which was expressed in her magical desire to solve all problems. Omnipotence was the real wonderland where Maria took refuge. Gradually, the depression lessened and after several sessions together with her mother, Maria began to take 'ownership' of her analysis, to the extent that in the end, she actually paid for some of her own sessions. The analytical experience took an important turn and I never worked with her mother directly again, nor did I ever see her father afterwards. This was the beginning of another period. Maria started to think about herself and work on herself, although there were several acting-outs: psychopathic activities, alcohol abuse, she ran away from home at night and stole money from her mother, saying ironically that 'stealing' was her family legacy. But then she felt guilty and lied about it. We even worked with the paradox that 'only when she lied, was she telling the truth.' During this time, the only constant was the inconsistency. The point of trauma repetition (the permanent abandonment) remained concentrated in the transference. Interpretations based on transference and countertransference opened the possibility for reconstructing herself.

As the end of her high-school years was approaching, the vitality of libidinal forces resurfaced. Soon afterwards, the field of sexuality became the center of her interest and concern. She started a relationship and claimed a sense of ownership over her body and emotions. Maria improved her academic performance and shared her plan to study abroad for a year with some friends. We agreed on a termination date and weeks after her graduation, we said goodbye. Two years later, she returned and we worked together for a few more years.

Sessions
First year session

Maria arrives feeling very sad; she is not wearing any make-up.

M – I failed physics. It was my birthday (I turned fourteen) and I didn't see my dad. There was no one to take me to his house and he didn't want to come pick me up. My mom.... I didn't know where she was, my friends stayed over on Saturday, my brothers didn't give me a present. I didn't go to school, I didn't feel like going, I'm not good at anything .... on Friday I was in history class, and they were talking about black people, and I thought they were talking about me, I heard voices....

Analyst – What did you hear?

M – I heard them saying, "Maria is black and she stinks like Negroes." I don't know what is wrong with me, but I feel that everybody is talking about me. My mom doesn't let me sleep in her room when I am scared. She keeps telling me to "rationalize your fears" (silence).... I like clubs because at night, kids don't see me well in the darkness. But I don't go anywhere near them anyway because since I smoke, I feel that my mouth smells. My friends are beautiful; they chose Paula for the cheerleading squad. I hate her so much! Boy, do I envy her! Since we were in kindergarten, she was always the güerita (blondie) and I was the negrita (black girl), and the teachers were so racist. Once when we were planning a school festival, I wanted to tango, but the teacher told me 'to stick to folk dancing.' As an indigenous person, I have the Indian complexion and when we go out together, I start imagining that everyone thinks that I am my friends' maid. That's why I behave so arrogantly, so that they won't mistake me for one. I would so love to do what Michael Jackson did.... as if he had been born white.

Analyst – It seems that not only do you fail physics, but that you also fail with your physique, isn't that right?

M – Yes, even on the inside I am bad. For instance, when I got my period, it was very irregular. When I went to the gynecologist, they told me that my ovaries were too big and that's why I bleed so much. Look at my knees, elbows and fingers! They are so crooked that they look like rods. I can't wait to turn eighteen and have a plastic surgery do-over everywhere. When I bled for the first time, I cried in pain, but my mother kept excitedly telling me, "You are a woman now." She never understood that I had menstrual cramps. I'm not built right and maybe that's why my friends stopped talking to me. Did I tell you that when I was little, I had no one to eat lunch with, I asked the girls if I could sit and eat with them, but they told me the space was taken. So, I ate with the teachers and then Laura, my best friend, stopped talking to me altogether, for no reason at all; and that's why I went to therapy for the first time when I was nine years old. I was left with the idea that if people get to know me more, they will no longer like me. My mom is always telling me, "Maria, you are so tiresome."

A – Do you feel the same way here? Considering that we see each other four times a week, do you feel that I could get tired of you?

M – No, I think that you are the only person who has faith in me. My parents don't have any, and I certainly don't either. I don't believe there is a cure for me. Only you believe in me, but it's useless if I don't believe in myself.

First session of the week – beginning of the second year

M – I flew to Miami for the weekend. I'm sorry I didn't tell you that I wasn't coming yesterday. My mom decided we were coming back yesterday at the last minute. As soon as we got off the plane, the school principal called her and told her that I had failed eight out of eleven subjects. If my dad finds out, he is going to kill me! What am I going to do? I had a good time when I was there but now, I am crying all the time for no reason. My mom doesn't help me with my school work. The only thing she has ever taught me was how to forge her signature. When I was very young, she told me, "Look Maria, I'll teach you how to sign as if you were me so you can do it for me." They are going to kick me out of school, Doctor. What am I going to do? On the plane back I told my mom that I felt ugly and her answer was, "Whatever problem you have with your self-esteem, it can be fixed with a plastic surgery." I continue to stay away from my friends because I feel that they look at me with pity.... My mom asks her friends for their grocery bills and puts them on my dad's expense account. The grocery bills are very inflated, and yet there is no milk in the house. She is taking antidepressants and sometimes I wonder if I should be taking them, too. Last weekend, our electricity was cut off; because they found that my mom was ripping off the electric company. She owes them seventy thousand and that is why we were cut off from the grid. I had to light candles at night.

A – What you are telling me is that you feel that your mother taught you the easy way out: forging, taking a miracle pill, plastic surgery or 'inflating' reality.

M – (Crying) Well, yes! I don't know any other way. My dad didn't teach me anything to begin with. I don't like what she does, but I don't know any other way. I don't want hers and I'm desperate.

A – Don't you feel that here we can learn another way that is not the easy way?

M – I want to, but I don't know how. I overslept and didn't go to school and I wasn't going to come here either, but I know I have to come. I'm going to be kicked out of school. I'm such a failure and you must be disappointed in me: either I don't come or I'm late. I'm like my mom, I play the victim.... I'm really tired, I can't move anymore. My dad wants to fly me to New York to buy me a prom dress. I was excited at first, but then I thought about telling him to give me the money for the trip instead. I can buy a cheaper one here and that way, I can give my mom the money to pay the electric bill. She told me that as soon as I move abroad after finishing high school, my dad is going to kick her out of the house. ... I'm scared and I feel very sad.

A – And yet, in spite of your sadness, you are here today.

M – (Smiling shyly). Yes, yes, every time I leave here, I feel some hope, but it lasts very little, it goes away quickly.

Third year session

M – I'm sad. ... Rather, I'm angry. ... Yesterday I didn't come because I had to study and today, they didn't let me take the exam because of all the absences I had. I got furious! I even felt like saying that there is no point in studying, because look at what happens when you do! But I know it's not like that. I know that it was because of my lack of responsibility that all of this happened.

A – It seems you are no longer blaming others. Now, you are playing a more active role in taking ownership of your actions and responding to what happens to you, isn't that so?

M – Yes, this was on me, on my lack of responsibility. But I am also very angry with everyone .... My dad wants to get back together with my mom. He needs her for his political campaign, and he is pretending to be sorry. My mom is taking advantage of the situation, telling him she has no money, and he ended up giving her money. ... I am worried because I do not want to fail. And yet, I told the teacher that I did not care. Why am I like that? Why do I pretend to be something I'm not?

A – Can we say that by asking 'why am I like this', you are demonstrating that you are starting to observe yourself more?

M – Yes, but I sometimes don't want to because it hurts (silence). In my house there is no food, when I really want a glass of milk, there is none. You see? I live in a golden cage, nobody would believe that somebody living in my upscale neighborhood wouldn't get a glass of milk. ... and I feel embarrassed to ask my friends to invite me over for dinner because there is no food in my house. Today, I had a piece of gum for breakfast and went back to sleep so as not to feel hungry. I already am like those homeless kids who take drugs just to not feel hungry. If I asked my dad for money to buy food, he would know that my mom is stealing his grocery money (silence). Pedro (the driver) lent me thirty pesos to buy a baguette... all I am is a mask with legs (a farce). Sometimes, I don't even know who I am.

A – During the last session you told me that you feel that your dad does a lot of pretending to get a job position, and that your mom pretends to 'be poor' so that everyone gives her money, and that you pretend to be 'rich', but you live as if you were 'poor', right? Like the poor rich kids play?

M – (Silence). Yes. When I was a small girl, there was a movie called the Truman Show, starring Jim Carrey. ... It was about a show that was similar to what you are saying. There was a fake city, he was an unknowing actor. It was like Big Brother, but without him knowing that the whole world was watching him. ... I felt like him. I thought that they were watching me, that there were cameras in my room and I danced and sang to them. I imagined that my whole family was watching what I was doing. Such nonsense! Or madness? I liked it a lot. ... In the show, when he realized that everyone was watching him, he ran away, because he didn't want to live a farce .... but I didn't want to leave. It still happens to me sometimes when I'm on a plane. I think there are cameras, I think they see me.... I don't want people to realize it is all in my imagination. They would make fun of me if they knew what goes on in my mind.

A – Maybe you don't want us to notice your loneliness?

M – (Crying) Well, yes. It's really crazy. When I was about six years old, I lived inside that illusion. I did for many years. I liked to imagine that they applauded me. It's really crazy that I had to invent a make-believe world where people would see me.

A – It is very sad.

M – Yes, it is. I've been remembering things from my childhood. Do you recall that I told you that I felt that I smelled? Well, I actually stank, for real. I would go into my bathroom, turn on the shower, wet my hair a little in the sink and sit down to read for ten minutes without washing myself. Nobody would notice. I swear, I stank horribly! Five days would easily go by without me showering. I didn't bathe.... I remember it was because there was a scary movie in which a monster would come out of the shower drain, so I would only bathe if the maid was around.... Why didn't my mom say anything? I remember sitting in the classroom, paralyzed, I couldn't move, I didn't go out for recess and I stayed alone in the classroom. Something was happening to me, and my mother didn't even notice it. How could she not notice, if I stank so horribly? I'm so dark-skinned that I am afraid people will see me all the way from the west coast. That's why I never sunbathe. I always hide myself because of my color, because of my smell.

A – Because of your pain?

M – Well.... Yes, maybe....

A – Could it be that the color of your skin only wrapped up your pain? Was it better to fear the monsters than to realize that you did not have the things you needed?

M – Yes, that sounds about right. Maybe that's why I felt I was like a zombie who was neither dead nor alive.

Session at the beginning of the fourth year

M – My mom fired the driver. She is so stupid! I didn't talk to her all weekend. I yelled at her that she was jealous of him because he took better care of me than my own mother. We live five minutes away from school, but when Pedro wasn't around, she would make me late!

A – You are truly angry.

M – Yes, I can't stand her! I want to live with my dad. It was so good to travel with him during his political campaign and to hear all the people shouting his name. I know they were paid off to give the impression that he is popular, but it doesn't matter! Life is like that, you pay and you get, if you don't pay for things, you don't get anything.... My mom told me, "He was just an employee, Maria. It is not normal for you to get all heated up like that just because I fired him." I told her, "Well, that employee took better care of me than you ever did." She then said, "He did that only because it was his job." That made me even angrier so I replied, "Oh! So that's why you don't look after me? Because you don't get paid? Now I understand everything." At that point, I stormed out to my room. So last night, I went out and drank heavily. I still feel hungover. I have a headache, and that's why I didn't come in yesterday.

A – Maybe you thought, "Why should I go to analysis, if my analyst is also paid to take care of me?"

M – (Opening her eyes in surprise). Well, to be honest, sometimes I get tired of coming here and talking about the past. My problem is my mom (silence). I don't know if I will ever get better, since whatever I do have, they take it away from me.

A – You don't want to risk losing anyone again?

M – Maybe. I ran away from home again. I went out with some friends, and we grabbed things from the supermarket without paying for them. You see? That's what I learned at home. It is the family model of 'stealing.'

A – Regardless of what your family does, the painful thing is that when you steal time from your sessions, you are robbing yourself of the opportunity to grow, Maria.

M – (Starts crying). I really got scared this time. We had done it before, about two years ago. We went to stores and stole things, just to wreak havoc. I haven't told you yet, but this time around, a policeman stopped my friend and took her to a room. I was terrified! I could have lost everything! I could imagine myself in jail. I was convinced my mom would just let me rot behind bars....

A – You seem bent on proving that we can't do anything for you. Could we say that if in the future you stopped coming, you would do it so that I would not leave you first? So that it wouldn't hurt so much?

M – I don't know, maybe. Do you remember the friend that was kidnapped? (Yes). Well, they can't find her, even though the ransom has been paid. Her parents believe she is still alive, but I don't think so. They just don't want to accept it (silence). I am afraid, I don't know how to stop this anger, and I don't know how to trust. When Pedro (the driver) was around, I could drink alcohol and I knew he would look after me. Have I told you that when I was a child, I used to call him 'Dad'? What am I going to do now? Sometimes, I worry that you will also get fed up of me and tell me to 'get out.'

A – It seems that the monsters are starting to come out of the sewage. Perhaps you feel that I am only wetting my hair, like you did, and that I am not really going to actually help you?

M – (Silence). I never saw it that way. But sometimes I do feel that whatever you do, I will never heal. I am the one who destroys what I build. I am the one who is sending you away every time I don't show up.

A – Yes. But you might also feel that I have already been paid a 'ransom' and yet, I cannot bring you back to life?

M – I don't know. I feel bad because you haven't done anything wrong. The truth is that I'm also afraid because now without Pedro, I'm going to have to learn how to drive.

A – It would seem so. But it's not just about driving a car, but also about being behind the wheel of your own life, right?

M – (Tilting her head and in a sad tone). Yes, that's true.

Fifth year session – two months before closing

M – Well, the deadline is approaching. We have twenty-three sessions left, but today I'm feeling sad. My dad is being attacked. Somebody published pornographic pictures of him (she breaks into tears). . . . He called me that night, he told me it was all a lie, that the pictures had been tampered with. First, I didn't know who was telling the truth. What is happening to me is horrible! But no matter what they tell me or what I see, it's not my problem anymore. I feel sorry for him because regardless of his shortcomings, he has always worked hard. He started supporting his family when he was ten years old, because his own father abandoned him. He has always struggled and maybe he has not been the best father, but he is still my father, and I love him. I can say that out loud in front of my mother and my brothers. Do you remember that I wanted to backpack for eight months and stay wherever? My dad arranged for me to go live with a family in Spain. At first, I didn't like it but now, I think it's for the best. He must know that I still need structure, and a family gives you structure, right? I have learned to accept the best they can give me .... And then I think of you. I will never stop thanking you for everything that you have done for me. If I am still alive, if I finished high school, and if I can laugh again, it's all because of you.

A – It's because of the both of us.

M – Yes, that is true. My poor mom! It's quite a miracle that she even became a mother in the first place. She told me that my grandmother used to scrub her with the brush they used to wash the horses when she misbehaved. I think that's why she put up with so much abuse from my father. Anyway, that is the dark side of the family. The bright side is that they have given me a trip to look forward to. The bright side is that I have a boyfriend, I finished high school, and I am already packing everything I am going to take with me. Paulina has already sent me the itinerary of the countries we are going to visit.

A – It seems you are doing the same here, packing what you will take with you, and deciding what to leave behind?

M – Yes. I know I am not healed; and that I still have a lot to work on. Can I come back? And maybe when I do, I will finally get to lie on the couch. Could I? Today I passed by a church and I remembered my first communion ceremony. I hadn't even learned the Lord's Prayer, but they let me do it because my parents had already paid for everything .... I couldn't see anything of what was written on the blackboard. That was about the time when I started wearing glasses. I was about eight years old and I couldn't see the blackboard, but my parents said that I squinted to draw attention to myself. You know? I am feeling a little scared. You have helped me follow a path and without you, I am afraid of going astray. But I am also confident, because you have been with me for more than five years. What I want to leave behind is the sadness with which I arrived. Do you remember? I wouldn't get out of bed until one in the afternoon, ate badly, turned on the TV but didn't watch any program in particular. I was hypnotized, neither paying attention to the TV nor to the outside world.

A – And now you are fully inside yourself, you use new glasses to write your life path, and you can also pack this experience inside your suitcase (pointing to the mind).

M – I also carry you in my mind and in my heart. (She smiles and cries with emotion. On her way to the door she says in a joking manner, "I no longer need to know the Lord's Prayer by heart."

A – (Laughs). Not anymore, it's inside you.

M – It is! Thank you very much.

Two years later – (Maria was almost twenty-one years old)

M – Well, I'm back! I'm now studying marketing. Things happened during my absence. Many people changed where my dad works, and my mom got back what my dad had taken away from her. She went back to Cancun to manage everything, while my brothers are studying abroad. Hugo (the oldest) is getting married in December with his high-school sweetheart. He is working with my dad, so I was left to live alone in the mansion (she laughs). I have a new boyfriend (we smile). His name is Rafael and what do you know? We are having sex and I love it! Before I stopped coming here, I was still Luis's girlfriend, do you remember? (Yes.)

M – Well, we broke up since he wanted to have sex before I left for my trip, and I was not ready back then. We still see each other. But Rafael is.... How can I say it? He is a real man in all the sense of the word. It's a good thing that I waited for him to be my first. I met others on the trip, but I didn't feel the way I do with him. I did not believe it would be possible to be with a man.

A – Well, I am not surprised. I see a woman in front of me (we smile).

M – Yes, I have grown up but I came back, because we had to make sure that I got to sit on that couch (laughing)! It's still hard for me to be constant with certain things. My mom wants me to move to London and finish my studies there. But I feel that I still need more stability, because this "being an adult" thing is still hard for me. In Europe, I got a little depressed, nothing like the depression I had when I first arrived with you, but it was still was hard for me. Remembering makes me sad. Something is happening to me because when I was finally able to get rid of my mother, when I found that I could be me, that I no longer needed to revolve around her.... And you see? I can barely talk about it now, because the anguish comes flooding back in. Something closes up inside of me and I get back that feeling of emptiness, of orphanhood that I felt when I was young and my mother was not there for me. Once again, I forget the things that are truly mine, what makes me happy, how difficult it was to differentiate me from others. Even though we have been doing this for years, I sometimes feel that I am moving backwards. So I am glad I came back. I also started working at a toy company. Yesterday, I was designing some toys, and it's funny that all the playing that I didn't do as a child, I am doing now, and I am getting paid for it! I feel like they are paying me to play (laughs). I saw my dad and I told him about my new job and he said, "Well, let's see how long this pleasure lasts, since you were not born to produce." You know what he's like. I went on a weekend trip with my friends and what do you know? I paid for my own expenses, and I can now afford to pay part of my therapy, too. I opened a bank account and I will be paying you from there. We are celebrating my birthday in advance.

A – Yes. It's your birthday tomorrow, right?

M – (Tearing up). Oh! I'm so touched you remember my birthday! That's why I came back. It's that feeling that someone "knows" your life and has you in their life, it's incredible. I never had that before! We'll continue tomorrow, I'm paying this session (she smiles). Oh! And I have a dog now (we smile). I'll bring him in one day so you can see him. I bought him with my money.

COMMENTARY 1

Through bits and pieces, as the tale of this analysis unwinds, we learn that Maria is the fourth child and only girl of a "by all outward indicators" wealthy family in Mexico. Although we can only attempt educated guesses about the disguised elements of this recounting, we discover clues about her life and her struggles as a thirteen-year-old girl, shared with us through the lens of the analyst's eye. Maria's family had a home or business in Cancun. Her father has run for political office and wishes to keep his positions. She spends most of her time with the domestic help. She needs to borrow pesos from their driver for food because the family's money is not real, at least not real enough to be useful to Maria and her mother. We also learn that Maria has the brown complexion of an *indigena* (an indigenous person or Indian in Mexico). Maria is described as a girl with a strong depression, suicidal ideation, not doing well at school, witness to her parents' violent home life, then separation. She is insightful but thin-skinned: the barrier between her anguish and the frustration-generating world is not thick enough to protect her. Maria's neglectful family is overwhelming in their absence, and we quickly learn that the consequences to Maria are profound.

The parents agree to begin a four times per week psychoanalysis, only to provoke a break in the treatment after two months due to non-payment. Maria is able to negotiate a return, but her father declares that he will only pay for three, then two, then one session a week. It is only on the precipice of Maria's failing the academic year, panic attacks, and nightmares that the analyst is able to obtain the father's commitment to the original analytic schedule and to not force Maria abroad for high school. Violent separations reverberated in this family.

At thirteen, we would hope that Maria would have the foundational developmental gains from latency that would provide her the supports required to undertake the upcoming tasks of adolescence. Based on what the analyst tells us, we know that her early relationships with her parents were "ambivalent" and with her siblings "adequate." Affection was not given freely nor unconditionally; most often it was bought. Maria was a lonely child whose parents were never home. She was well-aware of deficits in her parents and their ability to care for her from very early on. She had been close to the family driver since she was five: *Have I told you that when I was a child, I used to call him 'Dad'?* Her mother fires him one day, then wonders why Maria becomes enraged. *He took better care of me than you ever did.* Once, she watched a scary movie where a monster comes out of the shower, then goes for days without bathing, wanting her parents to notice her odor: *I would only bathe if the maid was around. Something was happening to me, and my mother didn't even notice it.* As an adult, Maria recounts "that feeling of emptiness, of orphanhood." Maria could describe herself as both her father's favorite child and also rejected and ignored by him. *I learned that everyone in the house altered reality.*

The analyst shares details of Maria's parents' efforts to manipulate and control perceived reality. Her family of pretenders lie and steal so much that lying and stealing are the only things that become "true". The façade is what matters: her parents feigning a happy marriage for her father's latest campaign; her mother wanting Maria to forge her signature, as a matter of course; plastic surgery to "fix" Maria's self-esteem; living in a wealthy neighborhood but not being able to afford food or electricity. The ruse was so extreme that when Maria was small she would imagine that her life was like *The Truman Show*, a movie about a young man who is completely unaware that his entire world is a television program, staged to convince him that it is real, where everyone in his life is just an actor. She tells the analyst that she loved imagining this. *I thought that they were watching me ... I imagined that my whole family was watching what I was doing.* Maria was desperate for her family's attention, in any form, even if in fantasy. The meaning that she does not articulate is her unconscious wish for another life and another family.

Which family is watching her? The family in front of her is not authentic and, perhaps, not real. Like the unhappy child who wishes to learn of an adoption, is there a wish for other unknown parents and another life that could have been- and would have been better? In *The Truman Show*, Truman is sacrificed as a baby to live out his life in the program. What is important is *the show*. Eventually, Truman runs away to find what is real, but Maria is afraid that all she can have is the fantasized attention. The real and the imagined family will only watch her and care through distant, hidden cameras. *I lived inside that illusion. I had to invent a make-believe world where people could see me.* She had to create a place where people seemed to care.

What does this mean to a child who is entering adolescence? Normally, we would expect the transition from latency to adolescence to be a bit bumpy. The late-latency child is struggling with the evolving ego and needs to return to borrow from the ego strengths of the parents. We would expect the child to supplement gaps and weaknesses in their newly forming and reforming ego by turning to the functioning of the parents. However, this assumes there is a functional ego from which to borrow. In Maria's case, her turn towards the parents is met with ego pathology and minimal object constancy from a very early age. She tells us that the only authentic and reliable objects were her driver and her maid. Additional questions then follow: What was the quality of Maria's first individuation as a toddler? Was Maria sufficiently able to work through the developmental tasks of latency in order to begin the next stage of development in adolescence? Was she well-prepared, or will she be pushed into the next stage ill-equipped? What will this mean for the second individuation marking her entry into adulthood?

Maria becomes one of the fortunate ones. At thirteen, she is offered a new object and a new developmental pathway through the analyst and the psychoanalysis. Although we might think that a new object is what we would normally consider for a younger child, Maria's deprivation has been so great that we are witness to the object hunger of a starving child in adolescence.

Literally and figuratively, Maria has been impoverished. She tells that us that her mother would not give her milk, did not have food in the house, was more concerned about forging inflated grocery bills to collect the money, while Maria ate gum for breakfast and was too embarrassed to ask to eat at a friend's house. She is deprived of physical and emotional nourishment. When Maria steals from the supermarket at seventeen, supposedly "just to wreak havoc", she is confronted with the terrifying awareness of real danger without her substitute father, her driver, who would normally have a watchful eye on her and keep her safe. She laments knowing that her mother would rather let her rot in jail than bail her out. Aware that this time was different, Maria associates to the kidnapping of her friend and believing her dead, even with the ransom already paid. There are real and perceived dangers in adolescence when more autonomous functioning is tested, with the surge in libidinal and aggressive drives, and with increase in narcissistic demands. How dangerous can they become in the chronic absence of the parents?

An additional and particular challenge for Maria, relates to questions about her developing identity, not just in how she experiences herself in the world, but in how she is reflected in the eyes of others. This becomes an internalized aspect of her psychic life. Will she believe she is "tiresome," as her mother repeatedly tells her? Will she believe she is worthy of anyone's time and attention, if her family has none for her? What is often put onto Maria by others outside of her family is the label *negrita*, black girl. At just fourteen, she tells her analyst about classmates talking about her: *Maria is black and she stinks like Negroes.* Maria's classmates insult her by calling her "Negro" and "black," demeaning both the indigenous, the African, and her. They perpetuate a colorism hierarchy that values lightness, subverting brownness, blackness, and darkness. Maria wonders what is wrong with her, then immediately shares that her mother no longer lets her sleep in her room when Maria is scared. Can her mother even tolerate her? Maria's reaction is to hide herself in the clubs at night, use her darkness as camouflage. She stays away from everyone, claiming that she smells from cigarettes. This is the second time we hear of Maria creating odors in herself. First, she did not wash, hoping to attract her parents' attention. Is she now manifesting the hostility of others' projections? At the same time, Maria is worried that her darkness makes her too visible. What if you can see her from across the country? She has to avoid being seen, not become darker, not sunbathe. Are her conflicts about closeness and acceptability making Maria keep everyone at bay?

Maria realizes that her teachers and classmates are racist, but this does not stop her from questioning whether there is something wrong *with her*, both inside and out. Her friend is glorified as Maria's opposite: *guerita*, blond girl. "She is beautiful" Maria exclaims. She was chosen for the cheerleading squad and is the kind of girl who gets to dance the tango in school. Maria is told to "stick to folk dancing" and worries she could be mistaken for her friend's maid. In Mexico, where class and race are inextricably linked and overtly acknowledged, it is clear who is favored within society. The residual effects of the colonial Spanish caste system that judged a person's position and value in society based on the amount of Spanish blood and the darkness of the complexion still persist. The expression of these values appear ubiquitously in popular cultural: *telenovelas* illustrate many of these persistent values of colonization. They capture the conflicts of class and its overlay of racial and ethnic tensions. The indigenous, Indian, or *moreno* (brown) actors are typically cast as the lower class, the criminals, the domestic help. They are the characters who aspire to a better lot in life, but are not born into it; nor are they ever offered an easy ride. Maria tells her analyst that sometimes she acts arrogantly, just to avoid being mistaken for a maid. She wishes she could "do what Michael Jackson did...as if he had been born white." Maybe Maria can change her color, then also change the reflection she perceives from others. Can there be a resolution for Maria? In order to avoid the judgement of race, she denies the class that has been her support and haven. How can she keep the love of her driver and maid if she is forced to reject them; if she, herself, has internalized the racism and classism that deny her and those closest to her? For now, only her analyst has faith in her and reflects to her who she is and could be.

The metaphor of skin runs throughout this analytic vignette. What do we know now of Maria's skin? It is too thin, too dark, too permeable to keep out the toxins around her. What is outside? What is inside? Are they connected? How? Early on we learn that Maria's brother has neurodermatitis, a condition she blames on the bad relationship with their father. The condition makes you itch, but the more you scratch, the worse it gets. The skin becomes irritated. Rather than soothe the itch, the scratching makes the skin darker, red, bumpy, raised. The momentary solution is an irritant and nothing but a fleeting wish for the problem to go away. Sometimes dark skin comes from illness. When Maria is eighteen, near the end of the first part of her treatment, she shares with her analyst that her mother suffered abuse as a child. When she misbehaved, she was scrubbed with the brush used to wash the horses. Did her mother's skin become red, irritated, and darkened from the abrasions? "That is the dark side of the family" Maria says. Can Maria, her brown skin, and her *indigena* identity be rescued from the pejorative "darkness" that so many have labeled her?

Maria's analyst tells us that the developmental milestones of Maria's adolescence will be hard fought and won. *If for most adolescents it is difficult to confront, integrate, and.... overcome the struggle of the psychological, physical, and emotional changes of that life stage, for this young patient, it was not only a challenge, but an almost impossible task....*" Although the adolescent must separate in both concrete and symbolic ways from the parents during the second individuation, this also offers alternate opportunities to form new attachments to those who are available, in the service of transitional growth towards adulthood. Maria had this opportunity with her analyst. As new object, substitute parental ego, ego ideal, and a stable and constant presence, the analyst was able to serve as surrogate. When profound deficits in the parents leave unfinished the development of latency and disrupt the psychic restructuring of adolescence, the analysis can restore, regenerate, and fortify growth. Necessary saving identifications were no longer limited to the family. In Maria's case, her work with her analyst allowed her to return at twenty-one as a vibrant young woman, excited to be in loving relationships, eager to take good care of herself, and no longer overwhelmed by abandonment and the task of survival. She is happy to been seen and known, and is also happy to know herself. At twenty-one she is finally able to play in ways that were never possible for her before and she can fully enjoy true pleasure, now *in reality*.

COMMENTARY 2

What a pleasure to read this experience-near, loving recollection of a sensitive, effective treatment. We meet the analyst with her lonely, tearful, desolate, and sometimes suicidal patient Maria at age 13, and (spoiler alert) reconnect with Maria when she is a 21-year-old in a second phase of treatment. Maria at 13 is deeply affected by her parents' separation, in addition to suffering cumulative hurt from years of early neglect, current abandonment, and duplicity in her wealthy family. But as she reminds her analyst, she is neglected currently as well. Maria, the child of a wealthy father, lives "in a golden cage" where there is no milk in the refrigerator, no electricity in the house because of her mother's overspending, and no secure attachment. Her mother, who is not attuned to her child's basic needs, allows her to sleep with her, which is overstimulating of need, and instead of fostering a slow transition to independence, she kicks her out of the bed. Neither parent gets it together to see Maria on her birthday, which leaves her feeling as if she has nothing good to take in from them or offer to them, and by extensions little to offer to friends or teachers. She feels like a failure at home and at school. Clearly, the adolescent analyst would be well advised to meet with the parents to create a partnership with them and counsel them in more effective ways of parenting or to arrange family meetings (K. Novick and J. Novick, 2002, D. Scharff and J. Scharff, 1987). Maria's mother did have her treatment for herself. But parents who cannot make it to a birthday cannot make a commitment to parent counseling for the sake of their child.

Maria is upset by her classmates' commenting on her body odor and her dark skin. I am not clear if she overhears them, or imagines that this is what they are saying about her. Either way she feels conspicuously dark, prefers to melt into a dark background so not to be noticed, and yet is desperate to be seen and noticed as good enough. She may be dealing with external racism, but the main problem to confront is her own internalized racism directed against her brown skin and Latin-American Indian culture. Her hatred of herself is compounded by her jealousy of her opposite, the popular blonde. The analyst makes the astute interpretation that Maria is focusing on the badness of her skin because it is too painful to focus on the badness that she feels inside her as a child who feels unloved. Maria agrees and offers her gynecological problems as further proof of internal badness. Maria confronts her use of an arrogant attitude when in company explaining it as a defense against the likelihood of her being assumed to be the maid. She is worried about being thought of as inferior, tiresome company. Astutely the analyst asks if Maria might worry that she will be tired of her. Maria corrects her, "Only you believe in me." And she adds with amazing insight, "But it's useless if I don't believe in myself."

Maria feels that her parents taught her nothing except how to take the easy way out. As parents her mother and father failed to notice Maria's poor hygiene and ignored her short sight even though it was interfering with her ability to attend and learn at school. As a child failing to wash or freshen her smoker's breath, Maria presented herself in ways that evoked comments of disparagement and disgust in others, which added to perceptions of her as a poor black girl, and so confirmed her sense of her badness. I see this self-presentation as an attempt to be noticed for her unkempt appearance and to fill the space around her with a bad smell, redolent of the badness in her family. Her unkempt appearance, alcohol abuse, and thieving behavior served as a rebuke to her parents and their wealthy, emotionally impoverished life. Her mother cannot relate to her daughter's sense of ugliness and promotes the magical idea that plastic surgery will cure her faults, but at the same time she does realize that the child needs treatment.

I was taken by the analyst's sensitive assessment of Maria's posture and muscle tone as physical expressions of her emotional state. Unlike Maria's mother, this woman does notice, putting her body awareness to use in the clinical situation. I am interested in the physical expressions of affect, culture and conflict (Rosenfeld and Scharff, 2021) and so this small sentence caught my attention. But the analyst could see the intelligent, sensitive and introspective girl and the anguish behind the depressed, slack exterior. This vision of who Maria can become is what would hold the treatment together.

Although Maria was her father's favorite, and she loved him, she also recognized his cruelty toward her mother. He was ambitious, highly visible in the community, and always at work, while her mother was supported to be an at-home mother who left the raising of her children to paid domestic help. Maria's story of the mother trading affection for money, appearing both to have money to spend and to be an impoverished victim, and pretending to have a husband in bed at home, seals the impression of a home where relationships were simulated, and reality altered. We learn very little about Maria's siblings, and yet I would have thought that with such parental neglect and conflict there would have been reason to seek comfort in the company of siblings or express rage at them for being inadequate substitutes.

When Maria's father, who controlled the money, reduced Maria's sessions, she fell into a panic, with persecutory nightmares, paralysis and failing grades: that secured the analysis. Good for her! In analysis, Maria was governed by unbridled primary process "which was expressed in her magical desire to solve all problems" without engaging in the slow process of mourning the loss of an intact parental couple. This manic defense, echoed in her preoccupation with the show of wealth, made her hard to reach, and left her analyst with nothing vital to connect to. How would she get through to Maria? How would she bring the desolate parts to life? The challenge left her feeling inept and hopeless. As the analyst worked to help Maria inhabit herself, the desolate parts in her patient's empty inner life came out in the form of acting out with alcohol, stealing, missing sessions, and running away from home. I can imagine the terror the analyst felt during this phase. So, how did she cope? With steady hand, reliable presence, and transformational interpretations she enabled this displaced drive activity to give way to coherent striving for academic achievement, sexual relatedness, and autonomy sufficient to allow for separation without total fear of abandonment. She asks Maria to consider therapy as a place for learning not to take the easy way out. Maria wants to, but she doesn't know how. She feels hopeful when she is with her analyst, but the feeling doesn't stay with her. Nevertheless, Maria is becoming aware of the mad pretense her parents promote, and observant of her own living in an illusion in which people see her in a positive light, at the same time always hiding herself because of her color and her smell.

Maria was angry when her mother suddenly fired the driver, a long-time employee. Maria was furious and probably scared and lonely without his support. Her mother thought Maria's attachment to him was ridiculous as if he could not be a real person of significance to her child when he was simply paid help to her. Immediately, the analyst picked up the resonance in the transference to her as someone paid to take care of Maria. Maria revealed the negative transference, admitting that she sometimes thinks of firing her. Certainly, Maria attacks the treatment by missing sessions, being late, and acting out by stealing, but she doesn't want to lose her. The analyst makes the point that by shortchanging the treatment Maria is robbing herself of the opportunity to grow. Perhaps she does this to leave before her analyst leaves her, or because she feels that her analyst is not able to help her. With amazing insight, Maria responds, "I am the one who is sending you away every time I don't show up." Maria is afraid without her trusted driver, and without analysis. How will she learn to take the wheel of her own life? But she does. She pulls up her grades, finishes high school, and becomes able to make a homestay abroad. She correctly realizes that all this is because of what her analyst has shown her. I am sure by her expression and tone the analyst graciously accepts Maria's gratitude. She reminds Maria that the two of them working together had achieved this movement to the point where Maria can have empathy for her parents and individuate from them, and can dare to try being abroad without the support of her analyst. I love the analyst's parting metaphor of Maria's taking the analytic relationship in her suitcase, and Maria's understanding of its relevance to her, as she concluded, "I also carry you in my mind and in my heart."

Indeed, analyst and patient carried each other in mind. Maria returned for another period in analysis to secure her adult development, and the analyst, now as the author, preserved her experience of the first treatment to share with us. The author, who had the immensely satisfying experience of working with Maria again at the next life stage, re-introduces Maria, now an independent woman with a job, an ambition for further study and cultural experience, and a boyfriend with whom she has discovered sexual pleasure and desire. She is still in touch with anguish when she thinks of the absent mother of her childhood, but it no longer defines her. Maria has built on her gains in analysis, is now capable of accepting her parents' kind of love, such as it is, and has returned to her life-affirming analyst, eager for more knowledge of her self.

EDITORIAL REFLECTIONS

This chapter brings us clear illustrations of several important psychoanalytic concepts useful for understanding adolescent conflicts and bringing about therapeutic change.

Shengold (1979) movingly described the impact of actual events of abuse as soul murder. Wurmser (1994, 1996) and we have said that the precursor to soul murder and abuse is soul blindness (Novick J. and Novick, K.K. 1994,2005). We wrote that externalizations on to others are fueled by wishes to get rid of hated or conflictual aspects of the self; externalization is only possible in the context of denial of the reality of the other person, a blindness to who they really are and what they really are like (Novick, J. and Novick, K.K. 1994, 2005). Children who are the targets of externalizations often become externalizers themselves. Maria's mother was punished by her mother with a brush used for horses, and she, in turn, could not see the ordinary needs her child had for food, for recognition, and for love. On Maria's birthday neither parent could find some way to see her which as one commentator says "... leaves her feeling she has nothing good to take in from them or offer to them, and by extension little to offer to friends or teachers." The abuse occurs also in relation to the theme of skin color. Maria is brown-skinned pointing to a genetic message in one or both parents but they react by externalizing the genetic history and treat her as if she is responsible for her "smelly, disgusting color." The theme of continuous parental abuse clearly appears in small and large ways; we can look at what the analyst can do, and think about what this teaches us about adolescent development and treatment in general.

The main transference in the treatment of adolescents is the transference of defense. If the adolescent has been the target of externalization this will show up in the transference (Novick and Novick, 1996). In the first phase Maria drastically undercut the new relationship she had found with her analyst. Despite the fact that she had found someone who would listen to her justified complaints, the feeling she conveyed was of desolation and hopelessness – "... despair seeped in, session after session to the extent that I came to question my analytical approach."

The target of externalizations is often threatened with abandonment and is made to feel that they are a burden on the family. Maria said that her mother repeatedly complained, "Maria, you are so tiresome." But after two months of treatment father stopped paying and the analyst suspended the sessions. Maria convinced her father to pay but after a month he reduced the sessions to three, then two, and then one. Both Maria and the analyst had to resort to extreme measures to have the treatment resume. It is an axiom of family systems theory that the family needs someone, usually a child or adolescent, to be the patient designated to carry the family pathology. In this family Maria was the dark one, the one who carried the denigrated status of the indigena, the Indian in Mexico. After two months of analytic attention to her externalizing defenses, Maria was changing and this threatened the pathological stability of the family.

Ostensibly, parent work was not designed into the structure of Maria's treatment. After the parental attempt to end the treatment after two months, the analyst said that she never worked directly with the parents again. It is our impression that the fact that the analyst and Maria could stand up to the parents was a turning point and made the positive results possible. The father was probably carrying out mother's commands, but the analyst stood up to their manipulations as did Maria, probably encouraged by the analyst's assertion. The analyst was possibly also supported by Maria's intense response to the threat of her analysis ending. Maria had found her voice, had found something more important than pleasing her parents by being the denigrated Indian, and had found an ally in her analyst.

This underscores a technical necessity in parent work. Some child/ adolescent analysts are willing to undertake concurrent parent work but have not worked through their own fear of parents, a fear that has transference roots in the anxiety that this is the mother of infancy with the power to humiliate, scold, or abandon you. This residual transference anxiety that allocates undue power to parents can be a source of over-compliance with parents' defensive takeover of the treatment and its structure. This chapter gives us a vision of an alternate possibility, an assertive, not aggressive or competitive, stance with parents, rooted in conviction about the child's needs and the utility of the treatment.

A two-systems approach to treatment is not just a cataloguing of symptoms and focus on pathology, but mandates an engagement with the whole child, beyond her history of trauma and adverse childhood experiences. We look for and explore areas of competence, joy, strengths, success and so forth (Novick & Novick,2016). The analyst started the report on Maria by describing her as a tall, nice girl with brown skin. She was fashionably dressed, she was intelligent and, despite her emotional state, had the capacity for introspection and insight into the family dynamics. The analyst presents many examples of growing open-system functioning and we see this most clearly in the termination phase of the work.

It has been rare to read of an adolescent analysis that ends with a good goodbye. Maria, who was the target of externalizations, who at first made the analyst feel hopeless and useless, could end her analysis choosing instead to finish with realistic gratitude and love for her analyst, her analysis, her parents and herself. This is a good outcome of treatment, and a good example of the adolescent process, as Maria could set aside her omnipotent self-defeating solutions and move forward realistically, with pleasure, into the growth potential of the next stage of her life.

III

MIDDLE ADOLESCENCE

CHAPTER 8

NICK – age 16

Nick is a tall, handsome, articulate, and cerebral 16-year-old. Nick's adolescent development came to a screeching halt at age 15 when his father announced sudden plans to leave the marriage and family in search of happiness and romantic love far afield. This family trauma catalyzed Nick's mother to seek help for her son, whom she feared was depressed and suicidal.

Nick has two sisters, ages 8 and 10. His father is a journalist, and his mother a retired engineer. Nick previously lost his beloved grandparents and family friends, and he had been bullied by his peers in elementary school. Still, until the current family crisis, Nick had been making a name for himself at his private school, where he excelled as an honors student and basketball player. His grades nose-dived, and his athletic performance slipped. His social life resembled that of a latency-aged child; Nick played videogames with online friends, and shied away from same-aged peers both in and out of school.

At the outset, Nick asserted that he was impervious to feelings, and he denied any impactful changes in his life. Nick usually sat sullenly, in a frozen posture, and frequently gazed into my eyes in prolonged silence. Occasionally, in sessions, his anger would leak out at his father for dealing his mother a rotten hand. Or he would worry that he himself was burdening his grief-stricken mother.

During the early phase of our work, Nick despaired that he would never feel better; he expressed frank suicidal ideas without a plan or intent. I often felt deeply concerned by his suicidal despair; in efforts to reach him, I experienced helplessness and impotence. Occasionally he would emerge from a hiding place in which he could express his desperation metaphorically. Then we could briefly play with ideas in ways that gave him relief and that attenuated my worries about him.

Gradually, as he became more in touch with his feelings, he described generalized anxieties about potential catastrophes, such as a bridge collapsing under him, or getting trapped in an elevator. Such anxieties were mixed with depressive feelings, but he displayed no dissociative or psychotic thinking. Additionally, he revealed an ongoing traumatic situation involving an ex-girlfriend who began cyberbullying him, despite their amicable separation. Gradually, he disclosed having been engaged with her in a hypersexual relationship about which he felt pressured and uncomfortable.

As the therapy progressed, Nick narrated his worries about his parents' imminent divorce. He had never known his parents to suffer overt conflict, although he suspected their strife may have gone unnoticed because, in his view, no one talked openly or deeply. He expressed his anxiety in relation to other people: he worried about his seemingly depressed and shell-shocked mother; and he felt burdened by a heightened sense of responsibility for his abandoned sisters. He suffered longstanding insecurities about making friends, often stricken with social phobia and profound feelings of self-recrimination if he made the slightest gaffe. Frequently he would express a longing for more friends but felt paralyzed at the prospect of initiating social engagement, having convinced himself that he was unwelcome or outright rejected. A year into the treatment, Nick established a romantic relationship with Natalia, which began in a sexualized way but then reverted to being more platonic – a cause of ongoing inner turmoil, as he felt emasculated and rejected. She was his only close friend.

Over the past couple years, the treatment has included twice-weekly individual psychoanalytic psychotherapy with Nick, complemented by twice-monthly parent work with the mother and occasional family sessions – initially with the father present, and later with the reconstituted family without the father. Nick expressed a longing for the family sessions so that everyone could learn to communicate more meaningfully. He was also agreeable to his mother and me meeting regularly so I could support her in lieu of his having to do so. The parent meetings focused on recapitulations of her family traumatic history, which she now recognized was being reenacted within the nuclear family.

The themes in the therapy relate to Nick's self-recrimination about his body image and moderate excess weight from stress eating, and his academic decline and worries about failing to meet the family standard for acceptance at Ivy League colleges. He was also consumed by intense feelings of shame over his awkward style of relating to his peers and his girlfriend. We worked extensively on his recurrent belief that he was unworthy and unappealing to others, who he thought either (at best) tolerated him or (at worst) intensely disapproved of him.

For the first several months of the therapy, although his suicidal feelings abated, he described his life as void of excitement and pleasure. He likened himself to a robot who proceeded through life mechanically, with no emotional life. Gradually, Nick found a way to unveil his fantasy life to me, which allowed us to more deeply explore his fears, internal conflicts, and defenses and to work more directly in the transference. When Nick felt he stumbled socially, he would eagerly tell me about his anguish, yet he would be filled with self-loathing and criticism at his *faux pas* and at his retelling of it. Typically, he would apologize profusely, and eventually he could work in the transference by openly exploring his fear that I would disapprove of his social missteps.

The following two consecutive sessions occurred after he had been wrestling for several months as to whether to leave Natalia, given her apparent disinterest in resuming their prior sexual relating. Nick was convinced that she had already rejected him. Time and time again, he would come into the sessions driven and determined to call things off between them. We explored his pressured feelings and potential misperceptions of her.

The therapy steadied him, as we reflected upon his tendency to project his negative self-appraisal onto her. He responded well when I encouraged him to communicate his worries to her rather than simply escaping the relationship. Repeatedly, Nick felt reassured by these conversations with her, but such comfort was short-lived; within a few days he would again be tormented by this internal drama, in which he either felt rejected by her or wanted to leave her.

Session – two years into therapy

Nick: [He opens the session.] Lately, I've been feeling like I just want to be friends with Natalia. It feels like she'll never want to be intimate with me again. I feel for my own sake, I'd rather just be friends.

Therapist: It's been really tough to keep wanting more and to feel like your desires go unanswered.

Nick: [He gazes downward.] I feel like not much would change. It's not as if there has been any romantic relationship in my opinion.

Therapist: The way you put it, it's as if there would be no loss, because you say nothing has changed.

Nick: I don't really think it would be a change. I think it would be the same. I've been feeling a lot more lonely lately. So, for example, last night, I didn't have anyone to hang out with, even though I wanted to. I was lonely, then I was feeling – I don't know how to explain it – like what I was seeing wasn't real, if that makes sense.

Therapist: Like what you were seeing wasn't real?

Nick: Like, what if everything isn't real? What if *this* is a simulation?

Therapist: I'm really trying to understand what you're saying. You're trying really hard to tell me. [I was puzzled by his far-out description that seemed entirely uncharacteristic of him; I wondered if he was expressing a depersonalization experience for the first time.]

Nick: I've been getting these thoughts for a while. Billions of years from now, no one is going to even know the legacy of what's going on with this planet. I think my feelings are amplified because of the coronavirus. It feels like this is Step 1 – I'm already seeing the end of the world coming. I know COVID-19 isn't going to cause the end of the world, but there's still so much unrest.

Therapist: So much unrest. I'm really struck by your use of the word "simulation."

Nick: Everyone in the world is in on this thing, and they're watching me. It's very difficult to explain.

Therapist: We can work on it together.

Nick: I'll lay it out plain and simple. I could be this side character or [could be] created for this entire purpose of someone else. So my importance is nothing since I might be in this world only to impact someone else. Or everyone else might be created to impact my existence in one instant. It could be either way. By simulation, I mean everything could be unreal. I could wake up and everything could be really different. I could wake up on a spaceship.

Therapist: I think you're describing very, very colorfully a sense of feeling meaningless.

Nick: Definitely, I don't connect to the world around me.

Therapist: [I wished to come back to earth.] Today you began by telling me of your distress over Natalia's repeated physical rejection of you, and how lonely you feel generally, not just with Natalia.

Nick: Yeah, I mean, usually it starts more with I feel lonely. Then I start feeling disconnected from everything.

Therapist: Maybe you're also feeling defeated at being unable to recreate that romantic spark with Natalia after trying so hard and for so long.

Nick: For me, it's not all about Natalia. For me, I'm having trouble with assignments. Sometimes an assignment doesn't feel important because it's not going to matter 50 years from now, even though it will. I just don't feel like it will.

Therapist: So it comes back to your feeling of meaninglessness, as if you're drifting aimlessly in a spaceship. You're describing today a pervasive feeling that you don't matter.

Nick: [nods]

Therapist: [Given that we were working well together, I chose to risk making a transference interpretation.] Maybe, in a similar way, you're not sure you matter to me either.

Nick: Ah, yeah, it's not as if I'm making a big enough impact on you. Inevitably, the sun will explode, humanity will collapse, the earth will collide with another planet, or the natural elements will disappear. So it's like oblivion almost. Then the accomplishments we've all made will be for nothing.

Therapist: What about the meaning you and I are making right now? Maybe you feel it doesn't matter because it won't matter 50 billion years from now?

Nick: Yeah, that's my opinion.

Therapist: I'd like for us to focus on a couple of core elements in what you've been describing today. What you imagined possible with Natalia has not been realized – like a technicolor universe in your mind was just shattered?

Nick: What do you mean, a technicolor universe in my mind?

Therapist: I think your colorful fantasy of being in a sexual relationship with Natalia has collapsed.

Nick: Well, I'm not upset about Natalia. I'm not saying it's about Natalia. I never really made aspirations and goals with Natalia. I think we both mutually agreed we'd not date at college.

Therapist: But you *did* have aspirations for a more physically and emotionally involved relationship with Natalia.

Nick: Yeah.

Therapist: Time and time again, you wanted more intimacy, and that wasn't happening. You've been carrying an imaginative romantic fantasy with her that hasn't come to fruition as you hoped.

Nick: Yeah

Therapist: I think you're really hurting right now. I think you're trying to give expression to your hurt, right now, inside you, by describing your sense that you wouldn't matter in the universe 50 billion years from now.

Nick: That makes sense. The collapse of the fantasy and ideas make sense, and the presence of pain in me now, rather than 50 billion years from now, makes sense. I'll ask Natalia to hang out, but she says she can't, which is why I feel so lonely. I know this is my fault by putting all my eggs in one basket. Any time I want to hang out with her, she wants to do things with her other friends, or she just doesn't want to, or just wants to study. So, I think I'm upset because of the loneliness that stems from me. I get my hopes up and then get let down.

Therapist: So I think you're *now* acknowledging your upset about Natalia, whereas before you were denying that. I think you're not sure who to be upset at – Natalia, because you feel she rejects you; or yourself, because you have trouble making friends beyond Natalia. Let's see if we can come back to your ideas of this being a simulation.

Nick: I mean, it's like we're living in a fake world.

Therapist: And you said the feelings are amplified by COVID-19.

Nick: Yeah, that's because there's a lot of tension between world powers like the USA and Russia, or there's the nuclear Armageddon, or one form of world collapse or another.

Therapist: These images are telling us so much about the tensions inside you and the threat of collapse you're feeling under the sway of all these pressures in the world, but especially inside you, right now. Sometimes, I think when you're talking about things out there and then – in outer space and 50 billion years from now – it's your way of keeping at a distance your cauldron of painful feelings inside, here and now.

Nick: Yeah, that makes sense.

Therapist: I think that's your way of trying to cope with a lot of feelings inside that are very painful.

Nick: I think it's a strong hypothesis. It makes logical sense that I'd be attempting by using a scapegoat like the future to lessen the way I feel now.

Therapist: [I enjoyed his scientific reference to an emotional matter by using the word, "hypothesis" and engaged in some word play with him.] I think what we need to do now is to test the hypothesis – your word. We need to investigate if your personal feelings of obliviousness will recede once we delve into more your painful feelings together. (end of session)

Next session (two days later)

Nick: [First words of the session] I think I feel better than last time when I was feeling sad or upset. I ended up seeing Natalia, and it was fine. It was the way it always is. Instead, I was more excited to see her, and I didn't care. We "Netflixed" and chilled.

Therapist: Something opened up inside you after our previous session. Maybe you were able to find more room inside yourself to enjoy something new with her. I think you seesaw between thinking things are doomed to fail between you and her, and then you're able to feel things have righted themselves again.

Nick: I guess I'm just getting my hopes down. I guess I'm just getting a reality check, that my aspirations aren't really going to happen on anything going further with Natalia. I guess things are changing, but maybe not in the way I hoped, but they're still changing, like life still goes on, even if I wish for something to be a certain way, it might not always be that way. I guess we keep still progressing.

Therapist: Are there other ways you wish for life to be different that come to your mind right now?

Nick: I don't know.... Not really, honestly.

Therapist: It sounded like you were about to say something.

Nick: [In a halting manner, he spoke.] I'm just trying to think.... not really.... well.... I was wishing.... um, I'm just curious about what it would be like to live on the West Coast.

Therapist: The West Coast?

Nick: I don't know; I think they're a different crowd of people.

Therapist: How do you imagine they are different?

Nick: I think they're relaxed and not always in such a hurry. Or maybe they just see more, like maybe they see everything around them.

Therapist: Maybe a lot of things feel like a blur for you, because things are going so fast.

Nick: Yeah, it feels like this year just started.

Therapist: Really?

Nick: In a certain way, it kind of feels like so much has happened. So much has been packed into one year. It's hard to comprehend how all that could happen in 365 days.

Therapist: I'm thinking so much has been packed into your life especially over the past few years.

Nick: I guess I feel more observant. This year, it feels like it's only been a day, and then at other times, it also feels like it's been a lifetime.

Therapist: When you slow down, you observe things more, you feel more, and that can feel much harder.

Nick: That's how I feel sometimes. I feel, "Why do I have to see so much? Or why can't things be simple sometimes?"

Therapist: In here with me, I'm thinking there's a way that things slow down so we can think together. That brings up a lot of painful feelings in you.

Nick: Yeah, I guess it's just a time of processing what's been going on [brief silence] And then also yesterday, I was on the phone with my college counselor. I don't know.... I guess it was a big reality check. Yeah, it was kind of like he said: "Everything you've been doing has been wrong!"

Therapist: Really?

Nick: Because he asked me, "Why did you not take AP Biology this year? Why did you not take AP Physics, or that sort of thing?" Then I asked him if I would still have a chance to go to a really good college, like Yale. Then he said with my grades, there's no possibility. Luckily, he said, "There is a possibility if you took a gap year," and if I later applied with basketball, I could be recruited as an athlete.

Therapist: Our last session, you were speaking about the eventual collapse of the universe, and today you're imagining what life would be like on the West Coast. I think this is another example where you go "there and then" when the "here and now" feels unbearable for you – or if not unbearable, at least overwhelming.... Does that make sense to you – how your mind works?

Nick: It makes sense because I kind of picture the West Coast as an escape. It makes sense because I picture it like the way I want it to be.

Therapist: [I think privately about his father having escaped to another country in search of a blissful remake of his life.] Exactly. I think it's a way you release a kind of pressure valve inside you. I wonder if you felt more lonely, or disconnected, after meeting with the college counselor.

Nick: I didn't care. I thought: "Oh, well; now it's time to work again." But I felt [it] in a good way. He explained it to me, like a coach would say: "Now, it's time to get to work."

Therapist: So you went from feeling deflated to being hopeful.

Nick: Yeah.

Therapist: It's kind of like what we do in here. You bring in your feelings, we roll up our sleeves, and then we get to work, and then some of the time you feel more hopeful. Getting to work is so different than escaping to the West Coast. I think you're wrestling with many different feelings: your longing for more closeness with Natalia; your appreciation for what it is, even though it isn't fully what you wish it to be; and the big hurdle to get into the college you want.

Nick: I mean, all this is still going to carry into 2021. I don't think it's going to be that different. I wish a lot of stuff that's happened didn't carry over, but I know it will.

Therapist: Well, your understanding of yourself is growing, so maybe the next chapter can feel better for you.

Nick: Hopefully.

Therapist: Okay, we'll continue next year.

Nick: [He smiles.] Okay, see you next year!

COMMENTARY 1

This was an interesting case to read and the therapist's empathic attitude to Nick has certainly given some containment to Nick's distress, not only of his emergence into adolescence, but also his grief about the break-up of his parents' marriage.

I was struck by the therapist's use of the words "screeching halt" and "grief-stricken" and "shell-shocked" mother. This conveys on the one hand an obstacle that suddenly appears as one is driving along and putting on the brakes in panic to avoid a dangerous collision. Secondly, the suddenness, being taken by surprise, with no preparation whatsoever; being "struck" by grief, and having a bomb exploding in your face, both occurrences seemingly out of the blue. There does not seem to be any awareness of what has been going on for some time between the parents. Is it a collusion between mother and son to keep their "Eyes Wide Shut?" He expresses his "longing for family sessions," i.e., for there to be a family again. In the sessions presented, there is no mention of this, despite the associations that Nick is making. There is mention of a "repeat of mother's family traumatic history." It might have been interesting to know what it was, because Nick seems to be identified with his mother and his parental marital relationship. He seems to be trying hard to find his own separate space in his relationship with Natalia. However I find that the therapist is focusing on this emerging adolescent sexuality and Natalia, even when Nick seems to be trying to tell her that it is much bigger than Natalia. He even says "It is not all about Natalia," that he is trying

216

hard not to let his distress over his universe collapsing "matter".... that is not "meaningless." The Sun, which gives life to his world "earth" will expand dangerously, becomes a supernova, a red Giant, grow beyond sustainable size, implode on itself and become a white dwarf, cold and frozen. Instead of seeing that his whole world is threatened, the therapist keeps referring only to Natalia. He tries saying it's not about Natalia. The therapist responds "But you **did** have aspirations.... about Natalia." He gives up and says "Yeah".

I wonder whether the "suicide" is an attempt to escape being swallowed up by the mother, or this split-up relationship. Or is it a uniting phantasy in this place called paradise on the other side (west coast) of "the collapsed bridge" or "trapped in an elevator" that won't go up and is stuck? He needs also to be able to be friends with the more intimate and deeper part of his own feelings. I wonder whether being overtaken by mother and not in his own skin, makes him feel that he is not his real self.... that this is a simulation of his parental relationship, not his own. Whether his getting into the "hypersexual" relationship with Natalia might be replaying father's exit, as he has found a more exciting sexual partner. On the other hand feeling that he and Mother were not exciting enough for father to stay.

However, it is clear that the therapist has been able to help him and that the therapeutic relationship has been held in place for over a year as he struggles as an in-betweener; the child of the past and the adult of the future. Talking a bit more of the intersubjective relationship would give the reader a deeper and wider understanding of the case. Another specific instance that could be elaborated and explained was about what these "painful things" are; I would have liked more specific identification and nature of the feelings. The introduction is quite detailed, so I guess these issues have been covered in the past sessions and the sessions presented are particularly highlighting the adolescent struggle to emerge into manhood and the difficulty it presents because of the parents' break up and him being put into father's shoes with all its oedipal anxieties.

COMMENTARY 2

Thank you for the opportunity to read and make remarks about the snippet of a treatment of a 16-year- old boy whose adolescence was derailed when the parents' divorce was announced. His regression was to the earlier days when he was "bullied." He was left with a grieving mother with whom his oedipal conflicts were activated in the context of a sexual adolescent boy. He identified with his father in pursuit of love and "romance" while simultaneously having hate and murderous feelings towards his father, which tied to his own "suicidal despair." Certainly, the counterresponses of impotence and helplessness were acknowledged by the analyst. It seems that the family sessions clarified some of the unspoken known aspects of the breakdown in the marriage so the individual treatment could move forward.

Nick's analysis was facilitated through the use of metaphors, since he would not accept direct open discussion of familial conflicts which made the news of divorce so devastating for Nick. Instead of discussing the divorce and the parents, he enacted a parallel relationship with a girl, Natalia. Their ambivalent and conflictual relationship had components that were enactments of the parents' own conflict. I felt these were not clearly articulated in the case material. Nick confused sexual and romantic, including idealizing fantasies. The analyst did help him face when fantasy meets reality and the feelings that result: "unrest."

Clearly the patient felt that they were in a team endeavor. His feeling "disconnected" was an attempt to modulate unpleasant affects which were not all necessarily painful, as verbalized by the analyst. Some were related to uncomfortable anger and possibly sexual feelings and urges. His missing feeling of being "lonely" may have also connected to being alone with his feelings and thoughts as well as being rejected by his girlfriend.

It seemed that his transference-interpreted work was beneficial leading him back to the fact of being impotent in reuniting the family as well as making Natalia feel the same way about him as he does her. "I think your colorful fantasy of being sexual with Natalia has collapsed."

I saw how the analyst was working to get Nick to "express" feelings of "hurt." I find that helping the adolescent articulate a wider and more exact affect language facilitates reducing the affective discomfort being experienced as well as increasing the observing ego, which there was evidence was occurring. The patient even commented that they were "progressing" and not hopelessly fixated.

The treatment vignette ends with the realization that the future may not be the idealized wished-for fantasy, but it may still be an optimistic new chapter in his developmental emancipation process.

COMMENTARY 3

Among psychoanalytic educators and educational programs across the country there is a renewed interest in discussing the question "What indications are there in the treatment to demonstrate a psychoanalytic process is occurring?" In addition to the inevitable theoretical merits this discussion inspires, such conversations have a very practical implication. Matriculated students in various formal psychoanalytically oriented education programs need their control cases to count toward graduation. As many of these same training programs have expanded the scope of their educational offerings to include psychoanalytic-oriented psychotherapies, a serious-minded conversation has grown up around the question, "to what degree can a psychoanalytic process be demonstrated in a psychotherapy treatment?" Although this is not the forum to explore the substantive points of debate among various thoughtful educators and clinicians, reading the vignette of Nick, I am convinced we find evidence a psychoanalytic process is developing within this treatment.

In most forms of psychoanalytic-oriented therapy, the primary goal of the work may be conceived in this way – to create a shared space, perhaps better described as a shared relationship, in which two people can use their individual minds to *make contact* with, observe, explore and seek to understand the psychic reality of one of those two persons – the patient. Based on the therapist's thorough and rich affective description from two years of working together with Nick in twice a week psychoanalytic-oriented therapy, we read of the therapist's success in making contact with Nick as a person, with Nick's mind, and how it works, and with how Nick is experiencing his current solitary place in the universe. We also see examples of how the therapist introduces his/her individualized mind at specific junctures to further the explorative process.

Nick is an adolescent who, despite all his winsome qualities (ie.. being smart, attractive, and gifted athletically), finds himself moving through a vast psychic universe feeling confused, potentially suicidal, and devoid of meaning. To cite a TV series from the 1960's, Nick feels "Lost in Space." His father's desire to end the marriage with Nick's mother in search of personal happiness and fulfillment is presented as a significant and traumatic event for this young man on the cusp of adolescence. In the aftermath of his parent's separation, and the presumable diminishment of consistent contact with his father, Nick conveys he worries about his mother and feels responsible for supporting his two younger sisters. As the sole remaining male in the house, we get the sense it is a task for which he feels inadequate and ill-prepared.

The therapist's growing knowledge about Nick's internal world cannot be taken for granted in this, or any, treatment. Developing a personal understanding of a patient by the therapist reveals a profound accomplishment and evolution of any psychotherapeutic endeavor. In this vignette, we are told Nick begins the treatment highly reluctant, or perhaps unable, to observe and share his complex inner experience. The therapist provides a couple of vivid examples from early in the treatment by saying,

"Nick usually sat sullenly, in a frozen posture, and frequently gazed into my eyes in prolonged silence" and "He likened himself to a robot who proceeded through life mechanically, with no emotional life." However, as the treatment unfolds, we learn Nick is an adolescent who is increasingly *willing and able to access and share his vivid fantasy life with his therapist.*

In this evolving shift, we see a quintessential example of a burgeoning therapeutic alliance between the patient and the psychoanalytically oriented clinician. The clinician strives towards feeling with Nick, standing in Nick's shoes, seeing the world and the vastness of the universe through Nick's eyes. And equally essential, Nick has found a way to assist the therapist in knowing something about what he is feeling. Through the use of idiosyncratic metaphors and personal fantasies of space and time expressing his creative and unique cerebral personality, Nick offers verbal imagery that brings into focus a deep and painful affective reality that he lives with consistently. Nick feels he is clumsily moving through life – awkward, anxious, lonely, adrift, and with dwindling motivation for the challenges and pleasures ahead in life. In the two sessions that follow, we see with close process notes an example of the remarkable discoveries that can occur between an adolescent and a therapist when the therapist settles into this reflective stance, and the patient is willing and able to join into the exploration! In the two sessions presented in verbatim, we see glimpses of how the therapist and the patient are working to accomplish this monumental psychoanalytic achievement.

In the commentary that follows, I will use the close process from the vignette to reflect more closely on salient points of the interactions, particularly those interactions that suggest a psychoanalytic process is occurring within the treatment.

In session one, Nick's material begins centered around his flagging relationship with his girlfriend, Natalia. Natalia is presented as his primary, maybe only friend, and a friend whom he consistently and painfully feels disconnected from and deprived of the sexual contact he passionately desires. Of his own volition, he presents one of those creative, cerebral images characteristic of Nick – he suggests "nothing is real" and imagines himself as locked in a "simulation" in which "Everyone in the world is in on this thing, and they're watching me." I appreciate how the therapist lets us in on how worrisome it is to hear Nick describe himself in terms that may suggest a deeper, more profound pathologic disturbance. My experience in treating adolescents, especially those that are in significant distress, is they can express their feelings in ways that do sometimes lead to a concern within the therapist for their psychological well-being. Notably, we see the therapist is able to contain his/her fears and stay with Nick's language by showing a curiosity and expressing a wish to better understand his communication. The therapist then locates the work between them as a shared endeavor, saying, "We can work on it together."

Nick responds to this offer of sharing the load together by saying, "I'll lay it out plain and simple. I could be this side character or [I could be] created for this entire purpose of someone else. So, my importance is nothing since I might be in this world only to impact someone else. Or everyone else might be created to impact my existence in one instant. It could be either way. By simulation, I mean everything could be unreal. I could wake up and everything could be really different. I could wake up on a spaceship."

There is hardly much that is "plain and simple" in this complex communication. However, as the session progresses, the therapist is able to hear Nick's communication as pointing to a deeper level of internal experience. The therapist is able to capture in Nick's language something about how, in this imagery, Nick moves away from a shared moment between them to being far away "on a spaceship." Also, it is important to note here the therapist's self-observant, silent, internal, emotional experience of "wanting to come back to earth" which serves as a signal to the therapist of Nick's potential state of mind. Nick's associations continue to move away from Natalia to his schoolwork which he also finds pointless and which he posits will be "meaningless 50 billion years from now." The therapist describes taking a leap of faith in making a transference interpretation in the form of a question asking if his feelings might also apply to their shared relationship in the here and now. I think it was equally a leap of faith for the therapist to suggest to Nick that he was indeed moving away from the very real pain of being sexually frustrated with the unrequited passion for Natalia. And it was in this leap we see an example of how the therapist used his/her own vivid and evocative language.

Therapist: I'd like for us to focus on a couple of core elements in what you've been describing today. What you imagined possible with Natalia has not been realized – like a technicolor universe in your mind was just shattered?

This vivid language captures Nick's attention.

Nick: What do you mean, a technicolor universe in my mind?

Therapist: I think your colorful fantasy of being in a sexual relationship with Natalia has collapsed.

A little bit later in the same session, the therapist continues to attempt to fine tune the growing emotional tenor of Nick's communication related to Natalia.

Therapist: I think you're really hurting right now. I think you're trying to give expression to your hurt, right now, inside you, by describing your sense that you wouldn't matter in the universe 50 billion years from now.

Nick: That makes sense. The collapse of the fantasy and ideas make sense, and the presence of pain in me now, rather than 50 billion years from now, makes sense. I'll ask Natalia to hang out, but she says she can't, which is why I feel so lonely. I know this is my fault by putting all my eggs in one basket. Any time I want to hang out with her, she wants to do things with her other friends, or she just doesn't want to, or just wants to study. So, I think I'm upset because of the loneliness that stems from me. I get my hopes up and then get let down.

Nick agrees with the therapist's explicit understanding of his emotional communication. The pain is present in his life in the here and now. However, from the standpoint of answering the question, "Is there a psychoanalytic process unfolding here?" Nick's poignant observation, "I think I'm upset because of the loneliness that stems from me...." suggests Nick has joined the therapist in looking inward. Nick is reflecting on the context and tenor of what is inside of him. This observation demonstrates how Nick, with his therapist's assistance, is using their relationship to go beyond the external circumstances and people in his life, to explore himself. This is a hallmark of a therapeutic alliance, and a therapeutic alliance is an important element of an evolving psychoanalytic process.

In the 2nd session of the week, we begin to see the fuller impact of the first session as the themes are unpacked and expanded. Nick returns to the theme of wishing to be far away. Nick shares with his therapist a daydream of imagining himself moving to the West Coast. Nick elaborates, "I think they're relaxed and not always in such a hurry. Or maybe they just see more, like maybe they see everything around them." This daydream is presented in opposition to the way he is feeling in the present – where everything is so hard!

Returning to the verbatim:

Therapist: Maybe a lot of things feel like a blur for you, because things are going so fast.

Nick: Yeah, it feels like this year just started.

Therapist: Really?

Nick: In a certain way, it kind of feels like so much has happened. So much has been packed into one year. It's hard to comprehend how all that could happen in 365 days.

Therapist: I'm thinking so much has been packed into your life especially over the past few years.

Nick: I guess I feel more observant. This year, it feels like it's only been a day, and then at other times, it also feels like it's been a lifetime.

In this exchange, we see that the therapist attempts to expand the field beyond the last 365 days by referencing "the last few years." This reference could be an implicit reference to the separation of Nick's parents. However, in a fascinating response, a poker reference might apply. Nick sees the therapist's increase and raises the bet. Not only has a lot been going on in the last year, Nick adds, nor, the last few years, but "it also feels like it's been a lifetime." When I hear Nick make this statement, I can hear vibrations of his unconscious speaking. I hear his unconscious becoming more open to exploration. I hear him expanding the field where more aspects of his life are potentially available for thought and conversation. Another sign a psychoanalytic process is occurring.

Interestingly, just as quickly as Nick's response suggests he is willingly joining the alliance, he reminds us the road is long and the journey is hard.

Nick: That's how I feel sometimes. I feel, "Why do I have to see so much? Or why can't things be simple sometimes?"

Therapist: In here with me, I'm thinking there's a way that things slow down so we can think together. That brings up a lot of painful feelings in you.

Nick: Yeah, I guess it's just a time of processing what's been going on. [brief silence] And then also yesterday, I was on the phone with my college counselor. I don't know.... I guess it was a big reality check. Yeah, it was kind of like he said: "Everything you've been doing has been wrong!"

Therapist: Really?

Nick: Because he asked me, "Why did you not take AP Biology this year? Why did you not take AP Physics, or that sort of thing?" Then I asked him if I would still have a chance to go to a really good college, like Yale. Then he said with my grades, there's no possibility. Luckily, he said, "There is a possibility if you took a gap year," and if I later applied with basketball, I could be recruited as an athlete.

Therapist: Our last session, you were speaking about the eventual collapse of the universe, and today you're imagining what life would be like on the West Coast. I think this is another example where you go "there and then" when the "here and now" feels unbearable for you – or if not unbearable, at least overwhelming.... Does that make sense to you – how your mind works?

From an Ego psychological perspective, we see a lovely and clear defense interpretation by the therapist with this last comment. "You go 'there and then' when the 'here and now' feels unbearable, at least overwhelming...." Although it has not been my experience that most adolescents are intrigued by a comment explicitly teaching them how their "mind works," Nick may be a notable exception. One might argue the two sessions have been building up to this singular moment. The therapist presents Nick with multiple invitations to be in the present together in his loneliness and despair and Nick finds his mind blasting off to strange new places, and other galaxies, far, far away.

In the final segment of the vignette cited below, Nick confirms the defensive interpretation characterizing the West Coast fantasy as an "escape." In a testament to his growing capacity to reflect upon and own his own inner experience, Nick offers an analysis of himself, extending the defense interpretation by saying, in essence, "I think this way [about escape] because I am trying to deal with the many ways I am disappointed in the reality of what life is like for me."

Nick: It makes sense because I kind of picture the West Coast as an escape. It makes sense because I picture it like the way I want it to be.

Therapist: [I think privately about his father having escaped elsewhere in search of a blissful remake of his life.] Exactly. I think it's a way you release a kind of pressure valve inside you. I wonder if you felt more lonely, or disconnected, after meeting with the college counselor.

With the therapist's response above, we are made privy to the inner workings of the therapist's mind, too. The therapist thinks of Nick's father who also, one could argue, "escaped" to a reality that better suited the way he wished his life to be. For many of us, it would be very tempting when we make such a clear connection in our own minds to share it with the patient. And sometimes this may foster further linkages by the patient, like two persons working simultaneously on a jigsaw puzzle together with each adding a successive piece. However, from the standpoint of the therapeutic aim of expanding Nick's capacity to think for himself, to come to thoughts on his own timetable, to own his own thinking, and to becoming more sensitive to the nuances of his own unrepresented experiences, I think the therapist was rewarded by keeping the thought silent.

Nick: I didn't care. I thought: "Oh, well; now it's time to work again." But I felt [it] in a good way. He explained it to me, like a coach would say: "Now, it's time to get to work."

Nick's associations are to a coach who challenges him. There is more work to be done. There is more to be accomplished and Nick is motivated.

Therapist: So, you went from feeling deflated to being hopeful.

Nick: Yeah.

Therapist: It's kind of like what we do in here. You bring in your feelings, we roll up our sleeves, and then we get to work, and then some of the time you feel more hopeful. Getting to work is so different than escaping to the West Coast. I think you're wrestling with many different feelings: you're longing for more closeness with Natalia; your appreciation for what it is, even though it isn't fully what you wish it to be; and the big hurdle to get into the college you want.

In the above remark, the therapist becomes very explicit. In the language of Field Theory this might be considered a "saturated interpretation." There is so much packed into a single brief paragraph and we cannot be sure how the patient will digest or metabolize the remarks. The observations are presented explicitly, directly, and without much nuance. In so many words, the therapist says, "here is what I think is happening here" and proceeds to lay it out to Nick:

- You have many challenging feelings that are difficult to deal with.
- You are longing for more closeness with Natalia.
- You are growing to appreciate more of what you do have with her; even though it is often unsatisfying.
- You have hurdles to overcome with gaining admittance into the college you desire.
- You bring these feelings into our conversations and we get to work on understanding them, even though it is sometimes so much easier to pass the time in a fantasy escape to the West Coast.

If the patient is not in a psychic position to mentalize (think about his thinking), such dense interpretations tend to be experienced by the patient at best as being misunderstood, and at worst, as being attacked. If this pair did not have the two years of work under their belt and Nick had not shown such positive growth over the two years in his ability to think about himself, such an dense interpretation may not be not optimal. However, in this situation, we see a young man who is able to join the work. In fact, his response suggests there are reasons to believe he will be able to go further. Nick answers,

Nick: I mean, all this is still going to carry into next year. I don't think it's going to be that different. I wish a lot of stuff that's happened didn't carry over, but I know it will.

When Nick says, "I wish a lot of stuff that's happened didn't carry over, but I know it will," I think we see an example of Nick's preconscious communicating with his therapist. I hear this remark as Nick saying to his therapist, "Listen, I know there is more for me to work through from my past, and, no worries, I am up to the task. I am growing in my ability to recognize what I feel, explore what I think and feel, and in good time, when the time is right, I can continue to handle with greater dexterity, all that I notice within me."

In conclusion, in the vignette of Nick, we read an artful description of one therapeutic dyad's attempt to, in the words of Gene Roddenberry's famous introduction to the TV series, Star Trek, "boldly go where no [one] has gone before." In the case of Nick, we might argue the dyad is attempting to boldly go where this young man does not wish to go – into an experiential black hole of meaninglessness and despair! From my reading of this beautiful work, Nick and his therapist have managed to create a psychoanalytic process together that is helping Nick to locate himself in this vast universe. It is a pleasure to see the emotionally sensitive and astute young man Nick is becoming!

EDITORIAL REFLECTIONS

This chapter illustrates vividly the vicissitudes of pathological development in adolescence against the backdrop of earlier times and the impact of therapeutic intervention on a young person's choices of defenses and solutions.

Before Freud described infantile sexuality, his theory of neurosogenesis hinged on the idea of deferred action (nachtraglichkeit) (1895). Initially he used this theory in relation to puberty, later widening it to cover the whole span of childhood. Briefly summarized, the concept was that an experience in childhood may have little impact until the memory becomes linked with later adolescent sexual impulses. Freud cast his early view of adolescence in terms of the new realities of the phase, notably genital sexual development, the availability of a full panoply of sexual activity, and the choice of a love object; Anna Freud importantly added aggression to this list (1936, 1958).

In adolescence, trauma that is related neither to the intensity of current external exposure nor to revival of earlier traumatic experience can occur through deferred action. We think there are three aspects of adolescence that can make teenagers particularly vulnerable to trauma, including by deferred action. They are (1) increased internal stimulation simultaneous with decreased availability of auxiliary ego and superego figures; (2) the real possibility of putting wishes and fantasies into action, which was not available in childhood; and (3) the increased likelihood of traumatization by deferred action under the impact of this reality.

In light of such an epigenetic developmental perspective, we can see Nick's story in terms of his efforts to find adaptive solutions to conflicts and stressors. The author alludes to Nick being bullied in childhood, but then we hear that he seems to have surmounted this experience, finding success in academics, sports, and friendships in middle school, during the transition into adolescence. In our terms, he seems to have found an open-system solution to his school-aged troubles (Novick, J. and Novick, K. 2016).

And then in adolescence came the family trauma of his father's departure and the divorce, and Nick's open-system solutions broke down. He turned to self-defeating, closed-system responses, losing interest in school and athletics, reverting to sadomasochistic relationships with peers, struggling with plummeting self-esteem, and feeling extreme anxiety about almost everything. It seemed hard to tell the difference between the family trauma and Nick's own experience.

We suggest that this may be a prevalent pattern in adolescent breakdown, when, just in the middle of the process of consolidating identity, the young person is overwhelmed from inside and outside, the self battered by internal sexual and aggressive feelings and meanings and assailed by the emotions of those around them. All three commentators noted in different ways the intensity of emotion and anxiety swirling in this family. There is a typical pattern visible in most families, where parents react with ambivalence to their child's burgeoning opportunities for sexual and life growth and fulfilment. When parents are secure in their own sources of self-esteem, they can mostly welcome the potentials of puberty and adolescence, mourn and integrate their own aging. But, when they are not, there can be an escalating back-and-forth of sexual excitement, aggressive provocation, defensive responses, envy, jealousy, hostility and withdrawal. This is a time of heightened danger of parental acting out (midlife crisis), as Nick's case aptly demonstrates. In such a confusing situation, there is no safe space for the gradual unfolding of the adolescent's sexuality and a stepped mastery of any revived oedipal wishes and conflicts, resulting eventually in a capacity for independent mutual loving and sexual relationship with an appropriate peer object.

This leads to a further point of interest: whose feelings were they? We learned that Nick's mother had a "traumatic history." Although there were no details given in this brief vignette, it seems plausible that she too had a traumatized reaction to her husband's departure. Thus we see here another common aspect of pathological adolescent development in Nick's identifications. He seemed to select the worst aspects of each parent, in symbolically identifying with his father's leaving in his use of avoidance, withdrawal, and denial, and with his mother's experience of intense anxiety and catastrophizing at every turn.

Reversion to sadomasochistic relationships is another aspect typical of pathological adolescence, consistent with Nick's suicidality. Suicidal ideas, whether realized or remaining in thought, function as an omnipotent, closed-system defense against experienced or threatened traumatic helplessness. Their relative prevalence in adolescents speaks to the challenge of reality in this period of development to past, often effective, omnipotent solutions (Novick , J. and Novick, K.K 1996). When we conceptualize setting aside omnipotence as a major adolescent developmental task, we can also characterize achievement of more open-system, competent adaptations as a measure of therapeutic progress, a return to the path of progressive development.

This chapter illuminates another typical aspect of adolescent development in the theme of loneliness. Pathological loneliness stems from a conflation of separation and separateness. Every physical separation feels like a devastating loss, a confirmation of desolate aloneness. Then the young person finds the real essential separateness of every individual well-nigh unbearable. Some feel driven to assuage this existential panic with suicidality, pain, and control through pain; others, like Nick, may also kill off their subjective sense of reality with depersonalization and derealization. Experience of the alliance in the therapeutic relationship between two people who are actually separate can begin to make separateness a source of security that the patient can internalize, in contrast to the panic and terror that had impelled him to escape into pain or thoughts of killing himself.

Nick's passage from existential panic and flight into the future to finding meaning in collaborating with his analyst, his college counselor, and his coaches points to the importance of establishing a sturdy therapeutic alliance with adolescents. This chapter's vignette and commentaries all point to the stance of patience and openness as critical to the analyst being able to stay with a sullen, withdrawn young person, and gradually enlist his interest and intellect in the therapeutic tasks, also inspiring trust in the value of mutually respectful relationships.

We note also the analyst's judicious choices of when and how to make defense interpretations and articulate transference manifestations, and when to support the patient's own work to make sense of what is going on. This is true at all ages, but giving adolescents space to take ownership of their own psyches and what transpires in interaction with others seem central to identity consolidation.

This therapeutic work included restoration of the parent-child relationship, first, by working with each to better delineate who was responsible for what, and then addressing emotions and communication.

We see again the crucial importance for a successful outcome of the inclusion of regular dynamic parent work in the treatment design with adolescents.

CHAPTER 9

JAKE – age 16

Jake was only a high-school junior but his family's plan was for him to attend 2 years later the same prestigious university his father had. He was in turmoil, determined to fulfill the plan and leave home, but clearly unhappy and unready to do so. His parents took it for granted that Jake would follow in the family tradition and sought a referral to help him "pull himself together and get on with his life." As the evaluation proceeded it became apparent to both Jake and me that removal of the obstacles to his further development would require much more than just self-control and immediate effort. When Jake and I met together with his parents to discuss this and make a treatment plan, the parents expressed ostensible concern and support, but, at home, they told Jake they were profoundly disappointed in him and simply expected him to try harder.

The parents' need to maintain their initial treatment goal of getting Jake to college was a theme in the parent work and in Jake's treatment through the first few months. His conflicts with them became more intense. Jake was increasingly hurt and angry, but very quickly displaced his rage to his girl friend, whom he at one point encouraged to go out with another boy, and to me, whom he characterized as "a stereotypical Jew only interested in money and taking advantage of helpless people like the Palestinians."

He raged for weeks, broke up with his girlfriend and began hinting at thoughts of killing himself. I noted this and asked Jake if he was planning to kill himself, perhaps to punish his girlfriend and me. Jake said he had been having the thought of using one of his father's guns to blow his brains out at the entrance to my office, "so everyone will see how terrible and useless you are!"

Jake had an active suicide plan; I was especially concerned when he mentioned using his father's gun and when the anger was displaced from his parents to his girl friend and then to me. I told Jake that I thought he was in danger of killing himself and asked what could be done to help him stay alive. Did his parents know that he was suicidal? "Hell no," Jake shouted, "and if you tell them I'll sue you. You promised me that everything I say is confidential. So now you're a liar too!" I reminded Jake (and myself) that our initial discussions had stipulated that all Jake's thoughts and feelings were private, but that actions that posed a threat to his safety or to others would take precedence; his safety was the top priority. Everyone was then responsible for ensuring his safety.

I suggested that Jake start by telling me about father's guns and if he had access to them. Jake's anger subsided and he told me relatively calmly that his father was a gun collector. Most of the guns were kept in a locked display case, but Jake knew where the key was and besides, he had recently noticed that there were always other guns lying around. "Is this a message?" Jake wondered, then agreed that he needed help and that his parents should know his current suicidal state. He said he would speak with them right after the session. I said I would call Jake in a couple of hours to hear how it had gone and what was happening.

On the phone Jake said that his parents seemed to be avoiding him, breaking off the conversation when he said he needed to have a serious talk with them. He was relieved when I suggested a joint emergency meeting for that evening, at which Jake could tell his parents of his unbearable stress, his wish to please them yet his helplessness to do so. His hurt and anger and wish to kill himself felt like his only way out of the situation. His plan was to do it with one of his father's guns, so he needed his parents to take responsibility for suicide-proofing the house.

At the meeting, which the parents attended only under pressure from me, they first said that Jake was not serious, that he was being dramatic to manipulate both me and them in order to avoid his responsibilities. I said that I felt otherwise, that I was convinced that Jake would kill himself if his parents did not listen and take the danger seriously. They could demonstrate that they believed him by locking up the guns, keeping the ammunition in a separate place, and putting the keys to the gun case in their safe. I said that I was inserting a note that day into Jake's file, noting the danger of suicide and that the need to seal off access to the guns had been discussed with Jake's parents.

The parents were taken aback, then agreed to lock up the guns as suggested. I privately thought they were motivated as much by potential social embarrassment as by genuine concern for Jake, but their actions were critical to protecting Jake.

The work with both Jake and his parents intensified. With Jake I focused on the hostility of his suicidal wishes and his shift of his rage from his parents to his girl friend and to me. I first noted the significant change in being able to access his anger and we began to talk about anger as a signal rather than a weapon. We talked about how anger can let us know when something doesn't feel good or right, and also how it can sometimes stand in for other feelings. I then wondered about the source of his anger at his girl friend when he had first described her as so loving and caring. "Let's see if we can figure out why you're so angry at your girlfriend?"

I then again became the target of his anger and he ranted at me about a range of misdeeds. I complimented him on his verbal facility, saying that he may want to become a lawyer one day, but noted that we still had the same question about the change in his feelings about me. I reminded him of his initial positive reaction to working with me to figure out what <u>he</u> wanted, rather than seeing me as hired by his parents to make him comply with their wishes. As with his girl friend, his initial reaction to our work together had been very positive; it had been <u>his</u> wish to work 4 days a week rather than the once a week the parents wanted.

I wondered if his anger at me and his girl friend was related in some way to the unfamiliar feeling of our following his lead rather than imposing our needs on him. He paused and then described how difficult it is for him to take a compliment from teachers or friends; it makes him feel anxious. "That is strange," he said, "I never thought of that before." This led to a long period of work on how he protects others by turning the anger and disappointment he feels about them on to himself. I suggested that his forgetting the good feelings about his girl friend and about our initial work is kind of a "little suicide." He actually could not remember the good feelings he had about his girl friend or about me, killing off his memory just like wanting to kill himself to protect his parents from his anger.

The work with Jake's parents had a very rough start. At first they saw no reason to be seeing me. They had conveyed their wishes and clearly my job was to help him overcome his reluctance to apply to father's alma mater. Jake had the grades and, as the child of a graduate and generous donor, he would surely be accepted. The parents could not understand or accept that Jake might not want to follow their plan. Jake's suicide plan was, as noted, first seen by them as an attempt to manipulate them and me, but they did finally agree to regular weekly parent meetings.

They were surprised when I questioned their assumption that he not only had to attend father's university but even questioned the idea that he leave home to attend university when there were three excellent universities right here in the same city. It was taken for granted that their children and those of their friends would leave home and go to a place where they could "sow their wild oats" and establish the social connections that would help them as adults. The grandfather had gone to that prestigious university, as had father, and father had then worked in grandfather's firm and was now the C.E.O. Jake was expected to follow the family pattern. The parents then spent weeks exploring ways of making their plan more palatable, like paying for a "gap year" after high school or after college.

I said that it sounded like father had been expected to follow the family pattern just as Jake was now expected to. Jake was resisting this plan. Had father resisted when he was being groomed to follow in his father's footsteps? Father at first denied this, but mother laughed and said "Don't you remember telling me that you had fallen in love with the theater in college and wanted to change your major and make theater your career?" Father blushed, then said that he wanted to be a football player when he was a a kid. "We all have our dreams and then we grow up," he said with a note of sadness.

That evening he telephoned and said, "I think you noticed that my wife touched on something that was more than a childhood dream. I was serious about changing my major, not following the plans of my parents and grandparents, and there was a woman involved, a theater major. She and I were going out together and we had plans for starting a 'black box' theater in the Village in New York. I spoke to my parents and the whole family 'came down on me.' I loved my grandfather and I hated to disappoint him. I was in turmoil. I went into therapy and after a few months I calmed down, broke off the relationship, and took a graduate degree that would help me in my family firm. I thought that I had put this behind me but there is Jake and it's all come up again."

It took father many weeks of difficult work to realize that his powerful need to have Jake follow the same path he had taken was unrelated to meeting Jake's needs but to his own continuing need to protect his own father from his rage for stopping him from fulfilling his passion. The parents were now discussing between themselves and with me how and what to say to Jake.

Jake had been struggling with his own anger at his parents and grandparents for ignoring his needs and, as we saw in the suicide plan, he had shifted to a dangerous displacement of the anger which would allow him to kill himself without concern about the impact this would have on his parents. It took some time to engage with and move beyond his omnipotent rage and the desperate attempts to protect others. As we did so we could get to the realization that he had no idea what he would like to do – what were his passions? He couldn't allow himself any because he assumed that they would be frustrated and intensify his rage. In the summer he worked at a preschool and found that he had a talent for such work and seemed to enjoy it. The timing coincided with his father's decision to talk to Jake and tell him of his own struggles.

A few weeks later, they gave indications of greater investment as parents when they said to Jake that they realized that his attending a particular college was not as important as his survival and happiness. This gave us all a more realistic platform from which to explore Jake's own conflicts and uncertainties, as well as the defenses he had developed to deal with his hurt and rage. Jake had a lot more work to do in addressing his anger, his tendency to slide into self-destructive thoughts and impulses, his self-doubt and perfectionism and his treatment lasted several years more. As his treatment progressed, Jake and his parents became closer and more loving than at any time earlier in his adolescence.

COMMENTARY 1

Jake, a high-school junior, is grappling with the adolescent developmental task of separating from his parents as he prepares for the next stage of his life. Confronted with increasing anxiety stemming from conflicts around what he wants to do, where he wants to go and if he is even ready to leave home, he faces significant challenges from both intrapsychic pressures and external familial demands. Consolidating one's identity and becoming more autonomous, described as the second-individuation phase (Blos,1967), is never easy and Jake shows all the signs of an individual who is unsure of his future, as he faces the onslaught of destabilizing emotions and potential ruptures in his relationship with family and friends. The initial referral emanating from his parents has a singular objective, that of making sure that the analyst steers Jake in the right direction, i.e., attending the prestigious university, the alma mater of his highly successful father. The consultation however, reveals that the presenting issues are not that simple to overcome and that Jake, with thoughts, feelings and desires of his own, needs more intensive therapy. The parent meetings during the evaluation phase (Novick, et al, 2000) reveal a clinical bias on the analyst's part. This work in conjunction with the individual work conducted with Jake, however, reveals the quintessential importance of working with the family system, one that the analyst uses well to set the therapeutic stage for compliance and ensure long term treatment and a healthy prognosis for the troubled adolescent (Novick et al, 2000)

The second paragraph in this case report reveals Jake's organizing and troubling dynamics. He wonders if the analyst will be "a stereotypical Jew only interested in money and taking advantage of helpless people like the Palestinians." Was Jake using this (perhaps implying some socio-political and cultural struggles as well) to reveal an intrapsychic tension, between going for what he wants and yet feeling somewhat limited and inadequate? Or does it reveal a defensive organization that vacillates between the oppressed and oppressor or digging further, more sado-masochistic in structure? Could it be both? Would these emerge during the course of the treatment and how significant would it be to address issues pertaining to socio-political, class and cultural concerns?

Perusing through the case report, one learns that Jake uses displacement (along with other defenses) to address his uncomfortable feelings. Angry with his parents but unable to voice his feelings towards them he gets angry with his girlfriend who he has initially liked, to date someone else. As he continues to meet with the analyst who provides a holding environment for him, he regresses and voices suicidal thoughts. Sinking deeper into a depressive state that he cannot seem to control he sets in motion a series of interactions between the parents and the analyst, which illustrates perhaps at some level that Jake was desperately seeking some help for his parents as well. Here the analyst's work with managing the crisis and still maintaining a therapeutic alliance with the patient is essential. Jake threatens to harm himself using the guns available to him at home. The analyst, rightfully so, informs Jake that he would have to involve the parents as the patient's safety is paramount and no treatment can proceed with this threat in the air. The analyst then explores with Jake the external reality to ensure safety in his living situation. The guns, it appears are guns readily available as Jake's father is an avid gun collector. Though he keeps them locked up in a cabinet, there have been times when they have not been locked up. Furthermore, Jake knows where the keys are kept. When Jake wonders if there is a 'message' when his father leaves the guns lying around, he reveals a glimmer of insight and a sign that intensive treatment could be of help. While Jake is unaware of the internal dynamics this time, his recognition that there is more to the picture informs his decision to involve his parents and seek their help. The analyst's warm, empathic, caring yet firm stance and follow through marks the beginning of a healthy working relationship.

Upon learning from the follow up phone call that Jake was unable to have a talk with his parents (they seem to be avoiding me, he says) the analyst with an astute understanding of the need to establish control over the case, suggests a joint emergency meeting to discuss the seriousness of Jake's mental status. The parents, with pressure from the analyst, agree to meet and the session reveals the predominant family dynamics. The parents minimizing of Jake's emotional state, dismissing the seriousness of

Jake's threat to hurt himself, seeing him as a histrionic and dramatic child, is quickly refuted by the analyst who presents the parents with a plan of action that would ensure Jake's safety. Perhaps this is the first time that someone has heard Jake and taken a strong and firm hand with his father. The social and potentially legal implications of their failure to act are quite evident and perhaps not unnoticed by Jake himself. The analyst's forceful intervention averts the crisis precipitated by Jake's threats to commit suicide. The parents, perhaps in an act of social compliance and possibly showing the beginnings of some insight into their son's internal world, promise to lock up the guns and here we see the clinical implications of working with crisis situations in an immediate and effective manner. This would hold true no matter where the individual was in their life struggle. For Jake, it meant that his parents recognized the intensity of his feelings and were willing to engage with the therapeutic process.

The impact of the initial intervention on treatment appears to bear out both for the parents in their meetings with the analyst and for Jake in his individual work with the analyst. They now begin to explore and delve deeper into their internal world and complex family dynamics. The analyst, recognizing that Jake's anger brimming just below the surface would resurface addresses this immediately and introduces the notion of using anger as a 'signal' to identify other emotions. By bringing Jake's anger into the therapeutic space, it becomes something that the two can talk about, rather than act upon. Jake's response towards the analyst in the transference facilitates the process of working through his angry feelings, identifying his wishes and desires and building a reservoir of healthy ego functions as he begins the more intensive and painful feelings. The analyst draws Jake's attention to how quick he was to dismiss and destroy the positive feelings he had towards someone, as in his initial reactions to both the girlfriend and towards the analyst. Drawing Jake's anxiety to holding on to the 'good object' illustrates Jake's internal struggle to find 'good' in himself. While this would lead us to wonder about what happens internally, in the initial stages of any treatment, drawing the person's attention to the internal process and identifying the anxiety is crucial to the therapeutic alliance and to setting the stage for effectively working through the conflicts and defenses as they emerge.

Working with the parents however has a rocky start. Holding onto their initial wishes that Jake follow his father in his footsteps, the parents are confused and possibly angry that their participation in the therapeutic process is required. While this clinical approach may itself be a departure from a more conservative analytic stance in working with an adolescent, it illustrates how the skillful engagement of working the family system can identify significant strains of intergenerational expectations and possibly trauma. This work is challenging as the analyst is faced with the task of unearthing these hidden unconscious family narratives while also ensuring the integrity and safety of the clinical space they share with Jake. This is not always easy as fears and anxieties around what is being shared are bound to arise. Defenses unleashed in this set up (in parents as well as in Jake) could lead to ruptures and impasses.

But, in Jake's case, the parent work led to revelations about his father's internal world and his mother's observations and insistence (presented somewhat obliquely) about her husband's early college years. This moment is reflected in the father's wistful (though initially somewhat reluctant) recollection of a prior relationship with a young woman, someone he had fallen in love with, when he was interested in theatre. The father's recollection of 'lost dreams' and the wife's memory of this early romantic encounter, signifies that perhaps something has been lost by all. When the father later on that evening calls the analyst to inform him about his early dreams and acknowledges his lost dreams as he succumbed to his father's wishes, it reveals two things: his need to immediately tell the analyst, perhaps in an effort to help his son as well as a speculation that this revelation by the wife might have opened a door for the marital relationship as well. One wonders if the initial meeting with the analyst led to further discussions at home, perhaps a rekindling of desire, lost dreams and hurt feelings. Perhaps this nudging from his wife allows both going back in time and reflecting on the losses and transformations providing the necessary emotional scaffolding for the two to separate and let their son find himself in this journey of separation and individuation. The mother's mind is not available to us in the write-up and one wonders why. Was the analyst strategizing to establish a firm control on the case and, by working with the father, whose dreams are more readily available to us, establishing perhaps a hierarchy in the relationship that might also have been perceived by Jake? Would those complex identifications appear in the transference and would Jake's defenses and as noted 'his omnipotent rage' be worked through? Faimberg's concept of the 'telescoping of the generations' (Faimberg, 1988) which highlights the narcissistic links between generations and their explorations during clinical work comes to mind as we see the analyst work with these parents.

The analyst's work with Jake continues for several years. The therapeutic alliance is strong and Jake is able to tolerate the intensity of his feelings as he works towards a healthier outlook on his life, engaging with his defenses and accessing his internal world, with his desires, wishes and needs. This is not easy as his world is filled with uncertainties, and finding his voice in an increasingly challenging world is colored with self-doubt, rage, hurt and anger. The treatment as one would expect lasts several years and the initial emotional scaffolding provided by the parents is evident in its continuation. Further, as the parents become more 'loving' towards each other, one can only assume that the revelation of the father's dreams perhaps allowed for the parental dyad to reconnect with lost dreams, mutual passions and a shared interest in the recovery of their son.

This case highlights a treatment objective that emphasizes movement from a closed family system (Novick et al, 2001) that does not allow for another person's opinions and feelings to an open family system which embraces differences of opinions and a desire to live peacefully are clearly evident in the communications styles, the respect for another's dreams and feelings and a consideration that one's internal world with their choice of 'ego ideal' is an individual choice though undoubtedly shaped by external realities. The development of ego capacities that help an individual navigate through difficult emotional challenges is emphasized in what is referred to as 'emotional muscle' (Novick et al, 2001) which includes both parent work and a focus on helping an individual modulate their affect and develop ego-resiliency. Parent work (Novick et al, 2000) is essential to this process, to not only strengthen the therapeutic dyad or in this case, the triad, but also to set the stage for a positive long-term outcome. Some analysts might point to the inevitable challenges to maintain therapeutic alliance in this clinical and technical stance. Working with the numerous transferences that are bound to emerge, and preserving the confidentiality and essential boundaries with the family system for the work of treatment to proceed unhindered with the adolescent, may indeed prove challenging. In Jake's case, it appeared to have worked well as the analyst not only helped the couple become more loving towards each other, but Jake himself engaged in treatment, which while rocky nevertheless appears to have benefited him enormously.

COMMENTARY 2

Adolescents struggle with their wishes to remain dependent on their parents and the push to achieve independence and develop new relationships. Jake was conflicted about leaving home to attend his father's college. This conflict may have reflected issues from both adolescence and earlier issues with separation that this short vignette couldn't cover.

The writer noted a conflict between the parents' treatment goals and the analyst's and Jake's views. The parents wanted Jake to get to college through "self-control and immediate effort," which differed from the "removal of the obstacles to his further development." I was curious how the work with the parents began and proceeded both during the evaluation and during the first few months of treatment. How did the analyst make decisions about meeting with the parents? Did they do an evaluation with the parents before meeting with Jake, simultaneously with the evaluation of Jake or afterwards? What did the analyst tell the parents and Jake at the beginning of analysis about issues around privacy and confidentiality, particularly in terms of sharing or not sharing with Jake what happened in the parent work? How did the analyst work with the parents' resistance to Jake's and the analyst's approach to treatment? How did the analyst address the sources of the parents' disappointment in Jake and their expecting him to "try harder"?

Another theme in this treatment involves the importance of continuing to evaluate an adolescent's suicidality as well as the context of safety and risk in the home environment. Letting Jake, and presumably the parents, know of the limits to privacy and the importance of safety at the beginning of treatment was crucial to being able to keep Jake safe as treatment progressed. Was the analyst aware during the evaluation period of the guns in the house and Jake's access to them? The analyst balanced out the adolescent's need for independence with preserving his safety by giving him the responsibility to talk with his parents, but then followed up with a phone call. Having a joint emergency meeting provided a needed container for both the patient's and the family's crisis. Jake had a chance to communicate his acute distress, and his parents heard the analyst emphasize the seriousness of Jake's suicidal plans.

The analyst proceeded to explore the sources of Jake's current suicidal wishes and rage. The analyst first helped Jake examine his transferring his rage from his parents to his girlfriend. Then the analyst interpreted how Jake's reactions to his girlfriend were similar to Jake's feelings about the analyst: first Jake was positive and then his feelings turned completely opposite; he forgot any good feelings and turned them into anger. Jake's conflicts about figuring out "what he wanted" rather than responding to others' needs created anxiety. As a result, he had difficulty accepting compliments and turned the anger and disappointment he felt about others onto himself. Moreover, he couldn't get in touch with his passions and, I assume, interests, because he felt they would not be accepted and then he would feel more enraged.

Now I'd like to return, as the analyst did, to the analyst's work with the parents. It's not clear if the weekly parent meetings began regularly only after Jake's suicide plan was discussed. Did the analyst have the opportunity before the crisis to explore the parents' adolescence? In particular what were they like around Jake's age?

The case study acknowledges that Jake had more work to do in therapy after the focus on his plans for suicide. Jake's suicidal plan came to a head, not just in the relationship with his parents but in the transference to the analyst. It would not be surprising if this period of depression was a recurrence, and perhaps even a reworking, of past depressions in Jake's life. Jake's turning his anger against himself was a major coping mechanism that the analyst had to address. In addition, although Jake presented with acute depression and anxiety in his junior year of high school when he struggled to find himself in adolescence, these feelings likely accompanied conflicts from separation and individuation in early adolescence as well as dependence and independence even earlier in his life.

EDITORIAL REFLECTIONS

With this chapter we see clearly the impact of the reality potential of adolescence on developmental issues, as well as on clinical technique. The actuality of adolescents' capacity to make choices puts separateness and autonomy into center stage, which can evoke or revive parental conflicts stemming from the same issue or the same stage of their lives, to serious effect, as was so vivid in this case. This chapter also brings together thoughts and knowledge about adolescent suicide and the ancillary technical issues when the danger of suicide is registered by the analyst. Jake's material demonstrated the same sequence of psychological events and shifts as emerged from various psychoanalytic studies of suicidal adolescents, which likely contributed to the analyst's alertness and decision to act sooner rather than later (Novick, J. and Novick, K.K. 1996, Chapter 8).

The chapter illuminates issues around the necessity and desirability of active technique on the part of the analyst in this situation, both in relation to exploring the parents' own histories and their impact on their parenting and their child, but also in the immediacy of the danger of violent self-destruction. Jake was no longer an angry child who might threaten to run away or kill himself. He was an adolescent fully capable of forming a realistic plan and putting it into action. Should the analyst have stayed 'in the transference,' interpreted the rage directed at the analyst as representing an oppressor, and waited to see if this had any effect? This brings us to a central challenge of adolescent therapy, when the hierarchy of clinical values mandates putting safety ahead of confidentiality (Novick, J. and Novick, K.K. 2008).

That necessity for protecting the adolescent's survival, however, lands us squarely in the middle of the most acute controversies in this realm, as all adolescent therapists struggle with issues of maintaining privacy when dealing with an adolescent's secrets. We have said that it is important to protect privacy, but analyze secrecy, rather than colluding with it. When we add into the mix the need to involve parents for the child's safety, we also have to consider looking beyond crisis management to the question of ongoing concurrent dynamic parent work as an integral part of adolescent treatment (Novick, K.K. and Novick, J. 2013). One of the commentators raises the question of whether more should have been done with parents even earlier in the work, while the other notes the analyst's choice or "bias" toward such work, despite observing how apt it was in this case.

This shows us that there continues to be a live debate over how to maintain boundaries in adolescent work. Our sense is that this issue is heir to a continuing emphasis by some on separation as the developmental goal of adolescence rather than, as we see it, transformation of the relationship to oneself and to parents. A new alignment of the pleasure, reality, and growth principles is needed to effect this transformation and the work will continue throughout later stages of adult development. But adolescence is the crucial time to set aside old omnipotent solutions and find pleasure in that new realistic relationship among the organizing principles. When this is not accomplished, pathology or worse may ensue; when, as in Jake's case, the outcome was positive, it augurs well for his continued growth and vindicates the utility of intensive adolescent treatment.

CHAPTER 10

CLAUDE – age 16

Rhythm and Blues

16-year-old Claude shuffled into my office with his hoodie stretched over his bent head and rounded shoulders. For the next couple of months, he punctuated his verbal utterances with sobbing and copious tears and mucus. He used massive amounts of tissues to wipe his face. Claude could not finish a phrase or sentence without correcting his word choice, amending his idea, or undoing what he just said, over and over and over. I felt like I was witnessing the incessant caesuras of his thoughts struggling to emerge. And he could not look me in the eye. I felt I was already cast in the role of a potential judge who might criticize him and cause further shame and humiliation. His aggrieved parents felt that the prior once a week therapy and medication consultation were not adequate interventions for his anxious and depressed state and agreed to a four time a week analysis with frequent parent work.

In our second meeting, after a very long overture of anxious fits and starts, Claude mumbled that he writes down his dreams on his phone and picked it up. He then put down his phone on the chair and told me a disturbing dream without looking at it. *"There is a gym structure, like a tall jungle gym. I am climbing apart with my dad. I tell him what to do but he doesn't listen. He goes to put his foot up and misses and ends up straddling a bar. I think he is stable but he falls and lands on his head. I am upset and mad that he didn't listen. I keep climbing up, but I fall back and presumably die also."* He teared up and grabbed more Kleenex. I said quietly that it was a tragic dream. Claude made eye contact with me and nodded affirmatively. We set the next appointment and he began to leave. With a smile, I said that his phone was not quite ready to leave yet. He picked it up between the cushions and thanked me, but I was already alerted to potential refrains of being dropped or forgotten, neglected or lost.

Two months into the analysis, his father left a message that Claude was very upset over the weekend and they could not reach me. I could not fathom how neither his parents nor Claude could fail to follow the clear instructions on my office voicemail about how to contact me for urgent matters. Claude came to session looking exhausted and tearful and recounted that he had asked a girl to come over to his house over the weekend. They started to make out, she then stopped abruptly and asked to be taken home. He felt distressed but complied. A few hours later she posted on the High School Facebook page that he was "the most disgusting and grossest kisser ever." Claude was devastated and sobbed as he described the humiliation. I commented that he might have felt dropped by me as well since we were not able to successfully make contact either over the weekend. He nodded affirmatively. This painful episode of cyberbullying and humiliation paved the way for Claude and me to understand more about his many experiences of feeling disconnected, humiliated, degraded and shamed. He recounted a number of times where teachers and peers called him out publicly for his disruptive and grandiose behaviors. He and his parents labeled these incidents examples of him being "treated poorly," "misunderstood," or "underappreciated for his brilliance and creativity," but were oblivious to his initiation of provocative and contemptuous attacks.

This theme of not being able to make connections, put ideas together or understand meanings permeated the case as Claude and I, in various constellations of transference and countertransference, over the three-year treatment, attempted to compose meanings to create for Claude a more coherent sense of self from his fragmented experiences of multiple traumas, which he conveyed to me through erratic and surprising disclosures, actions and nonverbal communications throughout the treatment.

Although I had been told that Claude's father created art with a voyeuristic bent, I had not been told that Claude's parents, already parents to one child, could not conceive another. In fact, it was Claude who referred to himself a year into treatment as an IVF baby; his parents never told me about the failed infertility treatments that preceded the obviously successful one. Their focus was on a cardiac episode when Claude was two weeks old. I was distracted by their telling me about the diagnosis of an arrhythmia and successful treatment with a medication that the father always felt negatively impacted the boy. In retrospect, it is possible that this medication dampened Claude's normal physiologic experience of anxiety by not allowing the normal rise and fall of heart rate to early childhood and latency challenges. In addition, Claude's mother suffered from depression and intense and unpredictable rages during much of his childhood and adolescence focused mainly on Claude and his father.

At the age of 9, Claude had the definitive treatment for his heart problem, which was what the family called an "ablazion." It was, in reality, a radiofrequency "ablation" of the extra electrical pathway in his heart, done under sedation but not general anesthesia. To access the veins to the heart, the cardiologist put a catheter into the femoral vein in the groin and guided it to the septum of the heart where heat was applied to destroy the extra electrical pathway in the muscle. Unfortunately, no one alerted Claude who awoke to heaviness on his groin. As he was telling me this story, he stopped and was silent. I then filled in the gap and wondered if he must have been terrified that he had been castrated. He remembered waking up alone and feeling beyond panicked and alone and unable to move the heavy bags on his own to check his private parts. I explained they had been placed there to prevent excess bleeding and how his heart had been fixed through his groin. I asked the parents how they explained the procedure to Claude before and after the ablation. They looked at me blankly and said that the cardiologist explained it to them all and there was nothing to discuss once it was over since it was a success. I wondered to myself whether the "ablazion" was too hot and frightening for the parents to create an organizing narrative for themselves, let alone for their nine-year-old son.

Dysrhythmias, often in the form of fits and starts, were, in real time, being played out symptomatically as the treatment began to unfold, with Claude, an 11th grader, being picked up almost daily when he was feeling panicked, sick or tearful. His mother dutifully collected him, did his homework with him and for him, cooked his favorite meals and found him the best doctors and tutors. Once home, he would lie on the parents' bed and watch television and YouTube, stripped down to his underwear while she wrote at the desk nearby. Supremely self-conscious and identified with his father whom he felt was awkward and his mother complained was a hypochondriac, he worried constantly about his body – the moles, thin body type, big nose and extralong clavicle, characteristics they shared as well as flat feet, a funny gait and what was later diagnosed as scoliosis. He also worried that he was like his mother who had been a poor student and never finished college. Perhaps these days of panic and anxiety with his mother reenacted the early days with the mutual terror and overstimulation of dysrhythmic and dysregulating emotional episodes ricocheting back and forth from one to the other without an effectively present third. Now, in adolescence, Claude had lost developmental momentum and rhythm and felt like a failure, unable to function academically, socially, sexually, or creatively compared to his much older brother, peers and parents. He then retreated to a passive, depressive, narcissistic refuge where, helpless and ill, he could omnipotently control his objects with incessant demands and critiques.

In the safety of the consultation room, Claude found a rhythm in his attacks on me, as he questioned, doubted, mistrusted and criticized me. I focused on containing these negative bits, listening attentively, calmly and seriously and not responding defensively, even when he worried aloud that I would end up controlling his mind. I conjured Winnicott and allowed myself to "survive destruction by the subject" by tolerating his destructive attempts without retaliation or abandonment or rhythmic disruption. In response to him, I unconsciously dampened down my physical movements in my chair to minimize any disruption to his new flow, to the point that Claude commented that "I have not seen anyone sit so still." Eventually Claude and I were able to link his hypercritical judgment of me as a way of ridding himself of his feelings of inadequacy, imperfection and disgust by locating them in the other, especially me, especially at times where he felt that he desperately needed to make contact, even if it was through negative affects.

I began to notice that during pauses, Claude would drum his fingers and later hum. As he became less anxious and defensive, I began to see his musical creativity emerge in these forms in session as well as his increasing willingness not just to tell me his dreams but work with me on the possible communications and meanings. Clearly the analysis with its beating rhythm of regularity carved out a space of acceptance, safety and respect to allow the two of us to try to understand the contents and operations of his mind. Returning from a family vacation with his parents, Claude played for me an instrumental piece with dueling violins that he had written. It was the first orchestral composition I had heard about since he began treatment. I imagined him feeling alone as the third wheel as his parents were alternatively quibbling and loving. I said aloud that I couldn't tell if the violins were arguing or having sex. Claude gasped and then laughed as he said, "I guess people can interpret different things in music." He then played the piece again, attempting to listen for my perspective. I didn't say more since I felt the unsaturated interpretation left open the possibilities of a primal scene or

255

other transferential or historical construction. This piece was later performed in various venues to great accolades with him as the conductor. Along with a burst of creativity in musical composition, Claude also was taking piano lessons and teaching himself several other instruments.

About 4 months later, Claude was humming during a silence in a session where he recounted a surprising triumph, "special accommodations" for standardized test taking without any acknowledgment of the effort that his mother, school counselor and I had contributed. Trying to contain my irritation of feeling so dismissed, I asked him what that song was. He thought for a moment and said, "The guitar solo from a Metallica song." He looked it up on his phone and played it. It was called "Master of Puppets." He used his phone to display the lyrics. The refrain reads: "Master of Puppets, I'm pulling your strings, yeah, Twisting your mind and Smashing your dreams, Blinded by me, you can't see a thing. Just call my name, I'll hear your scream, Master, Master." As we both read them together, I was filled with a feeling of having been manipulated. I said, attempting to disguise the edge in my voice, "I believe your own music is coming through to us, you as the Master of Puppets, being in charge, giving orders." He responded, "You or me?" I said, "It sounds like it gets confusing for you who is directing whom, who is in control?" He sat up from the couch and made direct eye contact with me. "Give me examples." I listed several ways where, quite recently, both parents, teachers and even I had taken action to assist him in pre-college tasks. He responded, "Those are negative examples. There is a patronizing sound to it but puppeteering doesn't make a sound. I am also the conductor, the master. But someone is puppeting my life. I am the guy who schemes his way but can't fool the teacher, like when I don't do work. On the other hand, you are the puppeteer, you do a lot. You came up with those examples." I said, "Perhaps you are worried that you need to maneuver or else you will be out maneuvered." He said, "That's your view of me?" We sat in quiet together and a few minutes later he sighed, "You were right to call me on it."

Months later, after a successful trip to summer camp, he had a visit with a girlfriend from camp, he told me they had had sex, both for the first time, but it was disappointing. He was so ashamed that it took several weeks for him to tell me what was really on his mind, complaining in a hysterical manner that he lacked desire and couldn't find a rhythm. Eventually, leaning over the couch with his head in his hands, he confessed that he was addicted to porn on the Internet. He sobbed as he explained that it had been going on for years. He was worried that the women that he was attracted to were all porn stars and that he had permanently damaged his brain. He was terrified that he would never find a partner in whom he could tolerate their faults and imperfections and who could excite him. We looked at his outrageous standards for women who would invariably disappoint him. More poignantly, we then discussed his pervasive affect of disappointment that enveloped him that he would never please a woman: his mother who wrote at her desk and didn't perceive that he was desperate for her attention as he watched "SpongeBob" in his underwear on the parental bed; the girl who rejected him in such a brutal and humiliating way; and me, since I saw so clearly how he was defective in so many ways, including his artificial conception, his physique, his twisted mind, a defective boy from defective parents. He felt he could always rely on the porn images, to allow him to be the judge and choose the image and videos that would excite him, that he could control and repeat, or that he could dismiss in disgust or boredom. Not so, with real and frightening women with their own wishes, desires and power, he could not always be the puppeteer.

Just before Claude's departure for college, about 2 years into the treatment, his father announced on a Sunday that Claude should look at the father's early artwork, four erotic photography books. The father asked his son to page through them at the kitchen table while his father ate a sandwich. Claude felt compelled to obey and tried his best to look at and speak about the work artistically and intelligently. Claude came to session the next day shaken by the experience and alternated between two assessments of his father, that he was either "some kind of genius" or a "perverted voyeur" who "couldn't give a shit about the impact of this on in my mind." Some of the photos involved women hanging from furniture or ropes with genitalia exposed, being photographed from below. Another book was less explicit, with photographs of couples having sex, the images focused on their faces and expressions during the act. He talked about how couples would call his dad to come over when they were about to have sex, how it was spontaneous but not intimate. He worried what it meant when his father was perusing his face and reactions to the photos. He paused and quietly said, "Like he is a voyeur." He wondered what I thought. I asked him what he imagined. He seemed to ignore the question and said he felt trapped and couldn't even think to ask to look at the book later, alone. He felt taken by surprise, not wanting to disappoint his dad but also excited to be treated like he was an adult, finally. He repeated that he liked that part but wished his dad could think about the impact on him. I asked him where his mother was during this kitchen scene. He shrugged and said, "Somewhere, it doesn't matter to her."

As I look back now, there was always a tension between wishes to be seen and not seen that played out over the three-year period in the analytic treatment. For the first several months, Claude sat in the chair opposite me and only increasingly could make direct eye contact. He would break gaze when he was anxious or as we later came to understand "overwhelmed with shame." For several months, he asked to lie on the couch not facing me so that he could talk more freely without looking "at my face twitch." He talked about anticipating my judgment and reactions the way his mother overreacted. After a few months, he decided he wasn't comfortable "laying down next to me" since it was "too close" and sat up at the end of couch so he could look ahead and not at me but so I could still look at him. Before leaving for college, he asked to turn the original chair around so he could look out the window and not at me and have me not see his face. While in college, we conducted the treatment by phone since he didn't want to use a video call and be seen.

After a four-month break from treatment as he transitioned to college, Claude called me to restart treatment over the Thanksgiving holiday by phone. Although he had made a good transition with a circle of friends and academic success, he confessed his worry that he was impotent. The frantic tone resembled the earlier concern that he lacked desire. He was being pursued aggressively by young women on campus for sex and was convinced that he would be impotent and humiliated and was making excuses and avoiding them. He worried that perhaps he was gay. He revealed that he had had homosexual relations with another boy when he was around 12. He said he thought he had told me and was surprised I didn't remember. Tearfully, he then told me that they "did everything," although he didn't recall being anally penetrated. He was devastated after 4 or 5 wonderful encounters that he never saw the boy again. Claude wrapped himself in an obsessive and tormented worry that he might be gay. I felt tumbled and confused and questioned myself for not picking up on clearly homosexual, overstimulating or sexually traumatic elements. The rhythmic waves of pounding of doubt and confusion had been projected into me.

Claude described looking at girls and was worried that he didn't find them attractive since none of them looked like porn stars, except for this one girl in his dorm who wanted to have sex with him. With the new sophistication of a college student, he had researched the impact of porn on the brain on the internet and felt that he had poisoned his mind with those images. I commented that he had become quite confused about which images were his own desires and fantasies and which belonged to others.

Claude requested sessions 5 times per week while in college, an increase in frequency from the earlier years of treatment. He was determined to deal with these upsetting feelings that were impeding his sexual expectations. The rhythm of the sessions and the focus on the auditory dimension seemed to allow Claude an ability to talk about his body, sexual feelings and fantasies, and sexual components in his dreams in a less inhibited, less self-conscious way, a dramatic contrast to his stifled free associations at the beginning of treatment. He still was terrified of sex and the threat of impotence and poor performance. Slowly, over weeks, he and I put into words his "confusion" about what he was feeling when his heart rate went up – was it terror, sexual or another kind of excitement, fear of failure, expectation of my judgment or his, even a return to the cardiac arrhythmia? During this time, Claude was performing in music classes and at various campus cafes and talent shows exhibiting his gifts and stage presence with minimal performance anxiety.

He told me of a memory when he was young of being "washing machined" in waves on a beach and having his mother be oblivious to him and not rescue him. Once he extricated himself from the water, he screamed at her that "she just sat on her fat ass while he could have died." He recalled that she became so furious that she didn't speak to him for 2 whole days. I addressed his worry of needing me so much and being so angry and worried I would turn away and shut him out. He paused and associated to a mirror in the girl's room on his dorm floor. Strangely, he felt better making out with her in her room since she had a large mirror in her room where he could see himself. I wondered aloud if he unconsciously worried that he would be swallowed up during sex and lose himself. He was quiet for the last few minutes.

In the following session, he said that he had been thinking about not being seen and was ashamed to tell me that the previous summer, while I was away, he found a chat room with a webcam that allowed him to expose his genitals to other people, men and women, to see if he measured up. He assured me that he found a way to cover his face so his identity would be protected. He said he was focused on preparing himself for college so he would be more confident. Embedded in this chatroom model was an element of control, in that either viewer may choose to click the mouse and exit the chatroom into another random pairing, in essence spinning the wheel. Therefore, there was the opportunity not only for voyeurism, but also exhibitionism, appreciation, mutual masturbatory engagement, cruel criticism and rejection.

When Claude was using the webcam in this way, we identified that he was in that chatroom while I was away for summer break. I said, "It seems to me that you desperately needed to be seen and, while I was away, this was the substitute." He was quiet. Over the next several sessions, we were able to piece together his underlying anxieties: that he worried he might not be adequately equipped for college, compared to the other men, especially his dad and brother, and that his sense of defectiveness would overwhelm his developing ability to soothe himself and he would need to return home and to me as a failure and, most powerfully, if he was not seen or held in mind, that he might not survive.

Given the timing of the webcam the previous summer that led up to his hysterical anxiety of impotence and that his body again would fail him, I interpreted that the dramatic worry was possibly self-punishment for going into that chatroom and exposing himself, for allowing himself to be seen. Almost simultaneously we both thought of "La petite mort," a French term for the potential experience of sadness, denouement or shift in consciousness after orgasm. I said I was surprised that we both came up with it at the same time and wondered what we both meant by it. He took it as a challenge that I underestimated his sexual knowledge and saw him as a young, inexperienced boy. I interpreted not just his worry that I would judge and diminish him as an incompetent little boy but also that I could see his terror left over from childhood that he could die from the extreme excitement of orgasm. He associated to his being sick or broken as a mechanism to keep his mother's attention. I wondered aloud if he felt he needed to be ill to be loved. I think of it now as a kind of protective self-castration in the face of the more powerful woman, his mother, me and the sexually demanding young women at college.

Soon thereafter, Claude announced triumphantly that he and the girl down the hall had had sex successfully several times, and he thought that the mirror in her room helped him a lot. I chose not to interrupt his rhythm with my idea of the "vagina dentata" or remind him of the experience of waking up after the ablation.

Claude ended his analysis abruptly within a few weeks of these successful sexual relations with the young woman. He was excited and surprised that she was complimentary about his performance and the pleasure he brought her during sex. He and I both knew how much he worried about being a disappointment. He felt that he could manage his anxieties and did not feel compelled to spend the time 4 or 5 sessions a week anymore. He could not bring himself to say goodbye or to plan a termination phase in person that summer. Our last session began with a litany of angry complaints, then tears and 20 minutes of silence. I asked Claude if he remembered his earlier dream of separation in which he wished to take off and hang glide but the cliff he was on was crumbling and not stable enough to push off from. I decided to tell him a story from a recent vacation where I watched a hang glider successfully launch from black cliffs and fly serenely in circles over a bay. I added that I had thought of him and, on that variation in a major key, we said goodbye. His way of resolving the abrupt and dramatic ending was through music he wrote over the next several months, some vocal solos or duets with elegant harmonies, rhythms and instrumentation posted on his Instagram. The lyrics expressed possible references to the analytic treatment including evidence of a good internal object that was now "everywhere" with fresh images of himself as a resilient survivor of shame, critique and self-doubt.

I began to piece together the sequence of events that I had never been told in the right order, almost like hearing a piece of music that had been divided and rearranged. The boy with whom Claude had had the sexual liaison, although reported as a friend of Claude's, was actually a close friend of his much older brother, who had gone off to college leaving Claude bereft and isolated in middle school with these secret and overstimulating experiences and memories. I imagined that Claude was overwhelmed with feeling disconnected and depressed and tried to enliven himself in various ways – including some impulsive and grandiose moves. One of them was skateboarding with peers without much practice where Claude fell and badly broke his forearm. He required two surgeries for a definitive repair and had to stop playing clarinet for months. From his parents, I had heard about his punitive expulsion from the two advanced bands he was in but hadn't originally linked together his need for masochistic punishment for the homosexual liaison with his contemporaneous provocative and grandiose behaviors. He had told me that he hated the feel of the clarinet and didn't want to play it anymore, but only much later could I surmise that it might have been related to his experiences of oral sex. Only after the treatment ended was I able to hear the melody beyond the words that I and the analytic treatment needed to be left as he had been left years before when he was washing machined in the waves by his mother, by the older boy who left for college and as he had abandoned the clarinet, that time-old tale of turning passive into active.

Looking back at the three-year treatment, Claude clearly used me and the analytic process that we created together as a vehicle for movement, development, transformation and remodeling his internal objects. Part of the work in the rearrangement of his sense of himself was the work of "*Nachträglichkeit*," the construction and reconstruction of fresh and authentic narratives of his experiences and the detoxification and reshaping of many of the traumatic, overstimulating and unbearably painful ones. The intensive treatment intertwined with his creative musicality served as transitional phenomena that moved Claude not just through adolescence but through a reworking of the overwhelming early infantile experience that became sequestered in his defensive claustrum, a retreat against death, defectiveness, invisibility, shame and paralysis. He used the analyst and the analytic situation not just to separate from home and leave for college but to relinquish various defensive maneuvers, including the pseudo-independent world of cyberspace and cyberporn, to establish his own emotional equilibrium and to be able to accomplish in domains that so mattered to him, the social, academic, sexual and artistic.

COMMENTARY 1

The analysis of Claude, beginning at age 16, is a remarkable piece of clinical work, in which we see a deeply neglected and humiliated boy, burdened by feelings of physical defectiveness, rage and shame, blossom into a desirable young man on campus and a local musical celebrity. The analyst uses the leitmotif of rhythm – arrythmias, dysrhythmia, pounding hearts and waves, and sound alternating with silence – to scaffold the description and the experience of the work; these musical, oceanic and cardiac metaphors resonate with Claude's traumas as well as his emerging talent as a composer and musician and his growing sexual competence.

There is much to praise in the analyst's work with Claude. However, there are three arenas in this treatment that remain hidden, like an inaudible echo of the series of secrets that the patient gradually reveals. These are not secrets but rather unchartered territories. Whether they are unexamined due to the analyst's intentional exclusion for the sake of brevity in this write-up or not included because they were "not noticed" is not clear. First is the role of the brother. Described as *much* older, by my calculation he was likely 6 years older (since his predatory friend and presumably he himself went off to college when the patient was 12) – an age difference which certainly does not preclude a meaningful relationship. The fact that the brother's friend took on the role of exploiter, arouser and initiator has to be understood in relation to Claude's feelings, desires and wishes in regard to his brother, the collusion between brother and his predatory friend and so many other complexities

– the exploration of these might have deepened the evolving picture of the family constellation. The horizontal dimension in this family is simply not addressed despite the spotlight the predation at age 12 shines on it.

Second, there is little described about the contribution that the gender of the analyst made to the relationship. The analyst's inclusion of herself in a list of powerful women late in the write-up surprised me; I had been under the impression that the analyst was a man. There is no mention of the complexity of the transference/countertransference in regard to Claude's maternal deprivation and desire, his excitement in the room, briefly acknowledged when he lay down but not elaborated, and his view of his analyst as a woman he might disparage as not perfect like a porn star or idealize as a nurturing maternal figure.

Finally there are the unilateral terminations that the patient introduced at intervals, no doubt also fraught with significance and seemingly timed with events in his sexual life. It seems clear that this patient played different rhythms with his analyst – and the relationship of this to his sexuality is evident but unrevealed.

These are three areas worthy of exploration; my sense is that this young man will be back in treatment soon enough, so that more work can be done.

COMMENTARY 2

I have found this account of a three year analysis of a boy/man, Claude, both absorbing and intriguing. The analyst has done remarkably well in letting us into the intimacy and mystery of what analyst and adolescent went through together. Clearly, the analyst's sensitivity and perspicacity contributed greatly to what was a very important experience in Claude's life. For the purpose of this comment, I will focus mainly on two salient features of adolescents in general and in their presence in the experience of Claude's analysis – their isolation and narcissism.

Adam Phillips, the English psychoanalyst and writer, once wrote in his succinct account of Winnicott's work (1988) the following, "The paradox he had begun to formulate was that the infant – like the adolescent about whom he could only write authoritatively in the last decade of his life – was an isolate who needed the object, above all, to protect the privacy of his isolation" (p.145). A few years later, I wrote of the adolescent being buffeted about in a confusion of contradictions, no doubt arising from the fundamental adolescent predicament – sometimes a child, sometimes an adult and always neither. In other words, the adolescent needs to find his own way and not be too much called to account, yet he needs attention, guidance and someone to care about him. He does not want to be understood, and yet he does. He wants license, and yet he needs boundaries. Claude might well add another, he wants to be seen and not seen. It is this conundrum, alongside the adolescent's narcissism, that I believe shapes the details and contours of the analytic experience with adolescents – the analyst balancing his or her implicit though unrealistic aspiration to 'know all' and yet settling for knowing less, out of respect for the adolescent's privacy and singularity.

The idea of the adolescent as an isolate may well run counter to the popular vision of the gregarious teenage fun lover. But, in so many ways, adolescents do find themselves experientially very much alone in many respects for the first time in their lives – solitary both in their own bodily preoccupations and in the goings on in their minds. This sense of isolation can be seen to reside at the center of the separation/individuation process – individuals attempting to define themselves as distinctive, different or in opposition to whoever is deemed to know who they are. This is further sharpened in the sheer force of narcissism in the experience of adolescents – that peculiar all-consuming fascination with their selves, with their identities and their preservation. They say in effect: "I am unique, different, not to be pigeon holed or overly defined." "I know what I am and what I know." "Only me, not you, understands." There is in this the strong tone of individual assertion that strikes forth with a new sense of freedom yet holds firm from within a kind of narcissistic insistence on their certitude beyond the reach of any outsider. Adolescence is a time of vulnerability and heightened narcissism. It can be of no surprise that adolescents are peculiarly bothered about themselves. There is a great deal going on. The fundamental pubertal changes, combined with expanding cognitive capacities create an unprecedented state in the life of the individual. These changes occur in the context of shifting patterns and alliances within the family. There is by definition no stability in adolescents. They are curiously disconnected from all that has held them together in the past and confronted with all that is new and unfamiliar and potentially threatening in the future. They are unavoidably driven back into themselves and, for the time being, as they struggle to keep their balance and find a way forward, they take refuge as it were in the realm of narcissistic defense. The extent of such defense, of the retreat either into a grandiose or idealizing fantasy (Kohut 1968) clearly is determined by early childhood insecurities.

A prominent feature in Claude's personality was his narcissism. Despite his all too familiar presentation of himself, especially in the beginning, as weak, ill and inadequate, it became increasingly apparent that he was anything but timid or enfeebled. On the contrary, he often related to others in a provocative, contemptuous and imperious manner. For example, two music bands in which he played both expelled him because of this kind of behavior. His attraction to pornography in which he indulged for many years contained the fantasy that he had total control of all that went on in the various sexual scenes laid out before him.

In his analysis, his analyst observed that beneath his displays of his incapacities, he harbored an underlying omnipotence, an illusion of supremacy within what his analyst described as "a narcissistic refuge" – a refuge in which he could retreat and compose a position of control over all those who were around him. There was a moment in the analysis for example in which he played with the refrain of "Master of Puppets, I'm pulling all the strings . . . ." – more than a whiff here of his assumption of omnipotence, of his being in charge, giving the orders in the analysis. The analyst also described Claude's "protective self-castration" as a defense utilized against the potential destructive power of his grandiosity. Finally, I was struck by how often he spoke of enduring the experience of 'humiliation' in his life, a particularly agonizing emotional pain that is typically felt by many people with hypersensitive narcissistic sensibilities.

It is not clear from what is understood of his history what might have brought about such sensibilities. Claude's analyst refers to "multiple trauma" in his childhood and it may well be that serious cardiac illnesses, which occurred when he was 2 weeks and as an 11th grader, had profoundly disturbing effects on his development. It is tempting too to suggest that he suffered a great deal in the hands of a narcissistic mother whose ambivalence towards him as a special and gifted, yet imperfect, child caused him a great deal of confusion and fearfulness. This curious split maternal attitude seemed to characterize so much of her relationship with her son – at times for example, dismissive and angry (as when Claude nearly drowned, "washing machined in waves") yet at other times taking extra care of him, collecting him from school, doing his homework with him and for him, making him special meals and even finding the best doctors and tutors for him. It is also interesting to read of reports of her having vigorously defended her son at times from criticism, declaring how brilliant, creative and talented he was. Overall, in the midst of such contradictions, however, there did seem to prevail a particular closeness, both narcissistic and sexual, between them.

I have assumed that the sex of the analyst was female – a distinctly maternal ambience which I thought caught many of the strains that had existed in Claude's relationship to his mother. The image of Claude for example lying on his sofa at home in his underwear looking at television whilst his mother was at her desk nearby was most striking – and so clearly associated with the reality of him on the couch with his analyst nearby. This latter became for the adolescent "too close for comfort" – and maybe too, for the analyst. It seemed in general that there was a kind of tussle going on between Claude and his analyst, Claude repeating in many ways his entanglement with his mother – striving to separate but both excited by his mother's love yet fearful of his mother's criticism and dismissal. A moment occurred, for example, at one point in the analysis when Claude shared with his analyst his pleasure and pride in having composed his first orchestral compositions. He described one passage in the composition in particular involving the interplay of two violins, as being like "dueling violins." His analyst interpreted this in terms of the violins either arguing or having sex. Claude seemed taken aback by this association, but enough I think was registered to acknowledge the ambivalence in the analytic relationship.

The nature of this relationship was complex, one in which both analyst and adolescent seemed to constantly intertwine and struggle with each other. Certainly, in the early stages of the analysis, the analyst had to weather a formidable negative transference as Claude viewed her as mother with suspicion – doubting, mistrusting, criticizing and dismissing. But at other times, the analyst found herself recipient of more subtle kinds of projection. For example, she seemed occasionally to lose her footing. On one occasion, she felt piqued that he hadn't credited her with a recent success in his musical achievement. At other times, she spoke having been "tumbled" and manipulated by him – somehow drawn into some kind of compliance, arousing a sense of disappointment and betrayal in the countertransference. I think in many ways the analyst was very much caught in a highly ambivalent and complicated interaction with Claude, sometimes not unlike a cat and mouse game, drawing close, teasing and breaking away. Altogether a challenging place for the analyst to be in, not eased I would think by the fact that she was an adult woman in the presence of a male adolescent.

What I found most impressive was her readiness to engage with this adolescent. She was willing to put herself out, to reach across to him – however complicated this might have been in the context of the more embroiled atmosphere in the transference. She adopted in effect what is often referred to as a 'relational' analytic approach, that is to say, creating a co-operative relationship alongside the realm of transferences in the interest of building a working alliance. There were frequent references to phrases such as "the two of us" working "together" and on one occasion arriving "simultaneously" at a new insight. I found this approach refreshing – "creating together" the analysis, as the analyst put it in her conclusion as "a vehicle for movement, development, transformation and re-modelling his internal object." I think this is what Ogden (1997) and others have referred to as an 'analytic third:' the interplay of three, that of three subjectivities, that of the analyst, of the analysand, and the analytic third. Similarly, Aron (2006) has written of "the way that two people are continually influenced by the very patterns and rhythms that they have previously established with each other."

However, as much as was accomplished in this analysis, I am left with the impression that much was left untouched and not understood. Of course, this can be said of most analyses, but I think it is in the nature of adolescence that limits are set by the adolescent to what can be brought into the analysis. Unlike classical adult analysis, work with adolescents is more a two-way active process in which both parties are drawn into an unusual and often intense closeness. Both are exposed much more to each other's scrutinies which are difficult to avoid.

For the adolescent, things indeed may become too close for comfort in the transference and in close proximity to the adult analyst. And, behind the adolescent's co-operativeness and compliance, there may well prevail a more urgent narcissistic need to protect his or her privacy, separateness and isolation from those around him. He may need to keep his own counsel, to hold onto his or her own business, to keep others out, not to have him or self to be 'taken over.' A firm demarcation needs to be made by the adolescent on what is to be his alone – and to be appreciated and understood by the analyst. And so for example Claude kept to himself, for much of the time, his absorption in pornography, his homosexual experiences, chat-room exhibitionism and no matter what else beside. Additionally, he showed an abiding though diminishing reluctance to renounce his grandiose ideas about himself or allow the analyst any sense of potency or countenance any sort of implied criticism or disrespect of his narcissistic omnipotence.

This I believe is the essence of adolescent developmental resistance – quite different from the repression, transference and super ego resistances that Freud encountered during his lifetime – firmly setting against the full flowering of the analysis the "privacy of [the adolescent's] isolation" needs, as Adam Phillips suggests. The adolescent needs the object to protect this isolation – or, likewise, the analyst to respect this isolation.

EDITORIAL REFLECTIONS

The first task of early adolescent development is to come to terms with the fact of having a sexual body. This chapter offers a rich and complex illustration of the interference with that process that ensues when a young person enters adolescence with an existing history of both physical/medical impingement and sexual abuse. When these occur in the context of a family dynamic that included neglect and intense use of denial, along with adults acting out perverse impulses over many years, we understand the likelihood of intense confusion, massive defenses, and a burden of self-doubt and troubled functioning for the adolescent.

The analyst shares with us a sense that the treatment could be characterized in terms of "being seen and not seen," and this is a helpful organizer in thinking about what we learn about adolescent preoccupation with how they seem to themselves and others, and who they feel they really are, from this account of Claude's analysis and the commentators' responses. There are also technical lessons to consider about which modes of communication conduce to greater or lesser freedom of expression and communication, suggesting the usefulness of a flexible approach to these matters, in contrast to received ideas of what is standard, proper, or desirable. To the theme of seeing, we would add the corollary of what was "known and not known," as the treatment seems riddled with secrets, stories not told and hidden, indeed, great confusion over what is private and what is made secret. Just as the analyst grappled with being often shut out and also being "tumbled" by shocking revelations, the commentators note these challenges and raise questions that speak to our effort to understand what is particular to this case and what it illuminates for us about adolescents and adolescence in general.

Claude's specific medical problems may well have interacted with his psyche throughout his development to skew both his experience and regulation of his emotions, but those particularities underscore the importance of attending to aspects of a youngster's developmental history that parents may repress, suppress, or downplay. Such attention may alert the analyst of an adolescent to the operation of nachtraglichkeit, helping us to understand the traumatic intensity of the adolescent's present breakdown. Claude's parents, despite the analyst's efforts to do regular parent work, demonstrated powerful denial of any psychological meanings of Claude's various adverse childhood experiences, and remained capable of inflicting abusive intrusions on his mind and feelings. We could wonder about how much this limitation in the parent work affected the work with Claude; did his ambivalence and repeated leavings of the treatment, culminating in his unilateral premature termination, represent a lingering need to please and take care of his parents by inhibiting his own progression? This points up the ongoing dynamic impact of parents through and beyond adolescence, for good or ill (Novick, K.K. and Novick, J. 2013; Novick et al 2020). It also affects our assessment of outcomes in adolescent treatment, in that we may have to hope and trust that the adolescent will continue working on and working out the parent-child relationship, even when that work is truncated during the active analysis.

This returns our attention to the scope of work in the analysis itself. Claude's analyst demonstrated for us the exquisite sensitivity at conscious and unconscious (body too) levels needed to "tune in," to find a shared rhythm, to meet each young person where they are, even while living out a clearly-differentiated relationship of respect between two separate individuals. Differences or similarities between adolescent and adult analysis have long been debated. Here too we hear about a possible contrast between adolescent analysis as a two-way active process and adult technique (Wilson 1991). We relate this issue to the whole domain of the therapeutic alliance and the analyst's role in creating and nurturing it at each stage of treatment (Novick, J. and Novick, K.K. 2016). Working with the open-system functioning of the patient to co-create a cooperative relationship alongside the realm of transferences has ramifications for technique that we apply to patients of all ages, but may have special effectiveness in adolescent work, where the analyst as a developmental object carries multiple educational and identificatory functions and may be the agent of developmental repair.

The needs of disturbed adolescents mandate a comprehensive technical repertoire that reflects a multi-dimensional understanding and range of interventions. When a young person presents with the level of disarray seen in Claude, there is the ever-present worry about potential self-harm or suicide. Thus we return to the issue of privacy and secrecy, so central in our view to this treatment and that of most adolescents, linked as it is with safety, and with the existential reality of aloneness, which all adolescents have to grapple with (Novick, J. and Novick, K.K. 2008, 2015, 2019). One of the commentators underlines adolescents' need to protect their ownership of their experience with selective sharing, distinguishing this from resistances as traditionally defined (Wilson 1995). Perhaps the newness of full ownership of one's own mature body and psyche instigates a temporarily increased filtering, but we would hope that a treatment that went the full distance to a mutually-agreed termination would be able to address all domains and lead to young persons' pleasure in sharing their inner worlds.

Adolescent treatments very often end prematurely, to the surprise and dismay of therapists (Novick, J. and Novick, K.K. 2006). Claude's repeated experience throughout his whole life of being unseen, unheard, left out and left behind in the wake of his parents' self-absorption and excited, sexualized, sadomasochistic functioning came into his treatment from the very beginning – his analyst notes the potential refrain of being lost from the second session, and Claude repeatedly inflicts that experience on the analyst, in a complex intermingling of passive-to-active and externalizing defenses, along with repeated ruptures of the rhythm of the treatment. By its very nature, externalization is abusive, as it violates the reality of the other. School-aged children occasionally use externalization to avoid blame from their consciences, but this usually stops before adolescence. Disturbed teenagers, on the other hand, often beam powerful externalizations at their analysts. It's not hard for therapists to retain a realistic yardstick when young children do this, but adolescents get under one's skin; their externalizations carry not only violence, but often a sting of acute perception that hits close to home. Might this be one source of the general disinclination to treat adolescents in analysis?

There has been an historical tendency to rationalize the premature terminations of adolescent treatments in terms of developmental needs for separation and individuation, as if separating from one's analyst is an adequate displacement substitute for doing the actual work of transforming the relationship with parents. One could make a similar argument in Claude's case, bolstered by the reality of his history; we could posit that the only way he felt he could retain control of his destiny and not be manipulated by his analyst or anyone else was to leave first. We might also consider the risks inherent in unilateral termination for adolescents who have been traumatized or abused or who see themselves as unusual/defective from factors such as assisted reproduction, medical issues – do they feel they deserve to claim a mutually respectful ending? Does such a termination sow dangerous seeds for later relationships?

There are echoes here of Anna Freud's formulations about mourning in "About losing and being lost" (1967 [1953]); although she does not explicitly reference termination or adolescence, we suggest that adolescents go through analogous internal processes in their efforts to realign the pleasure, reality, and growth principles, setting aside omnipotent beliefs in favor of the joys of reality and maturity. Young people who have suffered neglect and abuse, as did Claude and many others, struggle with these tasks and may fear dependency more than the loneliness of proceeding on their own. Nevertheless, the work that has already been accomplished in treatment may equip them adequately.

CHAPTER 11

ANNE – age 17

The Analysis of a Silent Adolescent

I would like to describe the analysis of an adolescent girl, focusing on the difficulties emerging from the very beginning, my attempts to engage the patient, as well as the movement from a borderline type of functioning to a more neurotic one.

I will also like to stress the importance of seeing this patient remotely for a great part of her analysis after her move to University, based in another city. Contrary to our current practices of psychoanalysis in times of a pandemic, at that point that was a new way of approaching a young person, which was treated with fierce criticism from colleagues, who saw it as a serious departure from the usual setting. It was nevertheless of utmost importance to keep the analytic work going, as I knew this young woman would be left with no emotional support once she left home for College.

Anne was 18 years old when she started 4 times a week analysis, some years ago. The sessions were dominated by lengthy, enduring silences, emotional disconnection, replicating her experience of everyday life. She avoided eye contact, rarely conveyed her thoughts spontaneously, and it was only after a great deal of work on my part that she managed to say something, revealing the picture of a persecutory, cruel and ruthless internal world. At times, the contents of her mind seemed fragmented, she struggled to express her ruminations, at others, she remarked being distracted, obsessing over banal matters, e.g. making endless lists.

Background information

Anne is the older of two children, her brother is 3 years younger. Father, a businessman, seemed physically and emotionally absent and her mother was in charge of looking after the family. There was a significant history of mental health disorders in both families. Parents' relationship seemed unhappy; a colleague working with the parents conveyed that father was rather arrogant and in denial of the seriousness of his daughter's condition and mother, although depressed, expressed real concerns for her daughter.

Anne struggled with low moods, irritability, self-harm and suicidal ideation. She failed to engage with her peers, felt frequently lonely, was bulimic and was cutting herself. She had also taken an overdose of 17 Fluoxetine tablets after poor A-level exam results [Eds. – secondary school-leaving examinations].

On the initial assessment interview, she was very depressed, detached, spoke in a monotonous voice, and apart from conveying she felt lost, could not say more about herself. She cried whilst relating that she hallucinated, seeing ghosts, initially thinking that they were not real, then becoming unsure, as these appeared more frequently. These ghosts could be of her family, friends or people she did not know. She mentioned scary dreams, filled with death and violence, saying, "I never have normal dreams." Her dreams had become so disturbing that she became worried she would not wake up from them.

Anne could feel often very angry, eventually losing control, behaving aggressively in a frightening way towards others around her, taken over by murderous feelings. These intense responses frightened her and she wished being admitted to hospital. She had a difficult relationship with food, making herself throw up, especially after eating fatty meals. There were frequent references to suicidal ideas, but she tried to reassure me that she had no suicide plans.

The beginning of the analysis – trying to engage a silent adolescent

Anne decided delaying going to University for a year as we started the analysis and during this period the sessions took place in the consulting room. An attractive young woman, she hid her body, wearing mainly pajama-like trousers, long-sleeved tops, looking as if she had just got out of bed. As analysis progressed, she started showing greater care for her appearance.

She would start the sessions saying "Hi," silently sitting down, facing me, with a vacant facial expression, avoiding eye contact, anxiously rubbing her hands, playing with her hair or clothes. She looked drowsy, yawned throughout, claiming tiredness despite having slept for long hours. She would never initiate any communication, remaining mostly silent, seeming secretive. Sometimes she responded to my attempts to engage her with a humming sound, without further comments. This remained the pattern for a long period of time.

She disconnected, in response to something unsettling I might have said, especially after a reference to sexuality or the transference. The little she managed to convey, often peppered by swearing, revealed that she had never had an intimate relationship. She felt intensely envious of other girls' ability to socialize and develop relationships, dominated by feelings of humiliation and hatred.

She was punctual, did not miss sessions, and continued to sit on the chair facing me for over a year, glancing furtively from time to time at the couch, something I commented on.

These are a few short vignettes and descriptions from the beginning of the analysis:

In response to asking her what she had in mind she simply replied "nothing" and I interpreted that she had to empty her mind from painful, difficult thoughts.

Although silences predominated most of the time, she could say that she had 'random' thoughts, which seemed to be fragments she couldn't quite articulate. Later she said she had thought of taking a bus and not coming, expressing anxieties about what she could find in the room and in herself, all that was unknown. She hummed. She continued that she did not feel ready for lots of things, including her unreadiness to engage with me, her struggles to make friends and going to University. I suggested that she did not feel ready for life and she seemed afraid of the kind of life that could emerge in the analysis with me.

When I mentioned that I had noticed her looking at the couch, she responded that she could not lie down, as it would make her feel vulnerable having someone sitting behind her, adding: "and I could fall asleep." I suggested that she feared being exposed to my ideas, overwhelmed by them, fearing knowing about life inside herself . . . . and falling asleep could be a good way of evading "this situation."

At some point later in analysis, she described her awareness of her relationship with her brother having become difficult, they used to be closer in the past. I commented that she felt that she had been changing, she was growing up, which made her feel more anxious about relating not just to her brother, but to herself, the world around her, worrying about what could happen in the room with me.

In the following vignette, something more meaningful began to emerge:

On a Monday session after being silent for a long period, prompted by a comment I made, she told me she had not slept well. She woke up at 3 am hearing noises, footsteps close to her bedroom, thinking that someone was in their house, and felt too scared. Eventually she told me that she feared being attacked, overpowered by someone and kidnapped. I linked her experience to her coming to the session after the weekend and her anxiety about using the couch and getting closer to me. She confirmed she was anxious about coming to the session, and then told me that just as she was waking up she had a dream. In this dream, "she had broken into someone's house to steal a book." She struggled to say that on "the book's cover there was a house and a tree," she had been in this house before and knew where the book was kept. She added that the house was like mine and that tree was like the very tall tree in my garden.

I suggested that she may have wanted to steal something from me, something valuable she feels I have that she did not have during the weekend, perhaps my knowledge of how I could help her. She wanted to be able do the job by herself and the only way would be depriving me from what I knew, instead of engaging in the work with me, which she feels is dangerous. I added that she felt exposed and humiliated by the idea of having to return and depend on me to know more about herself. She agreed.

It was possible to understand her worries of being attacked, kidnapped in the night, in the weekend dream, also expressing her terrifying anxieties of being taken over by her analyst and the analysis and by her own desire to become engaged. My countertransference experience, intuition, and associations provided an auxiliary mental space, allowing me to process, making some sense and translating her non-verbal communications, her feelings or thoughts, but the question of how active I had to be, remained a central technical issue.

Later in the first year, she announced that she would be travelling abroad with a cousin, beginning with the Christmas break. Her cousin had already been abroad for some time and Anne would join her. This was a sign of improvement, considering that when we started she hardly left her bedroom or her house.

In the last session before this break, she said at first, that she was trying not to think about the break, feeling frightened, feeling often like giving up going away .... it was not a dream. I linked her fears that bad things could happen during the trip such as an imagined plane being highjacked, to her anxieties emerging from what the journey with me was doing to her mind. She worried about being with and without the analysis. We agreed she could get in touch if she needed.

After a few weeks' away her mother contacted me to let me know that Anne had asked if I could speak to her on Skype as she was not feeling well and we had two sessions on Skype. She was abroad, couldn't leave her room, feeling extremely anxious. By the end of the second Skype session she said she felt better and would contact me again if she needed, but she didn't. I became aware that she had been more communicative using Skype than when in the consulting room.

When she returned, she was concerned with her application to Universities, speaking about all the options. Although staying in the same city would mean she could continue the analysis, Anne wanted to have the experience of living away from home, looking at different prospects, but interestingly started to look at courses connected to the psychological world. She was clearly feeling more able to leave home and at the same time remaining closer and interested in learning about what I do and how I think about her.

Moving to the couch

One year into the analysis, as we continue to explore thoughts she felt progressively more able to share, it became clear that Anne was interested in using the couch, in changes which could take place if the analysis continued to progress.

On a session following one where these became more evident, she arrived 10 minutes late, apologized, she was blushing, and went straight to the couch. When I commented on this change, she confirmed it was intentional. "I thought it was time to do it. I felt I had to do it." However, as could be expected, she missed the following session as she "became sick."

Anne was offered a place at University, 2 hours away by train. I was concerned that would mean a premature ending of the analysis, as she remained in a rather fragile and isolated state, although recognizing that this move represented a desire for real change. She told me during this period that she had to stop switching off, try to socialise, she wanted to have a normal life. She had achieved an increased capacity to concentrate in her studies, which allowed her to get a place in the course she wanted, freer to use the couch, being less paranoid. However, I felt these improvements were far from sustainable, as there would be moments of regression and fragility alternating with a stronger capacity to function and relate.

With these concerns in mind, I suggested and she agreed to continue the analytic treatment, adapting to this new situation, by having two sessions using Skype on Mondays and Wednesdays, and on Thursdays and Fridays, in person, in my consulting room. Some colleagues with whom I discussed this case, opposed these changes. However, I thought that interrupting the analysis would be even more damaging to her emotional state which was far from stable.

Evidently changes in the setting took place, when she was at University. She sat on a chair or occasionally on her bed, in front of her computer in her room. She appeared more relaxed and communicative; perhaps it was safer than being with me in person.

An increased ability to socialize followed, she began accepting invitations to go out with her house mates, which she found exciting and frightening. She alternated between different states of mind, hoping that things could go well, that people were reliable or anticipating all kinds of disaster. When she became too anxious she resorted to locking herself up in her bedroom, with the excuse that she had to revise. I often linked these fears of catastrophes with internal processes of development and a greater ability to be more separate as a result of the analysis.

She started riding horses, revealing how more at ease she felt, enough to allow some physical contact with something more alive (or sexual?) in herself. She could visit a friend at another University, go out to parties with groups of friends which included a friend's male flatmate, with whom she exchanged kisses. She said it was fine but she would not do it again, expressing how it scared her. Anne also managed to travel abroad with her family, despite terrors of being kidnapped or assaulted, and could engage with members of her extended family and to have a good time. She spoke how being in analysis was difficult, but she wanted to be able to have a normal life, to relate to others and stop disconnecting.

Concerns about food, worrying anxieties about her weight and body shape, remained, which seemed linked to sexual phantasies. Anne described her relationship with her body worrying about what would be put inside her. I understood and interpreted her fears of getting fatter with growing up, becoming a sexual woman and possibly getting pregnant. I linked that with how unsafe she could feel listening to me, taking in what I offered to her, fearing what could come up, develop, in her mind if she allowed herself to engage further with the analysis.

As she returned to University, on her first session back, she said that she was hungry, without hesitation, unusually in a lively way. Later, she said: "When I came back here (University) on Sunday I felt quite emotional. I felt upset. I am not sure why, maybe it was leaving home." It was clear that Anne was not disconnected and that she was clearly upset for being away "from the home she had with me" by not having sessions in my consulting room.

During that period, she brought a dream in which she felt freer, without fears, to swim in a sea full of sharks, helping her brother to manage, reassuring him that he could swim together with her, as if giving evidence to her greater confidence in the analysis, and in herself, of being helped to swim, feeling more connected, and empowered. However, another dream followed, in which "she was being driven by her mother, who appeared inattentive, driving without much care, which provoked her anxieties and anger at her mother, screaming at her: you never look ahead, why can't you fucking drive?"

This second dream seemed to have exposed that although feeling better and safer, more supported, hopeful, she seemed to be worrying if "I, as the mother/ driver of this analysis, would be paying proper attention to what is going on now, or to what lies ahead? Will I continue helping you (her) to feel safe?"

Although still quite anxious, Anne appeared to be in a better frame of mind, and as we moved towards the third year of her analysis, further changes took place.

Initiating verbal communication, further development and setback

This was a period of greater development; Anne had become increasingly more able to express her feelings spontaneously even if they were difficult. She could initiate the session without being prompted. She managed to socialize with people of her age, started taking driving lessons and decided to concentrate on her analysis, which she clearly valued. She was working very hard, hoping for good results during her first year, expecting that the following two years would be harder.

In one of the first sessions during this period, she described how a much-feared trip on her own with her father, had gone well. Following her return, Anne had felt more confident and was able to allow some closeness with a male student, D., who seemed also interested in her.

However, as we resumed in the following term, it emerged that she had been making herself sick, as "she ate more than she should," which had not happened for a long time. I suggested that she felt she needed a big meal. I wondered if she felt desiring not only more food and academic achievements but also greater developments in her personal life, this led into her feeling that there was something wrong about wanting more, feeling hungrier. It felt like being poisoned or that she had put bad things inside her, and had to get rid of them. Long silence.

After a while she said that she was confused about the "guy" thing and that it was about D. She didn't know what was going on. To make things worse, she was worried that she could be thought as greedy, as if it was wrong and disturbing to have such feelings for someone. The preoccupations with feelings for this young man continued present and disturbing. Later on Anne realised that her feelings for D. were not reciprocated, he just wanted to be friends with her, which left her feeling confused. She struggled to share how upset she was feeling.

She then said, "…. I was also thinking that I haven't been in such a good place for quite a long time. Maybe I am trying to do too much, too fast. Pause. I need to know how to be with myself. Pause. Maybe I am saying that to feel better. I was thinking that before, anyway." It was clear how hard she found thinking about her emerging intense feelings, including sexual feelings, and how difficult it was talking to me, another man. Anne replied after a long silence: "I don't know anything about this shit. I don't have a fucking clue. Maybe I need a fucking manual. I don't know anything about dating."

Later on, she came to a session in a very anxious state, telling me in a confused way that something had happened to her, which came across in a very dramatic way. It took her a few sessions to be able to describe in part what had gone on in a way that I could make sense.

After arriving late to a session, with lots of silences in between, and gently helped by me, she described, with great difficulty, an incident which had taken place between her and D., and another girl, also called Anne. She and D. had been kissing and he proceeded to remove her top but nothing further happened. Some minutes later another girl (also Anne) arrived and D. immediately turned away from my patient. He and this other girl started "doing stuff" in front of her, which must have been clearly sexual, leaving her quite profoundly disturbed, to the extent that she ran away in a distressed state, leaving all her belongings including her shoes and phone behind.

Anne seemed to have witnessed something which evoked in her the primal scene, with the resurgence of anxieties, central to her inhibition, her emotional struggles to separate, affecting her capacities to develop.

After this experience, we went through a critical period. Although having had very good end of the year results, she returned to feeling very anxious, unable to concentrate and to study, convinced that she was going to fail. She was considering dropping out from University, and mentioned stopping the analysis or to reduce it to two weekly sessions. Although all this felt quite worrying, we managed to overcome these threats to her progress and to the continuation of the analytic work.

As we carried on working, I became increasingly aware of Anne's much better state, becoming less anxious, able to engage with her peers and the world around her, the disturbing feelings and behavior ceased, and in analysis she could communicate more freely without needing to be prompted. Despite having had disappointing grades which resulted in her deciding to defer her course for one year, she continued coming for her analysis regularly and work went on for years to come.

Conclusion

In this short account, I hope to have been able to describe the development of the analysis of a disturbed, very withdrawn and emotionally stuck late adolescent girl, who had been trapped in a self-destructive state, stealing from shops, suffering from bulimia, self-harming, and, at periods, suicidal. She had bouts of uncontrollable and unprovoked fury and aggression, attacking people around her. Initially these appeared as a manifestation of psychotic functioning with loss of contact with reality, resulting in serious enactments.

Anne was resistant, secretive and apparently did not seem interested in knowing more about herself. During the first period in her analysis, I had to tolerate long silences, her avoidance of contact, deep states of anxieties and had to adapt my approach by becoming more active and directive than usual to support her to slowly gain greater trust in her analyst's ability to bear her anxieties without falling apart.

Although for quite a long time she dismissed any references to sexual feelings and phantasies, as she progressively felt less threatened by her awareness of her sexually mature body, Anne slowly managed to open up and bring references to her experiences, albeit in a very limited way. As a setback to a difficult experience of being rejected by a young man, whom she seemed to like and was attracted to, as well as facing a number of separations from the analysis, she felt compelled to abandon the couch and return to the safety of the chair.

Anne seemed to have felt "forced" by this young man to experience intense sexual feelings quite unbearable for her and, as she could not advance to be sexually active with him, he rejected her; Anne was then forced to witness the equivalent of a primal scene, between him and a new girl with an upsurge of deep anxieties. The enactment evoked the witnessing of the primal scene experienced as cruel.

This appeared to parallel her experiences in the transference, with the analyst/father, to whom she had been getting closer, attracted to his mind, his helpful thinking, to what he had been offering, as well as having to be exposed to feelings of rejection every time he turned away from her, to be with someone else, or to have a life which excluded her, hence making closer contact dangerous.

My main concern with this account has been focused on the modification to the classical psychoanalytical approach, in order to engage a very fragile and inhibited adolescent patient. I am certain that my descriptions will evoke a number of theoretical ideas, which could be very interesting and useful in conceptualizing a formulation about what could have contributed to Anne's disturbances, which brought her into analysis. We do not know a great deal about Anne's early experiences as well as her emotional development growing up, but one feels inevitably tempted to fill in the gaps to gain some further understanding of her developmental difficulties._

However, Anne seemed to have managed to recover more quickly from the latest disruption experience, and although she made the decision to defer her last year at University, she chose to remain in analysis, returning to the couch, and the analytic work continued. I expected these movements back and forth to continue, albeit with less intensity, as Anne had made progress in several ways, was profoundly attached to the analysis and seemed genuinely grateful for the help she was still getting. Although we continued to struggle, it feels as if we crossed a barrier.

Anne finished her academic studies and the analysis ended after 5 years. She is now pursuing further development in her chosen carrier, which is related to our work. She is now in a stable relationship with a young man. We have been meeting for monthly consultation for the last year.

COMMENTARY 1

The Sounds of Silence

What are the sounds of Anne's silence that the analyst hears even though she has such difficulty putting words to her thoughts and feelings? The silences predominate in the first year of the analysis, but continue to some degree throughout the time described in this vignette. Anne does not speak much, thus eliciting a more active stance from the analyst as he attempts to understand her mind. She can hardly speak, but she comes regularly and punctually.

Anne has come to analysis on the cusp of a developmental transition that she so clearly, painfully does not feel prepared for. Though we hear little of her history, we do hear of some of the terrors of her emotional life. Having done poorly on A-levels, she made a suicide attempt which presumably has brought her to treatment and she postpones entering a university in favor of the analysis. In an early session, she tells the analyst "that she did not feel ready for lots of things," including engaging with him, making friends or going off to a university. The interpretation he makes is that she does not "feel ready for life." Indeed!

Then, the analyst notes, "something more meaningful began to emerge." After reporting nighttime fears, she tells him a dream in which she has broken into a home to steal a book with a cover picture of a house and a tree. There are obvious transference references and the analyst interprets her anxieties about his influence on her and her need for him. Perhaps the dream can also be understood as a commentary on his earlier remark that she is not ready for life. She needs the book of life, someone who knows how to drive, the trusted guide represented by the analyst so that she, like a tree in a garden, can grow. Later, in despair about her romantic life, she says, "I need a fucking manual." She does need a manual, the manual of the analytic relationship. Rather than acknowledging this need directly, she must put it in terms of instructions, as people and the person of the analyst remain too dangerous for her. Yet the wish for forward development can be heard through her silence and defensive disguise.

At the end of the vignette, the analyst comments that instead of exploring the factors contributing to Anne's severe difficulties, he has focused on the alterations he made to a classical psychoanalytic approach in his more active stance and his use of video technology. These concerns are sprinkled throughout the description of the treatment. As this analysis took place before the pandemic made tele-analysis more acceptable, colleagues warn him about breaking the rules when he decides to use Skype to continue the analysis. The analyst goes against accepted practice in order to support Anne's developmentally healthy choice to go away to school in order to try for, as she says, for "a normal life." As much as we hear about her symptoms and psychopathology, Anne's wish to be on the developmental pathway propels the analysis forward.

The analyst seems less ambivalent about the choice to use video technology than about the ongoing tension of how "active" to be with Anne. Challenged by her extended silences, he takes a more active role with her against the stricture of going against analytic rules and allows himself to be guided by what he understands Anne to need from him. Another contribution to the analyst's anxiety about being active is the theme in Anne's anxiety about being kidnapped and overpowered so he must balance her need to be connected to him with her sensitivity to intrusion by the other. They discover that the use of Skype from her university creates a distance that seems to free Anne to be more forthcoming. These instances of deviating from the "classical psychoanalytic approach" turn out to be just what this young woman needs as she moves from adolescence into young adulthood. Lucky for her that she had an analyst who could learn from her about what would help her deal with the ghosts alive in her mind and discover her version of a "normal life."

Anne did use her analysis to "get ready for life." Perhaps what the analyst referred to as "alterations" in accepted technique should rather be considered analytic technique, not deviations or modifications or alterations, in that they facilitate this adolescent's ability to use her analyst for her growth and development while allowing the analyst to analyze. Adolescents may have something to teach psychoanalysts about a broader understanding of technique that will help them rewrite the manual.

COMMENTARY 2

Working With While Working On

As child analysts we are attuned to development: what is present and what is not. Our goal is to re-set the developmental track. To accomplish this goal – to demonstrate the flexibility we wish to instill in our patients – we are especially alert to what the patient is able to incorporate and consolidate. As growth requires different conditions, so does our work. Anne gives us the opportunity to examine how the analyst's ability to enlarge his conception of the working space provided Anne with the conditions needed for her growth.

Peek-a-boo is thought of as one of the first interactive exchanges between baby and parents. It is the outward demonstration of a developing internal landscape. The child is on the road to understanding that objects have permanence, that they exist beyond the child. This is an essential element as a child begins to make sense of the world. The chaos and randomness can begin to recede as connections between things and places are experienced as permanent, predictable, and reliable. While a child is learning treasured people and objects are stable independent entities, they are also incorporating that they, too, have an independent, cohesive and reliable existence.

Adolescent Anne came to analysis displaying a host of impulsive and self-destructive behaviors. She described herself as feeling lost, unconnected, and detached. At times she could not even rely on her ability to separate reality from fantasized ghosts. Her internal world seemed chaotic. Words often failed her as she tried to understand and communicate her experience of herself and the world outside her. It was as if she is still playing peek-a-boo, unsure what the world would present to her and unsure how she was perceived by it. There is not room for her to contend with her thoughts and reactions, so she responded quickly and impulsively to whatever stimulus came to the fore. Anne had tantrums; she stole from shops. Her ability to knit together a coherent picture of the world had broken down to the extent that her eating was disordered, she harmed herself, and she was periodically suicidal.

At the beginning of Anne's work she appeared in pajama-like clothing, she hummed and did her best to disengage herself. She conveyed her envy of her peers' social connection by swearing, indicating both her struggle and her wishes to enjoy the connections she saw around her. She relied on her analyst to initiate any talking.

Faced with a mostly silent adolescent, the analyst is forced to guess what is needed, like a parent of an infant or toddler sensing what cannot be put into words. The question for the analyst is two-fold: what is stopping the words, and what can facilitate the use of them. These questions are not unique to working with children but as child analysts we are not only trying to understand a patient's internal world and what conflicts may be preventing them from more fully expressing that world, but we also assess the developmental capacity of the patient.

Here we struggle to understand our role as both a developmental object and a transference object for a patient (Chused 1982, Miller 2017, Sugarman 2003). Anne required her analyst to endure her silence, to remain connected, and to start the talking. If her analyst had merely thought of his actions in terms of the transference, a great deal of what Anne required might not have been addressed. Anne's difficulties outside the sessions were reproduced within it, but focusing attention only on the transferential or interpersonal aspects would lose the developmental repair that was occurring.

The working surface is a familiar concept (Busch 1993, Paniagua 1991). Without it we risk missing the mark, asking too much or too little of ourselves and our patients. We know the boundaries of the working surface when we have misjudged it. This requires us to retrench, renegotiate, or otherwise revise our thoughts and even our formulations. This re-thinking is often when we discover a more nuanced understanding. At the best of those moments, we are the embodiment of what we hope our patients can achieve: the capacity to observe, to take in what is working and what is not, to endure the disappointment, and then to regroup.

Adolescents often present a formidable wall requiring the analyst to be alert to small hints of accessibility. Anne's punctuality and attendance at her sessions were announcements of her investment in her treatment. Her need to reassure her analyst that she had no suicidal plans had many facets but one of those is her hopes and wishes for a better life for herself.

Despite Anne's silences, her analyst was able to attune himself to her reactions and to tolerate her silence, her dress, and her vagueness. He witnessed her need to withdraw when his comments were unsettling. His awareness engendered a change in outlook and a recognition of the need to modify his actions as well. As a parent notices that he has held up the blanket too long in the peek-a-boo game and has to regroup, so Anne's analyst noted what comments were overwhelming and allowed her to direct the pace. Anne could develop her own internal sense of boundary and solidity that enabled her to begin the process of being connected.

Anne's going off with her cousin was a major step forward in her work. Part of the experience was too much for her and she requested a Skype session. Her analyst noticed how much more communicative she was using Skype. There is a shift for both Anne and her analyst. The tools of connection are now expanded. Anne also wanted to expand her world and her connections in it. She could now express her experience of ambivalent and contradictory feelings, wanting to go to University and wanting to stay in analysis. Her difficulty in finding a solution was, again, a signal to her analyst that her gains were not yet consolidated. The idea for continuing the analysis partly in person and partly online demonstrates how the analyst was able to understand her need to proceed with a developmental phase while he needed to provide the flexible surface from which to accomplish it.

The offer of on-line work gave Anne an active experience of negotiating competing desires. She wanted to go to University and to have some separation but still needed her analyst to understand her concern that the separation would be too much. The on-line work itself was successful: it provided a distance that also revealed a working surface for the analysis. Approaching the on-line sessions as just that – sessions that occur on-line – allowed the work to continue at its pace. To have focused on the use of the computer and its possible defensive functions would have derailed the direction of the treatment in progress. Anne discovered activities, friends, and relationships, and she was articulate about them. In the midst of this she also says: "I need to know how to be with myself." This awareness of a solid internal self and the ability to articulate it is, indeed, a signal that Anne is gaining the internal and external skills she needs to regain her developmental pathway.

The work with Anne is a demonstration of the flexibility often required to work with a child or adolescent. Not only must one determine what is stuck, but also how to "unstick" it. There are many aspects that determined and shaped Anne's dilemmas but her initial disconnection and impulsive response to the world seem prominent to me.

My analogies to a child playing peek-a-boo and needing to find a sense of solidity in herself and the world around her may not have been what was in her analyst's mind. The metaphor does not seem as important as observing how the treatment progressed. Anne's analyst was able to tolerate her disconnection while he remained engaged and connected. This functioned as a reservoir for her, a sustenance that was available as she could use it. Recognizing the treatment would be done at her pace and that she was invested in it was a cornerstone from which the analytic pair could proceed.

In this case one can look at the analysis itself as the developmental object, not merely the analyst. Anne comes on time to sessions and rarely misses them. When she is away, she asks for a Skype meeting. Just as she is able to work more freely at a distance, perhaps initially she was able to allow connection with "the analysis" rather than a focus on the analyst. Her analyst is able to observe this and uses this knowledge to make the analysis available to her when she wishes to attend University.

This case required flexibility from the analyst to use new tools to continue treatment. That there are modifications to our approach to patients is not a new concept. Perhaps it is the newness and rapid evolution of computer technology and computer capacities that gives us pause. This is a tool much like the consulting room, the couch, or a play area. For each instance we try to understand the significance and meaning for each patient.

This case is a skillful working and blending of being attuned to conflict and transference dynamics while attending to the more immediate developmental needs of an adolescent. It underlines that developmental lacks must be restored in order for the adolescent to be able to approach the exploration of conflict and transference.

EDITORIAL REFLECTIONS

There is much to learn about the possibilities of adolescent analysis from this chapter. We hear again about a very disturbed young person who does well with psychoanalysis. This good outcome comes about, however, in large measure because of the analyst's steadfastness and conviction about the value of the endeavor, even in the face of what sounds like strong disapproval from the reference group of colleagues. In our experience, every practitioner needs support from colleagues; but working with adolescents can severely try the patience of therapists and elicit doubts and fears that demand the help of positive professional surrounds. This situation warrants unpacking and further understanding, since it seems to us to exemplify many of the issues that have long surrounded adolescent psychoanalysis.

Currently, analysis is often a treatment of last resort for adolescents who have not responded well to other therapeutic efforts, with long histories of disturbance stretching back into childhood, and lack of apparent response to medical, psychiatric interventions. In Anne's case, one wishes she had been able to access dynamic treatment sooner. This general narrowing of the diagnostic range can then be echoed in a narrowed model of technique that deprives patients and analysts of a comprehensive repertoire of interventions and responses that could inform all facets of the therapeutic relationship. We suggest that this constriction of potential in the clinical situation may have roots in a misguided effort on the part of child and adolescent therapists to replicate what is presented as standard adult technique, in hopes of justifying or validating the legitimacy of child and adolescent psychoanalysis.

Fortunately for Anne, her analyst was able to expand their repertoire, to be flexible, to be creative, to everyone's advantage. We would have to look back to the work of August Aichhorn to find comparable efforts of flexibility to individualize the alliance with each adolescent (1984 [1935]). Despite her admiration for Aichhorn, Anna Freud generally talked of adolescents as unanalyzable. We think that this may represent a defensive manoeuvre that avoids taking responsibility for the challenges of adolescent treatment. Rather than attribute the difficulty in analyzing to the nature of adolescence, we should consider the limitations imposed by narrow and rigid technical models. When technique is appropriately broadened, cases have good outcomes and adolescents show themselves to be eminently analyzable!

Rather than adhere to a "standard" technique based on the theory of work with adults, this analyst learned from the patient what she needed and could make good use of. The analyst prioritized the patient's needs and generated a hybrid treatment structure that addressed all aspects of the treatment relationship, including serving as a developmental object, a real object, and a transference object. Avoiding a sadomasochistic closed-system relationship that could have been elicited from the start by Anne's silences and disconnections, the analyst presented the option of a realistic, thoughtful, reflective and safe space in the therapeutic alliance, allowing for developmental repair, adjusting the working surface sensitively as they went along, which led to her eventual freedom to choose an open-system relationship with the analyst and others. Her progressive development – the growth principle, the open system of self-regulation – could be accessed because the analyst was listening for it, rather than choosing to be bogged down consistently in conflict and transference.

We would stress that this broad repertoire should represent what is psychoanalytic technique, rather than be seen as 'parameters' or 'deviations.' This chapter helps to establish a new standard, responsive to the needs of both people, and reflective of a metapsychological view of development and treatment.

CHAPTER 12

KELLY – age 17

I Get By With a Little Help From My Friends

What does it look like when an adolescent is in the throes of the developmental task of achieving significant transformations, both internally and externally, with regard to primary object relations? For many, a friend group comes to play an important role in altering the nature of object investments and revising both preoedipal and oedipal narratives about the self in relation to others. The last two years of Kelly's lengthy analysis provide an opportunity to observe this process at close hand. Although transference, countertransference, and enactments all served to further our analytic understanding, frequently the work revealed itself through displacements to goings on with her friends. My aim in this contribution to the casebook is not to give a complete account of the analysis. Instead I hope to follow the unfolding drama of anger and excitement, love and aggression that Kelly experienced, sometimes in relation to her family, sometimes in the context of her friends. This necessary adolescent process, however it unfolds, paves the way for passion and romance with new objects, while more attenuated feelings of tenderness, affection, admiration, and loyalty to parents can grow, relatively unimpeded by conflicts from earlier phases.

When Kelly came to treatment in early adolescence, she and her parents recognized that she was suffering from extremely low self-esteem and lack of confidence in herself. She had given up a competitive sport she enjoyed when physical changes in puberty made her less successful than she had been previously. She did well enough in school, but her teachers consistently noted that she was underachieving and failed to show initiative. Psychoanalysis offered the best chance of understanding what early experiences and psychic conflicts contributed to her unhappiness; the parents were supportive while Kelly herself was less enthusiastic. Over time, however, she realized that her problem with procrastination was interfering with some of the academic goals she was setting for herself. She had close girlfriends but had never had a serious boyfriend and she was intrigued by recurrent dreams of becoming pregnant without having sex.

Kelly returned from the summer analytic break at the start of her junior year of high school by announcing, "Things are not so good with my parents.... they bug me. I think it bothers my mother that I'm not around much." She described her mother as silly, overemotional, and rather dense about the kind of humor Kelly now liked. She did not feel like her mother understood her and complained that she did not approve of a girlfriend, Lexie, with whom Kelly was developing a new friendship. She observed that there was always some kind of brouhaha in her family, some fight over what seemed trivial matters and she wondered "why can't they be calm."

I observed and heard about how she and her next-younger brother Brandon, also a teenager, contributed to the stirred-up atmosphere at home through petty quarreling and uniting in defiance of their parents. In Kelly's view her parents did not know how to intervene effectively to contain the excitement. She said her mother was easy on Brandon and hard on her, while her father was tough on Brandon and usually gave her a pass. "It's not like it's a 'Daddy's Little Girl' thing," she disclaimed. She described her father wandering off physically and emotionally at home and noted derisively, "It's not like he's the man in the family. He takes a lot from my mom, then he yells at Brandon. How can he live with someone like that?" After a particularly angry tirade about her mother during one of our sessions, Kelly reported what was evidently a guilty dream: "I was saying, 'I don't want to die... I want to get married!'" This marked a renewed attempt on her part to come to terms with her parents as individuals with their unique strengths and weaknesses.

Her view of her parents' marriage at this point was that it was not very romantic or particularly satisfying. She told me that she used to worry that they would get divorced because they fought so much, but she no longer believed this would happen. She talked about how the two would go off to have "private talks" in their bedroom, the garage, or on car rides. She felt both excluded and intensely curious, sometimes eavesdropping to try to find out what was going on when she was not a part of the action. When I suggested that she might be wondering what their private relationship was like, in typical adolescent fashion she said she did not like to think about them having sex and asserted that "they're too boring to do anything." I had no reason to believe that Kelly had ever actually been exposed to a primal scene, but the daily upsets had a distinctively sexual quality from which there was seldom relief. While this material was prominent, I had a dream of Kelly in my kitchen with my family while I cleaned things up. At least in part this seemed to reflect a fantasy we may both have shared that I could offer some nurturance and escape from the overstimulation.

Lexie began to take on an increasing importance to Kelly. That her mother found Lexie somehow an unsuitable friend made her all the more interesting and attractive. Her parents were divorced and their lifestyles were much more unconventional and permissive than Kelly's. On the one hand Lexie represented freedom, but Kelly also understood that she had some neglectful and abusive experiences that left her hurt and vulnerable. She imagined rescuing Lexie by having her come live at her house (as I rescued her in my dream). I wondered with her whether there was a part of her that wished she could live elsewhere, but she rejected this idea out of hand. She was not conscious of the fact that Lexie was someone toward whom she could feel superior. The only problem I heard about in the friendship was that Kelly was appalled when Lexie would come over and be flirtatious with Brandon. "She's hitting on my brother... my *younger* brother. It's gross and disgusting! I don't want him in my space with my friends!" A few days later she told me she had told him to "fuck off" – the first time she used that expression with me.

As Homecoming celebrations approached that fall, Kelly told me, "My friends are heaven." She and her best guy friend, Randy, became a pair of leaders who organized where the group would go and what they would do. She described him as outgoing, with an infectious sense of humor. Randy seemed to serve as a new, more sophisticated partner to replace the antics with Brandon. Kelly repeatedly bemoaned the fact that she had no boyfriend and when she and friends went to see a psychic, she asked when she would find one. The psychic said one day she would have a beau named Otis. After telling me this she added, "That's a terrible name... oh, wait... is that your son's name?" Here the material led me to make the first of two interpretations that seemed correct to me, the second of which later proved untimely and disruptive to her. At this point I asked if she imagined that she and my son might get together and she was taken by surprise. "Eww, no!" Homecoming turned out to be less fun than she had hoped and there was some fighting among the friends afterward that spoiled the occasion, reminiscent of life at home.

Kelly was struggling that fall with Advanced Placement classes she had signed up for and she said, "We've got to work on this procrastination.... I think I'm addicted to it." We began to pay attention to how she not only put things off, but also sabotaged herself by losing notes or forgetting a needed book when she had an assignment due. She was plagued by negative thoughts about herself being stupid, incompetent, clumsy, and a failure. The idea that she might also be stopping herself from being successful entered into our work, though she was usually able to bring her grades up before report cards and actually did quite well. A new piece of work about her mother came after she said that her mother told her she dreamed that Kelly got all Bs – lower than she actually got. Kelly was insulted that her mother would dream this and recognized that her mother was ambivalent and perhaps envious and competitive about her doing well.

The switch to thinking about her mother may have been an effort to avoid the transferential meanings my son held for her. Nonetheless, there was important work ahead regarding her sense of her mother in the past and in the present. She asked me, "Do you think she's depressed?" Based on my knowledge of her mother over several years, I replied that I thought it was hard for her mother to feel good, that her worries and upsets about things protected her from sad feelings from her own childhood and adolescence. My hope was that Kelly would at some point begin to see her mother as a person in her own right.

Kelly then asked me if I thought *she* was unhappy. "Have I gotten happier than last year?" She felt she was having the best year of her life. She said that she thought she was taking a 17-year-old look at her mother and seeing her more realistically. She went on to reflect that her parents were good role models (unlike Lexie's), but she did not want a marriage like theirs. "They don't have fun, their romance ended when they had kids… But they do support one another." She contrasted them with her grandparents who she said were "a cute, affectionate couple." I took this as a sign of her hope that her own future might hold more promise.

Kelly began to try out some new experiences with her friends, including some drinking at parties. She was conflicted about this and I shared my thought that it was a way to keep away loneliness as she moved away from her family without yet having an intimate relationship of her own. I said she was "in between" and that her friends helped but were not yet enough to fulfill her longings. Her response to what I intended as a helpful clarification was, "I didn't understand a thing you said." She also brushed away my thought that there was always some kind of excitement that protected her family members from difficult feelings.

There was soon an example, however, that illustrated my point. I received a call from an upset Kelly on a Friday night. "My parents are driving me crazy." Her parents had planned a holiday trip without consulting the rest of the family. Kelly eagerly went online to purchase tickets to a concert at their destination. Again, without consulting the kids, the parents concluded they were not interested enough in the plan and they cancelled the reservations. Kelly and her brother were sorely disappointed. Then the plan was on again! Her father actually purchased tickets to a concert he thought all would enjoy and announced the news. Kelly was beginning to recognize a pattern of misattunement and crazy-making that characterized her childhood.

The family went on the excursion but on her return, Kelly told me that Brandon had spoiled the trip by misbehaving and fighting with their parents. "Fuck got said a lot!" She shared that she and Brandon had shared a room and said it bothered her that he had made a comment about how her breasts looked in a new outfit. I told her that I had a thought I would like to share but realized it might be difficult for her to hear it. She indicated that I should go ahead and I proceeded in a halting way to say that I thought she was letting us know that Brandon was having feelings in relation to her that we could try to understand.

Kelly reacted with shock to this second approach to an interpretation. "Are you suggesting incest? Next thing you'll say is that I want to sleep with my father!" (I had never brought up either of these ideas to her.) Her extreme upset lasted for weeks and I was fearful that I might have so breached her defenses that the analysis was threatened. At the same time, I was aware of how exaggerated her resistance was. To my chagrin, she told her family and friends what I had said and reported that they all felt I had made a mistake. She accused *me* of procrastinating so that I could keep her in treatment to talk about things she did not want to speak of.

Gradually she was able to settle down and began to report dreams again. The first was like many she had before: She had a baby.... two babies, a boy and a girl.... she had not had sex and the birth was easy. She returned to thoughts about her parents, saying she liked her father better when he was not with her mother. "He's like a girl, whipped." She asked him at one point, "Why do you let her do this to you?" She asked me sincerely, "Do you think my mother gets more upset, more often than other people?" She noticed that her mother was out-of-touch with current events and other kinds of common knowledge. For the first time she could admit that she thought she was smarter than her mother.

She told me that Randy had confided in her that he thought girls did not see him as "romantic material." "I can relate," she said ruefully. "Boys look at me and say 'Yuck!'" Her friends were having co-ed sleepovers, with several teens piling into one bed. At one point, after she ended up in the same bed with a friend of her brother, Brandon told her, "Now I know how you felt about Lexie flirting with me." I let this go, feeling too cautious, too reluctant to explore it any further, lest her resistance return in full force.

A shift in the relationship between Kelly and Lexie became apparent in the second half of their junior year. Kelly began to reveal that others in the friend group did not like Lexie and she began to point out ways in which she was always drawing attention to herself. After many months of keeping this secret, she let me know that she herself had a crush on Jack, a new member of the friend group. She brought many details about his gallant comments and treatment of her that gave her hints that he reciprocated her feelings. Characteristically, she did not take much of an active part in response to his overtures and she could verbalize her desire to be the pursued one. She perceived hints that Jack was going to ask her to a big school dance and was over the moon in anticipation. She was taken completely by surprise when, instead, Jack asked Lexie to be his date for the dance. She was deeply humiliated and told me that she had "zero self-esteem in any area." She could not bring herself to talk to Lexie about the situation, avoiding her at school and refusing to answer her calls. Lexie was more concerned to lose her friendship with Kelly than she was interested in dating Jack at this time. In the end, the two girls went out together on the night of the dance, retreating to a same-sexed twosome rather than competing in an oedipal triangle. After several weeks passed, Kelly claimed that she could tell she no longer had any feelings for Jack. She sought to prove this to herself by joining a kissing and disrobing game after drinking at a party. Afterwards, she reported a dream: "No one was paying attention to me."

During the summer between her junior and senior year, Kelly worked as a tutor for children with learning disabilities. Lexie and many of her other friends were away for the summer and she lamented that it felt like everyone was "dying or going away forever." When it came time to say goodbye to her students, she realized that she was trying to play on the emotions of one particularly remote girl so that she would express sadness about their impending separation. She told me poignantly "If you help, and they get better, you get left." (Something I knew well from my own experience as an analyst.) She and I were both aware that we would be saying our own goodbye over the year ahead.

She found her diaries from elementary school and wanted to tell me about what she had written so many years before. She said that she had really wanted a boyfriend, even back then, and was preoccupied with who liked who. She wrote about having a crush on a male teacher and being surprised to see him kiss a female co-worker. She said she had been very angry at her parents and did not like them. She noticed entries about her mother's hard time letting her grow up, something we had done much work on in our years together. In the present she began to talk about how her mother habitually refused to give her things she asked for, such as certain foods, then undid this by giving her too much of the wrong thing.

During that summer her parents celebrated their 20th wedding anniversary. Kelly acknowledged the value of this milestone in her comment, "I hope I'll be married that long." A softening appeared in her view of them when she admitted that her mom could be fun to be around and that her dad was "cool in his own way." She still denied they were sexually attracted to one another anymore, adding, "If they are, I don't want to know about it." She admitted that she and Brandon sometimes talked about this and said she felt sorry for her father for marrying someone who was "gorgeous" but then got old and out-of-shape. She returned to the contents of her diaries and asked, "Why do you think I have low self-esteem?" I asked her ideas about this and she said that she thought it had to do with boys not paying attention to her. She recalled middle school dances when no one asked her to dance. To myself I wondered how this might have been a displacement from feeling that neither her mother nor her father had paid sufficient attention to her and her needs from infancy through her oedipal development. Now she was resigned to the fact that "romance is still in the distance for me."

On Kelly's first day back after the August analytic break, she told me that her mother was driving her crazy. "She does too much that I don't need her to do." By contrast, she said her dad was more fun and had taken her on a college visit to a school she had fallen in love with. Almost as an afterthought she said that Jack and Lexie were "a thing" now, though she underscored that they never wanted to spend any time alone together. She, Lexie, and Jack spent a lot of time together as a threesome and Kelly denied any emotions about the situation.

Her anger and even murderous feelings, however, appeared in a dream she described as "the worst ever." In it her father and her brother stabbed her paternal grandmother, then her brother shot and killed her. In associating she said, "I could understand if it were my mother." "She's sucking the air out of me." She complained in her sessions that her mother was keeping secrets and leaving her out. She, in turn, infuriated her mother by excluding her from activities they formerly enjoyed together. She and her friends had a game "Marry, Fuck, Kill" that required each to say who they would like to do these things to. She also reported that several people in the group were using each other as "friends with [sexual] benefits." She described this as both "disgusting," and "incestuous."

Kelly and her close friend Randy talked about their mutual despair about their love life. He said she was the girl he would be most attracted to and best suited to, if they were not such close friends. She said people envied them their closeness. Like Kelly, Randy felt neither his family nor his friends saw him and valued him as he really was. After she remarked to me that he looked cute that day, I wondered with her whether there was something more developing between them; she said no. Since neither had a date, the two decided to go to their senior Homecoming dance together. Once again, it was disappointing and any hope she might have had about Randy was dashed when he told her he really liked another girl. He did offer her some advice, however, that she took to heart and brought for us to think about. He said she did not tell him how she really felt about things and she did not let other people "touch her" emotionally.

Her anger shifted from her mother to Lexie, then to me whenever I questioned her reactions to Lexie and Jack. She said, "I've decided not to tell you stuff about things you don't understand." She accused me of not liking Lexie, projecting her own negative feelings to me as she had done to her mother earlier. Previously in her analysis we had focused a great deal on her difficulty with anger and ambivalence, her conflicts over loving and hating the same person, and her fear that her angry wishes to get rid of someone could come true. Any insights she might have gained from that work went out the window now and she insisted that I was being mean.

As Kelly's 18th birthday approached, she became more reflective. She said she would like to know the future. "Will I find someone to love? No.... will I find someone to love me?" (Her words reminded me of the last scene in the movie *Rebel Without a Cause* when Judy says to Jim, "All my life, I've been waiting for someone to love me, and now I love someone. It's so easy now. Why is it so easy?" Kelly's distress was not yet eased as she found herself longing to love and be loved, but still had no one to give and receive love.) Her birthday wishes were for a boyfriend and to get into the college she liked.

She went to a college party and made out with an older guy, which brought her a little reassurance that she was not as "hideous" as she feared. For the first time she could talk more directly about her own sexual sensations and desires, but she felt anxious and unsure of herself. All of this, along with the parents' recollections, led us to a reconstruction of her early experiences as a baby and toddler, when her mother was devoted but anxious in her emotional responses and handling of Kelly's body. Later, her lack of confidence and disgust around diapering and toilet mastery contributed to Kelly feeling messy and incompetent. We talked about the need to rework feelings of disgust about her genitals in order to integrate them as a source of sexual pleasure. Kelly recalled being abruptly denied access to her parents' bed (on the advice of an analyst) as a preschooler, leaving her feeling deprived, left out, and as though she had done something wrong. She spoke with her parents who confirmed how things had been and added details. She found this work extremely helpful.

Slowly she could begin to admit that she was envious of Lexie for having a boyfriend and to complain that Lexie and Jack were "annoying" because they did not want to do things with the group of friends. She began one session by saying that Lexie was acting weird. She had borrowed a book and had not returned it by the time Kelly needed it for a test. Kelly tracked her down at Jack's house, went there, and brusquely reclaimed the book. She said Lexie was acting funny "but she didn't talk to me, so I didn't talk to her." According to Randy, Lexie said Kelly had walked away from her. When I tried to see what we could understand about her envy, left out feelings, and unkind treatment of Lexie she brushed me off, "Let's get back to me being messed up as a baby."

During this time in the analysis there were frequent jumps to the past to avoid anxiety in some present circumstance, from her original oedipal objects to the triangle with Jack and Lexie, from sibling dynamics between her and Brandon to excitement with Randy, and from oedipal level conflicts to preoedipal ones. At times Kelly's accounts were tedious. Certainly there was nothing particularly unique about her adolescent trials and tribulations, but I believe that bearing witness to them, hearing them with the ear of an analyst, addressing the conflicts that seemed most salient and available to explore, allowed her to gain insights and move ahead. There was evidence that some internal adjustments were underway. For one thing, her relationship with Brandon was improving and becoming more neutral. She and her mother went to visit her first-choice college and had fun together on the trip. She noticed that Lexie's parents were not helping her with the process of applying to college and she could appreciate the support her own parents were offering her, their troubles notwithstanding.

Kelly was more able to focus on her inner life after learning of her college acceptance. I could share my idea that her obsessive self-criticisms sometimes served both as companions when lonely and as masturbatory substitutes. She and Lexie expressed "sexual frustration" to one another, but Kelly was inhibited about exploring how she might give herself pleasure. She did tell me of her fantasy of being able to enchant and have power over an imagined admirer. Intrusive, persecutory thoughts revolved around herself as the ugly sidekick to a fancy girl. Any ideas about mutuality and reciprocity in love relations were notably absent in this phallic reverie. This ushered in new work on what being the center of attention signified to her.

She observed that she had a pattern of surrounding herself with extroverts, like an old girlfriend who made everything "all about her." She noticed some similarities between her mother and Lexie drawing attention to themselves, along with her own pattern of letting herself fade into the background. She was thinking about our approaching termination and was determined to work on this before our goodbye.

Over a long weekend, Kelly went to visit the "all about her" friend at her college. She went to a party and tried not to be so shy, but later she was left alone in the dorm when her friend went to her boyfriend's room. Lexie had told her that she would be available if needed, but Kelly tried to reach her numerous times throughout the night without success. She did not let herself know this might be a clue that Lexie and Jack were together and she told me it was "no big deal." Soon afterwards, however, she found out that Lexie and Jack were having sex. She initially said it made her feel "young," seeming to mean virginal and naïve, then reported a dream in which she was being accused of murder. A secondary revision was that the judge was a lesbian, suggesting she felt betrayed in both negative and positive oedipal positions.

Her anger at Lexie grew and she became quite vindictive. There was a confrontation with Kelly and Randy when they saw Lexie's car at Jack's house, after she had told them she could not go out with them one night. In their shared agitation, Randy expressed an urge to kiss Kelly and told her he had dreamed of having sex with her. This made her anxious and excited in equal parts. She was puzzled about why she did not dream about sex herself and shared that Lexie, who had a history of trauma, talked about incestuous dreams of sex with family members. Lexie's description of sex as painful reinforced Kelly's fears of penetration and ideas that sex was violent. Kelly's own fantasy was of lying in bed with Randy, staring into each other's eyes. She said that she used to think kissing Randy would be like kissing her brother but not anymore. She only wanted to kiss, though, anything else would feel "too weird."

For a short time, Jack and Lexie were matchmakers for Kelly and Randy. Kelly's hopes were raised about the possibility of the two of them going to the senior spring dance together, not just as friends this time. She did not take any lead in this, saying she did not like to chase people. The pair spent a lot of time together engaging in silly pranks and mischief. She had one dream of being in Randy's family and another one in which "a father has died." These seemed to reflect further psychic work on disentangling her libidinal ties from the past to make room for new ones in the future. Once again, like the year before when Kelly's dance hopes were dashed by Jack, she was disappointed. Randy asked a girl he had long liked to the dance and she accepted. Apparently there was some behind-the-scenes maneuvering among the friends with the result that another boy invited Kelly. She was happy to have a date, if not a boyfriend, and made the best of the event, actually ending up feeling pretty and enjoying herself.

Kelly had gradually started doing things with others outside the circle of her closest friends, moving away from the conflicts and regressive pull they represented. She was involved in school activities and was interested in people who were headed to colleges similar to the one she had chosen. She learned one girl was going to the same school and they bonded around this shared future. She noticed that these other kids' parents were fun to be around and reflected sadly that she did not think her parents were especially happy together in contrast. She talked about her wish that her mother would be able to find interesting and rewarding things to do with her talents after all her children were more independent. She saw how her father had hobbies and was successful in his career. She was more able to see qualities in each of them which she wanted to emulate.

Soon after we had determined the actual date for her last session, she brought a dream: You were in it. It was in your house, but smaller than this one. I was helping you with other kids. (I was struck by its similarity to my dream about her in my home the year before.) The dream expressed her identification with me as someone who helps children, but it also showed me in some ways diminished – the smaller house – no longer as much of an idealized or enviable woman as in the past but more an adult role model.

Kelly warded off the sadness she was feeling about all the goodbyes she was facing as her senior year ended and only slowly came to be able to talk with me about it. It was easier to leave everyone behind if she felt angry. We worked on this and she could acknowledge that it was hard to imagine what it was going to be like "without you being present." She realized that she was going to miss Lexie and her mother, as well as me. As her last session approached she said, "You're a staple, like milk." She was well aware that I was sad too, but I told her I thought she was ready for solid food and she agreed. One of her last reflections was, "I wish I knew when I'll get married. Can I let you know?"

COMMENTARY 1

"The music is not in the notes, but in the silence between." Mozart

…. "Certainly there was nothing particularly unique about her adolescent trials and tribulations," says the analyst about Kelly, a high school senior who struggles with "extremely low self-esteem and lack of confidence in herself." This comment brought to mind a conversation with my supervisor from a long time ago. I asked him: if everyone has unresolved oedipal and attachment issues, how come people are so different? He said: "It is all about nuances: think about ripples on the water – same water and light, but their different combinations make for unique ripples." With time I came to appreciate that psychoanalysis, by virtue of being a creative process, is a treatment best suited for helping our patients discover and expand their "ripples." Whether it is the analysis of a child, an adolescent, or an adult, the patient and the analyst are using their analytic playground to toss ideas around. Each session has a potential for a surprise; it is an irreproducible creation of the analytic couple. When surprise is gone from analytic work the boredom sets in; it frequently indicates that the patient and the analyst are participating in an enactment. Perhaps it is not an accident that the feeling that transpired in Kelly's dream ("no one was paying attention to me") fits so well with her analyst's comment.

The author introduced the paper by talking about the role of displacement in the treatment of adolescents and specifically in the clinical work that was about to be shared with us. The analyst explained that "although transference, countertransference and enactments all served to further [their] analytic understanding, frequently the work revealed itself through displacements to goings on with her friends." Work in displacement is an integral part of the psychoanalytic technique, particularly in the child and adolescent treatment. It is a useful tool helping patients manage the intensity of transferential feelings that exceeds their capacity for containing and verbalizing. The transition from working in the displacement to working in the transference happens gradually as patient's affective tolerance and capacity for symbolization improve. During this process the focus of the exploration shifts from the manifest content of the analytic material to the latent and the transference intensifies in parallel with the patient's growing ability to tolerate this intensity. As analysis progresses, direct work in the transference with all the "sound and fury" comes to play the central role in the treatment. The shared experience and exploration of the feelings that have been brought to the fore render the work of the analytic couple transformative.

Patients who use reality as their primary defense need a longer period of work in the displacement. Their thinking is concrete; they have to develop capacity to use their imagination and think metaphorically. These patients are incapable of playing with an idea; it is about them that Winnicott said "the work done by the therapist is directed toward bringing the patient from a state of not being able to play into a state of being able to play" (Winnicott 1971, p.38). The focus on the events rather than a complex emotional experience attached to these events can serve as an invitation for the analyst to limit the analytic work to the manifest content of the associations. This shift is subtle: the patient and the analyst may become involved in an enactment with both participants sailing smoothly through the sessions, not being aware of the tinge of emotional flatness or formulaic quality of some interventions. If this is the case, patient's ability to "digest" their feelings and their symbolizing and mentalizing capacities have little opportunity for growth, and formation of the observing ego and self-analyzing function become stalled.

Let's return to Kelly and her analysis. One striking feature of the clinical material presented in the paper is Kelly's lack of curiosity about herself. Kelly is relentlessly factual; she goes in great detail describing the actions and sometimes feelings that took place between her and her friends or her and her parents without using this material as a bridge to her inner world. Kelly's creative capacities remain untapped: we rarely hear Kelly reflecting on her thoughts; her descriptions of people and relationships are rather concrete and unnuanced as if her speech consisted of headlines with the story behind them being left untold. There are ways in which the treatment has been helpful to her: many accurate genetic interpretations have been made during Kelly's treatment, and she gained many insights, but it is hard to see how the analytic couple felt, thought, and played together, or how Kelly's capacity to feel, think and play with her thoughts has been expanded as a result of her analysis. It seems that despite the progress that Kelly has made in other areas of the treatment, she has not developed the instrument for thinking (Ferro and Foresti, 2013) essential for the maintenance of one's mental life.

Kelly's lack of curiosity about herself is multidetermined. Likely it has a lot to do with her perception of herself as "stupid, incompetent, clumsy and a failure." Kelly's friend made an astute observation that she "did not tell how she really felt about things and did not let other people touch her emotionally." Perhaps Kelly feared that she had nothing valuable to offer and hoped to avoid being "discovered" by keeping everyone, including her analyst, at a distance.

In addition to protecting her from narcissistic blows, Kelly's factualness is an overused and inflexible defense against the uncomfortable intensity of her feelings. Kelly's analysis is surprisingly stable – descriptions of missed sessions, self-destructive acting out, affective storms frequently wreaking havoc in the analysis of adolescents are conspicuously absent from the clinical material. Even the interpretation described by the analyst as "untimely and disruptive" seemed to only slightly rock the solid boat of this treatment. Kelly became "extremely upset" and the analyst "was fearful.... that the analysis was threatened," but "gradually Kelly was able to settle down." Sounds rather benign. What is the message that Kelly is communicating by being so consistent and dutiful? Are both the patient and the analyst so invested in preserving stability that they avoid new and unpredictable feelings that may challenge it?

Let me give an example: Kelly's analyst makes a clarification about her "drinking at the parties" as "a way to keep away loneliness as she moved away from her family without yet having an intimate relationship of her own." Kelly immediately rejects it with "I did not understand a thing you said." This response can have many meanings including: "I don't care to understand what you said," or "I am confused and overwhelmed by what you said," or "The connection between us is broken at this moment and until we rebuild it I will not be able to understand you and you will not be able to understand me." Without inquiring about any of these possibilities the analyst offered another insight about her family that Kelly not surprisingly "also brushed away."

This moment had a potential for a surprise; something unspoken that was taking place between Kelly and her analyst could be expressed in words; they might have had a fresh look at their work. If moments like that were unnoticed hidden behind many insights and intellectual discoveries, Kelly's emotions may have been left untouched by her treatment.

Here is another example. After returning from the summer break Kelly declared that "it bothers her mother that she is not around much" and proceeds to describe the mother as "silly, overemotional and rather dense." She complained that "she did not feel that her mother understood her" and observed that "there was always some kind of brouhaha in her family." Kelly was dealing with raw feelings, and the emotional temperature of the session must have been pretty high. The analyst responded by commenting on Kelly's and her brother's contribution to a stirred-up atmosphere at home. Kelly's retort that "her parents did not know how to intervene effectively to contain the excitement" suggests that though factually accurate this intervention has not helped Kelly to modulate her feelings and emotional temperature of the session remained high.

This clinical material can be heard in many different ways, I would like to mention some of them: not knowing how the session unfolded leaves room for imagination.

On the manifest level, Kelly spoke about her very real frustration with her mother, and her analyst responded by bringing to her attention her very real contributions to their fights. I think that Kelly heard her analyst's comment as an accusation of being a troublemaker in her family and defended herself by projecting the blame on her parents. The best outcome of this exchange could have been Kelly recognizing her role in the family discord and modifying her behavior; alternatively, the session could have been spent in throwing blame back and forth, like a hot potato.

Listening to this material in a different way, one could understand it as a reference to the transference: Kelly was wondering what she and her analyst are feeling about having not been around each other much and whether either of them was "bugged" by that. In this case Kelly might have experienced the analyst's comment as a suggestion that she is creating a "stirred-up atmosphere" in their analytic home and responded by complaining that she has not been helped with modulating her feelings.

One could argue that Kelly's analyst missed an opening for the transference interpretation afforded by this exchange. I think that the analyst anticipated that transference interpretation at this moment would overwhelm Kelly's self-regulating capacity and wisely stayed away from it.

Focusing on Kelly's difficulties expressing her inner world, this material can be heard as Kelly talking about her experience of different emotions: frustration, missing and being missed, and a disappointment of not being understood by an older woman who is supposed to be understanding (I am guessing that Kelly's analyst is a female). This approach offers certain advantages: clarifying Kelly's emotions and helping her express them with more nuanced, vivid, and metaphorically rich words would be a step towards the development of symbolization and integration of her feelings.

Whether Kelly heard her analyst's remark as an accusation of being a troublemaker in her family or in her analytic home she has not made use of it. For narcissistically vulnerable patients comments about their behavior easily lend themselves to being interpreted as criticisms and often lead to patients using maladaptive defenses, like projective identification or dissociation, to deal with their rage. Uncoupling Kelly's experience of being frustrated, disappointed, missing and being or not being missed from a concrete interaction with her mother would invite Kelly to reflect on these feelings with the minimal super-ego interference; one cannot be criticized for the way how they are experiencing their feelings. Antonino Ferro (Ferro, 2015) described this process as "de-concretization." For Kelly who used reality as her prevailing defense de-concretization of the factual material could have been particularly helpful. Shared exploration of the quality of feelings, their different shades and colors – an integral part of the process of de-concretization – becomes a fertile ground for discovering and expanding patient's "ripples." We rarely talk about the pleasures attached to even the most painful analytic experience; a pleasure of being creative together is one of them.

There is a beautiful example of an exchange that opened up the analytic space beyond the factual material at the end of the paper. "You are a staple, like milk" said the patient in one of the last sessions before leaving for college. The analyst responded by sharing with Kelly that she thought that Kelly is "ready for solid food." In a pithy way this metaphor allowed Kelly and her analyst to speak about and experience together many feelings associated with the termination of the long treatment. This metaphor is about the growth of the patient and about the analyst's encouragement of this growth. And about the vital importance that the analyst has had for the patient and about the analyst's accepting the reality of becoming only one of many foods, and inviting the patient to the feast at a grown-ups' table. This exchange was lighthearted; the goodbye was bittersweet, as good goodbyes usually are. Importantly, they resonated with each other emotionally: the patient was "well aware" that the analyst "was sad too." It is hard to know how Kelly and her analyst found their way to each other: I don't see any clues to it in the paper. As a reader, I am surprised and gratified to discover that they did and that the analyst and analysis have been instrumental in preparing Kelly for a new developmental step.

COMMENTARY 2

The link between development and loss is present in the vignette "I Get By with a Little Help from my Friends" from the beginning when we are informed that Kelly gave up a competitive sport due to physical changes making it difficult for her to be as successful as she had previously been. This movement away from 'being seen' as successful is coupled with her retreat from success through procrastination in other areas of her life. Procrastination is often associated with a fear of success when ambitions are viewed as an expression of hostility (Horney, 2007, Miller, 1994). Kelly's view of her mother as dominant over her father "it's not like he is the man in the family," and her father as overly passive, "he is like a girl, whipped" is in part suggestive of her concern that to be successful in a relationship is to subjugate the other, or be subjugated. Similarly, Kelly's dream about getting pregnant without having sex can be viewed as an expression of both her fear of becoming a sexually competitive woman and her wish to be a successfully creative woman. The vignette indicates that this dream begins to take on more realistic features first through incestuous exchanges within the safety of her family.

With the help of her analyst, Kelly begins to express her competitive feelings along with her wish and fear that it is her mother and not she who is out of control, silly and fearful of her increasing need to physically separate. Her statement that she thinks her mother does not approve of a friend that Kelly views as 'free' to do and feel as she pleases hints at Kelly's concerns about her own difficulty remaining calm as pubertal changes and the press for physical and sexual maturation take hold.

Kelly's dream in which she says, "I don't want to die…. I want to get married!" is interpreted by the analyst as a guilty dream. It also appears to express Kelly's wish to be sexually successful and a movement from a more 'paranoid' position to a more depressive position in which Kelly begins to realize that something is lost as she matures, but she is not yet able to move from the concrete fear that it is either her or her mother who must die. In her article "My Graduation is My Mother's Funeral": Transformation from the Paranoid-Schizoid to the Depressive Position in Fear of Success, and the Role of the Internal Saboteur" (2006) Susan Kavaler-Adler distinguishes neurotic guilt and existential guilt. Neurotic guilt is born out of a defensive process and a fear of retaliation for being successful. Once the fantasy of annihilation is relinquished the individual can achieve more success in their relationships. Existential guilt is "a grief that encompasses object loss within it" and is regarded as a natural developmental achievement (Kavaler-Adler,

2006 p. 118). Existential guilt allows for acceptance of the self and other in a more compassionate way through regret, loss and mourning.

This transition from neurotic guilt to existential guilt is apparent as Kelly transitions from her competitive envy of her brother to her wish to couple in a more intimate, yet not sexual, way with Randy. Although still in denial of her feelings of jealousy and envy Kelly begins to become aware that by denying her sexual longings, she is likely to miss out, possibly die. Although Kelly became furious at her analyst's interpretation of the incestuous feelings between Kelly and her brother, this interpretation assists the push for movement outward from the family to more oedipal longings outside of the family. Kelly's movement toward the 'depressive position' (Kavaler-Adler, 2006) and the beginning of her acceptance and compassion for her mother is demonstrated in Kelly's concern that her mother might be depressed. The analyst interprets the sadness that her mother may have experienced as a means of helping Kelly accept both her mother's and her own feelings of loss and sadness. Kelly also begins to accept her father as a person whom she can turn to in a non-sexualized but intimate relationship. The increased compassion for self and other becomes evident in her acceptance of her wish to be more passionately successful than her parents, and in her wish to be as affectionate as her grandparents. The vignette illustrates the emotional, and cognitive growth that occurs during adolescence if all goes well enough.

EDITORIAL REFLECTIONS

We suggest that most would agree that the developmental goal of adolescence is to transform relationships to self and others and to transform the relationship among the pleasure, reality, and growth principles. There may be less agreement about goals of treatment, however, with some asserting the primacy of achieving a transference neurosis through interpretation of transferences to the analyst, and others espousing restoration to the path of progressive development through applying a variety of techniques.

This chapter, with its description of a period late in Kelly's analysis, when she is in her last years of secondary school, brings us directly into this central issue about both adolescent development and technique in treating adolescents, with the three contributors speaking from differing perspectives on these matters. We hear about changes over time and can consider the various viewpoints articulated about what marks constructive change and constitutes substantive growth in the patient. It is worth noting that this chapter also offers a vivid example of how the same behaviors can have different meanings and serve different functions at various times.

Anna Freud, in her discussion of the relations between child and adult analysis, noted, "Not all the relations established or transferred by a child in analysis are object relations in the sense that the analyst becomes cathected with libido or aggression. Many are due to externalizations, i.e., to processes in which the person of the analyst is used to represent one or the other part of the patient's personality structure." She goes on to say, "To interpret such externalizations in terms of an object relationship within the transference would be a mistake, even though originally all conflicts within the structure have their source in earliest relationships. At the time of therapy, however, their importance lies in the fact that they reveal what happens in the child's inner world, in the relations between his internal agencies, as contrasted with the emotional relationships to objects in the external world." She concludes that section of the paper with the statement, "Understood in this manner, externalization is a sub-species of transference. Treated as such in interpretation and kept separate from transference proper, it is a valuable source of insight into the psychic structure" (1965, pp. 41, 42, 43).

This conceptualization encompasses the different perspectives exemplified in this chapter, and offers renewed understanding of the crucial role of adolescence as a fulcrum in the course of development. During her analysis, Kelly uses displacement to peer relationships sometimes defensively, in flight from feelings concentrated on the analyst and the experience of breaches in her defensive wall, but also as a bridge to a safe space in which to work on, work out, and work through emotions and wishes that were heretofore too hard to manage and regulate. She moves from a sadomasochistic mode of relating to more realistic engagement with herself and others. Kelly's growing capacity to see her parents' virtues and flaws (as well as her analyst's?) parallels her shift to newer friends who actually share her interests.

In considering varieties of transference manifestations in adolescent patients, we might also ask whether it is useful to parse the analyst's reactions or countertransferences. Are Kelly's analyst's dream of the patient in her kitchen, or the thought of the patient having amorous fantasies of the analyst's son, manifestations of countertransference per se, or do they represent a kind of parallel process, symbolic acts of empathy? Could they represent the shared operation of defenses against anxiety over the inevitable passage of time that leads to growing up – was the analyst seeing Kelly as a youngster needing nurturance in her house a parallel to Kelly's procrastination, an effort to put things on hold and stop time, sexuality, and separateness? Are there specific counter-reactions and/or countertransferences to adolescents? Do analysts dream more often of adolescent patients than younger ones? Do they somehow get inside us more?

This chapter underscores the validity and possibility of analysis as the treatment of choice, indeed, all the contributors agreed that Kelly needed and benefited from the work from early adolescence into emerging adulthood. We are left with the challenge, however, of defining what is normative for adolescents, whether the 'sturm und drang' of passionate transferences represent an ordinary and expectable developmental course or, alternatively, indicate the presence of pathology which, analyzed faithfully over time, as

Kelly and her analyst were able to do, yield to the real pleasures of relations with peers and transformed parent-child interactions.

CHAPTER 13

JIM – age 17

Jim is a young man of 17. The first time I hear about him is when his mother gives me a phone call. She tells me that she and her husband, Jim's father, are worried about their son. Jim has always been an active and quick-witted boy, she says, but lately he has been more and more listless. He does not go to school and he is losing touch with his schoolmates. Most of the time he stays at home in his room, listening to music or sometimes painting pictures. I offer an appointment to all three of them, Jim, his mother and his father.

First meeting

Jim and mother come to the first meeting. He is a tall, lanky boy. His fair hair is medium-long; it covers part of his face. He settles himself loosely in an armchair and looks around. Little by little he takes in the room. After a while he gives me a searching look, as though he wants to sit on the fence a little longer with regard to me. He smiles a little and fiddles at a clasp on the leg of his pants.

His mother is the first one to speak. She is a rather small, well-dressed woman with quick movements and a candid look. She looks grave and worried. She explains that father could not come; he is busy in his work.

She tells me that Jim nowadays does not go to school; he stays in his room all day long. His parents are worried that he misses school but even more worried that he is isolating himself from his schoolmates and from social life in general. His mother doesn't know what he does in his room. She knows that young people can spend hours at the computer, playing games and chatting on the Internet but she doesn't think Jim is doing such things. Jim shakes his head. No, all that computer stuff is of no great interest to him. His mother says that Jim is gifted in many ways; he is also very good at painting. She thinks he paints most of the time and listens to music. Jim nods. Yes, he paints a lot, but his paints are not very good he says. He wants some other kind of tools. Jim sounds sad and a bit whiney.

I say he sounds worried. I wonder how he is thinking. He looks at me. He seems a bit confused as if he is realizing for the first time that I am somehow connected to the conversation. He goes on with his negative comments about how his paintings are not really good. I ask him what he can do about it.

–Nothing.
–What do you do, then?
–I lie down on my bed.

We talk about how this doesn't seem to help; everything seems to be too much for him. After a while he adds that he sometimes thinks nothing matters anyway. I say he seems to have lots of problems, and they sometimes grow to be such a huge burden that he cannot stand it. So, there is nothing else to do but lie down on his bed. He nods and for the first time he becomes alert in his speech and his expressions. He says yes, that's the way it is, he can't stand it and then nothing matters.

Now I also get some information about the family and Jim's history from his mother. When Jim was younger, he was quick-witted and lively. His mother describes his early development as being without problems, but she does mention that he was more tied to her than his older brother was. His brother has always had more of a drive in him. When they had parties in the family his brother talked to everybody while Jim kept to his mother. When he started school at 7, he was a bit shy. He took a great interest in sports and played on a soccer team. When he was 12–13 his interest waned. He could be afraid of the ball and afraid of going on offense. At this time, he got several infections and had to stay home from school for long periods. He had no difficulties catching up on his schoolwork but felt left out of the team. He gave up on sports. His mother says that from this time onward she and her husband noticed that Jim was more uptight and reserved.

This semester Jim hasn't gone to school at all. After some weeks he gave it up and he has been at home for three months now. Maybe Jim could drop out of school officially and get a job. Jim and his parents have been talking about this idea but it is not easy for a boy of 17 to find a job. It is obvious that his mother is the one making a project of this. She looks at job ads on the Internet and gives her suggestions to Jim before she goes to work in the morning. When I ask what happens then, Jim answers with a hint of a smile that sometimes he checks the ads but mostly he stays in bed.

I say:

–Yes, you stay in bed and nothing matters. That sounds like a gloomy life. Perhaps you sometimes wonder how things could turn out this way.
Jim looks at me:
–Sometimes, yes.
After a while he adds:
–But then I lie down again.

At the end of our meeting Jim agrees to come and see me again. He also says that he wants to come alone. We decide that the contact will be between Jim and me and that when I have contact with the parents, Jim will be informed or join the meeting.

There was some liveliness in Jim's eyes when I expressed my understanding how his problems grow to be a burden he cannot stand. I also caught a glimpse of interest when I talked about how things could turn out this way. But very soon he passed on to his passive, dejected attitude: "But then I lie down again."

When Jim was 12 something changed. Puberty entered. His father seems not to have been present, it was mother and him. The drives threaten to overwhelm him. Maybe he got scared and regression was a way out. It is as if there is something wrong with him. He says that he has got the wrong colors. I get the idea that he wants to get out of his passivity, his depression, and he wants to put color, other colors to his world.

Analysis begins

Jim shows up for our first appointment. He says he might as well come to see me since he has nothing else to do. Besides, he adds, he enjoys riding the subway. (He must go by subway to get to my office.) He lets me know that he is going on with his passive way of life. He doesn't want to have a fixed schedule of appointments. For almost two months we have a kind of agreement to meet "one at a time." At every meeting we decide on the date for the next.

After some time, Jim finds it too complicated to keep making new appointments so he suggests: "That time at eleven is OK, it suits me. It gives me time to wake up and get going." So, we settle the arrangements and before long we have agreed on 4 sessions a week.

The sessions are slow with long silences. Often, he comes five minutes late to his appointments. He walks into the room with tardy steps and settles himself in his chair with his outdoor clothes on. He puts the hood on his coat over his head. He looks tired and gloomy. He always has these explanations for coming late: I slept, the subway was late, mum didn't wake me up etc. And I feel left out. He doesn't tell me about his thoughts; he just says, "I am tired." I also feel affection for him. Here he sits, looking like a small boy, somewhat shabby, tired. Suddenly Jim moves in his chair. He puts down his hood, shakes his head a little and makes it more comfortable. He says:

– This music is really good.
And he picks up his mobile and gives me the headphones. We talk about the music he listened to last night.

After some time, Jim tells me about his painting, especially his graffiti-painting. He brings his pad and shows me his sketches. They are non-figurative pictures in bright colors, which do not reflect much of his usual listlessness and heaviness. Many pictures consist of his own tag, his initials, three letters hidden in different patterns. Jim tells me enthusiastically about different tags and how he develops them. This is the first time I see him so animated and even excited.

Jim tells me more about his graffiti-painting. Now he tells me that he has come into contact with some guys, most of them older than he is. They often spend their nights in the subway or at the depot for subway trains painting graffiti on the trains. I now come to hear about a new part of Jim: a Jim full of life, active – and antisocial. In my countertransference I get into a dilemma. I have a patient who is involved in illegal activities. The risks are several. One risk is that I ally myself with him, somewhat exciting. And I can feel the allurement. Jim tells me that graffiti-painting is not really a crime. That standpoint is "merely Society's" and it is "narrow-minded." Painting is, after all, an art and he is, he informs me, one of the best graffiti-painters in the group. Another risk is that I moralize and threaten to report him. And then I don't know if I would have a patient anymore.

I do not compromise in stressing that what he is doing is a crime. I tell him so; he knows my standpoint. I also stress that this situation needs to be further investigated. To be sure, we have a moral and ethical dilemma but also a dilemma of quite a different kind, in relation to me in the transference.

Graffiti-pictures contain something very personal, the painter's own distinguishing-mark, and his initials. Jim's tags are made up of his own initials, shaped beyond recognition. They are ornamented in the picture and he can triumph. It is as if he is saying: "Ha, I am tricking you, you have my initials right under your nose and you can't see them." Jim's identity is woven into the picture. His identity at night is as a member of a criminal gang. In this gang he is somebody. This is a hidden identity but also an attack on his family, a seemingly well-functioning family. At the same time, he is looking for himself. He is to be found in the pictures but only by those who know his secret. There is also another secret, unknown to him. We will return to this.

Jim develops his graffiti-painting at night with his gang. This activity starts after some months in analysis. I see it as a plain acting out in the analysis and I look upon this acting out as a part of transference. There is a problem, though, since his acting out takes place outside the analytic setting. Other people can be involved, such as parents, police, and social authorities as well as society in general. I didn't talk to his parents about his illegal activities. I had two reasons; first, I think I would have lost my patient and second, his acting out was directed towards me in the transference and we had to work with it there.

After six months

This session comes after 6 months of analysis. Jim has been involved in illegal graffiti-painting for some time. Jim rushes into my room. He throws his bag in a corner and plunges into his armchair.

–Damn it! They busted me. Those assholes from the Falcons got me!
I wonder what's going on.
–They busted me. Oh, how could it happen? It's crazy!

He tells me the whole story. The past weekend he had been out with his gang, painting graffiti on trains and in the subway. They went out at night and painted on a train on a siding. They knew that the guards from the Falcons, a security guard company with a night patrol, could come at any moment, so they worked fast. One of them painted with the spray can and the others kept watch. Suddenly one of them gave the signal and they had to run. Jim and another guy took the cans in a bag and ran away. At two o'clock in the morning they were standing at the bus stop when the Falcons came by in their car. The guard patrol slowed down. Jim and his friend quickly threw the bag with spray cans into the bushes. But they were caught, the spray cans were found by the guards' dogs and the guards noticed paint on their hands and clothes. Jim is angry, upset and curses those "damned Falcons snooping about everywhere."

Now we have quite a new situation. Jim has been discovered; the Falcons have caught him more or less red-handed. When he speaks to me of this turn of events, Jim doesn't acknowledge his own responsibility. The guilt-feeling is split off. The Falcons are the guilty ones. He is the good one, the graffiti-painter, the artist. He is not the one doing something aggressive or destructive, no, the Falcons are! Those Falcons with their dogs are snooping about everywhere.

We talk more about what happened the night before and I ask:

–What did you think there in the middle of the night at the bus-stop?
–Think? What do you mean, what did I think?
He sounds irritated.
–Did you know that the Falcons were on their way?

331

–Yes, but . . .

He is silent for a moment.

–What the hell, we always get away. They were out last week and then there was no trouble. That time we made it.

–But not this time?

–No.

Silence.

–What are you thinking about?

He shrugs his shoulders.

I continue:

–So there you sat at the bus-stop waiting. And no bus came. You waited and who came instead? The Falcons and their dogs! What a thing!

Jim looks at me and suddenly he begins to laugh.

–My God! There we sat so fucking stupid. We were sitting ducks for those assholes! Wow, how could we be such idiots!

When I recall the situation in a dramatized way, Jim bursts out laughing, and the tension is released. After this laughter, I say to Jim:

–It is as if you yourself saw to it that you got caught.

Jim nods.

–Yes, it's crazy, completely crazy.

When Jim sees to it that he gets caught, he has been in analysis for half a year. It took him until now to feel safe enough to let himself be seen. When I help him to see the part he is playing, he is shaken. Now there is a space that allows us a closer look at him and at what he has done.

Now Jim's double life, where he has one life in the daytime and a secret one at night can be unmasked. At the beginning of analysis Jim was depressed, listless and withdrawn. He lay on his bed most of the time and the regression was obvious. During the first period of analysis his graffiti-painting increased, and he started painting subway-trains together with his pals. He could maintain a split between day life and night life. But now after half a year of analysis he was seeing to it that he gets caught, he brings the two worlds together. In this way, he also becomes visible.

We also come upon questions about morality and guilt, about crime and punishment. Here we can talk about something that sounds like a paradox. One can say that the guilt is in the intention rather than in the action. The crime becomes the result of guilt rather than the contrary. Freud makes this connection clear when he speaks about guilt leading to criminality, leading to punishment, leading to relief. To commit a crime is to unconsciously make the guilt-feeling comprehensible.

Jim continues with his graffiti in the subway. One session he comes and sits down in his chair, smiling a bit mysterious.

–Yesterday I was out all night.

–Hmm, doing graffiti as usual?

–Yes, I used the tag I showed you last week. It looks fabulous. I've been working on it for a long time, but this was the first time I painted it on the wall. Wow, what a kick it gave me to see it so big!

–You painted on the wall?

His mysterious look returns.

–Yes, this tag looks best on the wall, not on a train. The colors come out best that way. It's awesome! You can see it if you want.

–What do you mean?

–You can see it in the underground station. It's right around here.

–Around here?

–Yes, here! Just around the corner.

–You mean you have been painting here in my station?

–Yes, I saw it when I arrived just now. Smashing! You can have a look, too, if you want.

I am a bit taken aback by this information. Lots of thoughts whirl around in my head. At first, I feel an excitement; there he was at my station in the middle of the night spray-painting his initials. I also feel some repudiation as if he has been intrusive, penetrating me. I look at him. He sits there observing me closely. He looks eager and expectant. I say:

–I see. So, you have been doing your graffiti-painting in my subway station. What do you think about that?
–Think, think, that's what you say over and over again. For Christ's sake! This is not about thinking, this is action, real action. Don't you see? You never understand anything! You're just too …
He throws his arms about and shows that he is quite upset.
–Well, I can see it is about action, yes, it is. You are quite right about that.
There is a silence. We look squarely at each other.
He says:
–Well, you can look at it if you want.
–There's hardly a chance I'll miss it, is there?
–No.
He gives me a grim smile.
–So, it has something to do with me? I mean painting your tag here near my office?
–Well, perhaps.
–I think you want to tell me something by doing this.
–I just paint, that's all.
–Yes, but this time you painted so I wouldn't miss it.
–Uh-huh.

–OK. Perhaps you want to show me something. You want to say, look what I've been doing, what I have created. Often you show me your tags as sketches but this time…

He fills in:

–This time it's for real.

–Yes. And this time you really want to crash into my place.

Next session Jim tells me that they have wiped out his tags in the subway. He says:

– They are crazy. These were the best I've ever done. The others were much more childish. But these were really good. They don't understand anything.

–So, you think they don't understand your paintings.

After a while I add:

– Maybe you think that I don't understand or appreciate your paintings.

– Well, I think you saw my tags, but…

– But perhaps you have expected something more. I mean, you get my attention, my interest and you know that I care. But sometimes that isn't enough; you would like something more. And then you get disappointed.

I add:

–I think you get disappointed when you see that what you are making does not hold. It can be wiped out just like that! And you are not a child anymore, you don't want to be ignored. You want to create something that lasts.

Jim's acting out is full of different meanings. It is an aggressive attack on me but there is also a libidinal sexual meaning to it. He wants to spray-paint my walls. He wants to come into me and leave his mark. We have touched upon the moral problem that I have a patient engaged in illegal activities.

But there is another side of the coin. When Jim tells me about his raids in the night, he wants to pull me into an exciting game. He is quite fired up when he describes the tension and thrill as he and his gang stand there painting rapidly before the Falcons start to hunt them. In transference Jim is acting out his infantile desires. It is as if he is saying: I hate/love you mother-analyst! His guilt emanates from this forbidden incestuous love. Right here we get the opportunity to work with it in the transference.

COMMENTARY 1

In clinical work over the years, I have become especially interested in trying to help therapists and patients be curious about their patients and themselves: childhood antecedents, current feelings and actions, dynamics, and so on. This is in order to enhance self-reflection and self-understanding in their patients and in themselves (e.g., How did you feel? Wounded? And then angry? What did the anger feel like, in your mind and body? What did you do? What were your actions? What did it remind you of? Was I involved somehow?).

As we know from the existence of a multitude of clinical perspectives and uniqueness of individuals, there may be many ways to skin a cat – and this multiplicity is related to the distinctive capacities and character structures of both the therapist and the patient. Given this, establishing a self-analytic function, a capacity for introspection, becomes crucial – in both patient and therapist. I mention the above because this case of 17-year-old Jim strikes me as quite intriguing on a number of levels, and much of my response will be in the form of curiosity and questions.

Let me first start with a brief overall remark of the process of the analysis, and then I will discuss some specific areas of content.

With respect to the overall process: The analyst (gender? sexual identity?) seems to establish a relationship with mother and Jim fairly readily. Jim agrees to see the analyst and soon is meeting four sessions a week. From this beginning phase, an alliance appears to develop. Jim seems slowly but increasingly trusting of and attached to the analyst, and the analyst is able to help Jim become more curious and introspective about his actions and internal world. The analysis seems to move into a middle phase with increased openness and transference material.

Turning now to some reflections on content, the focus will be on three aspects – the initial assessment phase; the beginning and next months of the analysis; and the episode of Jim's graffiti-bust.

With respect to the initial assessment phase, more information would be useful (and perhaps the analyst obtained it but did not report it in this write-up). I think gathering information would help ascertain if analysis is the best treatment option for Jim at this point, and I do not believe it would impair the beginning of an analytic process. I would want to know information about: the depth of Jim's current regression and depression; was he suicidal or cutting/hurting himself; any evidence of psychosis or schizophrenia, drug/alcohol use or illegal actions/trouble with the law; any physical problems or medications considered or tried; the nature of his changes at about 12 years old and puberty, e.g., sexual identity issues; his developmental history and childhood antecedents. Granted, much of this will emerge in the course of the analysis, but some of this information may be important to know in the beginning re treatment options.

Another important area for consideration in this initial phase concerns the work with the parents. Structured involvement of the parents in the analysis of adolescents can be a tremendous benefit (e.g., Novick & Novick, 2005; Novick, et al., 2020). The analyst writes that "when I have contact with the parents, Jim will be informed or join the meeting" – were there such meetings? Much of child and adolescent pathology can be understood via the character structures of the parents and their interactions with their children. Therefore, work with both parents could help one better understand Jim's relationships and internal world. Such work can also enhance understandings of Jim's internalizations and identifications with his parents, as well as areas of distortions and empathy in the parent-child interactions. In addition, the parent work often has a very positive impact on the parents' pathology, with consequent benefits for the child. Finally, the transferences and countertransferences involved in the parents-analyst interactions can be very useful in shedding light on both the parents' and child's issues.

Next, let's look briefly at some aspects of the analysis prior to the graffiti-bust. These involve Jim's affective life, his understanding of his internal world, and his capacities for introspection and self-reflection. I would suggest that Jim may be a person similar to those described by Katan (1961), Yanof (1996), Gedo (alexithymia) (2005), Tyson (2010), Holinger (2016) – those people who don't understand their own affects and consequently are terribly confused about their actions, motives, and sense of self. In these situations, specifically interpreting Jim's affects might enhance his capacities for self-reflection and understanding. His dreams, creativity, grandiosity, and anger also would be worth exploring. For example, the one area in which Jim seems to experience a sense of aliveness and energy is in his art, color, and so on – his art in a large, visible arena as connected with action (i.e., delinquency at this point of his development).

Third, we turn to the issue of the graffiti-bust. Jim gets busted, and shortly thereafter does graffiti near the analyst's office. Following these events, Jim and his analyst apparently make significant strides with respect to his denial, disavowal, and reality-processing (e.g., Basch, 1983). The analyst seems to entertain many possible childhood antecedents and motives, transference and otherwise: guilt, punishment, relief; acting out "infantile desires"; ambivalence towards "mother-analyst;" aggressive attack on the analyst; sexual meanings; feeling excited and alive; dealing with feelings of non-existence; wanting to be visible, seen, valued, of worth, appreciated, of interest to someone; struggling with his own interests, creativity, ambitions, and grandiosity; and more (e.g., Winnicott, 1965; Kohut, 1971; Pine, 1990).

Given these multiple aspects that arise from Jim's burst of action in his analysis, it's challenging to imagine the task of the analyst organizing the multi-faceted nature of intrapsychic motivation in his/her own mind to deal with the various transferences, affects, and contents as they emerge, with further enhancement of Jim's introspection and self-analytic functions.

It would be most interesting and exciting to see how this transpires.

COMMENTARY 2

Analysis is endlessly interesting in almost every way. The analyst never knows which of the many layers of brain and mind functioning in meaning making, formation and deformation, will be encountered in a particular analysis and which will determine the ways in which pain and adaptation co-habitate. In child analysis, the parents are often initial framers of what is to be considered. In adult analysis, they rarely perform this role. In adolescent analysis, their impact is always enormous and their actual framing role quite variable.

In thinking about the case of Jim, I began with two questions, if Jim were up all night playing with a gang of guys, all artists, why would his day time exhaustion be called a regression and then where was Jim's father? I followed with awe the ways in which Jim brought his issues into his analyst's office and then the ways in which she experienced them and then conceptualized them in the transference. Adolescence had made still more urgent his incestuous wishes (the triadic dilemmas encountered in all family constellations which always tutor both dyadic closenesses and sexual longings) toward his mother and actualized them in the art form which he chose, symbolizing both his wish for actual intercourse with his mother=analyst and his overwhelming need for a father, The Falcons, to intervene and help him modulate his now possible, previously unconscious wishes. I wondered, technically, if these interpretive thoughts and formulations would remain in the transference or whether they would be more clearly articulated about primary objects. I wondered what impact and long term effects the analyst's words would have on Jim. Then my thoughts turned to Leonard.

Leonard was referred to me by his mother's therapist when he was 11. His private school was threatening to ask him to leave. There were not academic problems but Leonard was drawing graffiti all over the school's blackboards. Also, even more disturbingly, he is imitating Michael Jackson's dance moves during class. Both activities are considered disruptive and disrespectful. Leonard has a younger sister who is a stellar student, as is he, and whose behavior is "completely appropriate." His parents are both academics; his father is a scientist and his mother a scholar of theoretical physics. Each finds Leonard's troubles in school almost incomprehensible. He is so smart; he should know better is their consensus. Mother is quite subdued, almost silent in this meeting. Father is more "fraternal." He comments that he knows my wife's research and that we both have married Jewish women. I listen.

Leonard and I embark on an analysis. In my office, he begins by singing. The song that keeps calling to him is from Carousel. "When you walk through a storm, hold your head up high," followed by "You never will walk alone." He intones this again and again. His voice has not yet changed and the clear soprano tones ring out clearly. Often he wants to open a window in my office as if the song should be able to travel, to where and to whom, I wonder. The school reports that the disruptive dancing has abated. Perhaps the graffiti has as well. They are very impressed with the effects of Leonard's work in analysis. The parents are thrilled and suggest that we should be congratulated and wind down. I suggest that even with a settling down of the major stressor, his tenure at the school having been threatened, it would be useful for us to continue. The parents end the treatment. Leonard does not express an opinion. He does say , however, that I was the only one who could hear his song. I say that I am always willing to hear him.

Four months after we interrupted, Leonard is back. He has been expelled from school. He has punched the music, dance and art teacher, lightly but very rapidly seven times in her buttocks and upper thighs, causing her to lose her balance and fall over. Far from being appalled by this outburst, he has triumphantly crowed, "I have felled the witch and Pinocchio can't do a fucking thing about it." Horrifyingly, the rest of the class has laughed and cheered. Leonard is immediately asked to leave and his little sister is also asked to depart. The school wishes to expunge the family. The parents are speechless. Very rapidly his sister is enrolled in another school and Leonard begins at the public school. Word of his adventure has preceded him and he is greeted as something of a hero.

Leonard starts to sing to me again, this time about the witch. I recognize that he is singing something that is quite similar to Humperdinck's Hansel and Gretel, both melodically and thematically. He does not sing but tells me that Pinocchio is the name he has given the headmaster who lies and has a very long nose. "I think that he is dickless," he now states. In the singing, I can hear that his voice has begun to change. He is now a tenor. I am trying to conceptualize what has happened. I decide to ask Leonard. He starts to tell me about someone he calls Dr. Upper Bum Cut. He demarcates all of the syllables very clearly. Dr. Upper Bum Cut, we soon learn, cannot tell his elbow from his asshole. That is not quite right. He mis-names every body part. He is sort of like Mrs. Malaprop. Thus I learn that Leonard is doing a lot of reading. I realize that Leonard is, indeed, answering my question, but in a very artful form.

We learn more. Dr. Upper Bum Cut, he considers, is lying about his confusion regarding naming body parts. The problem is actually deeper. He really does not know what is what. I am considering that Leonard is painting with words a self portrait. Is this the new transformation of the graffiti? I also consider that he is describing some felt experience of either or both of his parents either separately or together. The anatomical aspects of the "attack" at school are probably relevant as is the likelihood that the fact that the teacher was female and the headmaster, male, might be a representation of the parental couple. I can also hear that Leonard has become something of a rap artist in his vocabulary. He favors slang expression for body parts. At this point there is no expressed remorse for what has happened and no expressed concern for Ms. J, the teacher. There is a great deal of scorn for Headmaster Y.

The parents request a psychopharmacology consultation. I, of course, agree. Our consultant says that she has nothing to offer except an anti-psychotic which the parents decline. Leonard says that he found the psychopharmacologist cute. When he says this he smiles at me in a conspiratorial fashion. I wonder if he is asking if we think the same things. He answers by singing again from Carousel. "I know that you are listening to my song," he states.

Our work continues. The Doctor of curious appellation continues to be our chief protagonist. I do not try to shift Leonard's play mode. We learn that the Doctor has had a very painful childhood. He was a foster child never adopted by a family until he was 12. I note that Leonard is now 12. The doctor begins to tell about all of the women in his various foster families. One is more terrible than the next. I note that he does not describe any of the men. I do not say this. I do say, "They all sound like witches." Leonard looks directly at me. "Yeah," he says.

The external and the internal now converge. Mother's therapist calls me to say that her patient will leave her husband. Both children have been conceived with donor sperm and that the father and mother have never had intercourse. Now mother will seek an annulment. The therapist says that she assumes that this is very meaningful and only now does she have permission to share this information with me. I thank her. I think of the statement that Pinocchio is "dickless."

The separation occurs in the real world. Curiously, the parents do not communicate this to me directly. Leonard, however, does. Dr. Upper Bum Cut is instantaneously retired. Leonard is very upset. He says so. He also says that either he will need to bring his sister to our sessions or we will need to find her someone to see. She is inconsolable. This is a side of him that I have not previously encountered. He weeps in my office. The next day his mother brings both him and his sister. She stays in the car. Leonard is very parental with his sister. She asks me if I could find her a helper. Leonard says that she wants to see a woman. He then says that he understands this very well as he only wanted to see a man. This is followed by his directly wondering whether he should see me more (we are meeting 5 times a week). Shortly thereafter he articulates directly that he would like to move into my house. This is quickly followed by his stating that he needs actually to stay at home with his mother and sister. I learn that his father will move to California "for a better job."

We continued for two more years. Dr. Upper Bum Cut was called a very complicated character by Leonard and treated as a kind of art form. He considered many scenarios for his story. He called them Jazz, "you know improvisation." Then he said: "we are composing together." I learned from him that his mother now seemed always sad to him. I also learned that he missed his father and that he planned to visit him in California when he moved. Leonard sought out Ms. J. and profoundly apologized to her. He decided to tell her that his life had been in total turmoil. She wondered if he would like to come back to the private school. He responded by wondering if his sister was being invited too. Ms. J was moved to tears by their conversation and she embraced Leonard. He decided to stay in public school and his sister also decided not to return to the place where they had been expunged.

Leonard graduated from high school and went to college in California. He saw a lot of his father. He then went to graduate school. He came back to see me as a 30-year-old neuro-psychologist wondering about re-entering analysis. We met for almost 3 years during his post-doc days and as he launched his research endeavors. Now he told me his dreams and spoke about his sexual dilemmas. Each of his parents had new partners, his mother, sort of; his father very definitely. He said he liked both of them and he liked each of his parents better than ever. He now knew the story of his conception and of his sister's. They had each found the sperm donor. They had many many siblings.

Our work now focused on the transference. He now knew that he wanted me to have had a dick, and or a fist. These thoughts made him both excited and uncomfortable. He thought that what he wanted from me now was more related to his sexual confusions now than to his experiences when he was a boy. Then again he was not so sure. He felt that he wanted to help his father's dick. He began to feel very angry again with all of the witches. We reconstructed a narrative in which he understood more about the dancing and its relationship to the fixing rather than breaking of his Dad. "I think that some people would have called it break dancing," he said. "I didn't know that term then." With great pain he told me that he found it very difficult to trust his penis with a woman. We thought together that he might have thought that his mother played a role in his father's non sexuality at home. And then he told me that he had often thought about sex and love in my family. "I used to imagine that you and your wife loved to be together. I am back here to learn how that could be, can be."

Leonard is not Jim. Each analysand is his own person with his own play modes and unique sculpting. The adolescent's analyst learns from her or his analysand what similar symptoms might mean and where they might lead. Action and fantasy are differently deployed and differently available for each. Conversely, what combination of factors, intrapsychic, interactive and external may have led to the ways in which symbolization and action concur and occur in the analytic Spielraum and in a child's life, is always a question worth considering. It was only very late in the work that Leonard learned that his conception had required 7 "punches" from the sperm donor. Perhaps this was the origin of the light taps of Ms. J.

He also told me that he had helped his mother to consult the very same psychopharmacologist whom he had earlier met. Her previously untreated flagrant bipolar illness was not under control. We were learning more about the witches. But witches we were to learn were not just witches. They might suffer from depression or mania and actually be people who were ill. His father had told him about the work of Bruce Perry, M.D., Ph.D., and the concept of neurodevelopmental sequencing. He now also thought about his own psychology as reflecting developmental trauma, but this thought included the possibility that his father was describing aspects of Leonard's gestation that might have been adversely affected by his mother's illness. Was this fair on father's part, he wondered? In Palo Alto when he was there, he had gone into psychotherapy with an female analyst. He had studied the Oedipus in college and mostly noted that he felt terribly worried about his therapist. When she told him that she was very ill and must stop, he wondered if he were responsible. She told him certainly not and that everything that happened in his mind was of interest to her. He told her that he had learned that in his analysis as a child too. When she died soon thereafter, he experienced real grief. It was only then, he said that he learned that his therapist had a husband who survived her. Now, he spoke about how curious it was that he did not think of her sexuality but that he now did think of mine and of his.

Back in our home city and, in part, given his mother's gratifying response to mood stabilizers, he began the study of the safety of such drugs during pregnancy. His work in that area contributed very much to the field. He also applied for analytic training choosing, he said an Institute which understood that every Oedipus is different just as every analysand is different. "I celebrate that I know this from the inside and that I also know that the same drug can help every person whose affective life is dysregulated. I have arrived at the point of knowing that life is not either-or. It is always many, many different, I would say, unique components."

I choose to present another adolescent analysis to echo Leonard's observation. For me this highlights the wonderful work that Jim and his analyst are doing. Jim and his analyst are together understanding something between them and within him. May it help Jim to love, play and work more effectively and with greater freedom. Ultimately, may he, like Leonard, come to understand with compassion his play mode selections, their origins, and their meanings, and by so doing integrate and champion the fantastic gift which an analytic journey with an attuned and accompanying other always provides.

EDITORIAL REFLECTIONS

There is something about adolescence as a phase, something about this particular adolescent, and something about the flexibility and creativity of the analyst in this case that makes others respond creatively. One commentator shares his/her approach to work with adolescents giving us a brief and useful guide to assessment and focus in such work. The other commentator responds with a detailed association to his/her own case of a creative adolescent who ends up becoming a significant contributor to our field.

The history of the presenting problem brings to mind Freud's first theory of adolescent breakdown: deferred action or "Nachtraeglichkeit." Before Freud described infantile sexuality and consequent conflicts, his theory of neurosogenesis hinged on the idea of deferred action. Initially he used this theory in relation to puberty. Briefly summarized, his idea was that an experience in childhood may have little impact until the memory becomes linked with later adolescent sexual impulses (Novick, J. and Novick, K.K. 2001). We discussed this in relation to the case of Nick (Chapter 8) and here again, we have the case of Jim, who is described as active and quick-witted as a boy. He was enthusiastic in sports and had friends. Mother reports that "when he was twelve to thirteen his interest waned. He became afraid of the ball and afraid of going on offense."

The analyst also seems to focus on something happening at puberty: "The drives threaten to overwhelm him." In this volume and in our experience we have seen adolescents who carry childhood traumas through development and then the inner and external demands of adolescence lead to adolescent breakdown. But we have also seen cases in which there was no evidence of childhood trauma. In the paper referred to above we present a case which follows more along the lines described by Freud where the actuality of adolescent sexual or hostile wishes brings childhood memories, by deferred action, to a traumatic level. Jim may be one of those cases in which the reality of being able to put incestuous wishes into action led to a complete withdrawal from adolescent growth.

This is a vignette from an ongoing case. We are left wondering what the analyst eventually did with this incestuous wish. Was it interpreted in the transference and then linked to the mother? We have said that a major task at adolescence is the setting aside of omnipotent beliefs. It is a time when omnipotent beliefs may be most intensely reached for and relied on, serving multiple needs. But hanging on to such beliefs can lead to the most intense guilt and shame. The omnipotent belief at adolescence includes both the reality that physically they can put any sexual or hostile wishes into action, and the conviction that no one can or will stop them.

This can be a high intensity moment for the analyst also, whose memory of their own adolescent incestuous wishes may be awakened. In the countertransference the analyst may also institute a total affective shutdown and function as a tyrannical super ego reacting to the legal jeopardy of the boy with his acting out. This chapter also highlights the technical, moral, and ethical dilemmas that face the analyst whose patient is doing something illegal. How is this the same or different from facing the danger posed by suicidal potential, in terms of how the analyst responds. Should the parents have been involved actively at this point, as in the case of Jake (Chapter 9)? This analyst chose to verbalize the boy's behaviorally-expressed wish to be caught, thereby accessing the internal conflict. What we learn here is the benefit of holding on to a neutral stance, what Anna Freud called staying equidistant from the superego and the id, allying with the reality testing of the patient's ego. Such dilemmas arise more often with adolescents than any other age group and contribute to the challenge of working with them.

Despite our not knowing how this case will proceed and what the fates of these various wishes and defenses will be, this chapter gives us a vivid illustration of the specifically adolescent juxtaposition of creative potential for open-system growth and real achievement with the danger of closed-system co-opting of ego functions in the service of maintaining omnipotent defenses. The tension for both patient and analyst is palpable in the clinical vignette and the commentators respond in kind, resonating to the intensity of our shared therapeutic experience with this age group. Part of the joy and frustration of treating adolescents resides in the suspense over outcomes, the scope of the possibilities, and the way they evoke our own conflicts.

IV

LATE ADOLESCENCE

CHAPTER 14

FRED – age 18

History Of One's Own, Of Family, And Native Country

Fred came to see me after his severe suicidal developmental breakdown and 6 weeks of psychiatric hospitalization at the age of 18. He had graduated with distinction from high school and successfully applied for medical studies at the university, but could not start because of his hospitalization. He had consulted me two years before, because he had felt he was not sufficiently equipped intellectually to meet the requirements of his studies. After his breakdown, Fred had insisted on leaving the psychiatric clinic prematurely, hoping to start therapy with me. And so we started on our pathway of five years of psychoanalytic work (3 times per week).

When Fred was 28 months old his maternal grandfather had died unexpectedly. This grandfather had been the idol of his mother. She immediately moved with her first born child Fred to her mother for 5 months, leaving Fred's father far behind. The maternal grandmother had become very depressed and Fred was supposed to bring sunshine into her dark life. Around his third birthday Fred had to endure painful circumcision without having been prepared for it. Shortly afterwards his sister was born. Following the birth of her second child mother suffered a post partum depression for several months. Two years later a miscarriage in the fifth month of pregnancy triggered another long period of depression in the mother followed by the outbreak of her diabetes which got worse over time and could not be regulated sufficiently by her. Fred's active and successful

351

father shared few interests with the mother; he stayed mainly at home over weekends but had no interests in social contacts outside his family. Therefore, as Fred grew older, he was most often his mother's escort in public. This entailed his giving up sports where he had been very active before, as well as his involvement with his peer group outside school.

In the opening phase, good-looking, slim, and tall, Fred, with his romantic dark curly hair and deep dark eyes, surprised me again and again by starting grandiose projects which were beyond his actual capacities and resources and therefore had to be aborted repeatedly. He interrupted therapy several times because he felt the need to follow idealized philosophy or art-history teachers for weeks into foreign countries and he shared with me the neo-sexual, "perverse" longings his girl friend was not willing to satisfy. Obviously – to me – he was trying hard to test whether he was welcome to me and accepted by me the way he was and felt, and he hoped that I would not be jealous.

For quite some time we worked on his secret passion for watching boxing on TV at night and he described masochistic pleasure in identifying with the loser of the fight. In his dreams he often was the darling of outstanding statesmen or male geniuses, excluding the rest of the world. During the lengthy period when we had been working on his fears that I might rob of him all the treasures that he had recovered during the ongoing therapy, his relationship with his girl friend deepened, they moved in together, and he discovered new and mutual sexual pleasures with her. His capacities to tolerate conflicts and to solve them productively increased significantly. He chose a new focus in his university studies. With a big effort and much preparation he was accepted at the academy of fine arts of his choice. Although two years of treatment had helped him master important developmental milestones of late adolescence, he insisted on continuing in further psychoanalytic work.

In a session preceding a three-week break in therapy he remembered recurrent nightmares from the age of five on. He associated these dreams with actual political conflicts. In childhood often he had dreamed of a tank overrunning children in a tent. A few months later he came in deeply depressed and we wondered whether his sadness was due to having been left behind by an admired friend and artist who had gone abroad. Fred, however, linked his feelings to the student revolt in Beijing: "…. Do you remember my childhood dreams…. the tank…. it really happened…. tanks overrunning people in tents… I had to listen to a piece of music, which is so meaningful to me, in order to find some consolation…. but my mother interrupted me and my girlfriend found it ridiculous the way I cared for China." It seemed to me as if he felt degraded and chased away because of his yearnings, and I hoped that I could offer some refuge to him even though I had a certain uncanny feeling.

Therapist: "You link mass murder with people close to you who are not aware how deep an impact that mass murder had made on you and you feel that those people try to disrupt your way of coming to terms with mass murder."

F: "I had a discussion with my friend. We should shoot pictures, as many as possible…. to keep the public aware of it…. My girl friend hates pictures of dying or dead men…. Do you understand me? Without a witness, there is no apparent guilt, guilt disappears…."

T: (was I supposed to witness?) "This sounds to me as if you want me to understand that whenever guilt disappears for you and is not worked through it turns into deadly dangers" and to my surprise I hear myself say "Was this the reason why your graduation (from junior college) essay was on a famous resistance group?"

F: "In my dream…. and right now…. revenge makes no sense. We must stop people with the power to bring about disaster again. But the soldiers did follow the command to destroy.... In Roman times the army was not allowed to enter the city." He then remembered his paternal grandfather who had been a high ranking military person in World War II. That grandfather had painted the car of the young couple just married (F's parents) in military gray – "He turned their car into a war machine.... and my maternal grandfather was a dentist in camps in the East.... I do not know much about him.... they might have given me only little information on purpose.... or – I am not quite sure – I might not have been interested!"

T: "But in your nightmares again and again children in a tent, in a camp, become annihilated during war."

In the following session, quite unusually for him, he did not speak for the first 30 minutes.

Finally I said that perhaps he was making me experience what he had experienced; terrible and devastating reports followed by a deadly silence. He began to talk about his mother's family. The atmosphere there always reminded him of a graveyard. His mother's two siblings never had children. And in the meantime his sister became very disturbed and had tried to commit suicide twice.

Over the following 10 sessions his depression became nearly unbearable for him and for me, and I tried hard not to lose hope for the two of us. Then he informed me that he would travel to the US for several months but was not sure whether he would come back. I told him how important it is for the two of us, that the two of us take his words seriously, accept the fact that we could not know whether he would return to analytic work. The following day, he told me that deep down in himself he felt himself changing. I had taken him seriously and shared with him the uncertainty whether he would come back or not.

During his 4-month stay in the US his maternal grandmother died. In the second session after his return to treatment he remembered the dream he had in California in the morning before his father had called him to let him know that grandma had died:

F: "I was sitting with my family in the living room. On the sofa there was my grandmother's head (without her body). The others could not handle this, they could not understand what she was saying. I understood her well. I only touched her with my hands. Then somebody was buried, but it was not grandma."

He then associated to the stories he had heard about his grandma and his mother as a child: being persecuted, running through burning cities, leaving their hometown and escaping to the West. He hinted at war crimes in World War II, in Vietnam, all over the world. And he felt terrible pain, because his friend, an artist – a father figure for him – had gone away. I did not verbalize to him my thought that for him I had been "gone" during his stay in the US.

F: "There is no image for this terribly overwhelming pain – sort of hot rays penetrating my body, a blowtorch burning out my wound .... It is utmost painful, only burning out can bring about a solution. I do not want to pretend any longer. I want to shoot true pictures, brutal pictures which contain and present all the phases of human hate." (suddenly quiet and pensive) "Most of what I speak about I did not experience myself."

T: "You did not experience it yourself but it seems to me you are haunted by it."

F: "It is dangerous enough."

And I wondered to myself what sort of dangers the both of us will be confronted with.

With many recurrent difficulties and resistances during the next period, we approached his increasing sense of how much his depression was due to transgenerationally-burdened conflicts. Working through dreams and murderous feelings in the transference and countertransference we finally found words for the uncanny feeling that, in spite of the conspiracy of silence in his family, he "knew" about his grandfathers – the high-ranking soldier and the dentist – with their guilty involvements during World War II in camps in Poland and Russia by which Fred felt "touched and infected." He confronted me again – in case I should have forgotten – with information he had given me in the beginning of therapy. Weeks before his psychiatric hospitalisation he had felt compelled obsessively to construct miniature gallows and he was terribly convinced the military police would come in order to kill him. Now he was convinced that his maternal grandfather had committed suicide in order to prevent accusation and trial.

His global identification with this grandfather had helped him in my view to split off murderous feelings towards his sister, toward his father who had made mother bring that child into the world and simultaneously to hold on to an omnipotent illusion to cure his mother's depression by being her son and her father simultaneously, in this way also to deny the differences of generations and the facts of life.

Working through his trans-generationally burdened conflicts had helped Fred to better integrate his early object relations and to loosen his resistances to becoming aware of these infantile affects, memories, and fantasies.

Some months later, he shared with me his dream from the previous night:

"I am in a theater and I am supposed to meet an actor backstage. It was difficult to find my way through the basement. But I know the stage is above me. I enter the dressing room. Suddenly they want me to participate in the play. I try very hard to memorize my part and put on a red T-shirt. The curtain opens and I am in the limelight. Suddenly I realize that I had put on the T-shirt inside out and I say to myself: that does not matter on the stage. I am in the limelight and my shirt is inside out. I want to present my lines well." As he continues through the theater he meets an old friend who is searching the auditorium. Fred tells him that he is in a hurry, and the friend has to find his way alone by himself. Especially the scene with the T shirt, Fred emphasized, he remembered very intensely. "What was under the T-shirt, that was more important. As if my skin contained all of me."

T: "Your skin underneath made you feel great...."

Fred smiled and for the first time he was able to mention masturbation, associated it to memories of his circumcision, and hinted at dreams he had reported much earlier in therapy, in which he had lain in wait for dangerously attractive couples dancing in the dark, had watched fireworks and movies. And, seemingly changing topic: "I am quite surprised – and angry – that one of my teachers invited me into his family home, but he did not want me to find out more about himself. Anyway, even with you, I never inquired about your family and your background." I was impressed with how much independent analytic thinking was emerging.

A few sessions later, he recalled joining his parents in their bed whenever he woke up in the night full of terror because of his dreams where children were going to be killed .... " I also wanted you to know, that the color of my T-shirt was a deep dark red."

T: "It seems to me, you are proud of it and you want to make it quite clear to me: It is hot and quite becoming."

Fred (laughing): "Sure.... quite strong.... Red like leaves in Indian summer.... like heavy red wine.... sort of erotic.... sort of autoerotic."

357

(It seemed clear to me that Fred's vital sensuous feelings and his anger – perhaps also pain of loss – were sort of interdependent.)

The following session he came back to his T-shirt dream. A girl friend, who in some of his dreams appeared as his passionate lover, in reality yesterday wore exactly that red T-shirt he had been wearing in his dream.

F: "In the dream I wore it inside out, but it was my own shirt and the fit was perfect. And there was this feeling: Life is ok, though transitory, as if my part was in the last scene."

T: "Last scene as if the play came to an end?"

F: "It seems to me that we're talking about our relationship, our work. For some time now I've been feeling more secure, with a feeling of continuity in my work, perhaps since we have talked about my deep emotional closeness to my older friend. My mind tells me the feeling of continuity might be interrupted now and then, yet inwardly I am sure and secure."

Fred did respect the privacy of my background and my history. He never explicitly asked to know. But now he looked back to the course of our work, in spite its many interruptions, and found his own interpretation for it. He then linked the therapeutic process to his own individual development since childhood, to the history since of the days of his grandparents in World War II and to the actual current wave of xenophobia and racism.

F: "The past is still alive, the past in the present, that is what history is to me all about, still alive and not dead, unlike history in history books."

Fred experienced intense and painful feelings about parting, which he seemed never to have felt (or re-experienced) in puberty. "Parting brings about overwhelming pain.... But there is also something good about parting.... to let go in search of something new.... leaving and being left.... so painful.... But saying good bye is no catastrophic rupture.... The history of our therapeutic journey will remain alive inside of me.... I made therapy much more my own.... In the beginning it was nearly impossible to include therapy into that part of my life I dared to show to others and to myself."

Fred pointed out what impact our analytic work had made on his life outside the consulting room. He did not deny his therapy and his past any longer. More and more he found it very helpful to think about the past – near and distant – and reflecting about it.

F: " When I feel depressed now I can wait till tomorrow and postpone my judgement till tomorrow. Sure, I often have sad feelings, but now I am quite sure those sad feelings will be limited in time and pass."

It became important to him that not only he but I as well should be able to differentiate the past from history. It had become clear to him, in a way that he found rather surprising: "In history as well as in therapy there is always the chance to transform what was passed on to you."

He began interviewing relatives and he had the impression the way the events of the past were reported by them was as important and meaningful as the facts reported.

F: "Family history comes about – it is an invention – but it only gains true meanings seen in the light of general history.... Similar to the way I tell you my history in order for you to listen to me, then I can grasp it myself und understand its meaning."

During the two weeks preceding our last summer break, for the first time actually during a session (and not in between sessions) Fred felt and could verbalize how much he hated me because I (shall) leave him during difficult times. Tears were running down his cheeks, but he remained mute and motionless for quite some time. Finally with his shoulders he tried to wipe off his tears as if there was no consoling hand allowed to touch his head, unlike in the dream where he had understood and consoled his grandmother by touching her. Later on we could talk about it and understand how devastating it would have been for him if I – after such a long time – had not felt how deep his despair had been in that session. His despair now reminded him of those days when he was close to killing himself. In those days however there was nobody who tried to get in contact with him.

In our last sequence of analytic work he could tell me how alive he was all alone by himself, but with his girl friend as well, about his intense way of dreaming and working, integrating his looking to the world outside and into his own inside. Troubles might come up now and then, but they would not bring about deep depression and inactivity in him any more. It had taken him a long time to realize and to give up his conviction that he only had a right to live when he is perfect and is doing hard labor.

During our summer break he obtained a commission from an interesting important publication and he had done already a big part of the work for it. He even had conceptualized his project for his final exam at the university of fine arts as well. He planned to shoot a sequence of photos presenting memorials in honour of the murdered European Jews – each memorial in complete isolation. This series of photos will contrast to another series where those memorials are documented from a new perspective, integrated in their actual surroundings. With a voice both gentle and determined, he explained to me, "Perhaps also my photos can show that our life is really true, is more creative, whenever we are not afraid to transform and think anew about what had been passed on to us without harmonizing it with our present reality!"

Letting Fred go and saying goodbye to him was not that easy. I had to contain my own painful and loving emotions for him as well as my memories to World War II when I had been a small child, which the work with Fred had brought back to me. But wholeheartedly I could thank him for his confidence in our mutual explorative work over the years in which we continuously came to know each other better and more intimately. Of course I will remember him not only with sad, but also with good and grateful feelings, sure that he is on a good path as an artist and young man who is able to apply his analytic mind to his relationships and to the further development of his art.

COMMENTARY 1

The narrative describing Fred's psychoanalytic treatment is a moving testament to the healing power of psychoanalytic treatment of adolescents and emerging adults. When the adolescent and his or her analyst are able to form a solid partnership, the way Fred and his analyst were able to do, the curative effect of the analytic engagement is set into motion. Reading this rich and nuanced case report, we can see that when an analyst is able to fully receive the youngster's actions, enactments, and repetitions, even when they are initially inexplicable, or may appear to be "resistances" to the treatment, the therapeutic process unfolds organically.

My impression is that Fred was a traumatized yet gifted youngster, who perhaps was unconsciously selected by the previous generations, his parents and grandparents, to represent an un-representable trauma that had silently infected his entire family. I will elaborate on this idea later on. In my view it is important that Fred was able to take his own initiative, and that he was able to trust his intuition and "escape" the psychiatric hospital after six weeks, so that he could begin the second phase of his treatment. His previous encounter with his analyst, two years before this hospitalization at the age of eighteen, had given Fred the taste of what he really needed. I speculate that Fred knew that what he required at that time was not further hospitalization, but an intimate dialogue with a psychoanalyst who could receive him fully and accept his unique idiom and expressive actions.

As I read the narrative of Fred's treatment I thought to myself that Fred's analyst was able to follow Fred's lead and accompany him in a steady and sensitive way, without relying too much on theoretical constructs, and without delivering heavy handed interpretations, a technique that may have only impeded Fred's courageous attempt to re-work his early losses, and the narcissistic deformation he suffered due to his family's skewed Oedipal constellation. From an early age Fred's was squeezed into a warped Oedipal triangulation that forced him to become too close to his mother, without the mitigating impact of a present, involved and effective father. The accompanying that Fred's analyst, who I assume was a male analyst, provided him, enabled Fred to re-work these early deformations.

Fred's analyst's condensed story of Fred's analytic treatment introduces the reader, in a palpable and experience-near way, to the important milestones of this five-years-long analysis, an analysis that was carried out at a three times a week frequency. From the outset the analyst let us know that all along he kept in mind the significance of the traumatic nature of Fred's early object relations. The analyst informs us that by the time Fred was five years old he suffered from a number of traumatic impingements. He was subjected to a prolonged separation from his father, between the age of 28 months and 33 months. A few months after reuniting with his father, when Fred and his mother returned to their home, Fred underwent a painful circumcision. Soon after this traumatic procedure, that was carried out without preparation, Fred's mother gave birth to a sister and subsequently fell into a postpartum depression that lasted for a few months. Two years later, when Fred was now five years old, his mother suffered yet again from another significant depression following a late stage miscarriage. This second long period of depression was followed by the outbreak of mother's diabetes, a condition that she was unable to regulate sufficiently by herself, and that only worsened over time.

Fred, therefore, endured three significant early losses. The first was a prolonged separation from his father when his mother left his father to join her own bereaved mother who suffered from deep depression following the sudden death of her husband – mother's idealized father. The analyst notes that Fred's father was "left far behind." This separation occurred during a period when Fred, like all boys his age, needed his father's active presence to consolidate his sense of self and form a solid masculine identification.

Soon after the reunion with his father, Fred suffered from two additional significant blows. He lost his mother's vitality during two prolonged depressive episodes. Even after his mother recovered from her depression it appears that the family constellation was far from optimal. All along Fred's parents' marriage seemed to have been rather constricted and we learn that, when Fred was older, his father avoided social interactions and Fred was forced to become his mother's escort. Fred had to sacrifice his involvement with sports and with optimal social interactions and friendships with children his age, so that he could accompany his mother to her social activities. These traumatic losses and the misuse he suffered by his needy, sickly and lonely mother appear to have shaped Fred's early development and his unconscious phantasies, and led later to a severe and suicidal breakdown in adolescence.

During the first two years of his psychoanalytic treatment, Fred brought to his analyst the aftermath of this breakdown. He seems to have suffered from an intense "father hunger." He searched to identify with male figures, with "idealized philosophy or art-history teachers." We learn that Fred would interrupt his treatment and would follow these men into foreign countries for weeks at a time. When taking these excursions to follow idealized male mentors, Fred left his analyst as well. Fred may have been turning passive into active. He was now the one who was leaving rather than the one who was being left. Perhaps he wished to make his analyst suffer the pain he had suffered as a young boy when he was taken away from his father for what, we can imagine, he had experienced as an endless period.

Toward the end of his analysis, two weeks before the final summer break, Fred was able to share so poignantly with his analyst the anguish and rage he felt when he was left without containment by his analyst. I am assuming that Fred may have felt dropped by his analyst four days out of each week, a long gap for a fragmented and fragile youngster. Fred most likely felt helpless and abandoned during these weekly gaps and during all the other holidays and vacations that his analyst naturally had taken. A patient like Fred may have felt more held and contained in a five, or four sessions a week analytic frequency.

During the first two years of his analysis, in his dreams, Fred often imagined himself as "the darling of outstanding statesmen or male geniuses." Fred seems to have craved the attention, the recognition and the love of older men. I imagine that he needed the recognition and love of these outstanding father figures, so that he could differentiate himself, internally, from his too close and perhaps enveloping mother. He required this fatherly special attention for the formation of his separate identity and his masculinity. I assume that the analytic relationship, in the father transference, afforded Fred this needed recognition and affection from a father figure.

The frequent breaks in the treatment that Fred created, when he followed his idealized teachers to other countries, may have been, at the same time, attempts to distance himself from his analyst when he was in the throes of a maternal transference. It is possible that when the maternal transference to his analyst heated up, Fred may have felt his analyst to be needy and engulfing. He would then search for a male figure who could intervene and save him from being consumed by his mother in the maternal transference, punctuate the treatment, and force a break.

Fred's secret pleasure of watching boxing on the television at night, while identifying, in a masochistic way, with the loser, made me think of how frequently little boys love to wrestle and horse play with their fathers. A reciprocal and good natured rough and tumble play between a father and a son, helps the boy learn to self modulate his aggression and his excitement. The lack of this type of involvement and play between Fred and his father during parts of the second and third years of his life, and perhaps during later years, when he needed a more involved father, may have led him to lean into a more passive and masochistic masculine identification.

During the first two years of analysis Fred's analyst relates that he was surprised, if not taken aback, by watching Fred starting, again and again, grandiose projects, projects which were beyond his actual capacities and resources, and therefore had to be repeatedly aborted. One can attribute Fred's grandiosity to a narcissistic pathological organization. I prefer, however, to view his taking on projects that were beyond his capacity as a repetition of the impossible and omnipotent role that was assigned to him by his mother at a very tender age. Fred was expected to cure his grandmother, and perhaps also his own mother's depression, following his grandfather's sudden death. At age 28 months he was to bring "the sunshine" into his grandmother's dark depression.

I speculate that Fred was expected to lighten his mother's dark depression as well, as we learn that his mother had suddenly lost her idealized father. Only later in the treatment Fred and his analyst found out that this grandfather, a high ranking soldier, may have committed suicide in order to escape a trial against him for his possible participation in war crimes. What an impossible project Fred was assigned at a time that he himself lost the familiarity of his home and his relationship with his father! In the final phase of his analysis Fred discovered that unconsciously he had undertaken the impossible role of being like a father to his own struggling mother.

The analytic work during the first two years enabled Fred to deepen his relationship with his girlfriend and discover a mutually enjoyable sexual relationship with her. The two moved to live together. Fred developed more realistic and effective ways to deal with his conflicts. He also changed the course of his career. After working hard on the admission requirements, he was accepted to a fine art academy of his choice. He began to develop a meaningful artistic career.

Feeling that he needs to continue to build a stable psychological foundation, Fred, during the next three years undertook the painful, but necessary step to discover how his deep depression was linked also to transgenerational transmitted trauma. During this phase Fred recalled, with a renewed significance, that weeks before his hospitalization he was obsessively compelled to construct miniature gallows, and that he was convinced the military police would come after him in order to kill him. Fred realizes that he had identified with both his grandfathers who may have committed war crimes during the Second World War.

Following the work of the French child analysts François Davoine and Jean-Max Gaudillière, I speculate that Fred chose and was chosen by his family to represent the unspeakable horrors of the past. Un-symbolized traumas came to haunt him, while at the same time foreclosing free access to his familial and social history. At a certain point in his analysis Fred remembers his repeated childhood nightmares. From age five on he would often dream of a tank crushing children in a tent. This dream can be understood on a number of levels, but for Fred this dream signified the weight of the trans-generationally transmitted trauma. Fred became preoccupied with brutal crushing of the student uprising in China. During this period Fred shared with his analyst the excruciating pain he felt. "There is no image for this terribly overwhelming pain," he told his analyst in a heart wrenching way. The pain felt to Fred like "hot rays penetrating his body," as a blowtorch burning his wound. "It is utmost painful, only burning out can bring about a solution," he related to his analyst. "I do not want to pretend any longer," Fred continued, "I want to shoot true pictures, brutal pictures which contain and present all the phases of human hate."

Fred's earlier grandiosity can now also be understood as having to do with trans-generationally transmitted trauma. I speculate that Fred suffered from what Laub (1998) described as wounds without memory that children and grandchildren of survivors inherit from the previous generations. These transmitted memories often compel these children and grandchildren to find expression in the very shape of their lives for the sense of void, terror, loss that defies all comfort. The wounds without memories create a need for grandiose solutions. They are transmitted to these children and become interwoven with, and often overshadow, their normal developmental conflicts. Fred indeed discovers that his mother and his grandmother had to flee persecution, to escape through burning cities, leaving their hometown behind and escaping to the West.

Profound experiences marked the analytic phase in which Fred discovers how he was stamped by the trauma of the past generations. One profound experience was the deep depression that Fred sank into. During this acute depression, a depression that was hard for Fred and his analyst to bear, Fred recalled the heavy atmosphere in his mother's family, which felt like a "graveyard." Fred eventually decided to leave for the US for four months. He let his analyst know that he might not return to his analysis. His analyst accepted this painful possibility. Reading this section, I thought to myself that the threat was much more acute. I thought that Fred and his analyst, who reported having uncanny feelings, may have actually feared that Fred would not return because he would kill himself. They both may have needed to accept the reality of this possibility. At moments like this, a patient is confronted with the need to choose between living or committing suicide – between a destructive solution and a constructive choice to live and to prevail. The choice has to come from within the patient and cannot and should not be influenced by the analyst.

Before leaving for the US Fred described his sense that he was changing in a deep way. During a time like this, when a patient feels that he is transforming, he may be separating from an alien self that was formed and shaped through invasive traumatic identifications. This change may feel to the patient as though he is dying. This is a very frightening time for the patient and for the analyst. Fred chose to live, to continue his analysis, and to further distinguish himself from the trans-generationally transmitted traumatic identifications.

Fred persisted in discovering, and putting into words and images, the silent, yet pernicious trans-generationally transmitted trauma. I speculate that he had to sort out a confusing mixture of transmitted trauma of his victimized and perpetrator grandparents. Gampel (1998) described "radioactive residues," "unapproachable and nonrepresentable remnants" of memories of war and social violence that can be traced in psychoanalytic treatment, and eventually be noted, even though their original referent can no longer be spoken about, or described in words. These radioactive traces may have been the hot and burning rays that Fred felt were penetrating his body and like "a blowtorch burning his wounds."

Toward the end of his analysis Fred reports a complex dream in which he is wearing a dark red shirt, a shirt that fitted him perfectly. His associations to the red shirt indicated to me that with the help of his analyst Fred seemed to have developed a warm, comfortable and sensuous protective skin. This newly formed skin held him together, creating a more helpful separation between himself, his parents' and his grandparents' fates. Fred also developed a sense of a comfortable continuity and perspective. These developments enabled Fred to separate the past from the present. He was able to put the past where it belonged. He could now represent the atrocities of the past in his artistic and original documentations of the memorial for the persecuted Jews. Upon termination Fred seemed to have introjected his analyst as a good, protective and loving object that would accompany him into a promising future.

COMMENTARY 2

From multiple perspectives, this is an exceptional case. It seems to be a psychoanalytic treatment after one consultation, two years before the real treatment of 3 times a week started. The reason why – at that first moment – it didn't come to an analysis is unclear. It reminds me of Moses Laufer's warning, during his lectures in the Amsterdam child analytical seminars, to be aware of the possibility that the therapist to whom an adolescent asks for help, could be for him or her the last anchor to stay alive.

The delay may be out of the often-heard hesitation taking young adolescents in psychoanalysis, out of fear for the tumultuous developmental phase, fear for disintegration, for the usual heavy transference, or they themselves give the impression that 'all is in any case worthless.' Adolescence is often the heaviest last phase in the analysis of adults.

Fred's psychoanalytic treatment started after a *severe suicidal developmental breakdown and 6 weeks of hospitalization*. He left the hospital prematurely: *hoping to start therapy with me*; it sounds as if in a way he gives both the therapist and himself a second chance.

Fred was 16 when he consulted the therapist the first time, *because he had felt he was not sufficiently equipped to meet the requirements of his studies.* The reasons for asking help at 16, and again at 18 years old are in a way the same: the fear of becoming a medical doctor like his maternal grandfather who in Fred's judgment *had committed suicide in order to prevent accusation and trial.*

This is another reason why this is a special case: the transgenerational aspects of the seldom-reported treatments relating to the dark sides of the

369

spectrum of WWII-patients, the perpetrators. During the 1985 IPA-Congress in Hamburg, the first Congress in Germany since 1933, the question was raised why so few people came for treatment who had been voluntarily or forcibly active during the Nazi-period, although one could expect they must suffer a lot from their active or passive experiences, haunted by memory-images. Shame and fear of revenge or justified punishment were the easiest suppositions about their reasons for avoiding treatment, or a pre-existing developmental dysfunction of conscience.

The third reason why this is an exceptionally interesting case: it brings to the fore the importance of experiences known from infant-observation in connection with language acquisition. It is about feeling, imagination and language. Long before a child knows the words sadness, consolation, fear, it is able to feel sadness and consolation, it even is able to console. Long before the child can verbalize and verbally understand, it can feel the complex mental states, expressions and interactions of the surrounding adults, it can feel and experience the changing intensity of it. It can experience and internalize, without knowing the meaning, the unconsciously-expressed emotional load of a traumatized person. And if there are no images, the child makes them itself. Later the child tries to find connections, pictures or situations that can fill in, more or less adequately, the unverbalized internalized experiences of unbearable or overwhelming emotions, to make them understandable, give them images commensurate to the intensity of the transferred emotions, make it more or less understandable, and to make it – the most important – also psychically digestible.

Fred is looking for images of an intensity equal to what he can 'read' in his grandfather's emotional state, but also in his mother's, who as a child had to flee together with her mother because of bombings. The moment this maternal grandfather died, the then-pregnant mother fled with her 28-month-old Fred to her mother, to stay there for 5 months, *leaving Fred's father far behind*; repeating WWII's "Society without the Father," the famous post-war book by Alexander and Margarete Mitscherlich (1970).

The text of the case continues: *Fred was supposed to bring sunshine into her dark life*, an effective well known anti-depressive treatment for grandmothers: a grandchild-toddler to bring softness in a family where the horror-memories of the past have been felt and are emotionally readable, even and utmost by a toddler. It is excellently formulated by Fred, in the context of his grandmother and mother, running through burning, bombed cities: "*There is no image for this terrible overwhelming pain (...) I want to shoot true pictures, brutal pictures which contain and present all the phases of human hate.*" And the text continues: *(suddenly quiet and pensive)* "*Most of what I speak about I did not experience myself.*"

And at this point the analyst gives the crucial formulation of the transgenerational trauma: "*You did not experience it yourself, but it seems to me you are haunted by it.*" And Fred answers: "*It is dangerous enough.*" He is right, it has been the dangerous reality of suicide.

Fred and his psychoanalyst did a good job.

EDITORIAL REFLECTIONS

It's noteworthy that this very complex case, of a person who was not well served by psychiatric hospitalization, was significantly helped by psychoanalysis, as we see in several other cases in this volume. Rather than hurtling toward actual or psychic death the life forces of the pleasure principle, the reality principle, and the growth principle were integrated through psychoanalysis into a harmonious, future-oriented whole.

This chapter again brings adolescent suicide to the forefront. "Fred" was hospitalized at 18 for six weeks, a measure of how medically serious his suicide attempt was considered by hospital personnel. Suicide/murder has always been a risk for those working with adolescents. In 1924 Hermine Hug-

Hellmuth, the first child analyst, was murdered by her 18-year-old nephew Rolf, who many thought had been in analysis with her. The case became a public scandal with prominent psychiatrists taking the opportunity to publish warnings in popular newspapers about the dangers of psychoanalysis, especially with adolescents. Catipovic and Ladame (1998) suggest that the sensational murder made psychoanalysts place more emphasis on the perils than the benefits of analysis.

Yet the danger cannot be denied. As we have emphasized, the major difference between adolescents and younger children is that adolescents are capable of putting aggressive and sexual wishes into action. The suicide rate for adolescents in the U.S. in 2018 was 31/100,000, an increase of 57.4% since 2007. The case in this chapter suggests that psychoanalysis is effective as a treatment for serious suicide attempts and wishes.

Equally important is the demonstration that suicide is almost always the end point of a lifelong course of closed-system modes of self-regulation, often starting in infancy. With closed-system functioning, omnipotent beliefs, rather than realistic competent achievements, serve as a regulatory principle. From early on Fred was expected to do impossible things like cure his grandmother and mother of depression, be his mother's companion and escort and so forth. He spent the first part of his analysis embarked on grandiose tasks that he would fail. He acted out the belief that the analyst expected him to be omnipotent. We have said that the main dynamic task at adolescence is to put aside closed-system omnipotent modes of self-regulation and choose instead realistic, joyful, competent, creative and loving achievements which returns the young person to the "growth" track of progressive development.

Finally, as we focus on what this chapter tells us about adolescents and the technique of working with them, we come to the centrality of termination. It has generally been observed that most adolescents end therapy prematurely, usually by making a "unilateral" decision to leave or provoking the analyst to force an ending by various "gentle" and rationalized means or by a more forceful expression of hopelessness or acting out. Until collecting the contributions to this volume, it has seemed rare for a treatment to end by mutual agreement. There is little mention in the literature of the effect of premature endings on all the parties involved. It is likely that having been left so often and without explanation Fred experienced leaving as a sadistic act and he repeatedly left his analyst, for instance, early on when he asked for analysis at 16, but then didn't start until two years later after a serious suicide attempt.

Suicide, even the fantasy of suicide, is an omnipotent solution, carrying a belief that the important person can be controlled by threatening or actually attempting suicide. As Fred had improved in many areas the analyst suggested ending the treatment. Fred said no and it was a sign of how much Fred had changed and the analyst's continued attunement that the analysis kept going. Through this last bit of work the pair, working together in a fruitful alliance, got to the attraction of the omnipotent closed system. Only then could they face together the horrors both grandfathers represented but also Fred's omnipotent wish to protect them, keep them alive and available to identify with, and become a sadistic general rolling tanks over helpless children or pulling the gold from their teeth.

Part of the developmental work of adolescence is to locate and anchor the self in real time, but this can only be done when past and present are contrasted and differentiated. From this chapter we learn more about the way intergenerationally-transmitted trauma finds particular expression in adolescence, with its real potential for action, constructive or destructive. For an attuned analyst, the deep resonance of such material emerges in the almost uncanny (pre-conscious?) experience of revival of their own histories. Adolescents evoke such intense responses, perhaps precisely because of the seriousness of the psychic and behavioral choices they face.

CHAPTER 15

KARL – age 19

Karl, 19, came to see me at the end of his second university year. He said that he had been unhappy most of his life and now he was feeling anxious, overwhelmed and depressed. He had a difficult year with his roommates and in fact does not get along well with people. He described himself as hypercritical but he also believed that people were judging him. He began to cry as he told me that he had disappointed all the people who are important to him. He said that he had been on Ritalin and Prozac from an early age and had been in therapy, once per week, for many years. He was a very heavy marijuana user. During his first year at university he had become an active drug dealer and I gathered that he was known on campus as a major source of street drugs.

Karl was the middle child of artistic parents who divorced when he was 14. The initial picture was rather dire, especially his description of endless days in his darkened room, skipping class and stoned on marijuana from early morning. At the same time I felt that he was likeable, creative and intelligent.

I asked about what made him feel good, and a major conflict emerged. Karl said he felt uncomfortable about feeling good. When I suggested that he had some anxiety about feeling good, he said, "It doesn't make sense, yet that's so true." I said that this could be one of our goals of treatment, to help him hold on to good feelings.

In those initial sessions we also made some sense of his current anxiety. It was the end of the school year. I wondered if his anxiety had something to do with leaving, saying goodbye. He told me that, in preparation for going away to summer camp, his mother always took him out to shop for clothes. They would have a good time, then, inevitably, get into a horrendous shouting match. Karl would storm off in a rage, stay angry until he got to the camp, and then he would feel terribly homesick. I wondered if he was now having an intense reaction to saying goodbye to school, to his friends, to the town? Is there some big issue to saying goodbye? The next day he said that he was feeling calmer and thanked me for helping him. I said that saying goodbye could be another area to work on. We could try to find a better way to say goodbye than getting anxious or in a rage.

We then talked of all the therapy he had been through that he thought was totally worthless. He had been seen once per week for varying periods of time by different therapists since preschool. Mostly, he said, he figured out how to avoid doing anything or saying anything. He said that he finds it hard to say what he's thinking or feeling. "I always qualify my words. I say, 'I think, maybe.'" He believed this has helped him get along.

He told me a story about his uncle, who had sent him warm winter clothes, but the clothes were way too small. He was afraid to tell him and he ended up blaming himself. He said, "If I tell my uncle how disappointed I am, he'd never see me again." I said, "On the other hand you don't have warm winter clothes for walking to class or working in your cold apartment. Worst of all, you blame yourself. Looks like there are things to sort out there." "I never thought of that. I am so careful not to hurt people's feelings but then I end up hurting myself. By the way, how does therapy work?"

I said that, first of all, I don't work in the way he remembers his previous therapies. I said that therapy is a partnership where we each bring everything we've got to work out together what is stopping him from having a joyful, happy life. This is a unique relationship in that the entire focus is on him, rather than on what would make me happy. I said that this might be an initial hurdle for him since he takes care of other people's feelings, but therapy is also an opportunity to practice taking care of himself. He has told us that he is hyper-critical and also holds back his thoughts, so we could start by his telling me, honestly, what he doesn't like about me. He blushed, stammered, then said what he doesn't like is the "generation gap." I said that I could see how difficult it was for him to say something critical but I was impressed by his bravery. We will try to work on his fear that his critical thoughts will end a relationship, but it will take bravery on his part to do this work and I was glad to see that he had this quality.

He had told me that he was a musician. I gathered that he was a serious and accomplished trumpet player, so I asked how much he practiced. He said that he practiced as much as he could, 4 to 6 hours daily in addition to classes and gigs. I said "Well, you've got the stuff we need for therapy. You have the capacity for hard, sustained work, you don't expect instant results and you have the passion to succeed. But at the moment you have those muscles only for music. We will work toward helping you use those same muscles for emotional growth."

On the basis of the conflict I could discern between his severe, circular, closed-system pathology and his open-system competence, I recommended psychoanalysis. I said that, if I could, I would see him 7 times a week, but all I have is 4 times per week. We'll see how that works.

Karl was an out-of-town student. He was 19; at first he felt that there was no reason to include his parents in his treatment, as his problems had nothing to do with them anymore. I explained the idea of dual goals of treatment and noted that, from what he told me, he has a very complex and difficult relationship with both his parents. One of our goals would be to help him and help them transform the relationship to one where they could be a life-long resource for each other and not continue the time-consuming dance they now do to avoid or manipulate each other. I said that I would be available to see his parents when they were in town or by phone or videoconference.

Karl's mother came to town at the end of his second week of analysis and the three of us met for a double session. She brought a stack of psychological, psychiatric and neurological reports dating back to when Karl was 3 years old. I said that I would read them closely later but I glanced through the first report. He had been referred at 3 for psychological testing. The tester arrived at the diagnosis of ADHD and a recommendation for psychiatric evaluation for medication. Karl was put on medication soon after. Karl's mother did want me to know that all these experts agreed that he had neurological and other biological disorders.

I shared my puzzlement that the psychologist made no mention of family issues. For example, he had a sister 4 years older who was, according to Karl, "insanely jealous and always getting into physical battles." The family moved across the country when Karl was 10 months old and the next day his father, a businessman, left for a job that kept him away for a year. Father returned periodically and the parents would get into screaming rows. Karl's earliest memories were of standing outside his parents' bedroom listening to their battles.

In the report the psychologist described 3-year-old Karl requiring frequent breaks from the testing to "shout at or wrestle with the dolls" and the psychologist took this as an example of Karl's inability to self-regulate and a sign of ADHD. I said that I wasn't necessarily questioning the diagnosis but wasn't it possible that Karl was showing the psychologist that everyone at home was constantly shouting and fighting? Karl and his mother were both struck by this.

Then I scanned the referral letter for his next evaluation at age 6 and I remarked, "Things seem to be getting worse. He is now on Ritalin 2x/

day, medication for allergies and asthma, and he is described as 'having behavior problems, aggressive toward other children, impulsive, stubborn, provocative, competitive, and needs to be the center of attention.'" They were both getting uncomfortable, so I put the reports down and didn't read out the end of the referral note that described him exhibiting his penis at home, demanding attention for it, and pressing his penis against his sister and parents.

I wondered aloud how we could square these reports with the fact that he seemed to be such a nice and caring person. That side of him must have come from somewhere. They both relaxed and I asked what Karl was like as an infant. I asked him if he had heard stories of his infancy and he said he did not think so. "Well," I said, "this is a chance to hear things that are in your bones but you can't remember." Mother smiled and described, with obvious love in her voice, a smooth pregnancy and a very joyful, easy infancy. She said that he was active, alert, fed well, slept and was "an absolute delight." Her love was reinforced by the contrast with the older child who had been an extremely difficult infant and toddler. I mentally registered this crucial information as it gave a reality basis for the intense jealousy of the older sister.

The atmosphere of the session changed. Both words and body language expressed a deep love between mother and son. Mother then began to speak of her own parents, the difficulty she always had with them, and how overwhelming it was now as they were old, but they frustrated all her efforts at helping them. Karl said some supportive and comforting words and mother began to cry. She then said, "I was Karl's age when I went into analysis and my therapist would have nothing to do with my parents. If I could have done then what you're doing now, perhaps things would be different for me and my parents."

The complex interaction of Karl's personal analysis and what can be called "treatment of the parent via the adolescent" can be illustrated in the transformations of Karl's relationship with each of his parents, and their corresponding changes. Karl had many discussions with his parents throughout his treatment, using his analytic insights to address long-standing troubles and clarify issues.

Karl's father had a major anger management problem. From his own analytic work, Karl began to empathize and see this as father's way to avoid feeling helpless. At the start of analysis, Karl said that he hated his father. When he was with him he did things that brought out the worst side of father, which then confirmed and intensified the negative interaction. The analytic work helped Karl understand that he provoked his father so as not to feel guilty for his own rage, rivalry and eventually his guilt for the feeling of triumph in relation to father. By the spring, Karl could have long talks with his father, share his feelings of hurt and eventually express his love and longing for his frequently absent father.

Karl's hypercritical attitude and fear of the impact of his anger was an issue he had shared at our first meeting. He had told me of his critical thought about the generation gap between us and there were other negative or even hostile thoughts. We first focused on the fact that uncontrolled anger and physical fights with his sister were daily events in his house. We came to call anger the "family language." It was clear that the "family language" wasn't just anger, but intense anger, like a racing car exploding from 0 to 100 in seconds.

The anger felt so intense that Karl had the belief from early childhood that it must be really powerful in its impact on the real world. I took this up in relation to his friends, and also in the analytic relationship, where Karl's criticism of me was first defended against, built up, and then felt so strong that, when it emerged following interpretation, for instance, of his lateness and sleeping through, he became very anxious that I would respond in kind and want to get rid of him. The explanation that anger can be simply an internal signal, leading to problem-solving rather than catastrophe, is a realistic intervention that often provides great relief to patients. We worked on anger as a signal rather than a weapon; Karl made adaptive use of this idea with friends and in sessions.

Karl sometimes experienced himself as "depressed and alone." Then he would call his mother and tell her his grievances about his roommates. She would get furious at them and then angry at him for not solving his problems. In this way Karl used mutual anger as his way to stay magically connected to his parents and sister.

Our work on these issues began to bear fruit. When he returned home for a holiday, Karl watched the anger dynamic at play among family members but did not get caught up. At the end of the vacation he told mother some of things he had learned about the family use of anger; he said that he would like to find a better way to stay connected with her. His mother worked well with this, took it to her own therapist, and she and Karl began to learn better ways to relate than by finding a third party to be angry at or being angry at each other.

The divorced parents had never agreed about anything but, at the end of the year, they agreed that the analysis was the best thing they had done for Karl and that it had changed their relationships with their son.

One interesting aspect of this case is the long-term impact of prescription drugs for children. As noted, Karl's mother had brought copies of Karl's evaluations starting at age 3 until 12. He was evaluated for ADHD, learning and behavior issues, and "strange symptoms" leading to neurological examinations. He was tested by neuropsychologists, pediatricians, educational psychologists and neurologists at 3, 6, 7, 9, 10, 12. He was on Ritalin before Kindergarten, had medication for asthma and allergies from age 6 on, and by 10 was diagnosed as bipolar and put on Prozac. By 10 he was showing "strange symptoms" which led to neurological testing to rule out a seizure disorder.

At 19 when I saw him, he was a heavy marijuana user, abused alcohol, and it wasn't clear whether he still actually used Ritalin and Prozac. He definitely had prescriptions for them, as he sold these drugs in addition to marijuana.

Karl said that at first the medications made him feel that there was something wrong with him, that his brain was not like anyone else's. But then he began to think "it's cool." He could recall talking to his friends as early as 8 years old and telling them that he had a "chemical imbalance." It made him feel special. It was a physiological thing; he said, "I had no control or responsibility. I couldn't help it. At first I hated it and then I began to act out to prove I needed medication."

We did not focus particularly on the drugs in the analytic work, but other changes affected his level of drug use. By the end of the year he seemed to use marijuana only to go to sleep. He was clearly very gifted musically; the analysis, especially of his anger, allowed for a surge of creativity. He was spending so much time producing, writing and playing music that, as he said, he had no interest in anything interfering with his mind.

I think he was also influenced, consciously and unconsciously, by my attitudes to medication for children. I had made it clear that I did not think he ever "had" ADHD or any of the other conditions he had been diagnosed with. I think that the quick acceptance by doctors, parents and patients of medications with no sound scientific basis may represent a wish and belief in quick, easy omnipotent solutions, rather than a realistic assessment of the work needed to resolve conflicts and find new, realistic ways to regulate the self.

It was clear from early on that he had never learned a competent way to regulate his anger. From an early age his parents had used medication for that purpose. As the treatment progressed, it emerged that he had a similar approach to regulating pleasure. Pleasure quickly became uncontrolled excitement regulated by getting angry and then regulating anger through medication. The heavy pot use, he said, was a direct continuation of the Ritalin. It had few side effects but served the same purpose of affect regulation.

Karl was a performer, an excellent one, but this complicated a concern he began to talk about near the end of his first year of analysis. To him, everything was a performance; he said that he had difficulty separating authentic states of being from performances. For example, he said that one reason for his sexual difficulties (lack of pleasure, frequent inability to have an orgasm) was that sex was a performance and he mainly focused on his impact on the woman. "It's like I would forget to have an orgasm, I was so busy making sure that she had one and she thought that I was terrific." Performing became another magical way of dealing with helplessness. Karl continued to confuse performance based on withholding, lies and "wild" behavior with performance based on competent functioning. He still didn't know how to differentiate genuine praise from a manipulated response: a well-received musical gig felt to him the same as fooling the doctors into thinking he had a chemical imbalance or even epilepsy.

By the end of the first year of treatment he had become an outstanding student and a very busy and creative musician and producer. With the diminution of Karl's belief in the omnipotence of his anger, we could focus once more on his closed-system defenses against pleasure and love, and his continuing vulnerability at times of separation.

Karl recalled his terrible homesickness at summer camp and how it felt weak, babyish and vulnerable to miss anyone. Sadness, he feared, would lead to depression and confirm that he had "bipolar disorder." I told him that sadness was very different from depression. Sadness comes from missing someone or something you love. There may be pain, but, supported by his love, he could gradually build up the emotional muscle to bear the sadness.

Karl's positive reaction to this intervention allowed us to assume that he had love in him, but that we would have to explore why he seems afraid to love. We first acknowledged the deep love between Karl and his mother, noting the mother-child bond. Only then could we examine the possessive love and triumphant sexual love he also felt for her. His accompanying anxiety, omnipotent beliefs and the powerful defenses he used to deny his love came into the work.

"Love," Karl said, "makes me feel vulnerable and childish. When you have a father who is always leaving, it's hard to keep love going. When he would return, it was like a great social event. Unlike my mother and sister, I didn't fight with him. He liked to spend time with me, but then he would leave and I felt thrown away like an unwanted toy."

But the real danger he experienced was the love between him and his mother. His sister's envy was a theme throughout, along with his constant need to defer to her, to placate her, to be the little boy who idealized his older sister. Karl went home on a holiday. There was a party he wanted to go to, where he would see a girl he liked. He asked his sister to come along, to get her opinion of the girl and to help him approach her. At the party his sister did introduce him to the girl he fancied. Karl asked her out and she accepted. He told me, "When she agreed to go out with me I went right off her. I figured that there must be something wrong with her if she's willing to go out with me."

Karl was 20 years old by this point, but we could see that his low self-esteem came not only from years of feeling like a neurologically-damaged child, but included his maintaining a negative self-image to avoid sexual success and the subsequent envious rage of his older sister. In the second year of treatment, work continued on an open-system alternative for regulating his anger and we began to address his significant sexual difficulties with women.

Karl's feeling that his mother preferred him to both his sister, younger brother, and his father had some reality basis. In adolescence, however, it evolved into a forbidden sexual love for his mother. This was contained in his masturbation fantasies. He recalled discovering masturbation in the bath as a young child. Once his father walked in while he was enjoying running the tap water over his penis. He remembered his father glowering at him and calling him a "sex boy."

Karl's mother expressed guilt over preferring him to her daughter; to Karl this confirmed his belief in his mother's exclusive love, including her sexual love. All these thoughts and feelings were vigorously defended against by the negative conviction that he was only special by being "chemically imbalanced and a performer who could fool all the doctors."

Clinical work on these issues, summarized and condensed here, gave Karl access to his open-system love. He went on toward the end of the year to have an emotionally rich and mutually sexually satisfying relationship with a talented young woman.

All was going well in most areas. Karl enjoyed and appreciated his sessions. I began to wonder to myself and then out loud why there was no mention of finishing. Karl said it had crossed his mind, but then he thought that I would be upset if he mentioned ending. He had never thought of therapy ending except by quitting, as had happened in his previous treatments.

I described to Karl that we were in a "pretermination" phase, a time when we can look together at the changes, the issues that require further work, and consider what we have to do to prepare for the work of a "goodbye time." He was thrilled with the idea of working together for the task of saying goodbye. He felt this idea made perfect sense and responded with a surge of growth and creativity.

One of the main indicators of change was Karl's increasingly realistic use of his anger as a signal. He had started analysis complaining of difficulties with his roommates. This was an understatement, as he would get into silent rages, nurse his anger and go to bed furious. He would stay up most of the night planning revenge and eventually need to control his heart-pounding fury by using marijuana.

385

Soon after we discussed the pretermination phase, with its task of putting insights into action, Karl proudly reported how he had dealt with an unpleasant incident. His female roommate insulted him when she looked at one of his baby pictures and said he had a "tiny penis." She had also added that he wasn't very muscular now. Karl began to get into a rage but stopped. He said to himself, "Okay, that's a signal that I'm pissed. Now I should use my mind and figure out what to do." He talked about his pride in controlling himself, as he realized that his roommate was drunk and just trying to provoke him. He also realized that she was too drunk to listen, so he would talk with her the following day. He felt good about his plan and went easily to sleep. The next day he engaged her, told her she had been totally inappropriate, and walked away feeling proud of how much he had grown. But he also felt a bit lost and insecure, without the familiar safety of his omnipotent rage.

In the spring of the second year, in the context of Karl's feeling of uncertainty and worry, he said, "Someone once said I had a 'God complex.' It made me feel very uncomfortable. But I do want to be great, I do want to be the center of the universe. I feel threatened when I can't be the center. But there are high stakes in that. I avoid doing things to avoid failure. I think I move in extremes – I'm either the one pulling all the strings or I don't have anything to do with it at all."

I said, "We have an opportunity here. This could be and is a collaboration. But you feel I'm the God pulling all the strings; other times you're the God."

"Right," said Karl. "There are times I feel you're in charge and it gets scary for me; I feel small and helpless. Other times I feel I'm in charge and I'm doing all the work and I resent you. Then I feel I don't need you and it's a waste of time." We began to look more closely at the price Karl paid for self-regulating by living at these extremes.

Work on his "God Complex" continued to the end of his treatment. We established how his "God Complex" pervaded his functioning and colored all his relationships including its ramifications in the treatment relationship. Karl said, "It's scary to think you might be wrong. My father is a wrathful god, so I must be afraid of your wrath too. When my father criticizes my music, I can't say he's wrong. I agree with him and then I'm resentful." I suggested that treatment is a place to practice another way to have a relationship.

Karl said, "I have great difficulty being with people I disagree with. I build relationships based on the God complex, on people saying yes to me. But then I get stuck." We talked about the alternative of cooperative relationships, where people share responsibility. "Oh," Karl exclaimed, "there's only one god, god doesn't share. But I've been enjoying cooperating. I should look at my feelings. Being a god or having a god is worship, not pleasure. Pleasure should be my signal and motivator."

From a session very near the end of Karl's school year, the second year of treatment:

"So my thesis is due in 8 days – I'm kinda stressed out about it. I've not got as far as I hoped. I wanted 5 tracks of music – I'll have 4. Don't know how it will affect my grade. I was talking to my girlfriend June, telling her I was upset. Last time you and I were talking about the "God Complex." My upset is part of it. If I had to get something done I would stay up and not sleep for days and get it done. I would then feel, wow! I had some super power. I'm disappointed in myself. I'm comparing myself to others. My thesis won't be the best.

"But now I have another feeling, something different. Having only 4 tracks allows me to look at it and see that 'it is what it is.' But I keep going back and forth – feeling like a failure and feeling OK.

"I don't know if it relates, but recently I notice that I need to perform around June. I notice that I have self-doubt about her. I saw her coming out of her house, all dressed up – she looked so beautiful! I immediately felt that she's too good for me. I was surprised. I told her how I perform for people but I felt vulnerable telling her. Then she'll know I'm performing and I don't want her to call me on it. I was getting manic around her but after I told her our relationship is calmer."

(Brave to tell her but what are you covering up?)

"That I'm not good enough."

(If I know something you don't know then I'm God and you're the scared little kid. But if you know something I don't know, then you're God and you feel resentful, as you sound now.)

"Yeah, well I <u>did</u> tell you that I felt that I'm not good enough."

(But that doesn't make sense. You brought up the God Complex and I think that you're covering up that you are not really God.)

"I didn't mention that I won the Merit Scholarship. $5,000 and you know the work I put in."

(Congratulations! But that's not very God-like. God doesn't have to work. It's interesting that you tell me of a real accomplishment that needed real work when we said that you're covering up that you're not really God.)

"I was talking to June about doctors and how that's a profession in which there is no room for mistakes. When I'm God there's no room for mistakes, there's only one chance, so that's when I start performing."

(The God idea is an old stand-by to protect yourself – we've talked about how great it feels, how it's like being your dad and connects you with him instead of fighting him, but you're now beginning to see the cost of this protective system. Let me suggest an alternative, which you hinted at when you described your 4-track recording as "it is what it is." The alternative is being "good enough." I'm a doctor; I don't feel that I have no room for mistakes because you're there to correct me. I'm happy to be good enough.)

"That is a new idea. My recording is not God-like, it's good enough."
(I don't think that June loves you because you're God. You're a human being who is very hard-working, creative and you have other nice human qualities. You're good enough.)
"Ouch! That's hard to take. I don't want to be good enough for June. I want to be the best. It's hard to give up."
(You always have the God way – like being a stoner, once you've lived that way you can always do that. But now you have alternatives – like being competent, loving and creative)
"Hmm. I was planning the transition – what was I going to do when this semester ends. My first thought was to get totally stoned. To smoke weed all day. I know how I don't feel good doing that, yet here I was planning to get stoned. I was really planning to have the kind of day I had every day when we first started. Sit all alone in a dark room smoking weed and watching old movies and eating junk."
(What do you think?)
"My first thought is that I like to spoil good times. I had an extraordinary year, in every area including June."
(What do you think other people feel when you're God?)
"Resentful, jealous – and I feel guilty."
(If you're God then all that you've accomplished is not through hard work and emotional muscle, but because you're God.)
"I was talking to my Dad about talent. I hate the word 'talent.' People explain success as due to talent, as if it's genetic and you don't have to do anything but let it come out like a daffodil in spring. All the 'talented' people I know have worked hours and hours and years and years. It's funny hearing you saying the same thing I said to my dad, only it's me you're talking about and I'm doing to myself the thing I hate people saying about successful artists."

(Great! You now have a conflict inside your head. You have a choice. You can think you're God with the rush of feeling that goes with that, or you can be real and acknowledge all the hard work and effort you put into your accomplishments and feel good about that.)

"I can't believe I was planning on getting stoned. Like I don't know what to do in transitions."

(Talk to you tomorrow)

Soon after we began to talk about an ending date, making sure we would have enough time to have a good goodbye.

Very near the end of our work, Karl attended a family event, which gave him a chance to observe his mother and her sisters interacting with their father, his grandfather. Karl noticed that the sisters were all out of touch with their own feelings; they didn't seem to feel allowed to express things directly but became upset and preoccupied about minor and irrelevant things. The feelings could only come out in disguise. Karl linked this to his own previous need to hide his true self behind performance.

This insight about his mother went beyond our previous understandings about her. Karl had become, as I said, "a better therapist for himself than I had been." He could now figure out more than we had before. I described this as a goal of treatment, the result of our cooperative work and his setting aside his belief that either he or I had to be an omniscient and omnipotent God.

COMMENTARY 1

I was glad to see that the analyst acknowledged, right at the beginning, that he found Karl to be a likeable chap. It seems to me that this early and intuitive sense contributed to the analyst's ability to opine to Karl that he might profit from analytic work.

This reminds me of a paper I read perhaps 50 years ago in which skilled psychiatric diagnosticians were asked to give a tentative diagnosis at the 5-minute point in an initial interview, and then again at the end of a series of diagnostic interviews. The 5-minute impressions turned out to be as accurate and helpful for treatment planning as those formed after a much more lengthy assessment. All of which is to say that there's a lot of processing that goes on between analyst and analysand in those first few minutes.

The work done by Karl and the analyst illustrates the complementary relationship between the two goals of this treatment: (1) to get Karl back onto an age-appropriate developmental track and (2) to help Karl and his parents build mutually-rewarding relationships that might sustain them in the future.

The past tendency by drive-theory analysts (and others) to prohibit any involvement with parents amounts to a bit of denial of the roles played by the objects of the drives. These people affect drive expression in ongoing, interactive ways; ignoring that reality does not make it less true.

The analyst's work on helping Karl to observe his internal affective and behavioral signals (e.g., his anger, or his inability to say his thoughts out loud) stands in stark contrast to those therapies which ignore or try to paper over these valuable signals with psychotropic drugs or cognitive-behavioral techniques.

Karl's comment early on that he felt uncomfortable about feeling good led to a question that both Karl and the analyst could ponder seriously: "What keeps you from enjoying your life?" The search for an answer to that question became a mutually-endorsed goal of the treatment, a treatment that was to be a partnership.

The analyst put Karl to the test early on with his question about what Karl didn't like about the analyst; and Karl watched to see how the analyst would respond to his answer. Karl's concern about the "generation gap" seemed genuine and the analyst complimented Karl for his bravery (rather than sitting in non-neutral silence). They already were building their partnership.

Work with Karl and his mother quickly led to a rich vein when the analyst asked mother how child-rearing issues were handled in her family when she was growing up. This evocation of the ghosts in mother's attic proved to be very helpful as both mother and Karl began to see how her past had affected her relationship with Karl.

This work, which the analyst terms "treatment of the parent via the adolescent," turns the Hanna Perkins model of "treatment [of the child] via the parent" (Furman, 1981) on its head. Both phrases acknowledge that analytic work with an individual person always occurs within a matrix of relationships. Just as Winnicott (1960) could say "there is no such thing as an infant [unless there is a mother caring for that infant]," we can say "there is no such thing as an adolescent [unless there are parents – both internalized and external – who are interacting with and caring for that adolescent]."

It was important to discover that Karl's mother had not lost her connection to Karl; seeing that, the analyst could make use of her wish to forge a new, better relationship with her son. Had this not been true, the analyst and Karl might have had to re-assess their goal of building a bridge between Karl and his mother.

The analyst also helped Karl to begin to think about his father – especially about how his father's mind works. The clarifications of how his family used anger as a kind of language put Karl into a position where he could observe his parents anew. Explosive anger could be replaced by "signal anger" – a feeling which could alert Karl to dangers and then allow him to think about adaptive ways to respond to those dangers.

The analyst's open disdain for the various diagnoses that had been used with Karl conveyed a sense that the analyst did not see Karl as either a "defective brain" person or a "special brain" person – images that had bedeviled Karl since early childhood.

The analyst also helped Karl to draw a boundary between sadness and depression. Sadness is evidence of love and exists only in that context. Like anger, it is another signal affect (as well as a bodily experience). Sadness is a normal, healthy response to loss, not a pathological symptom to be blunted with drugs or denied.

The Novicks' (Novick, J. & Novick, K., 2013) earlier elaboration of open and closed systems of defenses sheds light on Karl's use of an image of himself as God. As a child, this image helped him survive some of the attacks he experienced from his parents (especially his father). In the long run, however, this image cost him dearly. First, it imposed God-like standards of perfection that Karl could not meet. Second, it implied that Karl was responsible (like God) for everything that happens, both good and bad. The analyst's ability to tolerate his own imperfections, coupled with his belief that Karl would put him right if the analyst said something that was off base ["I'm a doctor; I don't feel that I have no room for mistakes because you're there to correct me. I'm happy to be good enough."] conveyed the analyst's own comfort with not being God; and along with that, he was openly willing to partner with non-God Karl. Two non-Gods were able to do the kind of work that helped Karl to set aside (though probably not completely) the pleasures of God-head.

This "good enough" analysis, conducted by a "good enough" analyst and an analysand who eventually could tolerate being "good enough," stands as a fine example of what psychoanalysis has to offer. It is not freedom from conflicts; it is the ability to acknowledge conflicts for what they are – neither more nor less – and to use one's mind in a flexible, open way to chart a path forward.

COMMENTARY 2

It takes courage in this day and age of psychiatric medications and brief, usually behaviorally-oriented treatments, to recommend psychanalysis. I usually find myself hesitating for a least a few moments and needing to muster the fortitude to recommend a treatment that I anticipate the young person – and his or her parents – are likely to react to with perplexity and disbelief. At the same time, like this analyst, I see analysis (or multiple-times-week therapy) as the treatment of choice for young people struggling with longstanding neurotic conflicts. I find that young people, despite initial reservations, find the recommendation for intensive treatment relieving because it conveys I understand the depth of their distress – crucial because the people around them rarely do. In addition, it communicates that I am open to hearing about their suffering, which reassures them (at least partly) that I want to create a space to really get to know them in all their complexity. It's noteworthy that this analyst tells the young man he'd prefer to see him daily, which communicates receptivity to the young man's suffering and commitment to helping him.

I was intrigued by the analyst's early explicit invitation to Karl to say to the analyst what Karl didn't like about him or her. I think it's crucial to convey to our patients that we can tolerate their awareness of our shortcomings and limitations, especially because most, like Karl, believe their disappointment in others is damaging. One could have a lively discussion of technique in this context. I wonder, for instance, if the direct invitation to express a criticism bypasses the patient's defenses. On the other hand, it offers a chance to show Karl in real time how anxiety-provoking he finds his critical thoughts to be. I wondered how that particular transference reaction to the analyst's age played out over the course of the treatment for Karl – and for the analyst.

I appreciate the analyst's deliberate focus on goals at the outset. In my experience, analysts tend to give goals short shrift, and that can hinder the development of the treatment alliance. I also valued the analyst's focus on psychiatric medication, which I grapple with frequently, especially with college students, most of whom come for treatment on at least one medication. I agree that the quick movement toward medication in Karl's case – and in many of mine – reflects a lack of affect tolerance in the people in children's and adolescents' surround, mainly parents and mental health professionals. I agree, too, that it can create the sense in children that they are damaged – biologically and beyond repair. I often find it hard to know what stance would be optimal, especially with medications for depression and anxiety. While, like this analyst, I tend to be skeptical about psychiatric meds in circumstances like Karl's, I also wonder if some of my patients derive at least some benefit from them. I often recommend a careful review of medications with a psychiatrist I trust (because she believes in therapy and is conservative about meds), which includes consideration of whether medications are needed at all.

The issue of marijuana, too, comes up frequently with college students, many of whom, like Karl, have used it regularly for years and underestimate its long-term negative impact on their functioning. I find that young people who have used marijuana steadily for years are often severely stunted in their emotional growth because they've avoided the essential task of dealing with difficult affect states. Like this analyst, I frame pot use to my young patients as an easy way to deal with difficult feelings, such as anxiety and despondency, and suggest that, in the long run, it will be crucial to develop other means for addressing such feelings. Young people expect a judgmental approach to their substance use, reflecting how their parents have dealt with it as well as an exernalization of their own self-judgment. They appreciate a non-critical, commonsense approach. The implication in the case report is that Karl greatly reduced his marijuana use, though there's some ambiguity about it. I work hard to establish an open communication with young people about their use, which is often hard to track. It's tricky because direct queries tend to get bound up with intrusive parental transferences, which must be addressed.

Many analysts would eschew work with parents, given Karl's age. I'm inclined in working with college students to work with parents when there's significant tension that serves as a developmental interference. I'm not sure

I would have done parent work in Karl's case, but I believe from the case description that I would have missed an important opportunity. I valued the analyst's assertion that resolving conflicts between "child" and parent can help the young person continue to use his or her parents as a resource across the life cycle, an idea that many of us underestimate or ignore. I think therapists working with young people lose track of this crucial reality in their quest to establish the importance of the therapy or to bolster their own sense of importance.

The analyst focuses in the write-up on omnipotence, which provides a coherent and useful framework in which to consider Karl's difficulties traversing late adolescence and moving on constructively with his life. I find that many talented young people who have managed childhood's challenges easily, and are encouraged by parents who, in an ostensibly supportive stance, tell them they can do "anything," face excruciating difficulties when they try to navigate the more substantive challenges of sexual intimacy and competitive college coursework. They stumble and need help figuring out why. The painful acceptance of one's limitations and the limitations of others, including the analyst, facilitate ongoing development, as shown so richly here.

When I think of analytic work, I think of the moments, on display here, when analyst and patient establish a comfortable meeting of minds. In addition, I think about the many tough moments when I feel puzzled, stuck, and grapple with powerful, often painful emotions stirred by the work. In keeping with much contemporary writing on psychoanalytic process, I find that dealing with confusing enactments stimulated by patients' projective identifications becomes central to the therapeutic task. In working with young people in particular, I often find myself struggling with the need to take myself back to painful times in my own late adolescence in order to relate to theirs, as well as an acute awareness of the passage of time and envy of my young patients' having most of their lives in front of them. Karl's analyst alludes to tough moments when Karl came late or slept through sessions, but moves past them quickly. More open reflection on the emotional challenges of the work with Karl would have drawn me deeper into the case.

EDITORIAL REFLECTIONS

This chapter brings us a demonstration of the therapeutic potential of a particular technical approach to an adolescent who was in dire straits. The analyst and commentators all note that this young man's longstanding difficulties and current struggles made intensive work the treatment of choice, but they also point out the early and complex mutual processing initiated by the analyst from the beginning of the exploratory sessions. Immediate trial interpretations led to articulation of core conflicts around pleasure and description of characteristic defenses that were targeted in setting treatment goals.

This analyst introduced the idea of dual overall goals for this treatment, which proved very important to the effectiveness of the work. Both the adolescent patient and his parents spoke to the ongoing value of the parent work for them all. In the context of historical psychoanalytic denial of the importance of <u>real</u> objects, that is, parents and other significant adults in a child's life, this chapter brings us to a fuller theoretical appreciation of the developmental importance of paying attention to intergenerational patterns as they play out in the interaction of the pleasure, reality, and growth principles. Individual work always takes place within a matrix of actual relationships. Technically, this mandates concurrent parent work with a view to transforming and restoring the parent-child relationship to a lifelong positive resource for both parents and child.

Omnipotence can be seen as a frame of this treatment; the patient's closed-system use of medications, drugs, and image of himself as a god brought together his childhood history and his crucial pivot from shame to entitlement to avoid internal conflict and narcissistic injury. Reconstruction of the sequence he experienced inside when pleasure led to excitement that felt uncontrollable, which he tried to regulate with rage that his parents then sought to control with medication, allowed for expanding the field of attention. The analyst and patient could then explore central adolescent challenges of sexuality, authenticity, and competence.

Like the commentators, we were struck with the success of this treatment in the relatively short time of two years. We would do well to compare and contrast those cases where there is a positive outcome after a relatively short time with those that span many years and often several phases of development. Relevant technical lessons reside in the analyst's active approach, the even-handed attention to fluctuations in pathological solutions <u>and</u> positive ego capacities and functions (a two-systems stance), explicit fostering of a therapeutic alliance with the patient encouraged to share and then take on responsibility for the momentum of the work, especially in the pre-termination and termination phases, and conscious effort to hold the goals of growth in mind. Without explicit focus on the patient's drug use, the work of the analysis radically diminished the addiction to marijuana that had followed on the lifelong extensive use of psychostimulant and psychotropic medications to regulate feelings for this young man.

CHAPTER 16

MEGAN – age 19

Less than half way through her freshman year of college, Megan, an intelligent 19-year-old female, withdrew from classes and returned home. Though preparing for this transition had occupied much of the two years of twice-weekly psychotherapy that preceded this attempt, no one had been particularly surprised by the outcome. Megan had worked hard in therapy, but issues of safety and weekly crises had dominated the treatment, making progress difficult. While we had explored the possibility of more intensive work a couple of times during the two years, there were always barriers to moving forward. After Megan settled back into her childhood home, and as she began to consider the possibility of a second launch, we were finally able to transition into psychoanalytic treatment. Once we did, both of us were struck by how quickly this change in frame and frequency enabled us to expand and deepen our understanding of the painful dynamics that had plagued her from early childhood.

Megan had just started her junior year of high school when we first met, and both she and her mother described Megan as having a long history of disproportionately large reactions to a whole range of obstacles and challenges. As she grew, academics had become the main venue for these "storms." While Megan was clearly quite bright, she had always displayed a pattern of avoidance and procrastination. Large assignments were painfully pulled together over the final early morning hours before a due date, or completed through extensions and other accommodations. No volume of study skills courses or other external supports had shifted this pattern. In fact, when faced with a deadline, Megan frequently dissolved into tears and angry outbursts, sure that she would fail each time. Accomplishing anything often became a family affair, with her mother and sometimes her older siblings helping her to calm herself and organize her thinking. Megan herself expressed frustration that "I just can't seem to get my brain to work, though I am often proud of the final product when I can get there."

Anxiety around these dynamics increased as she aged, and was compounded by tensions in the family related to her father's increasing absences due to overseas work obligations. With more family responsibilities falling to her mother, Megan felt increasingly burdensome when she required support from her mother, castigating herself for her needs, and ultimately turning to thoughts that "my family would be better off without me." Her belief that she was a burden on both parents was amplified when marital tensions and talk of separation began just after she entered therapy. Faced with open displays of emotional need from both parents, needs that were notably separate from her own, Megan reacted with rage and shame. She was furious that her family was "shattering beneath me," and sure her own needs would bury each newly saddled parent. Though her parents ultimately reconciled, tensions and uncertainty certainly amplified Megan's already conflictual feelings around the transition away from home.

Megan had grown up in an upper middle-class home, the third child and second daughter of active, adventurous parents with a lukewarm romantic relationship, and parenting responsibilities that fell largely to the mother as the father spent long stretches overseas on work assignments, a situation that became more regular after Megan's birth. Megan's older siblings, a brother and sister, were born just 18 months apart from one another and shared a close relationship. They were also very similar to one another, devoted to the same individual sport, high achieving academically, and "very different from me," Megan explained. Megan was born 3 years later, unexpectedly, preferred art and music to sport, but also craved her siblings' attention. She recalls being frequently banished from their games and crying for her mother to demand they include her. Quite early she was found to be a talented musician and in this area she thrived, both in terms of skill development and genuine enjoyment. Talent and passion propelled her fairly far, and she seemed more able to both devote consistent effort to this pursuit and derive considerable positive self-regard from her success. By the time we met, Megan was engaged in more than one, rather high-profile, performance groups, though even in this realm she was struggling to keep up with the demands of preparation and practice.

Megan's mother would confirm that, given the father's frequent absences and the stress of raising three highly scheduled children, she saw herself as the fixer in the family. She would fix whatever needed fixing, as efficiently as possible, even if what needed fixing was someone else's feelings, which it often was with Megan. Other times, this meant taking the path of least resistance and functioning for her children rather than taking the time to teach them the steps to function for themselves. Her actions were confounded by a more overt message that independence was the ideal, which she herself displayed and lauded in her older children. In our first meeting, she confessed with a pained expression that though she knew Megan often felt overwhelmed, she worried that her daughter used her pain to make things happen around her, and she was clearly dismayed by this tendency in her child. Megan's father, on the other hand, responded to his daughter's emotional distress by making intermittent large gestures to punctuate his general absence. These were typically highly desired purchases, like electronics or a car. As these purchases were rarely thought through, he often became resentful of the long-term costs, contributing to Megan's feelings of guilt and burdensomeness.

Beginning psychotherapy two years prior to analysis, Megan was quick to lean into the treatment. She never missed a session and she had no difficulty filling the hours with material, from her anger at her parents, to her academic struggles, to her frustrations over the workings of her own mind. A positive transference quickly developed as Megan was used to seeking help from others and receiving support. My stance of neutral non-judgment served to deepen her trust. I also came to enjoy and look forward to the sessions. Megan was engaged and clearly in need of help. The sessions initially felt productive and there was much to address. I noticed that I felt useful.

By the end of the first year, however, it also became clear that Megan carried little forward between sessions. I noticed hints of irritation alongside my hopeful anticipation as each week began to feel like the containment of a new crisis. Megan would also remain fixated on external, unalterable factors, and it was a challenge to interpret her resistance to exploring internal barriers to change when I had to wait a week to address any feelings of hurt or anger that such an exploration might generate. Though we were able to wade into conflicts around dependency and Megan's difficulty in tolerating her awareness of her mother's separate internal world and priorities, Megan tended to use insight as an opportunity to dig deeper into a wound, rather than as a building block towards a more solid internal structure. Distress remained high, for both Megan and her family. While the therapeutic relationship seemed to prevent a worsening of the situation, there was not enough time or structure to really address the underlying dynamics which kept affects running high.

Soon we were immersed in the world of college preparation, applications, and the school selection process. The nearer we drew to college itself, the more anxious Megan became about her prospects of functioning independently. Her terror about leaving home amplified and the pull to curl up and retreat into childhood consciously dominated sessions, while at home Megan fought fiercely with her parents and pushed against rules and limits. Music fell into the background and nothing felt meaningful. Though Megan ultimately made the transition to college, she returned home part way through the first semester, paralyzed by anxiety, plagued by self-doubt, and preoccupied by intrusive suicidal thoughts. It was at that time, after a couple of months of rest, when Megan seriously began to consider a reentry into college, that she and I began to discuss the possibility of psychoanalysis. Together we articulated a goal of "finally figuring out what's underneath all of these painful patterns, and why we haven't been able to shift them over the past couple of years of work together."

In preparation for analysis, Megan became anxious about how our increased sessions would impact the costs of treatment. Aware that she would not be able to manage a job with her history of academic struggles, she worried that any increased financial pressure would put too much strain on her parents' still fragile marriage. Would her needs be too much for them this time? After clarifying the financial details, and assuring Megan that I had done likewise with her parents, the increased frequency of analysis provided the opportunity and containment to allow us to peel back the layers of her anxiety rather than focus so much on soothing the affect to ensure safety throughout the rest of the week, as we had had to do in our weekly treatment.

While part of Megan's guilt was certainly tied to her father's long-standing mixed messaging around gifts and affection, she now was able to step outside of the anxious cascade during our sessions with early reassurance of non-judgement and a focus on furthering our understanding under our new model of psychoanalysis. New material arose around her own spending habits, substantial hidden debt, and the associated shame. It became clear that she moved so quickly from shame to feelings of worthlessness and suicidality that any useful degree of guilt, the amount that would have helped her think twice about making a purchase, was completely skipped over. It became clear to both of us that intense emotion had become an "off-ramp" for Megan, a way to unconsciously sidestep further exploration, engagement, or assumption of responsibility, both in conversations with her parents and previously in our work together. Megan was not only making decisions based on the size of her emotional reactions, but she was expecting those around her to act based on the size of her emotions as well. This was the same pattern occurring with each painful academic assignment and in other areas of her life. Shame and anxiety ballooned to an overwhelming degree and the experience was so unpleasant for her and those around her that everyone looked for an out. Unfortunately, relying so heavily on emotional intensity to determine life choices seemed to have diminished her access to other capacities that she once valued quite highly, such as her cognitive skills and musical talents. I made a mental note that rediscovering and enlivening these capacities would likely be a key component of our early work together.

First, however, I would fall into one of a series of enactments, whereby I not only fell into the trap of "acting" based on Megan's emotions, but I also began to experience another dynamic whereby Megan succeeded in externalizing her constructive cognitive functioning into me, as she had done with other trusted "helpers" throughout her life. As Megan was preparing to return to school for her second attempt at launching, I felt a mix of her anxiety and my own. I did not want her to experience failure once again, and I did not want to fail to help her make the transition a second time around. Though she was significantly more motivated this time, focused on how essential she knew it was to prepare on many levels for the transition, she struggled to organize herself and her thoughts. "It's like no matter how much time I set aside to pack or organize, I just sit there staring at everything and it all blurs together. I haven't made any progress and I'm running out of time." Just a few weeks into the analysis a strong sense of helplessness radiated from the couch. Megan began to cry, pulling my tissue box into her lap. I found myself asking "What if she was truly incapable of functioning in this way?" "What if she needs me to do this thinking at this stage of the treatment?" I

404

sprang into action, guided her through an organizing task and felt a strong sense of accomplishment as we "did together" and made a lot of progress.

The next day she arrived, and, to my surprise, slumped even further on the couch than the day prior. She described feeling defeated and even worse about herself. Seeing how easy it had been for me to generate a plan had shown her how "stupid and incapable" she really was. Luckily, we were able to examine this pattern together: how she generated a strong air of helplessness, inducing others (me in this case) to act for her, leading her to feel even more inept and even resentful. Megan was able to trace this pattern far back into her childhood to times when she was struggling with an assignment or chore and one of her older siblings would swoop in and take over, or her mother would "fire ideas at me faster than I could think." The dynamic, however, was complex and fraught with a deeper conflict, because Megan also derived considerable positive feelings from her ability to ask for help and from the perceived close connections she generated from receiving emotionally charged support from others. What was lacking was a sense of awareness of, or empathy for, the other. What might the other feel about being pulled into help when Megan was actually capable of doing for herself? At what developmental level was she identifying "needs"?

The week following the "doing for" incident in session, Megan told the following vignette: "So my friends and I finally did that hike we had been planning. We got up really early, it was gorgeous. Then, about halfway up the mountain, there was a boulder field. I slipped on a loose boulder and pitched way off the trail! I ultimately stopped falling and miraculously didn't hit my head or break anything, but I was so terrified. There was no way I could finish the hike. I was just too shaken." She then described how one of her friends agreed to walk back down the mountain with her, rather than summiting with the others, checking in on her every few minutes, resting with her often. Megan emphasized how lovingly cared for she had felt. In contrast, I found myself wondering how her friend truly felt about having

405

to miss out on the summit to tend to Megan's big feelings. I felt less lovingly towards her and more irritated myself. I did not feel that it would be fruitful to utilize my countertransference directly in that early session, but it did help me clarify her mother's observation that Megan "used her pain to make things happen around her," which irritated her mother as well, though she only revealed this through her facial expressions. Ultimately, I was able to bring this back into session with Megan while decreasing the potential for shame, by framing the dynamic as the dilemma that it was: while Megan was absolutely entitled to her authentic, often strong affective responses to her life experiences, these responses inevitably impacted those around her as well, and she would fare better interpersonally if she could acknowledge and take responsibility for those impacts.

As our work progressed in the opening phase, it became more and more clear that Megan was attempting to enlist me in the role of rescuer, a role that held powerful affective charge for her. In a household where her father was mostly absent, her siblings were functioning quite well and separate from her, and her mother was preoccupied with manning the ship, Megan, flailing internally, could achieve a sense of cohesion by pulling everyone together around her with her big needs and feelings. She was attempting to generate the same affective experience with me in analysis. As I stepped back from accepting my assigned role of rescuer in sessions and declined to function for Megan as she made slow progress packing for school and making travel plans, she vacillated between taking more ownership over these tasks and describing "waves of anxiety, I'm just overwhelmed." Having identified that Megan would only feel more incompetent if I jumped into function for her, we were able to focus on the overwhelmed feeling itself. We talked about the wave as beginning as a stream of water composed of her emotions, which initially served important signal functions: in this case, anxiety alerting her that "there's still more to do to get ready before you move." However, Megan often fed the stream so that it grew into a wave that obliterated any path forward. She then could not think and ultimately used the wave and the flooded aftermath to pull others into acting for her, thinking for her, ultimately leading her to feel even worse about her ability to think and act on her own, as she'd done with me. Recognizing this pattern, Megan was able to shift back into a functional action mode.

In the final week leading up the start of her reentry into college, Megan remained focused on logistical preparations with notable persistence of motivation and even excitement. However, she had difficulty trusting the positive feelings she was experiencing. "What if I've just been pushing the bad feelings aside and they are all going to come flooding back?" With more exploration of these anxieties, Megan was able to identify that she had often become stuck, academically and otherwise, when she encountered projects or situations that were more difficult than she had expected, whether it be a project for school or packing for college. She seemed to freeze in these situations, preoccupied by self-doubt. Given that Megan had always been seen as a very bright child, gifted in music and other areas, and reminded as such, it is likely that she equated "things coming easily" with intelligence. When she encountered more difficult challenges, rather than trying harder, she questioned her own capacities and undermined her own potential efforts. In other words: It felt bad, she must be bad at it, so there was no point in trying and feeling worse. In addition, inherent in her anxiety around becoming suddenly flooded and overwhelmed by previously split off negative affects was the assumption that these affects would be inherently unbearable and even as unsurvivable as they had always felt. Megan and I explored both of these ideas and she found that they were both very accurate descriptions of her experience. We now understood even more about what drove her to take the emotional off-ramp, and both she and I could look together at the logical conclusion that she would likely need to live the experience of survivable affects before she could trust that "feeling bad" didn't mean being "bad at" and "incapable."

Megan successfully transitioned to college and was able to keep up with assignments without too much difficulty for the first couple of weeks. Though she often began a week feeling the workload was too much to handle, she was able to articulate the affective pull of the experience and the avoidant function: "I see all the assignments and it feels like too much. I start to tell myself that none of it matters, that I'm a failure, that I don't deserve to be here after all. Then I feel like I don't deserve to be alive. I can see I'm taking the suicide off ramp again, but it is a powerful pull." "But now you are here, walking me through all of those steps that you can see yourself taking, instead of just being immersed in it, lost in it." "That is a huge difference, isn't it?!" she replied. "It does feel really different. "And I didn't quit this time, I actually did some work, even though I wasn't sure I could."

A few weeks into the semester, Megan also surprised both of us by responding to a very stressful event in a responsible and independent manner. Her father had bought her a car for school, which had become a point of tension given that the city where she attended school had little affordable parking. One weekend, however, she was involved in a minor but frightening accident in the early morning hours. When she returned to session on Monday Megan relayed, with high emotion, how she had exchanged insurance information, spoken with police, taken her car for an appropriate inspection, and addressed her own mild whiplash with her physician, all on her own. As she relayed her experience with great distress, worried that the emotional impact might derail her academic semester, I was struck by the discord between her affect and her actions. I expressed appropriate empathy regarding her frightening experience and also reflected the mature and appropriate nature of her response, how she had used her anxiety to spur her to action, while avoiding pulling a roommate out of bed or asking a parent to drive several hours to help her navigate the situation. She could likewise take some control over the proportion of her emotional response moving forward, I suggested, so that her fear over the accident didn't prevent her from continuing to engage academically in college. Megan was able to use this framing to balance her time over the following week to devote appropriate time resting her shaken body, getting minor car repairs, and also refocusing on the academic tasks ahead of her so that she did not fall behind as feared.

She also found herself struggling, however, to make basic decisions around the care of her own body, vacillating, for example, over when and how much to eat, whether to take a break from homework to have a snack, or whether to push through and complete a task. She doubted her ability to make such judgements and found herself wondering what I would recommend. She brought this dilemma up in session, both able to recognize her discomfort with her own uncertainty while simultaneously asking me to decide for her. I was reminded of her mother's stories about Megan's difficulties in reading her own signals and planning ahead when she was little. In a frantic effort to make it through the days, her mother had elected to scoop Megan up mid-play and carry her out the door half dressed, only to feed, dress, and otherwise prepare her in transit rather than engage in the much lengthier process of helping her learn to anticipate and plan ahead. Even knowing this I still felt the now familiar pull to function for Megan, to help her think through when she had last eaten, to help her use other indicators to determine if her urge to eat was truly hunger or avoidance. As I resisted this urge, we explored the transference dynamics as well as how her use of my image outside of session could be thought of as a sign of her investment in the still new process of analysis. In addition, however, I think that her regression to asking me to feed her, as if she were a small child in a very dependent relationship, was a reaction to her disappointment that I had not joined her around her pain and fear in regards to the car accident, but around her mature functioning. I believe she herself experienced very little positive self-regard as a result of her mature independent functioning and therefore had difficulty feeling connected to me via this avenue. Though she could see intellectually how "well" she functioned, she did not derive the same sense of closeness and omnipotent control that she was so used to feeling when she generated feelings of helplessness and subsequent rescue from others. I have experienced her cognitive capacities, and it is hard to see her miss out on the opportunity to derive pleasure from her own competence. I believe that it is this pleasure, however, that will ultimately allow her to let go of the omnipotent gratification of being done for.

While there is not room to discuss it in depth, I have also worked closely with both of Megan's parents throughout the opening phase of analysis and plan to continue to do so throughout her treatment. We meet every other week and the emotional availability of each parent has mirrored their physical availability during Megan's childhood. Her mother has shown notable willingness to examine ways that her choices and compromises may have contributed to Megan's difficulties. She was fairly aware of the way that Megan unconsciously used big feeling to pull for rescue, but she had not understood how her (and others') rescuing actions served to leave Megan feeling even more inferior. She was subsequently able to shift to holding a supportive and curious stance when Megan came to her feeling upset, leading to growth in their relationship. In addition, once out of the "weekly crisis" phase of treatment, I found that there was much more time for Megan's mother to associate to earlier experiences from Megan's childhood that strongly supported my understanding of Megan's conflicts. Interestingly, I also found that once Megan began to function with enough improved capacity that she was no longer turning to her mother for such consistent rescue, her mother, in turn, found herself without an off ramp from her own emotional life and her own conflicts. She was more likely to fill sessions with her anger towards Megan's father and her own affective experiences.

Work with Megan's father largely consisted of his expression of a couple of concerns about current dynamics and requests that I reassure him that choices he had made were helpful to his daughter. I was able to better understand that, given the helplessness he felt when faced with Megan's needs, he acted to address the urgency of the moment, later angered when each moment held a fresh set of urgent demands. Both parents expressed relief at the notable decrease in overall urgency once Megan entered analysis. With the structure of four sessions per week, there were only three days each week when she did not have a predictable, safe, containing place to discuss her distress and the ways that she was trying to manage it. "She's more durable," they remarked. "The big feelings are still there, but she bounces back faster and she is able to talk about what's going on, rather than saying it's all too much."

Interestingly, Megan herself became quite interested in psychoanalysis as a discipline as she began to experience it working for her. She was fascinated when she found herself reflecting on her emotions and what she did with them rather than just reacting, and she enjoyed making connections between current relational patterns and earlier familial patterns. In fact, this may be the first area in which she is allowing herself to take pleasure in the use of her cognitive capacities. She has been keeping up with her assignments in a more regular fashion and though issues of avoidance arise, we are more able to discuss them early on. I believe this is because we are working more directly with the psychological conflicts that had become entangled with her academic pursuits. A few months into the analysis, Megan made a notable shift from focusing firmly on the unmovable external barriers to change her thinking about her internal psychological world, becoming eager to understand herself and grow in a way that will allow her to achieve her goals.

As the defensive mental fog clears, and Megan recognizes that her failure to achieve academically is not as much an issue of "can't," she has begun to grapple with the painful question of why her peers seem able to accomplish consistent work, even as they express similar frustrations with the expectations and challenges of college. "Maybe I'm just lazy. I never learned to persevere." She presses me for my view. "I just don't see it in those terms," I explain. I remind her of our discovery that, for her, challenges generate significant negative emotion, and that the urge to flee that emotion predominates over the desire to conquer the challenge. In addition, her tendency to induce others to navigate a challenge for her, means that she rarely learns what she's capable of. "Perhaps that's why it's so hard to feel good about doing something on my own," she surmises. Continuing to ponder this thought, Megan was actually quite productive over the weekend, yet returned on Monday without a feeling of accomplishment. "Even if I can get work done on my own," she was saying, "it doesn't mean I'm ok." Her curiosity about these dynamics remains, however, generated by the analytic process.

COMMENTARY 1

This is a lovely and frank account of the initial stages of the analytic treatment of 19-year-old Megan. The case illustrates the thoughtful and slow entrance into treatment, the issues of transference and counter-transference, and the careful approach to complex defensive structures that are indicative both of the stage of development in general, and the individual history of conflict in particular. This vignette offers us a way of thinking about how to assess and approach developmental conflicts and to differentiate them from more neurotic, embedded conflicts. This is a challenge for the therapist, and in this case, the therapist was able to identify how her own responses provided information about what was going on inside her patient.

Because this case began as a psychotherapy, it offers us an opportunity to observe elements of entry into analytic work that are sequential on one hand (one kind of therapy preceding another kind of therapy), and intricately combined on the other (balancing and promoting current development while at the same time understanding the interferences in that development). The initial psychotherapy, offering support and observation, established a working alliance between Megan and the therapist, during which a positive transference occurred. They focused on the "now," noting and solving current problems to encourage and enable forward development. At the same time, the emotional landscape became clearer, leading both therapist and Megan to understand that she was carrying her fears and conflicts with her and within her. Though triggered by external circumstances and developmental demands and shifts, the root causes to her panics were internal. Once the transition to an in-depth therapy occurred, work began around defenses, around engaging the observational ego, and exploring the inner, the "then" of the neurotic origins.

But the starting point to the treatment was Megan's relationship to the therapist. The non-judgmental responses to Megan's struggles permitted Megan's guilt to stay within rather than be externalized out. This kind and thoughtful response helped mitigate Megan's pattern of avoidance; by not being a harsh, judgmental, externalized superego, the therapist was able to develop a relationship that felt safe. The alliance that was formed in the preliminary work permitted the movement towards more depth work. Megan didn't need to defend against the therapy, so that her need and curiosity could be engaged in a productive way.

As the therapy transitioned to more frequency, permitting a change of focus, what becomes clearer are Megan's defense mechanisms, developed since early childhood, that were an attempt to manage huge affects and fears, some in response to her external environment and some in response to her internal world. Megan paid a price for her mechanisms of externalization and avoidance, as her panic and distress demonstrate. But these mechanisms all managed to engage her parents in a connection that was important and necessary to Megan, albeit dysfunctional.

Once analytic treatment began, the transference was extremely useful in understanding Megan's way of engaging the important objects in her life. The therapist's understanding of her own responses to Megan's panic and helplessness, the pressure she felt to rescue and fix, became the gateway for understanding the feeling states and mechanisms of protection experienced by Megan. It also became a way of understanding more about the family that had so influenced Megan's development. Her family looked functional in some ways, but was highly challenged and challenging in other ways. Megan's being the youngest, and the third wheel to her siblings' relationship, certainly contributed to her feelings of difference and exclusion, feelings that are part of the developmental arc, but were exacerbated by experience. The troubled relationship between her parents must also have played a role in Megan's insecurities and conflicts. Megan's mother's rushing in to do for Megan rather than help with mastery and promote the growth of self was perhaps a reflection of her own helplessness, a feeling and/or a fact likely taken in by the young Megan. And Megan's helplessness became a way of staying connected, attached, controlling something that felt out of control.

This dynamic of the interplay around helplessness was played out in the therapy, becoming a way for the therapist to understand earlier dynamics that were unclear to Megan or her parents, including her aggression toward her family. The issue of her aggression is observable again through understanding her defenses and the transference experienced by the therapist. Megan's intense feelings of helplessness, of being overwhelmed and unprepared, of confusion, were externalized onto the parents and the therapist. She would engage their support and involvement, but also provoke their irritation and anger in response; she unconsciously got them to feel what she was feeling. Often with children, if you want to know how they feel, see how they are getting you to feel. This element of externalization is observable in normal adolescent development as a common defense against superego struggles, a developmental conflict prototypical of adolescence. Megan not only externalized her anger and her guilt, but also her helplessness and panic around accomplishment and mastery. The therapist's ability to observe her own reactions was the gateway to understanding what was being accomplished by the defense: the unacceptable feeling was handed off to, and experienced by, the external objects (parents, therapists, siblings, friends). What was so hard and confusing for Megan was how unconscious this was, as seen in her sabotage of her friend's hike.

The therapist was able to engage Megan's ego observational capacity to look at the disparity between her affective responses versus the reality of what was going on in the external situation. For the therapist, this meant wearing two hats: straddling the roles of support and problem-solving (with the negative connotations to Megan of being rescued, which was supposed to supply relief, but instead created the opposite response) on the one hand, while trying to learn with Megan about her inner world on the other.

This work made it possible for Megan to function more appropriately on the ego level, while being able to observe and experience previously warded off feelings, particularly that of being alone. This important work, with Megan identifying a painful affect, illustrates the double nature of adolescent work. Developmentally, adolescents can experience intense loneliness as they remove from their original objects; the sense of loss can be intense. But at the same time, Megan's complicated relationships with the core objects of her life remained unresolved and markedly intensified by her developmental stage. Thus, in helping with separation and growth, the therapist is straddling the past world and the current world, a demanding but fascinating and fruitful position.

What this vignette offers, then, is an example of how treatment of an adolescent is often a balance between now and then, support and insight, outside and inside. This balancing act is a challenge for the therapist since it means constantly assessing what is going on, what to address about what's going on, and how to keep the therapeutic alliance functioning as the therapeutic focus varies. As this vignette demonstrates, awareness of transference and counter-transference is a major vehicle for understanding affect and conflict. The therapist's ability to initially start where Megan was, to identify the anxiety engendered in her by Megan's panic, and to move the focus from current functioning to the internal interferences in current functioning, set up an excellent platform for analysis.

COMMENTARY 2

This beautiful case presentation demonstrates the enduring power of psychoanalysis. Two years of weekly psychotherapy with the same skilled clinician failed to mobilize sufficient resources within Megan to successfully launch to college. When treatment converted to four-times-a-week psychoanalysis, success ensued. The pair's emergent articulation of "finally figuring out what's underneath all of these painful patterns, and why we haven't been able to shift them over the past couple of years of work together" powerfully organizes the importance of the conversion, which Megan fortunately endured.

Psychoanalysis as a gift

Megan and her family survived the initial anxieties of this event. The offer of psychoanalysis appeared rightly understood by the family as a profound gift. What may have been wrongly understood were its implications as based on the functions of gifts within the family.

Gifts had previously foreclosed exchanges of meaning within the family. Would psychoanalysis only offer more of the same, and thus be ultimately comfortable but meaningless? In contrast, the preparatory work had undoubtedly positioned psychoanalysis as an opportunity for opening meaning. Would psychoanalysis shatter the family's entrenched means of relating, and thus be uncomfortable and something to be feared? The likely simultaneous holding of both registers, and the conflict between these models, appeared to create some initial symptoms within the family.

Pre-existing fissures within the parental subsystem yielded to the strain to produce a marital disagreement about the fee. Though little detail is provided, the author notes that these disagreements were the product of a misunderstanding, suggesting potentially the operation of some type of blocking of thinking. The misunderstanding's quick resolution suggests that the issue may not have been very complex rationally, but perhaps much more so emotionally so as to create confusion and tension even over a basic pragmatic matter.

Megan, specifically, was "wracked with anxiety over the financial tensions." Maintaining initially the position within the family as the helpless child to the powerful parents, she continued to hold the stance of a dependent, perhaps as one who could not see herself as managing independently from the parental sphere in college.

As the finances of gifts were a comfortable area for fixation for Megan, these may have been an easy defensive stand-in for her bigger fears. Might her trusted provider's willingness to invest personalized attention and care in her serve the same purpose as her father's gifts? Megan did not yet know how to receive such a gift, and might her provider's faith in Megan's competencies to be able to create meaning be wrong, and ultimately lead to a disappointment? Would psychoanalysis ultimately be just like another "study skills course" and lead to both her dissolution into tears and anger and, ultimately, to failure?

This event of offering the psychoanalysis, of course, appears to retroactively create the potentialities for a new reaction to gift-receiving for Megan, of mobilizing potentials for meaning-making, and within this potential space the work unfolds.

Developmental help in emerging adulthood

One of the areas of the psychoanalytic work which warrants underscoring is the informed decision of the analyst to "rediscover and enliven" Megan's creative capacities in her cognitive skills and musical talents. This identification of developmentally-thwarted capabilities and the early choice to focus on their expansion in the work I believe comes more easily to a psychoanalyst trained in working with children and adolescents. At age 19, Megan is legally an adult, yet an exclusive focus on the tools of psychoanalysis with adults may complicate the ease with which this goal can be pursued.

The author shares that the path towards providing developmental help can be fraught. The author names as an enactment her assumption of the "study skills course" function, and highlights its effect of undercutting Megan's capability to learn that she could independently function. In addition to the potential effect of this action to debase the psychoanalysis to being just more of the same, the author highlights its impact upon her dependency conflicts. Yet, providing developmental help ultimately will provide some supportive functions, even if the work is clothed through interpretations.

Megan underscores what is on the line when she follows this "'doing for' incident" by the tale of her nearly falling on a hike. She underscores the potential for her to have "hit her head or break anything," including her neck. While the author emphasizes this may have been precipitated by her failure to avoid a supportive enactment, part of Megan's communication may have also been to reply to her analyst's self-incriminations that Megan, a late teenager with prior suicidal tendencies, did in fact, at times, need someone to step-in for her in order to keep her safe. Though with predominantly neurotic conflicts, Megan's presentation suggested areas where supports seemed needed to maintain her safety. The challenge of the work is illustrated here to require a delicate balance between traditional psychoanalytic work and developmental help. The balancing act can be made easier through freely and without concern providing the developmental help while also lending attention to its meaning. Authors within the enactment literature, including those who maintain that they are unavoidable and even valuable, often maintain this stance.

Megan had a reappraisal of her message to the analyst in her slipping on her hike within the car accident she later sustains. After the author's balancing of both functions of psychoanalysis within the developmental phase of emerging adulthood, Megan now shares the potential for harm without any allusion to the real risk of bodily harm. The accident is positioned as minor, and her capability to seek the help of appropriate supports in the form of a medical doctor for whiplash and a policeman for the accident pragmatics. Megan's recounting of the story in some ways underscores how she will continue to need help from those around her, yet she will interact with those supports in an adult manner, without a need to seek recourse upon the parents, a roommate, or the analyst. Only through providing these supportive developmental functions in the temporary transitional space of developmental help may Megan have been able to meet this achievement.

Following the content of the car accident, the author underscores how Megan continued to struggle over basic decisions around her own body, such as eating and resting. Pockets of deficits in need of developmental support will remain embedded within a strengthened structure, though with basic safety secured, the analyst was freer to interpret the genetic underpinnings within the maternal transference of Megan's pull towards an enactment, while also taking pleasure in the expanded capacities in her competency.

Families

Though the author emphasizes that the space limitations of the piece restrict a fuller depiction of the work with the parents, a child and adolescent psychoanalytic perspective also supplements traditional psychoanalytic work through an openness to working directly with the parents. This openness is fortunately increasing through the works of several leaders in the field, with a resultant productive overcoming of the unnecessarily dogmatic boundaries between family and systems therapy and psychoanalysis.

A frequency of every-other-week parent meetings clearly benefitted this family. Mother directly engaged in insight-oriented work in relation to her contributions to Megan's deficits without recriminations, while father's engagement is presented as more limited. Just as father may have experienced gains from directly observing mother's engagement in the work, certainly he may have as well indirectly through Megan. The positioning of Megan as a teacher of her father helps to break down the rigid parent-child subsystem boundary that kept Megan as a dependent, too scared to function alone in college. Through the benefits of her work, Megan is now capable of imparting to her parents her own lessons by her practices and choices in life, and thus arrives at greater equivalence in positioning within the family system. This is more characteristic of an adult daughter within a generational advancement of the family system, she is no longer even after a brief time of work the child-like daughter in an uncomfortable adult's body, and thus in this way indirectly advances the health of the entire family.

Conclusion

The joy Megan is described to behold in the psychoanalytic work suggests the promises of enduring value of this work. Megan will continue to find her own discoveries as she traverses her twenties, and her parents will continue to see their daughter make meaning and grab life in her own, independent way. With the work continuing at the time of writing, these processes will only further strengthen and unfold. This piece is a testament to the power of such work, which reveals itself in every patient-analyst dyad in its own, unique way.

EDITORIAL REFLECTIONS

This chapter highlights a number of important issues of technique in work with adolescents: the impact of different frequencies, the role and nature of parent work in adolescent treatment and the importance of including fathers, the range of techniques and aspects of the therapeutic relationship, and the power of love in the therapeutic alliance.

This case allows us to use the research method of "subjects as their own controls" to consider the impact of different frequencies on the course of therapy and to examine the relationship of frequency to delineating treatment goals. The patient had started therapy once a week at the age of 17. At 19 she started college but was not able to deal with this developmental move. She felt overwhelmed, anxious, suicidal and withdrew from college. The failure to launch enabled the analyst to effect the increase to four times per week including regular concurrent work with the parents. This change had an immediate and profound impact on the process, which patient and analyst each noted. The focus shifted from the repetitive expression of symptoms (anxiety, feeling overwhelmed) and a concern about safety (suicide) to understanding the meaning, purpose and history of the symptoms. At once a week the patient carried little forward between sessions and the analyst found it hard to wait a full week to take up resistances and verbalize underlying dynamics. At four times a week defenses, especially externalization, could be clearly seen and interpreted: transference of the rescuer, the organizer, and, in the counterreaction, the externalization of the annoyed, exasperated superego.

Megan's experience and presentation of herself as helpless served multiple functions, both of attachment and defense. The helplessness was also externalized and this became the background to potential sadomasochistic power dynamics; the gratification involved in forcing others to rescue her began to emerge, and likely played an even greater role as the treatment progressed. Here, as in several other chapters, we note the question of what represents a pathological, closed-system solution and what might be considered expectable in adolescence. One commentator describes this in wondering whether there is an expectable temporary externalization of the superego in adolescence, as there often is for schoolaged children, or are we seeing in Megan defensive disowning and externalization of her ego functions?

One commentator links the concurrent parent work with the approaches of family therapy and dynamic systems theory. It is time for someone familiar with both to contrast, compare, and amalgamate. The parent work with the mother was insight-oriented and led to dynamic shifts in the mother. This depth of work contrasted with the father's less intense engagement and we can assume that this had dynamic meaning and impact. As we have now seen with numerous cases, fathers are very important in the progressive development of adolescents (Novick, K.K. and Novick, J. 2013). A major finding exemplified in this chapter is that parent work is effective because of its dynamic content and is not limited by the age of the patient.

It is clear from the comments and the nimble flexibility of the analyst that experience in child and adolescent work is of great benefit in work with "emerging adults." It is what we have called open-system technique. It adds to the standard adult emphasis on transference/countertransference the analyst as an object for identification, for inspiration, developmental help, support, validation, witness, teacher and co-creator of a life story and so forth. We might suggest that a 'full' therapeutic relationship ideally includes all these elements, not only for children and adolescents, but also for adults.

Lastly, we note that each commentator starts their comments with similar words: "This beautiful case presentation..."; "This is a lovely and frank account of..." We think that this is not only a positive response to the vivid writing style and empathic clinical work of the analyst but also a response to the analyst's pleasure in the work and the objective love both analyst and patient have for each other. This is something not frequently discussed by analysts, but many of the cases described in this volume speak to the importance of the devotion, investment, and love evoked in the analyst by their adolescent patients (Novick J. and Novick, K.K. 2000b).

V

EMERGING ADULTHOOD

CHAPTER 17

CHRISTIAN – age 20

Intimacy and Separateness

I would like to present extracts from the course of psychoanalytic treatment over several years of a young man who came to see me a few months before his school leaving examination, the German "Abitur." Christian, as I will call him, had just turned 20, a slight, blonde, young man. He opened the first conversation with the words:

"I don't know who I am anymore. I am afraid to show myself. The others might think something negative of me, as if I don't want to be seen".

The upcoming Abitur does not cause him any problems. He is a good student. He wants to study here in the place where I practice, and had come to me on the recommendation of his mother's analyst in order to secure a therapy place with me as a precaution. He complained of compulsive brooding that removed him completely from reality. His head was going crazy, he kept thinking and couldn't stop, lost in the theater in his head. This distanced him from reality. Sometimes he does not feel at all. He also has many fears: fears of illness, fears of falling asleep. His biggest fear is that he will never find a girlfriend.

The way he feels now has become so extreme since he was rejected three months ago by a schoolmate he had fallen in love with. It was the first time he had been interested in a girl and fallen in love. Now he is constantly thinking about what he did wrong. He had been very successful in "Jugend forscht," a German science research competition for young people, which had given him security and also brought him considerable social recognition. He described how, together with a fellow pupil, he had done many projects involving safety systems in the technical field. He felt safe working with computers and technical equipment, which is why he wanted to choose this field of study.

In his childhood and youth he had moved many times, often changing schools, and had always been very shy and withdrawn; it was only at secondary school and with the success of his projects at "Jugend forscht" that things had improved. Currently, a new problem has arisen: a problem with "clothes stuff," and especially with trousers. He has to compulsively change his clothes many times in front of the mirror, and his trousers must not be creased. He only feels comfortable in jogging trousers, where you can't see the shape. He says:

> "I am afraid that I could change by wearing different clothes or, especially, that I could be seen negatively by young women and be labelled from the start. But I'm also afraid of trying something new because in theory, I could make mistakes."

These first accounts by Christian convey to me his search for identity, combined with a great uncertainty as to how he could endure his longings for love and give them form. The conflictual tension between his need for recognition of his sexual, male body and the simultaneously mobilised regressive desires to slip back into a childlike body becomes clear. When he spoke of the jogging trousers, I involuntarily thought of baby rompers. For me it became very noticeable how insecure he feels in his male body and how much shame is associated with this. I then learn that he is in a difficult and tense conflict with his parents. His mother is his most important point of contact and she has always supported him. He describes his father rather disparagingly, saying that he is selfish, thinks only of himself and is constantly afraid of becoming poor. His mother now wants to move out into her own flat. She always looks to Christian for support against his father and he too is horrified by his father's behaviour. Christian, however, tries to play down his stress to me, probably in order not to show up his parents too much, who have very heated arguments about finances because of the impending separation.

At the start of his degree course, Christian contacted me again. As a precaution, he had secured a place in therapy and in the meantime had kept in touch with me. But now it was difficult to find an appointment for therapy sessions. He brought his diary with his semester schedule and told me which appointments would suit him. I understood this as a necessary preservation of his independence at the beginning and as his need to negotiate with me on an equal footing. At the time, I did not pick up on the deep-seated fear of renewed dependence which this expressed. I told him that I thought analytical therapy would be useful, but I agreed to start with one hour of psychotherapy.

On the practical level, Christian had managed to move out of the family home, find a flat and organise the start of his course. Internally, he is under a lot of pressure and has developed new symptoms: an involuntary eye twitch and trembling leg movements. These tics make him feel very ashamed. In addition, his problem with "clothes stuff" has intensified considerably. He frequently and compulsively has to change his clothes in front of the mirror, the trousers must not wrinkle, and especially from the back they should fit perfectly. He would prefer to wear only jogging trousers. Again, I have to think of rompers. Once again I can feel how insecure he feels in his male body and how much shame this involves.

Sheltered by a mild positive transference, he begins to settle into student life. He wanted my recognition and sought support from me for his work at the university and the organisation of his everyday life. But whereas he could do without concrete support in the therapy sessions, he still discussed many things with his mother and sought her opinion. He spoke to her several times a day on the phone. His science subject interested him and he was initially happy with his choice. This technical, predictable world was probably familiar to him from his "Jugend forscht" days. He became friends with a fellow student who took over auxiliary ego functions for his social contacts in the first two semesters, while he helped her with her studies and explained the study material to her. In the early days, he only went to university when he knew Nina would be there too. However, he quickly felt overwhelmed by the social contacts. He played through every encounter with other people in his head for a long time beforehand: What they might say, what they might think of him and how he should behave. But he struggled with himself and his fears. He understands from me in the therapy how much he has to control everything and how little he can stand uncertainty.

For a long time he always came in the same trousers because he couldn't manage to buy new ones. He used to go clothes shopping with his mum and she would choose them for him. When in one session he suddenly appeared in a new shirt and I asked him about it, he confessed that he had left the price tag on to test whether I liked the shirt. Elements of his adhesive mother relationship with me were undoubtedly present in this scene, but I picked up that he was showing me his need to want to be attractive. He then wanted to find out what sports at the university I thought would be good for him and whether I would trust him to do them. He tried out various things, always with a lot of pondering and considerable fear. Finally, he decided on a water sport. This turned out to be a great challenge for him. All the male students there were musclemen, but he could keep up with the women. The water was his medium.

When working at his studies, it became clear how much he was looking for a certainty that did not exist. He always wanted to be optimally prepared and to be sure of getting the grade he wanted in the exams at the end of the semester. He couldn't take breaks while studying, couldn't detach himself from the subject matter, so to speak. Then he often couldn't sleep and described nightmares in which he was haunted.

Now, after half a year, the first holiday break was coming up. I was worried, because I could really feel his effort to hold himself together. After the holidays, I learned that he had had a stomach bug that got so bad that he had to be hospitalized. His mother had come to take care of him. On top of the infection there had been severe anxiety and panic attacks. He could no longer sleep and felt very insecure. He became aware that he really needed the therapy and urgently asked to increase the frequency now. We agreed on analytical therapy with three sessions per week.

I will now describe a session from this period:

The patient arrives on the dot, as he almost always does. He seems particularly pale and thin today. He puts his bulging backpack on the foot end of the couch. Then he carefully fetches a water bottle, twists it open and drinks with his back turned to me. He sits down on his chair.
Patient): I'm feeling really bad. Everything is difficult at the moment. I am thinking all the time again. I play through every situation, every action in my mind. So I am never in the present. So I don't know how I feel, what I feel. I can't relax at all, I can't sleep either. I'm having panic attacks again, today too.
Analyst): How were the panic attacks today?
P): I didn't feel well when I woke up. I didn't want to get up at all. I did everything mechanically and then went to the university. I was sitting in the cafeteria with another student when I saw Jenny and some others pass by out of the corner of my eye. (Jenny is a fellow student who he

likes and can imagine being a good match for him. He has gone for a walk with her once so far). *Then it immediately went off in my head: Should I have stood up and approached her? Would that have been right? In the end I had the feeling that I had done everything wrong again. I judged myself all over again. I started to panic. I had to go home immediately and that's when it got a little better. I can only run or drive home immediately in such situations. At home I was able to calm down a bit and then I came to see you for the session now.*

The weekend was also terrible. I couldn't relax, do anything, just think nothing for a change. I plan and think about everything down to the smallest detail. For example, when I go to the pharmacy I think about exactly what I will say, when, how, and what the reaction will be. I am constantly afraid of doing something wrong. I have to get it really right. I know that this is the wrong way and that it won't help. But I can't turn it off. I can't free myself from it. When I'm not under so much stress, I can push the thoughts away.

A): *You expect yourself to be able to function like a computer. Everything is pre-programmed.*

P): *Yes, I know that I do that. I want myself to feel the way I do and not constantly judge myself for doing something wrong. I've been doing this for a long time. Ever since Sabrina rejected me in my Abitur class, I've noticed it in myself. I still have almost every scene with her in my head, what I said and how she reacted. I've been through the scenes 100 times. I get so caught up in it and then really beat myself up about it. It got much better and sometimes I was really happy. But when I'm in a state like I was at the weekend, I feel hopeless and think it will never get better.*

A): *You can't calm yourself down at all. I think of a baby or a toddler. The mother and the baby become more and more agitated and the mother cannot calm it down because she is so stressed herself. You can imagine a small child experiencing this as a rejection, not getting an answer, not getting a response and not being able to calm itself down.*

After a pause: *You often call your mother when you are feeling bad and seek reassurance there.*

P): It doesn't calm me down when I call my mother. But I do it anyway. It's a relief when I can talk. It is also so important that I can talk to you here. It makes the inner critic weaker and I feel a little better. I am always happy when there are sessions here. You gave the example of the baby. That makes sense to me. My mother was really extremely stressed during pregnancy and also constantly when I was little. She was with my father once before, then they broke up and got back together again. I think that was because she felt sorry for him. Then I was born. I guess I was supposed to stabilize the relationship. But my mother was probably always burdened by her father and her brother. They are just assholes.

A): It is important that you notice how bad it is when you cannot calm down. But it is so crucial that you can ease up on your self-judgement. I told you about the baby to help you find a way into yourself; to see that it's not just an inability, a disorder of yours, but that it has to be understood in a relational context. After a pause, I add: *"When someone speaks, it becomes light," a little boy who was afraid of the dark once said.*

P): It was already quite different and much better. The panic states were gone. I sometimes had a feeling of happiness and could just sit and listen to music and relax by playing the guitar.

A): We have both noticed that interruptions in the regularity of the sessions, longer breaks, do you no good.

P): Yes, that's true. It took me a while to admit this to myself. At the beginning I thought I would find an explanation with your help and then I would have the key to my problems and be able to eliminate them. Do you remember my dream with the key? The dream just came

433

to my mind. In the dream I was in a dark corridor and at the end was a door. I wanted to open the door, but I couldn't find the key. That's when I woke up. I have to find the key to my conditions. I want to be able to turn them off.

A): These conditions are not easy to stop. A first step is not to judge them solely as your own failures and to blame only yourself for them. Your demand that you have to do everything right, that there is only right or wrong, puts you under pressure. You tried to find a practical key, a method, when you signed up for the student counselling group. What actually came of it?

P): This group was no use. It was not suitable for me at all. They were noisy people who had all really needed therapy and always saw their problems as being in others. They all wanted to be taught a method to get rid of their fears. That was not for me. My fears and my difficulties have to do with me and I can't let others make them go away. Most of all, the group really upset me. I dropped it again.

I have problems with myself. The new thing is dizziness. I can't take things in properly. Today with you I also feel confused. I have mixed everything up. There was no line in it. I experienced everything as if through a tunnel. I see nothing on the left and nothing on the right. I can't feel anything. I can't remember anything. I've already told you how awful it was at the weekend. I am obsessed again with the idea that I will never find a girlfriend. But I know very well that a girlfriend wouldn't solve my problems.

A): A girlfriend would not solve your problems, but we could also translate your need to find a girlfriend as a need to get out of your prison, to find resonance, to have someone you can talk to.

P): Do you know the book "Schachnovelle" (a novella by Stefan Zweig)? *The protagonist walks up and down and talks to himself as if he were in a prison. He thinks about a chess move and then he goes back and forth again. I do the same at home. I would go back and forth here too if I didn't have to sit on the chair.*

A): Like a tiger in a cage. (When I hear myself say this, I wonder. Tiger – I have chosen a powerful animal.)

P): Yes, but after all I make the cage myself. But it does me good to talk to you. These conditions had already improved a lot. But today I can't absorb so much. I wonder if you could even understand what I was saying in such a jumbled way. It all seems very confused and jumbled to me.

A): I didn't think it was so jumbled. I think I could understand and absorb something of your condition. But I think right now your inner fault-finder is striking again.

P): My mother is always surprised that her analyst can understand something of what she is saying.

A): I think it would be necessary for you to come more often. I'm thinking three times a week. Then we could stay closer to the action and watch how your sensitivities change and when your inner fault-finder strikes.

P): Yes, three sessions would be fine with me. I often find that talking to you helps me a lot. I could arrange that. I have already told you all my free times.

A): You have to check with your health insurance provider and have them send you the application forms. Then we can discuss it further on Thursday.

As the three times weekly sessions began, Christian confided more about his body fears and shame about his body: *"I really don't have broad shoulders and I'm not muscular, so I'm not what you'd imagine a real man to be. With my funnel chest, I can't show myself."* Later he can confess to me that he is afraid his penis is much too small and also stands at an angle. I learned that he has been masturbating every day since he was five years old and that even now he pleasures himself extremely often, especially when he feels anxious and insecure. I thought of a lonely boy who sought refuge in onanism to get rid of the bewildering dependency through arousal and also to comfort himself. Christian told me rather desperately: *"The two sides, reason and drivenness, confuse me a lot. I simply cannot bring these two things together. Masturbation is not a pleasurable satisfaction, but a compulsion."*

In the sessions that followed, Christian described to me with much shame that masturbation was about what sensations a woman would have.

> *"It's practically all about the sensations a woman would have. In my fantasies, I find it extremely difficult to consider my own sensations. I somehow still have the feeling that what can be offered physically is not enough for a woman anyway. That's why it's extremely difficult for me to come up with an arousing image through my own fantasy."*
>
> *"So why can't I find a girlfriend?"* he asked me again, insistently. I said to Christian: *"I think it scares you to be so close to someone, to penetrate someone. Then you get very afraid of dissolving into the woman, of losing the boundaries of your body and any stability you have."* After a pause, I added, *"When you masturbate, you are alone with yourself and in control – but you fantasise the aroused woman as well."* I understood this to mean that during his sexual acts, Christian was desperately trying to externalise a part of himself, to make space for the woman. It was no longer he who was aroused, it was about the woman's arousal. I thought that Christian was looking for something that belongs to sexuality: to experience it in the other.

A few weeks later I received an e-mail from Christian telling me that he watches porn on the Internet to get excited. He was totally conflicted about this because he found men who did it appalling. I would like to mention here that I had made an agreement with Christian that if he felt very pressured, he could send me an email; I would not answer it, but we would refer to it in the next session. He told me that it gave him great relief when he could formulate his feelings in an email and know that I would read it.

In the session he said, *"The porn I watched was sort of anime videos. So not real people. But violent. I get very excited by violence sometimes. But I don't want that because it's just not right, and I don't want to accept it as a part of me, that sometimes violence excites me. It is just wrong. Every time I get aroused by violence (even in my fantasies), I feel like a bad person. Sometimes I hate myself for doing it. At the moment, I would love to throw my PC out of the window so that I could no longer get porn. But of course I don't do that. I think it's sad that there's a side of me at the moment that finds violence arousing and I can't deal with that side."*

I assumed that watching arousing porn was a "means" by which Christian could detach himself from his mother's body and feel his own. But this "means" did not really help him. The compulsive masturbation became more and more of a burden for him. He had to control himself incessantly and severely judged himself, as the discrepancy with his ideals became unbearable for him. During this time, Christian had a "terrible dream" which was "about his mother."

The dream: *There were people who were living beings made of glowing, liquid stones, who lived in deserts of rock and lava. There were very frequent explosions. I myself grew larger and larger in human form, but I don't know exactly why that was. People could take on a human form, but they were still living beings made of glowing, liquid stones. My family was always being caught in such an explosion. I was mostly spared. Whenever Mum was caught, I was terrified that she had not survived. I didn't care much about Dad. At the end, Mum was hit again by a rather violent explosion, but before that I was still holding her in my arms and telling her how much I loved her. I was afraid that something had happened to her and ran down the hill, crying: "Mother, mother!" When I reached the bottom, I saw that her liquid stone had almost turned cold and solid and that only a little bit of it was still glowing. So she was still alive. Then I woke up.*

In the dream, the existential threat to his own bodily boundaries and those of his mother becomes frighteningly clear. His own sexuality – the explosions – are a threat to his relationship, indeed to his mother's existence. The father is eliminated: "I didn't really care about him." For me, it became very noticeable how much Christian had to put a distance between himself and me again and again, and how he first had to tell me something threatening by e-mail. As if he had to test whether his sexual desires, which were very much mixed with a hatred of his mother, were damaging me. When he then came to the next session and perceived me undamaged, he was relieved.

Christian was in a very bad way in the period that followed. He no longer left his flat and could no longer concentrate when studying. He found everything pointless and hardly ate anything any more. His anxiety attacks increased again and he suffered from severe insomnia. He had to fall asleep with the light on again. But he came regularly to his sessions and afterwards felt better for a short time. On his course, he had to cancel exams because he was unable to study.

With the help of other dreams, it was easy to work out which existential fears Christian associated with his sexual needs. Becoming an adult, feeling more like a man, threatened his dependent relationship with his mother. It became clear to him how attached he was to her and how strongly he felt that he could not make it without her. His relationship with his mother and his dependence on her now came to the fore. He tried to detach himself more from his mother, to stop calling her several times a day. Then, when she went on holiday, he realised how much it scared him when he couldn't reach her. "I am very attached to my mother because sometimes at the moment I feel I can't manage without her. She is always there when I need her." To me, the unconscious hatred that he made disappear by idealizing his mother was also apparent.

It was now becoming increasingly clear that Christian's mother had a completely devalued inner image of the father, and of men in general. This was related above all to the fact that Christian's father had had many sexual relationships before her. Christian lived, so to speak, in a projective identification with his mother's devaluing image of men. In this prison, he had to be the better, even the ideal man, but a man without sexuality and without aggression.

As the treatment went on, the critical examination of the relationship with his mother continued to take center stage. At first he held on to the idealization of her, as he also did in the transference to me. His father continued to receive all the negative valuations. The fact that he had taken over his mother's devalued image of men and also projected it into his father now became apparent, and could be worked with. Here, too, dreams were a great help, in which Christian, together with the analyst, could see his tendencies to exclude his father and avoid triangulation. He realised that he saw his father through his mother's eyes, and said that *"Maybe my father is not as bad as my mother makes him out to be."*

Christian discovered his musical interests. He formed a band with two women and a man, all students, in which he played the guitar and also sang. They met every week. Christian had found in music an important area for him. He could now – when he was well – stay quietly in his flat, play the guitar and compose his own songs. In the transference-countertransference situation, Christian was also able to get through and work on conflicts with the analyst. Examples would include requests to reschedule sessions and frustrations with the detailed and laborious therapeutic work. He became willing to take on more responsibility and, after the summer holidays, to earn part of the financial contribution to the therapy by tutoring. But then I realised retrospectively that I had underestimated the extent of the anxiety which stemmed from the critical distancing from his father and a massive confrontation with him. Christian had taken his mother's side in his parents' financial disputes, in which, in my opinion too, his father had acted criminally. In my counter-transference, I had probably shown too much (unspoken) solidarity with Christian. But he took this to mean that he could survive a confrontation with his father.

After the next summer holidays, Christian surprised me by announcing that he wanted to end the therapy. His argument was that his health insurance provider was asking for a co-payment. His father would not pay the difference and Christian could not. I was disappointed and also annoyed, because we had discussed and fixed everything before the holidays. But I sensed that in Christian's mind there was a great fear of dependence on me and his massive disappointment in his father had become acute. He told me he had come through the holidays well after all, and now he wanted to try it on his own. I said that I was pleased that he had survived the holidays well. It was not a contradiction to manage something on your own and at the same time stay in therapy. But that was his decision. I would want to continue working with him and I thought it was necessary and made sense. I had to work very hard with myself to give him the freedom to end the therapy. He suggested a termination date in two months time. I replied that we could use this period to understand his wish to end and only then decide. He agreed.

Some time after the argument about continuing the therapy, when I unexpectedly had to cancel the therapy for a fortnight because of illness, I received an email in which he told me that he could no longer attend the Tuesday sessions. After the therapy resumed, I found out that he now had a singing lesson with a singing teacher instead of the therapy session. I pointed out to him that it was precisely the therapy appointment he had changed to a singing lesson. Well, he was perhaps trying out whether he could risk the freedom to find his own way. It was a question of whether I could tolerate that, whether I was willing to continue working with him. We found an alternative date.

A specific kind of side-transference developed with the singing teacher, concerning breathing and sensory sensations, which we could usefully take up and work on in the analysis sessions. Sensory sensations and perceptual modalities, hearing and seeing, now took up a lot of space in the sessions. In the therapy there was a very regressive period which was concerned with smelling and stinking, and with an at times intense sensitivity to sounds. He came to one of the sessions distraught, reporting that he had not been able to sleep because a baby had been crying for a terrifyingly long time in the flat next door and no one had come. I told him that I could imagine that the crying had touched something in him from his early life, as it had shaken him so much.

He asked his mother and his maternal grandmother, with whom he had a trusting relationship, about his early days. He learned that his mother had been very stressed and depressed during her pregnancy with him. There had been a lot of quarrelling and arguments in the parental home, especially with his father. His maternal grandfather had been very negative about his mother's pregnancy and had advised her to have an abortion so as not to jeopardise her professional career. His mother had to lie down during the last weeks of her pregnancy and had been given so much diazepam that she had difficulty speaking. His maternal grandmother told him this in the strictest confidence. Because labor began prematurely, the mother then had to go to hospital for the delivery. He is said to have been a very sensitive and restless baby. His mother had also been depressed after his birth and had had to take medication, so she had only breast-fed him for a short time. His extreme sensitivity to noise was striking and continues to this day.

He had known some of these things before, but had never let them touch him emotionally as he did now. We could both now understand that he must early on have tried to hold himself together by "thinking". Christian decided to continue the therapy. He began to deal further with his parents, daring to see them more critically and to form his own view. On an unconscious level, the confrontation became clear through dreams. For example, he dreamt that his father was in his room with him and deleted from his computer his network connections with all his personal data. He had cried in the dream. In another dream, his father inoculated him against his will with a syringe. He was not sure whether his father was not inoculating him with something deadly.

To illustrate this, I will present an excerpt from a session in this phase of the therapy.

P): I notice that my mother's bad image of men affects me a lot. My mother only sees my father in a bad way. I really see my father the way my mother sees him.

A): In the last session you thought about taking care of your mother because your father doesn't want to give her money. After a short pause: You are not your mother's partner, responsible for her.

P): My mother has a very ideal picture of how a man should be. There is no such man. My mother is in her early 40s, but she could be 20 years old. She is not so mature. She looks 30 years old.

A): It's very tempting for the mother to be so important and for you to be the only good man (I said with a smile).

P): Yes – I am locked in there and don't allow myself any sexual experiences. I feel such anger now. Thoughtfully: Maybe it has something to do with the violent porn?

A): It's about detaching more from your mother. The violent porn is maybe an outlet because it's so hard to rely on yourself and to leave *your mother out of it. I would say: to be able to think your mother away when she is present.*

P): Then I'm afraid of becoming like my father. But maybe he's not only bad, which is how my mother sees him because he had lots of girlfriends before her.

A): You are really caught between the two parents: Either you are the ideal man for your mother or you become the "asshole" father. It's all about finding your own way.

P): That's why I want to do an internship in Finland or England. I want to go far away.

A): Going away won't get rid of your inner mother. But an internship abroad allows you to have your own, new experiences. (I convey in my tone of voice that I trust the patient to do an internship abroad.)

P): Andrea, who I'm going to visit in Finland, said I should just try something. I can speak English well. I want to try it out.

A): Try something out and risk something. Even risk cancelling sessions here to go away.

P): I am so afraid of making mistakes. I am also very afraid that the anxiety will increase again and I won't be able to sleep. I can't stand that for more than two days. I still have a prescription for Tavor (a tranquiliser) *from my mother. I can take that with me.*

A): Then you again take something concrete from your mother abroad.

But it is more important that you can believe that I trust you to be able to go away and that we then continue to work together to accommodate your wishes and also your fears.

P): Yes – I'll be back.

A): Then see you tomorrow.

Christian did an internship abroad. He was very afraid. But he dared to do it and came back without having experienced massive anxiety there.

The gradual distinction between sadistic impulses and phallic strength and potency created the basis for Christian to develop towards a more stable masculine identity.

He became more interested in his studies and was also quite successful in his exams. Now a wide variety of women appeared, and he fell in love with them. One of them, Vera, he really finds suitable for him in every way. She finds him likeable, but is not in love with him. This is very upsetting for him, but he gets through it. He comes to terms with his high, idealistic expectations of women. He only wants to sleep with a woman if he is absolutely sure that she is the woman for life. He also plays – at first in his imagination – with different life plans. Technology, the scientific subjects, do not fill him up completely. He is still enthusiastic about his studies, but he asks himself whether he really wants to work in business. Maybe he could go to "Engineers Without Borders". He would have to find something that really made sense.

He then decides to go to a student cultural group. He comes back excited from the weekend with the group. Two weeks later, I hear from him that he had met a woman and spent a very nice evening with her. His head was going crazy at the moment. He told the girl that he thought she was sweet and she hugged him and they became very close. Soon after, he started crying because he just couldn't stand it any more. The stress of the exams probably played a role. He had not cried for a long time, especially not when someone else saw him. But Jana, the girl, fully understood it. *"I can't get her out of my mind now and I feel closer to her than to many other people I have known for years. On the one hand, I'm happy about it and the feeling is nice. On the other hand, it's really hard for me. It's just so new. It's something I've never felt before, which is nice, but it's also scary and makes me feel insecure. University is also very stressful, which adds to it. I'm confused."*

Christian now had a steady girlfriend. They sleep together. The first time he doesn't have an orgasm, but he doesn't have to see it as self-devaluing and

444

as an embarrassment. During one of the following intimate scenes, his guitar falls on his penis and he becomes tremendously anxious. In the following therapy session we can process this and also understand that he might have experienced it as a punishment, a castration threat. His relationship with Jana brings him into conflict with his need to be on his own and not always to want to "cuddle" with her.

Christian said: *"It is very important to me that I can stay with my feelings and not give myself away completely, as I did with Sabrina* (the schoolmate who rejected him). *When I think about how I ran after her, in retrospect I feel really embarrassed. I don't have the idea now that having a girlfriend will radically change my life, that I'll become a completely different person and then everything will be fine."*

We talked about how being in love makes you feel. About how at first you project a lot into the other person, you see in them something you want or something of yourself, and then you gradually take it back. Then you can experience the other person as very familiar, but also strange. Christian was very annoyed when he noticed that it was too much for him with Jana, that he wanted to have time for himself. He was then immediately afraid that this was the end of love. His dreams also showed how he was changing. They were now much more focused on relationships and fewer persecuting, frightening figures appeared. For example, he dreamt that Jana was crying a lot because something had happened to her parents during the holidays. He had felt very close to her. He felt for her and in the dream they both cried.

Christian decided to stay in therapy. It was important for him right now to have another support, and he would finance this with private tutoring and another contribution from his health insurance provider. He could now admit to himself that he still needed therapy and he was no longer so afraid of becoming dependent.

I will now end this account of passages from Christian's therapy. Christian had had to go through a lengthy process in order to be able to *"wistfully greet the person he wants to be"* and now feels more comfortable with who he is in the process of becoming.

He was in therapy for a total of four-and-a-half years. He completed his studies very successfully and with happiness. His inner and outer relationships with his parents had changed significantly. He felt more secure in his masculine identity and he knew his strengths as well as his weaknesses. His inner "fault finder" had lost power, as his ego was no longer caught in a quandary between an overdemanding ego ideal and a persecuting superego.

COMMENTARY 1

Discussing this chapter is both a pleasure and a problem.

The outcome of the 4 ½ years of work by the analyst and patient could not have been better. That was a pleasure to read. However, the first thought that sprang to mind when I finished reading the last paragraph of this clinical account was, "How did he/she do it?" Answering that question was the problem.

My preliminary answer to that question was that he/she did it by addressing several factors, such as Christian's developmental progress and environmental improvements, which the analyst did not bring about but worked with the adolescent to enable him to use positively. There were also shifts in the family dynamics, especially with the father, which I think were a consequence of the father's awareness of changes that were going on in his son. Finally, and at a fundamental level, there were psychic conflicts that the analyst had to understand and interpret.

This multi-dimensional nature of the adolescent's life is broader and more complex than the lived life of the adult. Although I don't have the space to consider the impact that various factors have on the child and adolescent's development, I think a child and adolescent analyst needs to have a wide lens and awareness of the breadth of the many contemporary factors that are in flux and impinging on the adolescent's psychic life, something that the analyst of an adult patient does not normally face.

The analyst begins the account of the 20-year-old male patient's fear, precipitated by development, that he will never find a girl friend. He had just been rejected by his first girl friend. Interestingly, he was very interested in safety systems. I tend to focus on sequence as a way of seeing how the patient and/or the analyst is consciously or unconsciously making connections between cause and effect. The analyst's next association was to the patient's moving and often changing schools as he was growing up. This led to the analyst reporting that the young man was anxious about his trousers as though they would betray to women something negative about him. The analyst's association was to baby rompers and the patient's insecurity and shame about his male body. This patient appears to have little contact with peers. "His mother is his most important point of contact." Father is disparaged as narcissistic and afraid of becoming poor. His mother wants to move into her own flat and looks to Christian for support. The Oedipal triangle, which was never strong, appears to be collapsing at the time he is starting therapy.

What the adult and adolescent psychoanalyst share is a focus on the unconscious through which their patient's fears and anxieties are processed. Freud (1910) maintained that the aim of psychoanalysis was the analysis of resistance in the form of the transference and to the process of analysis. If we can identify a resistance (a defence) in an analytic session it will help us identify anxieties that are being defended against.

Looking back on the start of once weekly therapy, the analyst notices that he/she didn't pick up Christian's "deep seated fear of renewed dependence." The analyst may have wondered later what might have contributed to his/her missing this in the transference. When I catch up with myself on this kind of thing I try to consider what I missed as a consequence of the patient's impact on me. Sandler's (1977) idea is that an unconscious enactment, my missing something that I see later, is the result of an overlap of my pathology and the patient's.

I imagine that Christian was ambivalent, at an unconscious level, about becoming dependent on his analyst, at this time his mother in the transference. The analyst was aware of Christian's adhesive relationship with his mother and a collusion that enabled her to take over his body, choose his clothes. Christian had to be hospitalised with a stomach bug during the first summer holiday and his mother came to take care of him. Christian's anxiety increased. He suffered from panic attacks and could no longer sleep. He asked to increase his sessions to 3 times a week.

In any case, Christian's effort to be more independent by moving out of his family home, getting a flat for himself and organising the start of his course, all efforts to do something about his dependence, led to new symptoms: an involuntary eye twitch and trembling leg movements. The conflicts about his gender identity intensified as he became more anxious that trousers fit perfectly over his buttocks. Again, the analyst thought of rompers. I thought of adolescent unconscious homosexual anxiety, and wondered if that contributed to Christian's anxiety about using the couch and choosing, instead, to sit on a chair where he can keep his eye on the analyst. Importantly, the analyst picks up how insecure Christian is in this male body and the shame this involves.

Seeing Jenny, whom he likes, triggers a panic attack that he had done something wrong. My impression is that Christian's self-persecution is aroused when he separates from his mother, perhaps intensified by guilt about not rescuing mother from father. A severe prohibitive super-ego, which he describes as beating himself up, is only relieved when he comes to his session. However, when he goes home for the weekend he has to mobilise obsessional defences to ward off fears of misbehaving.

The analyst's view of Christian as a baby or toddler may illustrate the persistence of unresolved infantile conflicts, which undermine adolescent development, especially the revival of Oedipal anxieties. Christian explains that calling his mother does not calm him down, but he does it anyway. I wonder if calling his mother is an unconscious, but implicit, criticism of her for his inability to separate from her and for breaking up with his father. Christian notices that after calling his mother his inner critic is weaker and he feels better. At this point Christian associates to his fantasy that his role in the family was to stabilize the parental relationship. While this may be every little boy's fantasy about his place in the Oedipal triangle, the precarious marriage, mother's attachment and father's distance may have reinforced an enactment of that fantasy. In any case, Christian becomes anxious when he leaves his mother or tries to form a couple with a non-incestuous partner.

Returning to Freud's emphasis on the analysis of resistance, I notice that at this point in the session the analyst begins to give the patient advice, and tells Christian that his "disorder" needs to be understood in a relational context. I wonder if the analyst has picked up an intensification of a libidinal dimension to the transference relationship, and reacted by avoiding the patient's anxieties about feeling closer to the analyst. I say this because Christian seems to respond by distancing himself and saying he was "already quite different and much better." Although the analyst counters by saying that interruptions "do you no good," he/she stays away from wondering why Christian stays away. Could it have something to do with how he is feeling about his analyst?

Christian returns to his wish for "a key to my conditions. I want to be able to turn them off." The analyst gives him some advice: don't judge, don't blame yourself. Christian's response is to associate to a student counselling group where everyone wanted to be taught a method to get rid of their fears, which I heard as Christian voicing his anxieties that the analyst was teaching him a method to get rid of his fears. Christian now feels dizzy, confused and mixed-up. He can't feel anything and he can't remember anything. Is he identifying with his analyst who at this point is not relating to Christian's feelings? I have the impression that the analyst's return to thinking that Christian's search for a girl friend is motivated by a need to get out of his personal prison by finding someone to talk to because the analyst is now presenting himself as that person.

He/she takes up Christian's going back and forth at home as "like a tiger in a cage." My association was to the patient's aggression. Christian's association was to making the cage himself. Did he put himself in a cage because of his anxiety about his aggression? Christian's response was to feel confused and jumbled, which I took as a sign that Christian is anxious about his aggression. However, the analyst does not take up the patient's state of mind, but reassures Christian that he can understand his condition. It is at this point that the analyst says it will be "necessary" for Christian to come 3 times a week. This sounds very prescriptive and I'm not sure who it is necessary for, Christian or the analyst, but it is clear that the insurance company should be involved.

With the intensification of sessions I would imagine that there was an intensification of the transference. In any case, Christian began to talk about his unmasculine body, small penis and, "with much shame," daily compulsive masturbation to fantasies about "sensations women would have." Christian is identified with the woman's vagina and feels shame. I wondered if Christian's identification led him to masturbate anally, which may be another source of shame.

At this point Christian admitted that he found violent pornography arousing. The analyst thought that the violent pornography was a means of detaching himself from his mother's body in order to feel his own. However, the guilt about his compulsive masturbation became unbearable. At this time Christian reported a disturbing dream which struck me as an effort to disguise his violence towards her by holding her and telling her how much he loved her while she was hit by violent explosions, while Christian's aggression towards his mother was projected in the dream and in his fears that he wouldn't survive if he separated from her. Idealizing mother and identifying with her denigration of his father defended against his unconscious hatred and fear of her.

A turning point in the analysis occurred when Christian realised that he saw his father through his mother's eyes and said, "Maybe my father is not as bad as my mother makes him out to be." I wondered if this new found recognition of and attachment to his father intensified the transference and generated homosexual anxieties, which Christian dealt with by splitting the transference with a singing teacher and wanting to end his therapy, thereby provoking a row with his analyst and creating more distance.

This new relationship with his father led to associations to Christian's babyhood; his mother's depression during and after her pregnancy, pressure to have an abortion, and a prematurely terminated breast feeding. This opened up a fuller picture of his mother; her seduction of him, negation of his father, and a working through of the Oedipal dynamics. The violent porn may have been the medium for Christian to 'play out' his incestuous anxieties.

I tend to think of psychoanalysis as led by a technique that addresses Freud's view that analysis is the analysis of resistance. I try to identify resistance when it appears in a session. For instance, a pause, a deadening of affect, a sudden departure from a line of inquiry may indicate that something has entered the patient's mind that has made them anxious, which in turn, triggers a defensive reaction, like a silence, etc. This defensive reaction would alert me to the presence of an anxiety and set me wondering what it might be. I also give priority to the patient's self-analysis. Did they notice the pause? Were they aware of an anxiety that interrupted a process? Are they able to wonder about what might have made them anxious at that point? These are aspects of a session that we can follow, to some extent, in the analyst's verbatim account; a sequence of associations, a process of cause and effect. But our accounts of sessions will always be to some extent inaccurate. I don't think we ever report the content and sequence accurately. It is always difficult to resist the temptation to make sense of that part of a session we can't remember, or order the material so that it is easier to understand, or to improve on what we actually said.

Although my technique differs from that used by Christian's analyst, I can't honestly say that my approach would have resulted in as good an outcome. No, the answer to my original question: How did he/she do it? must include the analysis described above. Although Freud (1910) warns us that even apparently positive outcomes can be expressions of resistance to real change, in this case, the outcome of the analysis seems authentic and validates the analyst's work with the patient. But there is another element in most successful analyses that is more difficult to include in verbatim write-up of cases. It is an element that has its roots in the inherently dyadic organization of the individual.

Braten (1987) proposes that, within the central nervous system of the newborn, there are circuits that specify the immediate co-presence of a complementary participant, which he terms the "virtual other," in place of which the actual other may step. The virtual other is a "felt prospective, an as yet unrealized otherness that is realized by the actual other taking their place in the dialogic circle" (Murray 1991, page 221). Research (Brazleton, Koslowski, and Main, 1974; Stern, 1974; Trevarthen, 1979) elucidates the infant's capacity to cue a response from the parent from as early as two months which suggests that the infant has the ability to attract or stimulate into life the object it is seeking. This 'felt prospective,' a virtual other, confirms what the infant has been looking for; the presence of an actual object who will nurture the infant's development.

There is an inter-subjective dimension to the patient-analyst relationship that has its roots in the earlier infant-mother relationship, which emerges in the transference and counter-transference. Our analytic attitude of non-judgemental neutrality with minimum self-exposure facilitates the patient's transference to us. But because we can never erase ourselves our patients will also perceive aspects of our actual selves that co-exist with the transference object that the patient has projected on to us. The patient's perception of us will always be based on various mixtures of the transference and our actual selves. When the analyst allows himself or herself to be a *receptive* actual object, the patient and the analyst can work in and through the transference. It is the actual analyst's capacity to identify the transference, not necessarily to name the transference object he or she represents, that enables the patient and the analyst to work *in* the transference.

The results of Christian's analysis confirm the validity of his analyst's way of working, which enabled Christian to experience his analyst as a 'felt prospective,' an actual other who he felt could help him, as Christian's analyst says, to "wistfully greet the person he wants to be."

COMMENTARY 2

Oedipus Wrecks

The most prominent feature of this patient's difficulties is his pervasive anxiety which manifests as brooding and ruminations. The case report suggests that this anxiety ranges over virtually the whole landscape of early childhood calamities including separation anxiety, castration anxiety and anxiety about being the Oedipal winner and the destruction of the father, i.e., anxiety over superego condemnation. This last phase also seems linked to the patient's feeling that he is an exception and that the ordinary rules do not apply to him because of his mother's widespread indulgences of him, in the context of vilifying the father, thus producing a narcissistic inclination in his personality, an unconscious attitude of his specialness belied by his frequent self-derogation.

The case study is entitled *Intimacy and Separateness* and focuses almost entirely on the impact of developments during the pre-oedipal period, and in particular, on anxiety arising out of the mother-infant dyad, re-experienced and re-encountered later in the mother-child and "mother-grown-up child" dyads, all of which are ostensibly connected to early separation distress and maternal anxiety. A significant question is whether the manifestations of what appears to be pre-oedipal infantile anxiety are due primarily to early disturbances in the mother-child relationship or whether, while acknowledging the impact of this period, they are the result of an affective regression in the form of a failure of signal anxiety, from higher levels of functioning at the phallic-Oedipal level in an ego that is otherwise relatively intact?

The history delineates the predominant role of the mother's anxiety in the patient's early life and his resulting irritability and sensitivity as an infant, with which this was apparently associated. The mother's use of diazepam during lactation does not appear to cause increased sensitivity or restlessness on the part of the infant but rather lethargy, sedation, and weight loss (Igbal & Sobham, 2002). However, myoclonus, seizures, and abnormal movements have also been reported (Glykys & Staley, 2015) but it is not clear whether this would explain the patient's sensitivity or restlessness during infancy. There appears to be no research on whether diazepam might be implicated in this patient's sensitivity to noise since infancy.

It appears significant, however, that despite this early history, which one might surmise from the case report would be associated with structural ego defects, there is no evidence in the report of any difficulties such as reality testing or thought disorder, rather routine manifestations of borderline or psychotic functioning which one would expect under such circumstances. This suggests that despite the mother's anxiety and depression, there was a good enough period in early infancy to establish fairly reliable ego functioning and reality testing. For example, the patient moved many times during his childhood and youth, often changing schools and had always been very shy and withdrawn. However, he appears to have blossomed in secondary school by his participation in a student research competition "which had given him security and also brought him considerable social recognition." Furthermore, the patient moved out of the family home, found a flat and organised the start of his course at the university, before the commencement of his treatment, although not without the emergence of new symptoms: an involuntary eye twitch and trembling leg movements. Although he felt these tics were shameful, his anxiety did not result in structural ego regression but rather an intensification of his preoccupation with his appearance and his clothes, which appear related to his castration anxiety, as will be discussed later.

This patient's significantly increased functioning both interpersonally and in relation to his social and academic development at the end of 4 ½ years of treatment, are noticeable developmental achievements and evidence the significant benefit he derived from this treatment within a relatively short period of time. Such a degree of improvement in functioning within that time would not be typical in a borderline or psychotic patient. There is also no report of the use of any psychotropic, especially anti-psychotic medication, which correlates with this.

For these reasons, this discussion will suggest that although the patient's early experiences predisposed him to increased sensitivity to anxiety and difficulty in affect tolerance, the primary locus of his anxiety appears to relate to the phallic-Oedipal period and the emotional intimacy between himself and his mother to the demeaning exclusion of his father, and to associated fantasies of sexuality and aggression. The picture of seeming early pathology which the narrative depicts, suggests a regression in ego functioning accompanied by difficulties with affect tolerance particularly anxiety and pathological narcissism. The latter could be due to a sense of entitlement since he has been treated by his mother as "the exception," as special and certainly far more important than the father. The most prominent affect associated with all of these events is some version of anxiety, depending on which developmental context is being considered.

The case suggests significant anxiety due to superego condemnation of the patient's unconscious sexual wishes for his mother and his fantasy that he successfully disposed of his father as a rival. The role of the analyst's countertransference and analytic stance in the patient's undoubted progress in this treatment, especially in the paternal transference, are also relevant (later).

The patient's predominant affect, besides anxiety, appears to be shame. It is often preceded by allusions to anxiety for example, the patient's sensitivity about his physical appearance, his insistence on having a crease at the back of his pants and, somewhat paradoxically, his preference for baggy jogging pants which do not, according to his own preference, reveal much of the shape of his body. He is often worried about what people think of him and presents an overall picture of extreme hesitancy, self-doubt, body and social self-consciousness and self-recrimination, all of which leave him feeling ashamed.

There are various situations which precipitate extreme anxiety and even panic attacks for this patient, upon separation from both the mother and the analyst. His anxiety concerning separations caused him to call his mother compulsively several times a day when away at college and he preferred that she select his clothing for him. He found his analyst on referral from his mother's analyst and arranged his treatment ahead of his entrance into university in the town in which his own analyst was practicing, which is described as a "precaution." This appears to be an attempt to manage separation anxiety occasioned by the separation from his mother to attend university. Also significant in this connection are the regression and emergence of panic levels of anxiety during the first vacation break in the treatment. The patient took ill with an apparent viral illness and had to be hospitalized, with his mother in attendance.

A similar pattern is revealed in his use of his friend Nina, once he was at university, to help him negotiate social relationships, using her as an "auxiliary ego", according to the writeup. None of these experiences are reported to have occasioned structural regressions in the ego. Rather they suggest significant distress and being flooded with anxiety which is managed through an affective regression and the ability to find an object of comfort and reassurance. This suggests the employment of an ego defense against anxiety which had been used successfully for many years in regard to his mother. It was in fact adaptive even though it was infantile. However, is it the early period that is determinative here?

The predominant contribution of the phallic-Oedipal phase to this patient's anxiety is suggested by the patient's awareness of his parents' discord and fights. These presumably contributed to his difficulties with affect tolerance (the report does not mention this as a factor) and it appears that his parents were so absorbed in this conflict that the patient's own experiences during those periods were apparently neglected. One cannot help but wonder if there was also exposure to the primal scene during this period and whether indeed the patient's recollections of parental fights is actually or partially a screen memory for witnessing the primal scene. The patient is also reported to have been sensitive to noise ever since he was an infant which might be an allusion to the impact of overhearing parental arguments. This possibility is not commented on in the report. The patient also reports commencing masturbation at the age of five which is described as compulsive and appears to be a reaction to intense anxiety, very likely in response to the parental conflict and castration anxiety.

The patient's wrestling with phallic-Oedipal period and superego aggression are quite noticeable as contributory as to his anxiety. Superego aggression is evident in his constant self-recriminations, his extreme sensitivity to his appearance and anxiety about his body shape, his compulsive masturbation and his guilt feelings concerning his closeness to his mother and their shared "horror" at his father's behavior regarding his drinking and liaisons with other women, producing the seeds of Oedipal guilt. He says "I am constantly afraid of doing something wrong, I have to get it really right." He berates himself for not approaching a girl Jenny whom he thinks would be a good match for him: "I judge myself all over again. I started to panic. I had to go home immediately and that's when I got a little bit better. I can only run or drive home immediately in such situations." These musings seem to be echoes of oedipal guilt which has put him on notice to be extremely vigilant in his actions, lest he transgress the oedipal barrier. As soon as he encounters an attractive woman, he has accordingly to retreat because she represents the forbidden Oedipal object and his castration anxiety becomes overwhelming. He appears to be pre-consciously aware of this, although not of his retreat from his sense of Oedipal victory, experienced with his mother.

His hyper-attentiveness to the arrangement of his pants suggests both a defensive exhibitionistic wish and extreme anxiety regarding the size of his penis which he acknowledges: He says: "I really don't have broad shoulders and I'm not muscular, so I'm not what you'd imagine a real man to be. With my funnel chest, I can't show myself." Later he confesses to his analyst that he is afraid his penis is much too small and stands at an angle. He goes on: "I somehow still have the feeling that what can be offered physically is not enough for a woman anyway." The patient is saying that in reality, he is just a baby boy with a very small penis and that he is unable to arouse a woman adequately because of that deficiency.

After acknowledging that he watches porn and gets very excited by the violence he observes, he reports a "terrible dream" about his mother. The dream involves people taking on the forms of glowing liquid stones. There is an explosion and, when his mother was involved, he reports being terrified that she might not have survived the explosion and acknowledges that "I didn't care much about dad." There is another violent explosion, he holds his mother in his arms and tells her how much he loves her. Then somehow, she reaches the bottom of a hill and when he finds her there she had turned almost cold and solid so that only a little bit was still glowing. She was still alive, and then he woke up. The patient is reported to have been in a "very bad way" immediately after this dream. He no longer left his flat and could not concentrate when he was studying. Everything felt pointless and he hardly ate anything. His anxiety attacks increased, he suffered severe insomnia and he had to cancel his exams because he was unable to study. This was interpreted by the analyst as the patient's anxiety about growing up, which would threaten his dependent relationship on his mother. However, it appears to accord with significant anxiety about possessing the mother to the exclusion of the father, who is destroyed in the process, as is clear in the dream. This appears to be a source of major anxiety in the dream and indicates an unconscious fantasy in which he saves his mother, leaves his father to die and then regresses and is overwhelmed by anxiety due to Oedipal guilt. His interest in violent pornography seems to relate to the contents of the dream which likely refer to primal scene fantasies and/or exposure in which he identifies with the sadistic father hurting the mother during intercourse. He identifies defensively with the father to mitigate his guilt at replacing the father as the aggressive intruder into his mother's body.

The analytic stance of the analyst and his or her response to the countertransference pressures in the treatment are also relevant here. The analyst's style is often quite directive, even professorial. One wonders whether this was considered in relation to the patient's paternal transference and his latent father-hunger due to the absence of support and approval for any masculinity or assertiveness. For example, the patient asks for the analyst's approval of a shirt he purchased; later, with the emergence of tics and an upsurge in anxiety after his hospitalization, the patient requests an increase in the frequency of his treatment, observing that he "really needed the therapy" which suggests a wish to have more of the analyst/father as a bulwark. The analyst had already proposed this earlier which suggests that the patient was initially ambivalent about accepting more from the father/analyst but his anxiety during the holiday break in the treatment persuaded him that he needed the father/analyst more than he had realized. The analyst's style and recommendation that he increase the frequency of his sessions, provide this bulwark very clearly.

The analyst also intervenes definitively in his Oedipal enmeshment with his mother. The analyst says: "You are not your mother's partner, [you are not] responsible for her." This is the father/analyst who puts up a barrier between the patient and his mother, in no uncertain terms, and challenges the patient to stand on his own two feet, and, in effect, to be a "man." The analyst is here acting as a developmental object in the treatment as the father who prohibits access to the mother, which also gratifies the positive side of the paternal transference with its longing for paternal reassurance and encouragement. The patient does later acknowledge that his mother's "bad image of men affects me a lot. My mother only sees my father in a bad way. I really see my father the way my mother sees him." He had earlier disparaged his father, saying that he was selfish, and thought only of himself, constantly afraid of becoming poor. His mother wanted to leave his father and is described as always looking to the patient for support against the father, horrified by his behavior.

However, the analyst reports that subsequently, through the clinical work, the patient realized that "Maybe my father is not as bad as my mother makes him out to be." This suggests a pivotal turn to the father/analyst in the treatment, presaged by the analyst's declaration that the patient was not responsible for his mother, thus installing the oedipal barrier. It also indicates a retreat from the position of replicating in the transference the relation to his mother as special and the "exception" (Freud, 1916) who can dictate to the analyst the times of his availability for treatment, as he had attempted to do at the beginning. Although initially insisting on his "specialness" in the maternal transference at the beginning of the treatment, he now gravitates towards the paternal transference of accepting the longed-for power and authority of the analyst/father and his significance for buttressing the patient's sense of masculinity and separating him from his mother's influence

Perhaps this turn is the reason the analyst reports being surprised that, after the following summer vacation, which the patient tolerated without regression, he announced that he wished to terminate the treatment. The patient's stated reason was that "he had come through the holidays well after all, and now he wanted to try it on his own." A termination date two months in the future was agreed upon and then almost immediately afterwards, the patient informed the analyst that he could no longer attend the Tuesday sessions because he had arranged for singing lessons. Although an alternative date was found so that the treatment was not interrupted like this, there is no discussion in the report about the meaning of the patient's wish to terminate beyond his stated purpose, nor of his sudden and unpredictable resistance to following through on this by arranging a singing lesson which conflicts with an analytic session. This raises the question as to whether this wish to terminate was due to anxiety about aggressive wishes in the Oedipal transference to the father as a rival becoming more prominent in the patient's mind in the gathering pace of the treatment, and as a fluctuation away from the positive transference to the analyst as someone who supported his masculinity but who now obstructed the patient's access to the mother such that his Oedipal wish to possess the mother and eliminate the father was once again transcendent. He has to cancel the treatment and take distance from the analyst/father by trying to cancel Tuesdays, thus protecting him from his oedipal aggression. This suggests that the patient is responding to his aggression towards his father as manifested in his dreams but not overtly acknowledged by him.

This marshalling of the evidence suggests, it is argued, that this patient's intense anxiety is predominantly about castration fear at being the Oedipal winner and destroyer of the father, i.e., anxiety over punishment for his oedipal success, transformed and internalized into superego condemnation.

Postscript:

In the middle of the night, after completing the above discussion, this author awoke, thunderstruck by the realization that he had completely overlooked consideration of the significance of the second separation-individuation phase of development, typical of adolescence. As is mentioned above, the main focus of the case report is early onset anxiety during infancy and early childhood. The above discussion focuses heavily, by contrast, on the contribution of the Oedipal period to the patient's dynamic picture.

Now, with the benefit of hindsight and a cup of hot chocolate, the following comes to mind: while the original discussion above emphasizes the role of the analyst's rather didactic style in contributing to the erection of an Oedipal barrier between himself and his mother, to forestall his incestuous wishes, it may also be the case that this facilitated the beginning of a much-delayed separation-individuation process primarily from the mother, in this patient's development. It is noticeable that aside from the sadistic sexual fantasies relating to his mother, evidenced in his dream and implied in his preoccupation with violent pornography, there is no aggression reported against either mother – or father for that matter. The patient ostensibly displays none of the usual at times frenetic, and often offensive adolescent attempts to distance himself from and belittle his parents' attitudes, wishes, ministrations and directives which one usually finds at this phase of development. This appears perhaps not only to be the case because when we first meet the patient he is 20 years of age, but there is also no evidence in the case report that such manifestations ever occurred. An adolescence without an aggressive thrust towards separation and individuation? Believable?

It seems reasonable to speculate on the basis of the evidence that is available, that the patient's regression towards anxiety and increased dependence on his mother was more clearly linked dynamically to castration anxiety, as is outlined in the discussion above, than to concerns about separation and individuation. On the contrary, he appears to have made the transition from home to university life without a major regression, although he did prearrange to have his analyst waiting for him, so to speak, in the university town to which he relocated. After that time, the only significant regression occurred after the interruption of the first holiday break. Although it is not clear from the report, one assumes that he returned home during this period because there is no report of any travel or other interests which suggest otherwise. The patient then appears to have experienced his breakdown, requiring hospitalization because of a serious viral illness, whilst under the care of his mother. This does not suggest a regression due to intense separation anxiety from the analyst. In that case, the mother's presence would have been far more reassuring than it appears to have been.

What seems more likely, however, is that once the vacation put him back in his mother's nest, his anxiety about the Oedipal implications of this proved overwhelming. If this formulation is accurate, it suggests the remarkable proposition that in this case the usual manifestations of the second separation individuation in adolescence were crowded out by the imperative nature of the patient's castration anxiety in relation to his all too available Oedipal object, with the exclusion and total absence of any paternal presence. Furthermore, the patient's aggression seems to have been recruited entirely in the service of his superego, vilifying several aspects of his personal appearance, habitus and character, belittling the size of his penis and sexual inadequacy with women, with none of it directed outwards towards either parent in the context of separation-individuation. The only evidence of such aggression appears in an Oedipal dream in which he manages to save his mother from burning up in an enormous conflagration and in which he acknowledges complete indifference to his father's fate, accompanied by sadomasochistic allusions to the primal scene.

By the end of the account of the treatment, the patient decides to remain with his analyst. He says he needs the additional support. But he has graduated from the University and has a steady girlfriend with whom he has a satisfying sexual relationship. His developmental attainments by the end of the 4 ½ period of treatment reported argue for a delayed but increasingly successful negotiation of separation-individuation, under the aegis of the analyst's treatment, however only after the full impact of the analyst's restriction of the patient's access to his mother, was able to take hold. With the analyst's help, he seems to have arrived there in the end, far more separate and individuated.

EDITORIAL REFLECTIONS

A major objective of this volume is to find out if psychoanalysis is relevant and useful for the treatment of adolescents. Christian, a 20-year-old "emerging adult" (Gilmore 2019) presented as seriously disturbed across every area of his life; the intensity of his anxiety when frustrated produced serious interference with ego functions, including independent functioning and reality testing. After four and a half years of psychoanalysis he was successful in all his endeavors and could then engage with and grow from a mutually agreed termination. This chapter affirms our view on the efficacy of psychoanalysis.

Noteworthy is the emphasis on development by the analyst and commentators. One comments on the "multi-dimensionality of the adolescent's life," the broad array of inner and outer forces an adolescent is struggling with. The analyst of adults deals with a much narrower range of influences and this creates major differences for how child and adolescent analysts work. Included in these forces are the developmental ones, with conflicts over growth itself often central. A wide range of techniques is needed, including reconstruction, now often neglected by adult-only analysts. In this chapter we hear of the therapeutic work on the continuing impact of early trauma, neglect, conflict occurring even prenatally and extending post-oedipally and into adolescence. One person remarks on the "second separation-individuation" occurring at adolescence (Blos 1967) as this adolescent is struggling with leaving his "adhesive" mother.

This chapter also perhaps offers an illustration of Freud's first theory of adolescent breakdown, the theory of deferred action or "nachtraglichkeit." Winnicott underscored the qualitative difference between childhood fantasies of death and the actual potential that ".... at adolescence there is contained murder" (1969, p.752). The impact of deferred action can raise that potential to traumatic intensity when inner and outer forces coincide and overwhelm the adolescent (Novick, J. and Novick, K.K. 2001a). In Christian's case, whatever the effects of the postnatal difficulties, childhood abuse, and all the other adverse childhood experiences, the full impact may not have appeared until he reached physical maturity and could put his sexual rage and omnipotent beliefs into action. He, like many disturbed adolescents, was terrified of growing up and insisted that his penis was small, that no woman could be interested in him, that he had to stay home and remain a dependent pre-adolescent forever.

Among the many directions of thought stimulated by this chapter, we note that there were a number of instances where the analyst chose to not to make a transference interpretation, but instead commented on the progressive component of Christian's behavior. For example, when he wanted the analyst's response to a shirt he had purchased, the analyst chose not to take up the transference of his dependent/sexual wish for approval from his mother, but instead commented on his progressive wish to be attractive to others. This is what we mean when we talk about using a "two systems" approach to psychoanalytic work, especially with adolescents, stressing the importance of supporting the action of the growth principle tending toward realistic, creative expansion. There will be other opportunities to take up both positive and negative transferences. Since 1996 we have asserted that the overriding task of adolescence is setting aside closed-system beliefs, choosing instead to be guided by open-system reality, pleasure, love, and creativity (Novick, J. and Novick, K.K. 1996). In a recent book, "Freedom to Choose" (Novick and Novick, 2016), we have elaborated on these ideas.

Both commentators note the patient's intense involvement with his parents and the analyst's focus on the dynamics of those relationships, but, unlike many of the adolescent cases in this book and our parent work casebook, this analyst did not work with either parent. It is, however, very clear that the analyst kept both parents in mind. Many interpretations involved the early mother and one of the crucial transformations resulting from treatment was Christian's changed perception of his father. This raises the question of whether, when, and how concurrent parent work is critical to effective treatment of adolescents, and what kind of difference it can make even if not necessary to the maintenance of the therapy.

CHAPTER 18

MARK – age 20

Mark's Analytic Journey from Imprisonment to Freedom

In describing my extended analytic journey with Mark, which began when he was six years old and has continued through adolescence and emerging adulthood, I will focus on the crucial role that following his interests and talents, particularly his musical gifts, has played in his remarkable transformation. Our work began with five times per week psychoanalytic therapy until he was eighteen, followed by three times per week treatment until he was twenty-four. After two years of twice-weekly work, he interrupted therapy for a year until beginning once-weekly therapy three years ago. He is now thirty. His musical talents have contributed immensely to his positive development – helping him explore his conflicts in the transference, overcoming social anxiety and isolation, forming relationships with other peers, and helping us explore his inner world. His music has played a major role in his emotional regulation, serving as a most adaptive defense (sublimation), as well as an important component of his identity and source of competence. His recent music explores themes related to his experience of emerging adulthood, including change and transformation, instability, forming relationships, and identity. In addition, work within the transference has been crucial. In fact, his lyrics reflect the central concerns in our transference-based work. Focusing on his conflicts regarding positive emotional connections and letting others help him, as well as separation, loss, and individuation has played a critical role in allowing him to use his musical gifts. I will briefly describe Mark at the beginning of treatment before moving to his music and later years.

Mark – age six

When six-year-old Mark's parents first consulted me, they considered him to be a child who, despite having significant strengths, was experiencing severe difficulties. He was a shy child who recently had begun meowing like a kitty when meeting new people. When engaged in conversation, he would also drift off and repeat the same word over and over. In addition, routines and rituals such as which foods were served and the way foods were arranged on his plate, were extremely important to Mark. For example, if the hamburger that he had wanted with catsup came with mustard, he would respond with a "meltdown" and likely throw the hamburger at a parent. He also engaged in repetitive, stereotyped behaviors, such as jumping up and down and gazing at his fingers. The *Star Wars* films and the sinking of the Titanic were extreme preoccupations and interests. Alongside these problematic areas, his parents both spoke of his considerable strengths, noting Mark's kindness toward and genuine concern for animals and other children, his creative imagination, and a gift for music.

Before our initial meeting, in the waiting room Mark drew the Titanic hitting the iceberg – a vivid image of his feelings of impending disaster. (Years later, he pointed out that he had drawn a vampire with fangs and evil eyes in the iceberg, making clear the role his destructive rage played in his troubles.) At first he was quite scared of me and meowed when he met me. He clawed at his mother's sweater and made other "cat sounds," and, despite my efforts to engage him, did not speak for five to ten minutes. His initial speech seemed immature and unclear. When he reached for a toy in my office he made sure his mother's hand enclosed his. He decided that we should play with the walkie-talkies. At first, he meowed into his walkie-talkie, but then he pretended that it was a gun and had a gunfight with me. He became quite animated, called 911 to report that people were fighting and had the police take the offenders to jail. Nevertheless, he was afraid that they would escape. In another play scenario we worked together to lock up some thieves. He hunted for food while I guarded the thieves. Next Mark loaded up a small table with toys and was concerned that it would collapse under the enormous weight because, as he explained, "people had forgotten to put in the nails." I understood this to represent his concern about having a psychological structure that was sturdy enough to manage his strong feelings and conflicts, his emotional burdens. While he was eager to return, as we were ending the first session, he clung to mother and placed the corner of her sweater in his mouth. I was impressed with a number of positive qualities in Mark who had a definite appeal. There was a sparkle in his eyes, and he exuded a certain warmth. Despite difficulties, he became quite emotionally connected, engaged in symbolic play and communicated in a meaningful way. Most importantly, he seemed to be aware of and concerned about his difficulties and to be eager for help with them

As part of my initial evaluation, Mark was referred for a psychological assessment. Projective testing revealed both an interest in people as well as anxiety about interactions. Story themes related to feeling abandoned and unprotected with characters who are killed or sucked into a whirlpool. One of his drawings was of a snake shooting poison from its mouth. The psychologist concluded that Mark was "expressing his feelings of being at the mercy of his own aggressive impulses, which he projects onto the environment. Feelings of being abandoned or unprotected originate from his own difficulty connecting with others and should not be interpreted as a criticism of his parents." While many responses revealed idiosyncratic perceptions and illogical thinking, other responses "suggested the presence of affective and cognitive resources, which, while not currently available to

Mark, could be made available to him through successful psychotherapy." His "social avoidance and adherence to routines" were felt to represent attempts to cope with a frightening inner world. The psychologist and I both considered him to have a mild autistic spectrum disorder.

My initial impression was that Mark's neurobiological difficulties had led to a predominant experience of feeling overwhelmed and therefore interfered with his feeling safe and protected as an infant and young child. This left him feeling alone, vulnerable, and terrified in a threatening world. Mark's excessive sense of danger led to his developing a rigid protective structure involving isolation, excessive hostility, and compensatory omnipotence, as well as his insistence on sameness and routine, to manage his overwhelming emotions. This protective shell interfered with his taking in the loving parental input and developmental assistance which was available and which he needed in order to develop a sound psychological structure and sense of self.

In addition, while he was both excessively dependent as well as isolated, any experience of true dependence or need as well as any experience of healthy separation or individuation was fought because of difficulties with tolerating and managing the normal emotions surrounding need, loss, and sadness. He felt overwhelmed and in a desperate panic, as if he were the table in my office that would collapse under his emotional burdens or the Titanic that would sink because of his hostility. It is somewhat amazing to me that at age twenty-eight, Mark confirmed these initial formulations to a significant extent. He said that when he was younger that he felt that there was "love up on the shelf but that he just couldn't reach it." He said that throwing his improperly prepared hamburgers at his parents was the only way he could express his extreme sadness and disappointment in life.

His loving and caring parents were puzzled and understandably quite concerned about Mark, unsure of how to help him, and were most willing to engage in a useful therapeutic process. While I felt that there was considerable goodness, strength, and talent hidden inside of Mark, I also felt that his parents had much to offer him. Through therapeutic engagement with Mark in intensive individual therapy and dealing with his internal conflicts about caring and helpful connections in the transference, I hoped to help him become better able to use more the loving care and developmental assistance that his parents were offering him. Aside from some extra emphasis on ways to engage and interact with Mark, I focused on helping them understand Mark at a deeper level and on affording parental guidance as needed. Over many years it was most important to support their exceptional dedication to Mark and their most unusual efforts on his behalf, including bringing him to our early, before-school sessions five days a week and seeking out educational settings which would optimize his development. Helping them recognize Mark's hidden appreciation for their and my help was critical.

Understanding Mark's conflicts about feeling loved or loving and about progressive emotional development, including individuation and loss, helped them to not feel discouraged, when, repeatedly, after increased engagement with them or me and feelings of progress, he would forcibly assert that he would never come to see me again or angrily lash out at them, or withdraw into his own world, spending hours jumping or posing before a mirror. It was important that they could understand that Mark's anger at them, his anger at me and his withdrawal were all generally responses to feeling helped, cared about, and caring rather than to actually feeling disappointed or misunderstood. Also, I tried to help them maintain a realistic hope despite many difficulties and setbacks. During his high school years, we occasionally had emergency sessions involving parents alone or with Mark in order to deal with his threatening verbal outbursts of rage at home. With regard to music, I supported mother's successful efforts pushing him to take music lessons at a rock school despite his objections.

At twenty-one Mark completed a book describing his experience with Asperger's. In the chapter entitled "The Early Stages," Mark poignantly depicts his descent into Asperger's and the development of his most crippling defense – the repetitive behavior of jumping as a means of self-regulation when he was four to five years of age. In his words, after he saw *Return of the Jedi*, Mark started:

> ...bouncing up and down on the living room sofa and making these funny noises. What I was doing was imagining and acting out all of these dramatic fantasies while making sound effects with my mouth. I was pretending that I was having all of these fights involving guns, swords, light sabers, starships, soldiers, ships, hand-to-hand combat, all kinds of things relating to violence or conflict. After my mom eventually complained to me about wearing out her furniture with me always bouncing on it, I replaced that with going outside or someplace private and just jumping up and down on my own two feet while still acting out the same makeshift stories. This felt great! For a long time, there was nothing that gave me a better sense of satisfaction than this. Just escaping from the real world and creating and living in my own where I was in complete control was the best of anything. Literally jumping away reality. I didn't care how weird anyone who saw me thought I was or how much further isolated from the real world it made me.

I can't accurately convey how much trouble this retreat into jumping and his world of fantasy caused Mark and how much he resisted my trying to understand this with him. Right after graduation from high school and his twentieth birthday, he finally gave up jumping, much as one gives up an addiction. Mark had realized that living in his own world, a way of trying to escape from painful reality, actually imprisoned him.

It was crucial for me to be able to see the loving, worthwhile person who has something valuable to offer imprisoned within Mark's hard protective shell. I'll quote from Mark's book:

> Larry (how Mark refers to me) has had more access to my mind and feelings than anyone I know and he always seemed to see something in me that I didn't. He always appeared to have complete confidence in me even in my darkest days and I almost sensed that he could foresee a certain bright future ahead of me that I could not.

Six months into treatment he told his mother "when I get older I'm going to have a normal life like you and Dad," reflecting his real optimism that with his parents' and my help, coupled with his own effort, he could change. The analyst's realistic conviction that meaningful change is possible, not magically, but through hard work, is crucial.

Relationship: early years of treatment

Despite his desire for help, Mark feared needing people. He protected himself by acting like he didn't care, trashing our work, refusing to cooperate, and retreating into his own world. A real emotional battle ensued because of his fears of vulnerability and loss if he depended on me. Mark rejected the help I offered. I worked hard to engage him. For example, he became quite interested in the Disney book telling the story of Pinocchio and for a time he would begin our sessions by running into my office ahead of me, grabbing the book, sitting in my large toy closet, closing the door and reading silently to himself. One day I playfully wrestled with him to keep him from entering the closet and closing the door while he read. The next day he again ran into the office ahead of me, but this time he sat in the toy closet with the door open and not reading. He looked at me spontaneously and said,

"Did you notice anything? I'm not reading!" However, engagement did not come without a price. Occasionally, after times of positive development and connectedness Mark would refuse to come into my office and, on a number of occasions, I had to conduct therapy through a closed car window in the parking lot across the street.

Reaction to my first vacation after four-five months of treatment and themes from the early years of treatment

Four to five months after beginning treatment Mark and I were working on his reaction to my first vacation which would begin in several weeks. He dreamt that he and his brother were in a pit and smashed through glass and there were monsters, bats, and snakes and when he woke he felt that the dream had been real. He mentioned that my soft hand puppet raccoon – which he was quite fond of and had named Wrinkles – was afraid of me. During these days he told Wrinkles to bite me and said that Wrinkles hated Dr. Larry who was stupid and ugly. I responded that he was treating me like he didn't care and that he hated me because he didn't want to be sad because I was leaving. When I wondered if he felt that Dr. Larry didn't care if Mark lived or died because I was going away, Mark responded by saying, "Dr. Larry is a piece of junk and he certainly won't be missed." We were able to talk about missing feelings involving Wrinkles and that Mark would miss Wrinkles, and Wrinkles would miss Mark. There were angry feelings and guns and shooting as well as play with themes involving fears of being left all alone in a scary world and being hurt. We discussed being mad instead of sad and of trying to control people and order people around so that they could not leave him. We also talked about how Mark meowed when he was angry because he felt that I did not do enough for him.

In one session, almost immediately before I left for vacation, Mark asked for a cup to get some water. After drinking the water, he tore the cup into bits shouting, "You only got me water! You didn't get me food!" I said that this was Mark's way of saying "Thank you." I think that you will recognize his difficulty with gratitude – receiving help and not throwing it away – since true gratitude interferes with a sense of omnipotence because it leads to feelings of need and to concerns about loss. Envy, greed, and destructive attacks on someone whom the child just experienced as helpful are most important pathological defenses. Such attacks on good people inside are extremely destructive to the child's internal world and damage the sense of having a loving self as well as loving others inside. I've found that it helps to interpret these ego-weakening protections and defenses. In his book, Mark reflects upon this incident "…. what I was doing was a disguised reflection on my distaste towards the world for what …. it had failed to give me [and] helped bring to light a major conflict in my personality…. A resentment towards life and a strong envy for those around me who had it so much easier."

During the second year of treatment Mark became even more attached to Wrinkles and decided to have a birthday party for him. He came in loaded with gifts – a handmade four-poster bed with a handmade quilt, monogrammed pajamas, along with hand-painted napkins and cupcakes – all for Wrinkles. The next day, Mark pretended to kill and eat Wrinkles whom he served boiled, roasted over a fire, and chopped and fried. Mark agreed when I said that after killing and eating Wrinkles whom he loved so much, he felt he would have him inside forever and never lose him – a vivid illustration of omnipotent control of others to avoid the passive experience of loss.

After a few years of treatment, we began to play out an ongoing story with Playmobil figures. I was assigned the role of Duke, a policeman. Mark played all the other parts, including Duke's enemy, the evil Zorn. During one episode, Duke helped Zorn and they were becoming friends. Then Zorn shot Duke. Mark announced "and for the first time Zorn felt shame." This represented a significant step toward the development of a helpful conscience. After a period of years, Duke evolved into a psychologist and a prison warden in a benevolent prison that helped criminals transform into loving people. This storyline provided many opportunities to confront issues relating to imprisonment and freedom.

Mark's Music

Following Mark's interest in music has been crucial in our work. As he moved into his teen years, exploring the lyrics of his favorite songs was extremely helpful entering into a dialogue dealing more directly with his emotional experience. Then, at sixteen, Mark began writing songs that provide a compelling road map to his inner life and growth in treatment.

One of his earliest was entitled *Let Me Out.* Though unfinished, the fragments are quite expressive of his difficulty with emotional regulation and his experience of emotional imprisonment:

I'm sitting on my ice-cold doorstep weeping away my love.
Thinking what's the value of this place that I call hell.
You can't unlock my chains.
So ice my thoughts down with fear
As I sit in this cold dark room.

Another song, *Past and Present,* accurately describes the early atmosphere of our work and his multiple forms of attack:

no doctor can stop me because I just don't care
not even with these stupid daily meetings
chorus: I'm just selfish
and just won't cooperate
I'm just a nightmare

I won't communicate
I'll just stay here inside my mind
just like a knot you can't unwind
because I don't know what will become of me

Written in his later high school years, *Burning Motivations* presents a compelling picture of Mark's resistance to positive development and change. Clearly the double meaning of the title *Burning Motivations* conveys not only strong determination but also the opposite, the impulse to destroy that determination. In Mark's words the song was about "doing something that you know is wrong and you want to stop but you're addicted to it and feel shackled." At the beginning of his senior year I had the pleasure of hearing Mark and his band perform *Burning Motivations* for the first time at a local bar. I even purchased a T-shirt with his band's name on it.

All the things that I've come so far for I'm wasting away
But I don't want that
The healing for the feeling is what I'm pushing back down below
And it takes me, and it breaks me, but I just won't let it go

Chorus:
'Cause it's that one that I know
And I'm a miserable fighter
All stuck down below
It's killing me but I don't want to stop
I can give it a shot but that's not enough
And I'm burning away the motivation inside
It's killing me but I just won't let it go

These moments of warm sharing were interspersed with intense work regarding attacks on me and on our work. For example, in his book Mark wrote this description of our work:

> His (Dr. Larry's) occasional failure to communicate properly sometimes led to tempestuous arguments during our later meetings, though these disputes also enabled us to examine the flaws in our connection and then move to close the loopholes in question. For an example, there was one particular meeting when we were discussing the concept of Asperger's Syndrome and Dr. Larry made an observation that I in turn misread as a derogatory sentiment. Whiffing the opportunity to play the high card and request that he clarify his comments, I succumbed to my frenetic impulse and fiercely chastised him; he then angrily responded that I was unfairly labeling him as an antagonist. For the next thirty minutes, tempers flared, fingers jabbed through the air and more f-bombs were dropped than at a Dane Cook stand-up. The following session however, we sat down and after bringing up the aggressive conversation from before, we burst out laughing. What had happened was that we had both taken our biggest conversational flaws and gone head to head with each other and though it was heated, it also illuminated the defects that we both needed to modify in order to enhance a therapeutic relationship; in this case his deficiency in conveying his analogies and my impulsive tendency to antagonize what was being said to me.

Mark's music began to tell a story of movement from feeling imprisoned and shut off from love to freedom and loving connections. Mark illustrated this process in his song, *With Me*, written for a school performance near high school graduation.

'cause I can feel you watchin', every time I turn out the lights

And I'm breathin', cause I feel you with me tonight

Mark ends with:

Your voice inside my head is still guiding me towards the distant light

However, after high school graduation, his journey was far from over. Mark had not applied for college, lived at home, was unable to hold a relatively simple job and had significant difficulty with his friends and family. This lasted for approximately 5 months until he gave up jumping. Mark would literally spend hours jumping by the side of the road or posturing and staring into the mirror. His song, *No Escape*, describes his realization that living in his own world as a way of trying to escape from painful reality actually imprisoned him:

Those times I'd spend staring in the mirror

and see my arms around you though there's no one there

Now I know, it's no escape no more

Mark later talked about what a crucial decision this was – to give up jumping. He said that he had to realize and accept that instead of helping him, jumping was actually hurting him. He added that he probably would not have been able to go to college had he not given up jumping.

Two months later, Mark entered a small university near his home where he did quite well while he lived with his parents, held various part-time jobs, and graduated with honors in psychology. During college he began dating but had a number of disappointing relationships. Since graduation he has continued to live at home and worked full-time in a residential rehabilitation facility. His difficulties in dating led to much hard work in treatment as evidenced by two songs which chronicle his growing capacity to bear sadness and endure the potential pain of loss of someone you love and need – a capacity necessary to form a loving relationship. The first of these, *Blueprint*, was written as Mark was preparing to risk pursuing a relationship:

> And when I finally show these tears, it's my blueprint for loving you.
> To have something that I can value and something I can miss

Mark said that this song indicated a psychological transformation for him. It meant accepting uncertainty and destroying a blueprint for disaster – trying to avoid painful experiences and staying on the sideline in life. He said that you can't find love if you live in a robotic world of anger. His blueprint for love involves accepting vulnerability and being able to be sad which he likened to being able to take a punch.

A few months later it became clear that he would not be able to successfully pursue this relationship. At this point Mark wrote *Hurricane of Hearts* expressing his growing capacity for adaptive emotional regulation in the face the emotional challenges of emerging adulthood:

> See the waves crash in front of your weary eyes, hear the sound of the wind cry inside your mind,
> Brace yourself, say a prayer for a miracle, as catastrophe it takes its toll, threatens to take your soul.
> So how do we build a hurricane of hearts, babe, in the eye of the storm.
> Board it up, protect your mind from the outside, others say there's nowhere to hide, that you can't decide.

Mark poignantly expressed his experience of this developmental phase and how to manage adaptively as he said:

You're in the eye of the storm. There's destruction all around you. There's been a disaster. Your heart is broken down. Notice that the guitar ends all by itself; this expresses an important idea – emptiness. How do you restructure this? How do you find optimism in such a time of despair. You have to build this within you by turning destructiveness into something like its opposite – love and joy. You need strength, courage, and perseverance. You can wind up feeling that even though you're in the middle of the storm – in distress and feel all alone – you still have the feeling that good times – what you're looking for – could still be around the corner.

What a description of adaptive emotional regulation or open system functioning to manage the pains of life as Kerry and Jack Novick have described!

A little later in his song, *You Take My Breath Away*, Mark poignantly expresses how terrifying it is to love and care for someone and the courage required to face such fears:

Long time waiting for a moment to say
The passion's rising in my heart today
Feels like thin ice breaking beneath your feet
Woke up this morning shaking from this Epiphany
The times we shared and what they still mean to me
I thought I could escape the truth
By being someone else pretending I didn't need you
But I still got lost in you,
Oh, I'm still so in love with you.

Over the past two to three years Mark has been involved in a satisfying relationship with a caring young woman with whom he recently went to

Europe, and he successfully finished the first semester of graduate school before deciding that this was not the right program for him. Mark recently completed an album entitled *Nebulae*, where stars die and are reborn-endings and beginnings. I'll close with the last song on this album *Dawn*:

Guided memories feel like broken bones
Static noises on the radio
Wasting time on what has come and gone
Innocence fades away into the sun

When the break of dawn changes what's left of who you are
Eternal fire now please spare me somehow
Don't you leave me to wake up on my own
Your dad's truck don't run like it used to
And the old Sand man no longer visits you
Mark closes with:
I try to embrace what I'm meant to be
Is that what it means to feel free

Of course *Dawn* represents a new beginning. Mark's thoughts about the songs on this album poignantly express his experience of emerging adulthood. "All the songs are about certain themes – change and adapting – adapting to the world but also to what's inside you. Also, they are about acceptance of yourself and changing your whole identity, who you are. You go through a physical puberty in your teens but there's a mental puberty in your twenty's. It's about becoming free."

In closing, Mark's music is playing a crucial role in his continuing development. Currently he is becoming more committed in his romantic relationship, planning to move out of his home and reevaluating his further education and vocational choices. As Mark proceeds, he has embarked on a new musical project which he feels will eclipse what he has done so far and will be even more introspective. He plans to revisit his autobiography, making music a more central, integrative theme that runs throughout his entire life. Mark intends to highlight his changed view of himself. Previously he described his life as representing a certain diagnostic category. Now he sees himself as a "misfit who has had difficulty finding his own voice and talents." In his revised autobiography, he plans a "retrospective consideration of the significant events" in his life. As befits his increasing sense of freedom, Mark looks forward to an expanding and exciting future.[4]

COMMENTARY 1

One way in which child psychoanalysis differs greatly from classical, narrow-scope, adult psychoanalysis is in the severity of conditions that can be treated. The intensity of psychoanalysis in childhood can provide the developing ego with strengths that result in the individual outperforming the prognosis associated with their underlying condition such as trauma, neuro-atypicality, or psychotic tendencies. Mark appears to be one such patient.

As described in the vignette of Mark's treatment starting at age six the analyst is both a transference object, a real object, a developmental object and a coach for Mark's parents whose child requires more than Winnicott's 'ordinary' or 'good enough' parental devotion.

Let us consider how, at age twenty-one, Mark looks back on his experiences with the analyst with the comment that the analyst "always seemed to see something in me that I didn't. He always appeared to have complete confidence in me even in my darkest days and I almost sensed that he could foresee a certain bright future ahead of me that I could not." Indeed, the analyst did see strengths in Mark and in his family that gave hope of a

---

4 The patient and his family have given me permission to use his material.

functioning and interpersonally satisfying adulthood. As the keeper of this hope, the analyst presented to Mark a real and a developmental object whose wisdom Mark felt he could rely on. This facilitating developmental object present from the assessment onward allowed Mark to internalize the analyst's vision and with hope identify with his parents in a manner typical for his age. Mark is reported to have said to his mother early in the treatment "when I get older I'm going to have a normal life like you and Dad." The ability of parents to envision their child as an adult in terms that are hopeful, positive and rewarding is very important to the normal child's development of self-esteem. However, it is also important for parents to let the child, especially as the child becomes an adolescent and young adult, revise and individualize their self-image and the accompanying ambitions.

One area where parents sometimes unwittingly fail to encourage change is in their off-springs' sibling relationships allowing siblings to remain intensely, and immaturely, rivalrous because they were so at the time the sibling entered the family. Psychoanalysis as a treatment is highly focused on the patient often to the point of barely reflecting on siblings. Mark's brother is mentioned only once in this brief summary of a very long and intense treatment. That mention is in the context of a dream in which he and his brother are "in a pit and smashed through glass and there were monsters, bats, and snakes and when he woke up he felt the dream had been real." Was his brother a companion to assist Mark in managing a terrifying world of monsters? Or was the brother an object of envy, perhaps with fewer difficulties of self-regulation and interpersonal engagement? Or was he both?

Throughout this long analysis Mark needed to unleash his anger upon the analyst as Mark struggled with being overwhelmed by all that churned inside him and his fears of being overwhelmed and isolated by that state. Mark's hunger for intimacy and his difficulties with self-regulation led him to behaviors that walled him off from others. From the time, as a child, he hurled his hamburger at his parents to episodes like the finger jabbing, and f-bombing argument of the adolescent Mark with the analyst, Mark attacked his parents and his analyst time and time again. The analyst helped the parents understand that Mark's tantrums were a sign of his desperation and longing for love as he wrote at 28 that he felt he knew there was "love up on the shelf but that he just couldn't reach it." Clearly by adolescence their work together had led to a deep trust that allowed them to laugh together at the next session over the angry words of the previous session's argument.

Is Mark's ability in his late teens to express anger at the analyst and to recover their warm bond soon after a result, at least in part, of the length and intensity of the treatment? Would Mark, as an adolescent, be able to recover in this fashion in a newly initiated treatment with a newly encountered analyst? Would a new analyst be as confident that the anger, which was multifactorial (part real gripe with the therapist, part frustration at being handed such a difficult neural system and, no doubt, part transferential) could be metabolized and the therapeutic relationship stabilized? The adolescent, under the developmental pressure to pursue greater independence and individuation, needs to create rifts with the most closely held libidinal objects, primarily the parents, but also with the analyst, both in the transference and with the real object due to the fear of regressive dependency. This need for conflict makes the ability of the therapeutic dyad to survive these conflicts of aggression critical to the treatment.

With Mark, the long treatment appears to be a significant asset. However, there are cases in which, as the patient enters young adulthood, it may be advantageous for the child analyst to encourage a move to a new therapist. The analyst who has seen the patient since early childhood may well recall the patient's childhood more clearly than the patient does. This may lead inadvertently to a situation where the dyad will not be motivated to have the patient recount past experiences as remembered by the patient despite the associations to the past that might come to mind in the context of the treatment. This avoidance of recounting the past can result in avoidance of a significant means to gaining a new, more mature perspective that would be a valuable effect of the treatment. Mark does revisit the past in a manner that encourages developing a more mature perspective by writing his autobiography.

Mark's meowing as a means of vocal engagement and his addiction-like dependency on jumping to soothe and stabilize his internal experiences are early signs of his neural atypicality. To the degree they are stigmatizing and off-putting to others, leading to social isolation, they may be seen by many clinicians, teachers and parents as weaknesses. But the analyst is able to also see them as strengths, as alternate neural pathways recruited to help Mark get where he needed to go. Meowing allowed Mark to communicate his wish for engagement when ordinary, pragmatic language was not within his reach. The very problematic jumping was a self-empowering means of control over both his churning internal environment and his overstimulation from the social environment albeit at a cost of further loneliness and isolation.

Mark did develop the capacity for both narrative and expository language as evidenced in his memoir writing. He also developed his gift for poetic expression. Now more than just a cryptic metaphoric meow, his lyrics were evocative and must have been meaningful to many in his audiences when performed with his band. Reading this vignette we do not actually hear the rhythm of his band performing but one can wonder if it may be understood as an alternate pathway to an inner rhythmicity formerly achieved through jumping.

COMMENTARY 2

A Blueprint for Love and Transformation

Introduction – Psychoanalytic treatment is recommended for ASDs

This is one of the most painful and beautiful accounts of child analysis I have ever read. It is painful for how sensitively the author conveys how terrified and abandoned Mark felt for so long. It is beautiful for how dedicated the parents, the analyst and, most importantly, Mark himself, have been to helping Mark become the soulful artist and loving human he is now. The analyst, called "Larry," began this transformative analytic journey with Mark at age 6 and has continued working with him to the present, age 30, with gradual reductions in frequency.

Mark was diagnosed with mild autism at age 6 by the author and a psychologist who evaluated him. His terrorizing internal world, determined largely by his neurobiology, resulted in behaviors that made relating a challenge: he meowed or repeated words to people, then might wander away; he would melt down and throw his burger when it came with mustard instead of catsup; he would jump for hours while making noises and staring at his hand, imagining scenes from *Return of the Jedi* to deflect feeling helpless. Alone in these incomplete and disconnected interactions made disaster feel imminent, as his drawing of the Titanic and the iceberg showed in his first session. During adolescence he had rages and regularly denounced his family, analyst and self as useless. Often Mark appeared unable to use the considerable warmth his devoted parents and analyst offered him.

The analyst was able to hold hope for both Mark and his parents that the kind and loving parts of Mark would prevail despite many excruciating periods when Mark sought to destroy his gains. The analyst presciently understood that when Mark rejected help, as when he tore the water cup before an interruption, angry that Larry had not brought food, that this reflected Mark's only known way to express gratitude, since approaching missing a person or feeling a need felt panicky since said person would not have been under Mark's control (as in a vacationing analyst). Putting words to feelings over many years of work eventually led to Mark being eloquent with words, lyrics, and prose. Mark has put to words the attraction he once had to jumping with omnipotent fantasies to his faltering moves towards having the strength to risk getting closer to people. Mark and his analyst – with rare courage and persistence – kept to that path of Mark having the strength to bear the prospect of unpredictability or loss in taking the risk to love a person not under his control. The report of this analysis shows the many transformations for this young man, the analyst and the parents. Below I highlight his difficulties in being grateful; his fright at relating (and how jumping protected him), and how words and love have amalgamated into an internal anchor that has transformed his previous sense of himself as an abandoned self.

No! I don't thank you. (I love/need you too much).

One of the most illuminating aspects of this analytic journey was this analyst's understanding of Mark's omnipotent defense against gratitude, along with Mark's late adolescent written reflection. Here they both comment on this aspect of the old Mark:

In one session, almost immediately before I left for vacation, Mark asked for a cup to get some water. After drinking the water, he tore the cup into bits shouting, "You only got me water! You didn't get me food!" I said that this was Mark's way of saying "Thank you." I think that you will recognize his difficulty with gratitude – receiving help and not throwing it away – since true gratitude interferes with a sense of omnipotence because it leads to feelings of need and to concerns about loss. Envy, greed, and destructive attacks on someone whom the child just experienced as helpful are most important pathological defenses. Such attacks on good people inside are extremely destructive to the child's internal world and damage the sense of having a loving self as well as loving others inside. I've found that it helps to interpret these ego-weakening protections and defenses. In his book, Mark reflects upon this incident "... what I was doing was a disguised reflection on my distaste towards the world for what ... it had failed to give me [and] helped bring to light a major conflict in my personality...A resentment towards life and a strong envy for those around me who had it so much easier."

As the author clarifies so helpfully, it was a most important interpretation to say 'thank you' in response to Mark's attacks on the analyst's helpful deeds or words, for without that profound interpretation Mark wrought damage to his "sense of having a loving self as well as loving others inside." When, as a young adult, Mark can put words to the abject feeling of resenting "life and a strong envy for those around me who had it so much easier" we hear his retrospective understanding of how experiencing needs, in this case hunger for an analyst about to go away, displaced onto food, was unbearable and made him rip up a cup. This reminds us that one of the many benefits for adolescents or children who have had a long analysis as children is that they often are able to meet with the exigencies of life with far more resiliency, as they have done the day by day acknowledging of what they have suffered and worked through alongside another mind in ways that make subsequent development less onerous. Mark was helped to carry the burden of how inadequate he felt to bear the ructions of real relating through the analyst's respectful understanding of his difficulties taking in the analyst's help.

Jumping away from and towards reality

Mark's jumping "addiction," as the author likens it to, was fascinating for how its use changed over development. It is so incredibly helpful to have Mark as a young adult able to comment upon it since so often children on the autistic spectrum are not able to become so self-aware with such eloquence, which is another reason this paper is unique in the child/adolescent analytic literature. Mark describes how it felt great to be in his own universe wielding light sabers and interacting as if in *The Return of the Jedi*. What could be better in the face of feeling socially and emotionally incapacitated than to be as if on the set of a blockbuster film fighting intergalactic baddies? The jumping and accompanying imaginary world under Mark's aegis eventually wore out the family couch so he took it outside. It seems that it was only through taking it outside that he could eventually see how others might view this odd and distancing behavior, and eventually realize the necessity of stopping it in order to make contact with real humans. However, before he made that crucial decision that enabled him to eventually go to college and make friends, he wrote,

> *For a long time, there was nothing that gave me a better sense of satisfaction than this. Just escaping from the real world and creating and living in my own where I was in complete control, was the best at anything. Literally jumping away reality. I didn't care how weird anyone who saw me thought I was or how much further isolated from the real world it made me.*

The analyst makes the point that Mark jumped until 20 and conveyed how enormously challenging it was for the two of them to help Mark see how unhelpful this symptom was. Ridding himself of jumping represented a watershed moment in Mark's analysis and development, for he emerged into reality alongside young adulthood.

The parent work

Owing to Mark's protective shell, strongly correlated to his neuro-biological divergence, according to this author and the evaluating psychologist, his well-meaning parents felt confused and helpless. A significant part of Mark's ability to resolve his difficulties of being in reality, relinquishing his omnipotent jumping behavior, feeling sturdy enough to risk having loving and vulnerable feelings, related to the analyst's ability to explain Mark to the parents, and hold hope alive for this family despite years of discouraging withdrawal. The author humbly writes "I focused on helping them understand Mark at a deeper level" though this does not adequately show how involved with Mark this analyst was in order to be so helpful to the parents. It was through experiencing how Mark retreated after getting a bit closer, or resorted to omnipotent defenses (from eating Wrinkles after his beautiful birthday party or when Mark as Zorn shot Duke, to his jumping retreats) following cooperative play *over many years* that this analyst could help the parents to understand that Mark's verbal rages or withdrawals actually meant he felt helped, cared about and the beginnings of gratitude.

This powerful intervention with the parents cannot be emphasized enough. It is a well-known truism that parents of children and adolescents with neurodevelopmental differences who take far longer to give back loving, validating feelings cause marriages to break up and vulnerable parents to flounder. That this author made himself available for emergency sessions and held hope for these parents, and indeed for Mark, was central to Mark's transformation. Further, the author's attendance at Mark's concert, band t-shirt in tow, highlights the necessity of having flexibility in child and adolescent analytic work.

Conclusion

The story of Mark's analytic treatment begins at age 6 and has carried on to the present. The dedication of Mark, his parents and this analyst are rare and yet it is also clear from this story of the analysis that Mark and his parents really needed this psychoanalytic treatment of many years' duration. Mark's transformation from being a boy who disintegrated in terrifying ways to being a bigger boy and teenager who escaped from reality via jumping and who then reached towards reality with increased self-awareness to finally risk being intimate with special people represents a tour de force of child and adolescent psychoanalytic work. From Mark's start as a child who felt he could not reach "love on the shelf," immobilized as he was from the internal sense of abandonment and terror that he could neither feel claimed nor claim a connection to his loving parents and warm analyst was portrayed in a way by the author that made the cold desultoriness inside him feel palpable. It is rare to hear of a child on the spectrum developing into such a sensitive, mature and related adult, and to this the analytic work – attended to so fully by analyst, Mark and his parents – was central for holding the hope alive for Mark and his family for years. As he writes of Larry,

> *Larry (how Mark refers to me) has had more access to my mind and feelings than anyone I know and he always seemed to see something in me that I didn't. He always appeared to have complete confidence in me even in my darkest days and I almost sensed that he could foresee a certain bright future ahead of me that I could not.*

Anna Freud writes of how important child analysis is for a child such as Mark with a mixed presentation. On the one hand, he presented as being on the autistic spectrum, if mildly so. On the other, he had kindness and a gleam inside the analyst early on detected. The analysis was able to recruit Mark's inborn poetic and musical lyricism and sensitivity. Anna Freud's words speak for the profound influence this analysis had on Mark:

"It is this mixed psychopathology of childhood for which the comprehensive method of child analysis is needed. Only in child analysis proper is the whole range of therapeutic possibilities kept available for the patient, and all parts of him are given the chance on the one hand to reveal and on the other to cure themselves" (Freud, A., 1965, p. 234).

EDITORIAL REFLECTIONS

This chapter illustrates, with moving clinical examples, issues about ASD (Autism Spectrum Disorder), modern epigenetic developmental issues, the role of a modern developmental theory in the long multi-phase work of this case (ages 6–30 and ongoing), the specific action of puberty and adolescence on the treatment, and the expansion of psychoanalytic theory and technique to include the successful treatment of such degrees of disturbance in all ages. This chapter is an inspiration to others to try an intensive psychoanalytic treatment, one which includes concurrent parent work, to test its efficacy for children, adolescents, and adults with "neuro-atypical symptoms." In 1965 a child at the Hampstead Clinic preschool was diagnosed as being autistic. The medical director (an analyst) said that the child should be institutionalized. Anna Freud suggested instead that this child should be in analysis. That case was equally successful and was followed by success at every stage of life as confirmed in follow up forty years after the end of treatment.

The main change since the 1960s has been the diagnosis of ASD, which has increased exponentially, and the construction and use of ASD tests and checklists. We doubt there has been a concomitant increase in the psychoanalytic treatment of ASD. Many clinicians feel hopeless when faced by such a case and psychoanalysis is usually not considered as the treatment of choice. It seems to us that the results of the treatment described in this chapter could not have been achieved by anything less than a full analysis with concurrent parent work. But this can and should be tested.

Modern developmental theory includes the idea of epigenesis. It is no longer nature vs. nurture but nature and nurture in constant interaction. The patient in treatment is not alone but brings a whole world of real and imagined relationships with him or her. In the brief vignette we see the developmental transformations of the patient, the parents, and the therapist.

In relation to puberty and adolescence, we see the impact of the physical and psychological changes on Mark's functioning. Mark is not only the patient but also the commentator on his own development, as reflected in his book and in the lyrics of his songs. He says at one point that physical puberty took place in his teens but his "mental puberty" took place at 20.[5] This insight relates to what we have emphasized as the central adolescent task of setting aside omnipotent beliefs and defenses and engaging in reality. At 20, Mark stopped the addictive behavior of jumping. Jumping was probably a manifestation of his need to self-regulate and be in control of his relationship with others. It was a closed-system omnipotent defense that became an addiction. His longstanding neuro-atypical symptoms kept others at a distance and could protect him from the danger of love, pleasure, and gratitude. These were dangerous because they depended on others and he couldn't trust others. The combination of years of patient, loving, authentic work by his analyst, the support for the parents to help them maintain their love and hope, and the pubertal push of the growth principle for him to use open-system creative capacities allowed for the emergence of a choice between closed- and open-system modes of self-regulation. He had always

---

5 Following Mark's lead, this is why we included him here in the section on emerging adulthood, rather than earlier in the volume, even though he began his analysis at age 6.

been interested in music but it was only after puberty that Mark, at 16, began writing songs. His songs follow his first tentative engagements with reality; as he becomes more secure he can at 20 give up his addiction to jumping and become someone more committed to loving, creative, open-system modes of self-regulation and relation to others.

CHAPTER 19

JULIAN – age 21

In the last few years I have treated four late adolescents presenting situations very similar to that of Julian. They were all blocked in their studies and activities after the transition from high school to University. They often felt sleepy and actually slept many more hours. Usually they felt in a melancholy mood, along with feeling severe narcissistic vulnerability. With a limited or practically nonexistent social life, they had few or no sexual relationships. They showed intense dependence on videogames and screens in general.

All these young men came from families of middle to high social class, and they were all enmeshed in their relations with their mothers, while their fathers were marginal figures, mainly devalued. With each of these young men I found it definitely difficult to establish a working alliance. As we worked together, there was slow progress (to different extents) with all of them, always with some oscillations.

The improvement took place above all through the work of mobilization and support of the youngster's exploratory resources, due, I believe, to an intensifying empathic and identificatory exchange. It was thus possible to strengthen progressively the recognition and transformation of stifling authoritarian internal identifications, a totalitarian aspect that prevented their access to their own vitality. The overall outcome of the therapies was good in terms of behavioral and symptomatic change. One treatment is ongoing, but the other three of the four treatments (as with Julian) were interrupted by the youngster, precisely when we were getting toward the conclusion.

Here is the story of Julian, as an example of one of these young men:

Julian was 21 years old when we met for the first time. He is a slim young man of average height, good-looking, with long hair reaching down to his shoulders. He dresses informally but neatly and moves slowly, with a slouch. He has a mild gaze, sometimes with an inquisitive look and sometimes evasive. He made me think of a character in a 19th-century romantic novel.

He had consulted me on the advice of his mother, a University professor. His father is a medical doctor, working as a general practitioner. He is an only son, living with his family, and is studying medicine in our city. In high school he was an average student. He was keen to tell me that he was, however, appreciated by his teachers, as he had many cultural interests, above all in movies and in theater.

At the moment, however, he felt blocked, finding it difficult to concentrate on his studies and most things. He had sat for only two of his exams and had not been going to classes for the last few months. He was also supposed to start a rotation in a hospital ward, but he said he had a "phobia of getting infected" and what sounded like hypochondriacal anxiety. He had become progressively isolated from his friends and companions and was spending a lot of time playing video games on the computer or watching films and TV series. He was also sleeping a lot, not only until late in the morning but also in the afternoon.

He told me, winking, that he did not use substances, but that he produced them himself.

"I am hibernating;" I perceived some complacency, some smugness or entitled feeling, in his words. "Perhaps I went the wrong way: I chose my father's and grandfather's work for expedient reasons of convenience. I was not clear-headed. I would have liked to be a film director, but was afraid I didn't have enough talent. In high school I had tried to make videos with a friend of mine, but then gave that up. All my fellow medical students are ahead of me with their exams. I feel like a failure."

During the sessions following this stage of assessment he told me how he felt that part of his anxieties was due to having been present three years earlier at the death of his maternal grandfather from a heart attack. He had received a phone call from his grandmother. Both the ambulance and his father, who was out of the house, arrived too late. Julian had felt helpless and guilty. He had continued to think about the situation, (it was an obsessive thought that came back to him even now), repeatedly wondering about what he could have done. At the end of his narration, he looked at me with a questioning attitude, as if he was waiting for my judgement.

His maternal grandparents live on another floor of the same building in which Julian lives with his family. Now only his grandmother remains and he is closely attached to her. He had always spent a lot of time with her, ever since he was a child, often in a holiday home at the seaside where they spent their summers. Julian said, "She is an educated and intelligent woman, but has never had a job; she took care of her family and her husband, who was a famous surgeon. My mother and her sister, too, adored him as a god. But of all his grandchildren I am the favorite."

Both his paternal grandparents are dead, but, even before they died, Julian did not see much of them. They lived in another city and his father did not have a good relationship with them. "Perhaps it is for this reason that my father seems to me to be a bit weak," Julian told me. "His work does not satisfy him, he has not made much of a career. My mother, on the other hand, is a strong woman, with many important positions. She thinks that she knows and understands everything and that she is always right. Even if this is not quite so." Since his early adolescence Julian has spent hours talking with his mother, mainly discussing the great topics of politics and philosophy. His father generally stays with them for a while, in silence, and then leaves them.

After the assessment I started a psychoanalytic psychotherapy with Julian at two sessions a week. At first Julian had asked to maintain the frequency of one session a week, saying that he didn't want to burden the family's finances. (In my country, for both economic and cultural reasons, the majority of psychotherapies with adolescents and young adults are done at this frequency of sessions).

When I suggested to Julian that he could lie on the couch, he asked firmly to continue "face to face." I thought at the time that the passive aspect of lying on the couch frightened him (probably inducing feelings of persecutory experiences and homosexual anxieties). I decided then to postpone further discussion about this issue until we could come to a deeper understanding of the meaning of his refusal.

He started to talk to me about his unease at being together with others. He felt judged by his new acquaintances at University but also by his old friends. He felt excluded and excluded himself by remaining in silence and at the edge of the group, with a growing feeling of extraneousness and discontent. He saw others as more cheerful, relaxed and casual than himself. With girls, too, he felt shy and less easy-going than everybody else. Throughout his high school years he had felt a "crush" on a female schoolmate. She was "the most beautiful" but Julian had never admitted anything to her. He acted as a confidant, listening to her and fretting when she talked to him about her flirts.

"So I reached my great age without ever having kissed a girl. Isn't that weird?" His irony and sarcasm about his feelings and behavior were a habitual manner for him.

The main theme of this first period of the treatment consisted of the severe hindrance in every initiative and in particular in his assertive activities. This hindrance suffused him with feelings of inadequacy and blame. The relationship between us, too, was weighed down and devitalized.

He often found it difficult to start talking; his discourse was repetitive and monotonous, full of regret due to lost opportunities .

I felt bored and prevented from reaching out to him: our sessions passed in a muffled and melancholic atmosphere that led back to Julian's experiences in his hours on his own. Some greater liveliness came from his tales of the movies he had seen and of his dreams. The movies were mainly horror movies with stories about evil beings, vampires and zombies. I told him how he seemed to put into the fight between the live and dead of these stories his conflict between the aspects of himself that were "alive" and those that he felt were paralyzing him and threatening him with "death."

We worked a lot on this subject; Julian recognised that the fact that he frequently felt himself sleeping or blocked was equivalent to obeying some sort of "internal propaganda" that he created on his own and which took his strength away.

The dead also appeared in his dreams. "I have never told anyone about them, they are so frightening!" In one dream Julian found himself in a house that reminded him of his maternal grandparents' seaside house, even if it was much larger; he was going around in the rooms, empty and as vast "as those of a palace, with marble columns: there was an old man lying on a marble bed in the middle of a hall. I was afraid that he might wake up from his apparent death and kill me. I would try to run away, but the doors and windows were shut."

I told him that talking to me about the dream was because he was starting to trust that there was an open window, in the therapy and in his relationship with me. In the transference, I was taking on a protective function. The majestic and vindictive man (who, in his associations, reminded him of the image of his maternal grandfather) was less looming and threatening. During some sessions a freer and more colloquial tone developed in our relationship, and the difficulty of finding topics decreased. During other sessions the attitude of keeping a distance, of absent-minded listening, returned.

501

I also felt that a provocative and challenging attitude was becoming more present. In that period I returned to the issue of a possible change in the setting, moving to lie down on the couch. He again refused firmly, saying that he would have been "too bewildered." He seemed very worried about leaving the setup in our relationship where he was developing growing confidence and trust. This was an area of security; he made me feel the deep importance for him to count on me as a real person and as an object of identification. Julian saw the shift to the couch as a potential regression.

After the time we discussed this issue, he started to often arrive late for his sessions (or even not to come at all), making excuses for himself with a pretended contrite air, saying that he had been sleeping and had not woken up. I interpreted his ambivalence about whoever, outside and within him, wanted to modify his control of the distance with the other and with his own feelings. He also made me think of the difficulties and failures in his connection with an unempathic mother. Was his stiff manner and inhibition a way of not "waking" the Oedipal conflict? Julian used to identify himself with his father, who stayed on the sidelines in life, excluded and perhaps humiliated by his powerful father-in-law and by his wife.

In the following months Julian started to talk to me about his sexual fantasies (before then he had been ashamed to confide them). They were fantasies of sadistic intercourse, in which the voyeuristic mode and anal sexuality prevailed. He spent a lot of time on pornographic sites. This was a way of guaranteeing his autarchy and cancelling the thrust (not waking up) to try sex with a girl "in flesh and blood." He denied genital primacy, privileging the sadomasochistic position and anal sexuality.

He admitted the desire for magical and omnipotent appropriation: "With Pornhub I have millions of women at my disposal, of all ages, of all races," he would say to me ironically. But he recognized that he was afraid of finding himself impotent, "when it came to the point" with a real woman.

I pointed out to him the similarity of this "propaganda" that blocked him in the exploration of a relationship with a real woman with what occurred in other aspects of his assertiveness, as if he were pre-emptively castrating himself, foreseeing his failure. It was Julian who associated this situation with the long "masturbatory" discussions with his mother, in which they got excited together talking about "great topics," leaving him exhausted and inconclusive.

In the meantime Julian had gone back to attending University, studying and sitting some exams, with good results. He had also started regularly attending a hospital ward; his phobias and his hypochondriacal anxieties had become weaker. "I find interest in taking care for other people, in listening to them." I said to him that now that he found it possible to take care of others, he could worry less about himself.

His identification with me came to the forefront: he asked me for a suggestion about a book on eating disorders because there was an anorexic girl hospitalized in the department he was attending and he was interested in understanding what was happening to her. On another occasion he told me: "I would not mind doing your job. Do you know that joke: a psychoanalyst is a Jewish doctor who is afraid of blood . . . ."

He resumed contacts with peers, for instance, with Richard, an old friend who in the past had made him very envious because "he knew how to get on with girls." With Richard he was planning to make some short films to put on You Tube. He felt motivated, and indeed some of the plots he told me about were amusing and creative. But when he had tried to go out with Richard's group of friends, he started feeling awkward and excluded again. His anger increased because Richard did not devote himself enough to their project (and to him).

"But I never get directly angry, I keep everything inside and ruminate on it." He did not attack others, so that the one who was "screwed" was him (and possibly the other felt guilty). He felt that his analyst, too, did not value his projects and his capacities sufficiently. We thought about the difficulty he had to find a different balance between activity and passivity: the condition of passivity, which he actually sought out, roused homosexual anxieties.

One day he had a violent exchange with Richard. In their fight he had broken one of Richard's fingers: this was something that had never happened to him before, and made him feel guilty but also excited. Richard and Julian stopped seeing each other. But then Julian went back to working on the short films. He found as partner a young man a bit older than him, who knew the technical aspects better than he did. He let himself be helped without entering into competition.

He had become more confident and no longer felt sluggish and melancholic. But with girls he was still "at the window." One evening he had managed to kiss a girl with whom he went to University, but things had not got any further than that. A few months later he had gone with a prostitute, but had not achieved an erection. At first he told me that he had "not minded much," but later he had been afraid, for some time, that he might have caught a disease. He repeatedly wanted to carry out HIV tests.

We thought about the return of the "propaganda" when he took the freedom of risking "touching and being touched." We talked about his wish to have the other (and the analyst) as a prostitute always at his disposal (so as not to feel need in the absence of the object of his need). And we articulated his fear of being "touched" by another person (and by the analyst), arousing emotions he found difficult to manage.

Before the summer holidays, at the end of his second year of treatment, he once again skipped a few sessions, informing me at the last moment, or even not informing me at all, putting me in a position of dependence and making me feel his abandonment. Upon return from the holidays he told me, with noticeable satisfaction and paying attention to my reaction, that during the summer he had met a girl slightly older than him, Barbara, and that they had got together. After some dates, they had sex, for the first times masturbating each other and later reaching complete sexual intercourse. "As a girl she is not particularly good-looking, a little plump, however I got over my doubts about other people's opinions. She tells me that she is very much in love and she accepts my perversions."

This relationship with Barbara became the main topic of the following months: at some sessions he made me take on a voyeuristic position on their sexual games (directed by him). On other occasions he said that he felt guilty because he was "taking advantage" of her deep attachment. One day he telephoned me asking me with urgency to bring our session forward. He was very upset when he arrived; he had just been informed by his father that his grandmother had been given a diagnosis of an advanced stage of leukaemia.

"I am so afraid she will die, she is the person I love most. The person who has been better with me than anyone else." He cried for a long time, in silence. I told him that I understood how deep his pain was and how he could now trust himself to let it come out. At the end of the session, without thinking about it, I reached out to shake his hand, which I do not usually do. Julian gave me an intense look, surprised, with gratitude.

During the next session he told me about a dream: "I could not find the road I was looking for. I was very shaken. Then a man, perhaps a taxi-driver, gave me a road map drawn on the plastic used to make coloured balloons, those that fly in the air, soft and as thin as a handkerchief. I liked that floppy cloth, with the map on it. But it was strange: strange to combine the professional map and the plastic of children's balloons."

I said that perhaps it was the feeling received with the handshake that seemed "strange" to him. But now, in our work, he felt he could be helped to find the road and together to see his childhood needs met (as if to recover a transitional object). Julian was discovering tender, spontaneous and restorative aspects inside himself. He showed me this when he told me about meetings with the patients on the hospital ward, especially elderly ones.

Barbara had a chronic disease and Julian would take care of her; they spent a lot of time together. In these months, he sat for many exams and had started to talk to me about concluding his University studies. These thoughts certainly also concerned the end of his therapy and we started to talk about this. He oscillated between recognising that he wanted to do things on his own and his fear "that he still had a lot to learn."

A few months later he said to me that he felt Barbara to be "too sticky," that he needed to feel freer. He wanted to get rid of his needy and dependent aspects. In a dream from that period he found himself "in a long corridor, like the one there is in my father's office. It was dark and I hit against a large aquarium containing two big lizards. I was afraid that the glass wall would break and that the lizards would get out and attack me." This was the primal scene, the one which Julian would hit up against in the dark.

In the transference his castration anxiety showed up in his fantasy that I would dissuade him from his project to become a psychotherapist and would consider him "someone who was not worth much." His doubt as to whether or not to leave Barbara had become obsessive, and even during our sessions this subject had taken over from all others. The fluidity and the pleasure of our analytic work appeared to have got jammed. His fear of moving forward temporarily overtook his progress.

I told him that we could consider to move toward thinking about termination of the treatment. We agreed to the fact that many changes had already occurred and that, in any case, we would reach a decision after the summer break. But at the return, in September, Julian did not turn up for the appointment that had been agreed to. I called him a few days later: Julian apologized that he had not warned me and told me that he was thinking of ending his therapy.

We reached an agreement for a meeting, but I had understood that he wanted to keep for himself the power of being the one to quit. He told me that during the holidays he had ended his relationship with Barbara. He said that he was very sorry for her being the one who felt abandoned. He was afraid about remaining on his own, but wanted to try new experiences.

We thought about the possible meaning of his "forging ahead" to this ending and about his stated fear of receiving criticism and obstacles from me (feeling abandoned). He was, however, confident that he would be able to find the door open if he felt the need, and I confirmed this to him.

I had also considered talking to him about the possibility of undergoing psychoanalysis in the future, in particular if his intention to become a psychotherapist became consolidated. But these were thoughts that I kept for myself.

I had the impression that Julian would have felt my intervention as a push in that direction in accordance to my expectations, and perhaps simultaneously as an attempt to keep him hooked, as a refusal of his separation.

At the end of the session he thanked me affectionately, and, after a sideways glance at the couch, he left.

COMMENTARY 1

We hear that the analyst has noticed similarities in four of the young adults whom the analyst has treated. They all, including Julian, demonstrate problems in their adolescent development, for example, inhibition in work and in the establishment of a sexual identity and good social relationships. All four manifest depression and specifically sleep difficulties. Their turning (which presumably exceeds normal usage levels) to video game and screen activity may be understood as an attempt to cope with their anxiety and low mood, as well as seeking of excitement rather like Julian's intense discussions with mother.

Interestingly all four young men share a family constellation of being enmeshed in their relationships with their mothers while they experienced their fathers as weak devalued marginal figures. In my work I have found that such a triangle is common in adolescents with perverse and narcissistic features.

The analyst raises the question of whether Julian's improvement was due to an intensifying empathic and identificatory exchange. The analyst argues that *it was possible to strengthen progressively the recognition and transformation of stifling authoritarian internal identifications, a totalitarian aspect that prevented their access to their own vitality.*

I will address this interesting question later in my commentary.

Julian

We hear that Julian is 21 when he first meets the analyst. He undergoes an assessment and then works twice weekly off the couch for three years. We do not know how many assessment sessions there were nor the details of how the fees were organised and arranged.

His initial body language conveys slow movement and a slouch perhaps reflecting not only his state of body but also his state of mind. His gaze moves between curiosity and evasiveness thereby foregrounding the difficulty he has in engaging with the analytic object.

Julian consults the analyst on the advice of his mother who is a powerful figure in his mind. We learn post-assessment that, "She thinks that she knows and understands everything and that she is always right, even if this is not quite so." Julian is an only son and is a medical student in identification with his father and grandfather who are both doctors.

It is interesting to know the living arrangement of Julian namely that he lives with his family in the same building as his maternal grandparents who live on another floor. As I imagined the psycho-geography of this, a line from a Paul Simon song came to my mind: "One man's ceiling is another man's floor." This perhaps reflects the dividing line between the two generations and the shared partition which has different functions for the different generations.

My association reveals my question about the quality of the space between the two generations in Julian's and his parents' minds. He is a member of an extended family with close physical and psychological contact with the older generation. I wondered about the cultural aspects of this, as well as perhaps a scenario where the separation-individuation between mother and her family has not been fully achieved, that is, in the eyes of someone from another culture. Julian, an only child, we are told, enjoys a particularly close relationship with his maternal grandmother who devoted herself to looking after her family and her husband, who was a famous surgeon. Maternal grandfather is reported to have been treated by Julian's mother and aunt as a God. Julian believes that he is "the favorite of all" this man's grandchildren. So it seems he experiences himself as special to an adored (particularly by female figures) and idealized grandfather. Interestingly, by contrast, there has been little or no contact between Julian's family and his paternal grandparents as they are reported to be dead, and the relationship between father and his family described as estranged.

Julian is an only child and therefore has not experienced sharing in his immediate family circle. He has not it seems had the opportunity to learn to love and hate, and appreciate sibling rivals. We do not learn whether there were other pregnancies, even miscarriages, and the reasons why he is an only child.

To return to the described assessment Julian tells the analyst that he was an average high school student. So, we know from the beginning that achievement is an important pre-occupation. Julian's need to impress the analyst is revealed in his eagerness to tell that he was appreciated by his teachers as he had many cultural interests particularly in the movies and the theatre. This is interesting because we see, as the material unfolds, the connection between his internal dramas, his dreams, his choice of films and his conflictual object relationships.

It is striking that Julian tells the analyst, while "winking," that he didn't use substances but produced them himself. This was unclear to me; I didn't know what he meant. However it is noteworthy that he *winks* at the analyst implying some flirtatiousness and perhaps a complicit secret. He refers to his hibernating which in my terms reveals a need to withdraw from excitation, aggression and his objects. Here we see the theme of the problem of inner vitality, something Ogden (1995) has written about. Julian reveals his aspiration to be a film director as well as his fear that he didn't have enough talent. There is some evidence that Julian is "wrecked by success" in that he needs to spoil his own creativity, thereby keeping himself as an equal with his father whom he experiences as a failure. It seems Julian fears to compete with his maternal grandfather who is successful at least in his work. So Oedipal themes are in the air.

Julian talks about being blocked, struggling to concentrate on his studies among many other things. He also describes his inability to sit his exams and reveals his lack of attendance at classes for several months. Julian refers to his "phobia of getting infected." He reports becoming progressively isolated from his friends and companions, and turning increasingly toward computer games or watching films or TV series. He therefore has regressed into a fantasy world. Julian also reports another withdrawal, namely sleeping a lot, not only until late in the morning, but also in the afternoon. Presumably he is awake at night, having reversed the day/night cycle.

Therefore in summary, the assessment reveals how this young man's development has been held up in the adolescent phase. He is a young adult caught up in adolescent issues, his identity lacks solidity; he is enmeshed with parental figures. Later we learn that he has not yet experienced his first kiss!!

Psychotherapy

Julian prefers once weekly but it is agreed twice weekly. The analyst does not tell us how this frequency was negotiated nor if his wish to deny himself getting sufficient resource was interpreted, for example, in relation to his depressive anxieties about asking or having too much for himself. The reasons for not using the couch are discussed as they evolved.

Julian reveals a precipitating event that seems to have triggered his (partial) adolescent developmental breakdown. Three years earlier when he was 18, he was present at the death of his maternal grandfather from a heart attack. Julian had received a phone call from his grandmother but the "too late" arrival of both the ambulance and his father who was out of the house left Julian feeling traumatized, "helpless and guilty." He could not process this traumatic experience and developed obsessive thoughts, perhaps punishing himself for his lack of action. Interestingly he sought with his questioning look that the analyst pardon him for this. This may also be understood as reflecting his guilt over his not doing more to save his grandfather, and may be associated with the underlying Oedipal wish that he die thereby allowing Julian to succeed as the special adored male. Unconsciously Julian may believe that such thoughts magically killed his grandfather. This links, I argue, to his inhibitions in his studies.

I wonder what this event/memory represented and meant for Julian. Were his murderous Oedipal wishes towards his grandfather realised or actualised (Sandler, 1976), leaving him with his beloved grandmother? On the other hand he would no longer occupy the very special place of being the favourite grandson to this revered man? Interestingly the father arrives too late – perhaps again experienced by Julian as absent when needed and ineffectual as the ambulance arrives too late? Julian faces the reality of time and of death of a loved relative – even he, a famous surgeon, is not immune from heart failure .

With impressively sensitive and empathic analytic technique, we see how Julian very gradually comes to trust the analyst. Throughout I was struck by the analyst's awareness of the delicate narcissistic issues and the balance required between listening and healthy versus over-interest thereby not repeating the overinvolved mother-son relationship. I formed the impression of a disturbed mother who at times was absent to her son and at other moments "in his face," so to speak, indulging together in exciting yet inconclusive conversations about hot topics. Julian seems to have internalized such oscillations which we see in the analytic relationship and in his other relationships. He struggles to titrate the distance between himself and his objects. The concept of the invasive object (Williams, 2004) is pertinent here as is Glasser's (1979) concept of the core complex.

Julian struggles to think reflectively; at times he acts or does not act, that is, is paralyzed or frozen in a marginalised position, witnessing a scene, for example, a primal scene, which he longs to be included in. The cause of his inhibitions seems to lie in his fear of the power of his instincts (Anna Freud, 1965). And there is evidence of how his instincts break through into violent action, i.e. the breaking of Richard's finger during a fight. There seems to be little evidence of an internal protective figure which can contain or provide symbolic representation of such bodily action. It is interesting that he chooses a girlfriend who has a chronic disease and their relationship seems to be one that includes looking after one another. By caring for her Julian vicariously cares for himself. We do hear something about a primitive sexual atmosphere in the consulting room; is it safer to keep sexuality outside? I wonder about a lateral transference (Nicolo, 2016) to Barbara, the first lover?

Blood is a theme – the grandmother is diagnosed with leukaemia. The joke, "A psychoanalyst is a Jewish doctor who is afraid of blood," conveys Julian's growing identification with the analyst and perhaps the analytic process, and has other meanings. Is blood linked to castration fears? Another meaning of blood is life itself, something which Julian struggles to grasp in his own hands.

The expression "grasping the nettle" comes to mind, implying the capacity to be assertively decisive no matter the relative unpleasure and discomfort. This is a quality needed by a competent doctor and we recall that his father is a general practitioner and his late grandfather was a surgeon. Blood is also linked to hurt and pain, and we hear how Julian is more in touch with the pain of imminent loss when he finds out about the serious illness of his grandmother, the most important person in his life. Something he can do little about. He feels and is helpless. His omnipotence is challenged and he faces one of the facts of life (Money-Kyrle, 1968). There are limits; nothing and more particularly, no relationship, is infinite (see Lombardi, 2016).

The authoritarian propaganda to my mind seems to be an internalization and identification of and with the mother's rigidly held beliefs and omniscience. Julian has constructed his own propaganda which does not serve him well. This internal organisation kicks in at the brink of success: he becomes anxious, perhaps at the thought of becoming more powerful than some of his male objects, and has to undermine himself with self-doubt and disbelief in his talents and ability to make things happen. That is, in psychoanalytic terms, to bring both parents together in a creative intercourse.

The handshake is so interesting. It occurs after a powerful session when the maternal transference has deepened. The analyst and the analysand touch. We do not know if the analyst is male or female in psychical or material reality. I understood the offering of the handshake as a sign of the analyst's concern and empathy. Words, it seems, are insufficient at this juncture. Is the handshake a physical connection at the moment of separation after a session of much affect? Why were words not enough? Was the analyst too identified with Julian? Such an action was talked about in the subsequent sessions aided by the bringing of the dream. I wondered about the balloons – the skin – might one hypothesise something about balloons – breasts that float away out of reach? This seems linked perhaps to the experience of the tantalizingly absent mother, seen but beyond reach.

Julian allows himself to travel through adolescence and free himself to experience the world beyond his first ever girlfriend. I particularly admired the analyst's holding back on referring to future psychoanalysis as this reflected to me a deep understanding of not becoming the narcissistic parent seeking to satisfy her/his own needs. Julian announces his ending. I wondered whether he had to wrench himself away from the analyst to whom he clearly felt deeply attached; was there a grandmother, the person who mattered most to him, transference? I think it is a turning point when, confronted by the potential loss of his grandmother who has been diagnosed with advanced leukemia, that he requests his session to be moved forward, and then can acknowledge his love and sense of loss – he cries silently for a long time – with the help of the analytic process and facilitated by the receptive empathic therapist. To my mind, the calm, containing, listening and making-meaning analyst has provided more than one "window" of possibilities and it seems has served and been used by young adult Julian as a developmental object (Hurry, 1998). Julian has found new ways of relating to himself and the Other, the pleasures of sexuality and tenderness, as well as discovering new ways of thinking, moving away from repetitive screen activity and grandiose certitude to curiosity, more creative pursuits of his own, and the tolerance of uncertainty. Interestingly, when he leaves the consulting room for the last time, Julian looks sideways at the couch – acknowledging perhaps what he missed and what he might try some day? The future beckons.

COMMENTARY 2

There are several aspects of this clinical vignette that I find valuable. The analyst immediately establishes a developmental orientation, identifies his conceptual assumptions regarding what is mutative in the work, and provides a compelling description of the arc of his experience in the room with Julian over time.

In the university town in which I practice, young people of Julian's age frequently seek treatment with conflicts that are recognizable to me in this account. Within this group, the manifest narratives are comparable: They have devoted considerable efforts in high school with the aim of excelling academically and building a *resume* in order to get into and then to excel at college. At the point of seeking treatment, they recognize that they are moving towards the end of college and find themselves in a state of *not knowing*, with no idea about what they want to do and limited awareness of their inner worlds to make use of in order to imagine themselves into the future. This unknown terrain is unsurprising given the perpetual focus of their families on goals to be achieved during adolescence. School work may be flagging, knowledge about themselves sexually and in relationships, impoverished. They feel isolated and certain that their peers are living more successful lives, a view seemingly confirmed in the universe of social media. Some additionally contend with parents' idealized memories of college as the "best years of their lives." Often relying heavily on their parents and in very close contact, such parental musings infuse a sense of even deeper failure and dread.[6]

These patients (like Julian) don't tend to enter more frequent treatment and often terminate sooner. Nevertheless, many seem to make extremely good use of the treatment, even those initially appearing quite lost. I have puzzled over this, and fretted. Is their apparent improvement wishful thinking on their part and/or mine? Will they soon come bumping back into themselves or fall apart? Did I defensively fail to engage these patients at a deeper level? For me, concerns are exacerbated by an awareness that I find myself adopting a lighter touch with these young people. I work closely within their chosen metaphors and provide more generous use of myself

---

6 I have thought to myself that these young people sound like they are plummeting into a midlife crisis rather than embarking on their lives. In a perverse twist, 21 becomes the new 40, while older adults insist that they have the *joie de vivre* of someone twenty years younger.

as a developmental object. All of these questions and doubts, while useful to reflect upon, give voice to stirrings of my psychoanalytic superego.[7] The plain truth is that I *enjoy* working with these young people. Am I having too good a time?

A growing literature relating to emerging adulthood may offer a way to conceptualize the presentation and accelerated course of treatment with these young patients. Consisting of young people roughly between twenty-two and twenty-nine years of age, a salient characteristic of this group is the continued exploration of identity issues traditionally expected to be more settled, according to most of our extant developmental theory. They are not at all ready to settle, still actively exploring aspects in life arenas such as career choice, financial independence, place of residence and deepened relationships.[8] This, in turn, has implications for notions of the expectable tasks and achievements of late adolescence as representing only an entry phase in identity explorations.

I think that this model better matches what I observe clinically. The 21-year-old Julian who entered therapy – isolated, inhibited sexually, enmeshed with his mother and distant from his father, symptomatic and suffering, might be seen as an individual experiencing a developmental snag rather than a more pervasive and pathological shutdown. I do not think that Julian's analyst is promoting a pathologized view. Rather, I am suggesting here that our developmental model may create a pull to view these young people as more pathological than they actually are.

Relatedly, the perception of parents of young people Julian's age as "enmeshed" may be overstated. While some undoubtedly are enmeshed,

---

7 Not the loving one described by Schafer (1960)!

8 For a fuller discussion supporting the designation of "Emerging Adulthood" as a psychoanalytically relevant developmental phase, see Gilmore, 2019. She specifically argues in favor of an expansion of our conceptualization of developmental stages to incorporate cultural factors including societal-level change.

many are ready to allow their relationship with their child to move forward. They, like their child, see a significant gap between traditional pictures of what a post-college young person should look like and the view they have of their child. They are scared and know that their child needs help and that they cannot provide this help given the natural pull toward regression (in the child and the relationship) in times of stress. In addition to supporting the young person's self-exploration, the therapist can help to unfreeze the parent-child relationship and help it to grow into one more suitable for the young person's age.

The warmth of the analyst's feelings for Julian are apparent in this vignette. I think there is a particular pleasure in work with young people this age as they become unfettered and expand their capacity to imagine possibilities. This contains elements of the imaginative play of work with young children. In child work, there is an interesting point when the analyst must accept that the child has shifted the play, even when she loves that play that the two have engaged in. I think that the analyst accepts with grace a similar shift when he resists the temptation to suggest a future analysis to Julian in their last session.

In closing, I suggest that we reconsider our developmental theory and allow *it* to move forward. As clinicians we work to meet the patient where s/he lives, taking into account a variety of factors. The description of Julian's treatment suggests that this is what occurred. Expectations based upon outdated normative models can burden treatments or distort our diagnostic picture and treatment recommendations. One suggested update would be to more thoroughly integrate changing cultural factors in our theory (e.g., views of adolescence and adulthood, race, gender, class) to better help clinicians to conceptualize and assess their work.

EDITORIAL REFLECTIONS

This chapter offers an important consideration of how we think about developmental phases and how we formulate normality and pathology. Given the history of the psychoanalytic and general cultural tendency to normalize adolescent pathology, we also consider here how to assess the seriousness of interruptions of progressive development, how blocking of the growth principle is implicated in pathology. We also have to factor in the data of good clinical outcome despite the sense of incomplete work.

A plausible traditional formulation of this case (and the other young men the analyst describes) would include the idea of deferred action (nachtraglichkeit): earlier oedipal wishes and fantasies became overwhelming to Julian in adolescence when they could be actualized, and indeed were validated by his mother's excited involvement in intense discussions with him that excluded his father. Feelings of inadequacy to achieve the status of the idealized grandfather and disappointment in his own father's efficacy may also have led to conflict for Julian around his achievements and capacities. His response was extreme passivity; his withdrawal of vitality from interactions was initially reflected in his empty and boring sessions. Defensive regression to an anal universe appeared in his fantasies and choices of porn sites.

In thinking about these patients and others in this age group, we can consider the status and functioning of the three motivating principles of mental life. We can think about normality and pathology in terms of assessing the operation of the pleasure, reality, and growth principles, and harmony among them. Is the young person on the path of progressive development, that is, is growth proceeding in a way that leads to positive transformations in life, relationships, expectations, work, and sexuality? Adolescents are faced with figuring out realistic sources of pleasure, how they want to be sexual and with whom. In this era the pervasiveness and universal accessibility of pornography, all of which contains sadomasochistic elements, can contribute to a young person being thrown back on evoked childhood sexual theories and fantasies, many of which confuse sexuality and aggression. Many young adolescent boys grapple with conscious incestuous sexual fantasies, which contributes to defensive symptom formation. To what extent has a young adult moved beyond incestuous infantile sexual relationships? Is there pleasure in mastery of reality challenges instead of omnipotent fantasy gratification through control of others?

This chapter also offers a consideration of the impact of standard practices in any particular locale on the framework of treatment, where the choices about frequency of sessions are overdetermined by the patient's defenses and the prevailing professional customs. Would a different technical approach, for example, establishing a preliminary or exploratory or trial phase of work before fixing on the framework of the treatment plan, make a difference?

CONCLUSIONS AND FUTURE DIRECTIONS

In the introductory chapter, we said that our focus in this volume is the psychoanalytic treatment of adolescents and emerging adults. We set out to understand more about how clinicians are actually working with young people in this age group and stage of development, how they are thinking about that work, what feels effective, where the pitfalls occur. The impetus for undertaking this study came from our sense of increasing needs for mental health attention to adolescent populations, while, at the same time, existing psychoanalytic models of normal and pathological adolescence seem at odds with what we were seeing and hearing in the world and in our practices. We asked five questions:

1. Are people treating adolescents psychoanalytically?
2. Is psychoanalysis an effective treatment for adolescent disturbances?
3. How do the contributors to this volume think about adolescence as a phase of development?
4. What are the techniques being used in adolescent treatments?
5. Does the material in this volume point us to useful revisions of the psychoanalytic model of adolescent development and our understandings about adolescent treatment?

We hoped to use the material collected in this volume to challenge, refine, and further elaborate an evolving model of adolescent development and treatment. In this concluding chapter, we will try to collate and summarize points arising from the editorial reflections of each of the clinical chapters. We will think about particular elements of what emerges from these accounts of real adolescent work (as opposed to theorizing or generalizing from other sources) to better understand normal and pathological adolescent development and functioning, and see how the work described in this book refines, elaborates, refutes, redirects, or challenges earlier assumptions and findings.

What have we learned?

The material in this volume demonstrates that the general pessimism and negativity about adolescents and adolescent treatment is ill-founded.

As we invited colleagues around the world to share samples of their clinical work, and asked others to comment on those vignettes, we encountered enthusiasm, devotion, and some relief that adolescent treatment can be considered seriously among psychoanalysts. Contributors came from all regions of the world, with varied training backgrounds and theoretical orientations, and spanned all levels of experience. Despite these differences, we found three commonalities that feel significant:

Everyone in this large group of psychoanalysts (58 in all) likes teenagers! Appreciation and affection come through in every clinical account and commentary, despite moments or patches of exasperation, doubt, anxiety, and confusion. This may be partly related to the vocational self-selection of training in child and adolescent analysis, but we have written about the profound and specific importance of open-system, objective love in the therapeutic alliance as a mutative factor in a shift from sadomasochistic, closed-system patterns of relating to mutually-enhancing and growth-promoting relationships grounded in realistic perception of each person (Novick, J. and Novick, K.K. 2000b, Winnicott 1949, Loewald 1957). We suggest that the capacity and courage to love the patient in this way may have contributed substantively to the unexpectedly high proportion of good outcomes in this sample.

A second common factor relates to the conviction, commitment, confidence, and competence of the analysts involved. Given the era of this book, almost all the contributors were formed professionally in the context of a psychoanalytic culture of negativity about adolescence and adolescent analysis, as we described in the introduction. The prevailing definition of analysis in most training centers also takes adult psychoanalysis as the norm, often with narrow definitions of suitability and technical approach. In contrast, the contributors in this volume display conviction that analysis can be the treatment of choice even for seriously disturbed young people; they maintain commitment to the process in the face of resistance or discouragement; they have confidence in the relevance of the approach; and they are competent in a wide range of interventions. To do all this, they need what we have called "emotional muscles for therapists," the ego strengths that provide sturdy internal resources and protect against burnout (Novick, J. and Novick, K.K. 2012). These are maintained in the face of a larger professional and social culture rife with teenism.

From the resource of those emotional muscles comes the third factor we noted in common – flexibility. These contributors adapt to the needs of the adolescents they are working with, rather than being constricted by biases of the culture or mainstream psychoanalysis. Thus we see a wide range of techniques that goes beyond an oversimplified or over-generalized transference/countertransference paradigm.

Looking demographically at the clinical vignettes, we gathered a broad and varied sample of young people, with eleven boys and eight girls, whose ages at the beginning of treatment ranged from 6 to 21 years old.[9] Five of them began treatment before or just at puberty, and several ended in their twenties. Thus we had examples of young people going through the transitions into and/or out of adolescence. Therapies lasted at least 2 years to ongoing after a long time, with most others spanning 3 to 5 years. Seven cases are ongoing, but, of the remaining twelve, ten went to a mutually-agreed termination. This is a startling finding, given the usually-reported high rates of premature and unilateral terminations in adolescent treatments. Only one or two of the young people in this sample ended their treatments in an abrupt way. All but one were at session frequencies of 3-5 times per week. Six of the nineteen patients came from families of divorce, one had lost both parents to death, and the rest lived with two parents. Regular parent work was done at various intervals in eleven of the cases, a surprising proportion in an arena where there remains controversy; four had no parent work beyond initial evaluation meetings; in the remaining four cases, parent work was either intermittent or done by someone other than the adolescent's therapist.

The patients in this sample were all seriously troubled, with forward development stalled in sometimes profound ways, and symptoms ranged from severe self-destructive or injurious behaviors, including suicidal danger, to shutdown or inhibition of activity and achievement. Relationships within and beyond the family were disrupted or avoided and all these young people evoked grave concern in those around them, including their therapists. In those treatments where the termination was described, most had positive outcomes, with no one lost to suicide or hospitalization.

---

9 The Parent Work Casebook (Novick et al 2020) included vignettes of nine cases in treatment during adolescence. Course of treatment, termination, and outcomes were generally similar to those described in the sample in this volume. Despite the different focus of the Parent Work Casebook, there is enough material included there to consider pooling the two samples of cases to increase the numbers described here to 28 cases.

In response to our initial two questions, we can conclude that adolescents are indeed being treated psychoanalytically, and those treatments are effective, with positive outcomes leading to restoration to the path of progressive development.

Moving to our third question, we are trying to discern how these contributors are thinking about adolescence as a phase of development. What emerged from this collection of perspectives that speaks to generating a coherent set of assumptions that reflects the reality of the young people and their passage through this crucial time in their lives? We were struck by the fact that all of the vignettes describe a process that underscores the centrality of adolescence as a point of successful intervention and a phase that integrates and consolidates prior positive or negative solutions and sets the stage for adult health or pathology. The epigenetic interaction of nature and nurture is vivid in these adolescents, when the physiological push of growth coincides with changes in social norms and expectations and internal expansion of psychological capacities.

One specific aspect of this phase, as described in this material, which differentiates adolescence from either childhood or adulthood, is the very much broader range of influences that can affect young people for good or ill; with this in mind, we conclude that adults can and should remain important in teenagers' lives, for support, containment, companionship and inspiration. Adolescents can use displacement to peer relationships sometimes defensively, in flight from feelings concentrated on the analyst or other adults, but also as a bridge to a safe space in which to work on, work out, and work through emotions and wishes that were heretofore too hard to manage and regulate. They thereby move from a sadomasochistic mode of relating to more realistic engagement with themselves and others. The conventional wisdom that adolescents *should* be expected to shift all their attention and intensity of involvement to friends, an idea unfortunately derived from the exclusive psychoanalytic focus on separation as the goal of adolescence, is contradicted in the material in this volume.

Similarly, we see in these chapters a growing emphasis on the importance of differentiating separation from separateness in adolescence, when loneliness becomes a major emotional and developmental challenge. The peak times for the experience of loneliness seem to be adolescence and old age. This makes sense, when we acknowledge that those are the two phases that bring the greatest demand for adaptation to change and loss. For adolescents, there can be terrible fear of the loss of an earlier self experienced as omnipotent, that served them well enough in childhood when reality was not very demanding. A major characteristic of adolescence is the increasing impingement of reality from inside and outside. If adolescents cannot find a new resolution of the relationship of the pleasure and the reality principles, they can feel helpless, with no alternatives. We see this dynamic described in many of the chapters, where we discern growth stalled and the young person clinging to omnipotent defenses. The interaction and integration of the pleasure, reality and growth principles coalesce in adolescence; these cases demonstrate that identifications with the worst aspects of parents stops or slows growth, while identification with positive aspects of parents and the analyst promotes growth.

This brings us to summarize the findings about pathogenesis and protective factors in this sample. It appears to us that there are two pathways described. In this volume and in our experience we have seen adolescents who carry childhood traumas and struggle throughout development and then the inner and external demands of adolescence lead to adolescent breakdown. Then there are cases that follow more along the lines described by Freud, where the actuality of adolescent sexual or hostile wishes brings childhood memories, by deferred action (nachtraglichkeit), to a traumatic level.

Many of the chapters point to grave difficulties in the young people's histories and/or their parents' functioning. While there were no instances of outright acts of physical or sexual abuse, we think it is important to underscore the pervasiveness of what we have characterized as "soul blindness" (Wurmser 1994, 1996; Novick, J. and Novick, K.K. 2005). We have described families in which the parents were blind to the real personalities of their children, where parents used the defense of externalization to deal with their own anxiety or pain (Novick, J. and Novick, K.K. 1970). Externalization is the attribution to another, for instance a child, of parts of one's own personality, irrespective of the child's characteristics. Since externalization violates the child's existing and developing personality, it constitutes an abuse in itself. Our early studies indicated that children who are the objects of parental externalizations show severe disturbance in their self-esteem and difficulty integrating positive aspects of their functioning, along with interference in developing a realistic self-image. Not only are these children unseen by those around them, they also lose the capacity to see themselves clearly.

In the context of adolescent identity formation, the operation of familial externalizations and consequent soul blindness becomes a severe interference. A pervasive etiologic factor was parental difficulty, from various sources, with acknowledging the separateness of their child. In Solms' 2021 volume examining the origins of consciousness, he cites studies relating to visual agnosia, a condition associated with lesions to the occipital cortex, which leads to a person being unable to ascribe meaning to what or whom they see. He describes the discoveries of Hermann Munk in the late 1800s that led to the first description of "mind blindness" (ibid., p. 63). But those people were mind-blind to everything, in sharp contrast to some of the parents described in our sample, whose soul blindness appeared to have emotional/psychological roots. Their externalizations and denial of individuality were specifically targeted to their child or children. That soul blindness, seemingly intractable in some of the cases (for instance, Maria or Kaitlyn), yielded to some extent in others, where parents were more accessible to dynamic parent work and could transform their image and relationships with their children, and appreciate them for who they really were.

This thread is central to our findings in this volume: most contributors continued to use the traditional language of 'separation' or 'separation-individuation' in relation to the goals of adolescence, even while describing case after case where the results of treatment actually constituted *transformations* of relationships to self and others. In many cases those transformations encompassed acknowledgment by parents and young people of their essential separateness along with ongoing mutual appreciation, interdependence, and love, but at a new level commensurate with the adolescent or emerging adult's changing capacities. Separateness was no longer conflated with separation.

We should also think about what mutative factors seem active in generating the good outcomes described here. As noted above, identification with the analyst, or, perhaps more precisely, with aspects of the analyst's stance or attitudes, seems significant. We mentioned above the emotional muscles the therapists used actively, and this emphasis directs our attention to our fourth question, to those aspects of technique that emerge from these chapters and seem specific to effective work with adolescents. Our conclusion is that important new ideas for technique abound in this volume; they deserve to be incorporated in every clinician's repertoire.

To list some instances:

- Dynamic parent work was part of the majority of cases, and dual goals for the treatment were often articulated with both patient and parents; where parents were not seen regularly or at all, they were kept in the analyst's mind. These were not only the parents of the past, but also the parents of the *present,* indicating a sophisticated awareness of the complex operation of time in the psychic functioning of adolescents.

This also allowed for access to understanding the intergenerational transmission of trauma, pathology, and defenses in many cases.

- Privacy and secrecy were differentiated and there was active engagement with issues of confidentiality.
- Safety was a paramount clinical value.
- We saw that the contributors worked actively to generate a therapeutic alliance and paid attention to it throughout the treatments.
- Analysts worked to maintain equidistance from patient and parents, as well as among agencies of the mind.
- Active intervention from the very beginning was critical in some cases, while others demanded patience and frustration tolerance. The point here relates again to flexibility of technique – there is no one standard technique with teenagers.
- Even before pandemic requirements for alternative modalities of maintaining treatment, many of these contributors found that flexibility in modes of communication and the structure of the analytic frame was central to the success of the treatment.
- Consistent support of reality-testing, for instance, in relation to parental pathology.
- Many contributors pointed explicitly to the importance of noting and verbalizing the patient's strengths, capacities and achievements, with the emphasis on the whole person, not just pathology.
- Reference to levels of consciousness, that is, use of the topographical metapsychological perspective, is helpful and grounding to adolescents.
- Higher frequency of sessions came through as significant for development of the therapeutic relationship.
- Analysts of these adolescents were comfortable in moving among different roles in the therapeutic relationship, serving as transference objects from both past and present, and also as developmental objects,

authoritative resources of knowledge, collaborator in the work, real separate people with their own perspectives and opinions, and crucially as guardians of the therapeutic alliance.

- In general, terminations were addressed from inside the treatment, rather than externally determined, thus becoming part of the adolescent's growth.

Summary conclusions and future directions

Harking back to our introductory description of the traditional psychoanalytic model of adolescent development, we are challenged now to consider the fifth question in our list. The material in this volume suggests the need to revise the way psychoanalysts characterize adolescent normality and pathology. It also suggests that radical revision and expansion of the technical repertoire leads to effective analytic treatment of young people. Nevertheless, we did not generally see contributors articulating new models or describing using them. Adolescent analysts now are doing new things that work, but don't seem to have a current, coherent, explicit model for developmental theory or technique. They are using the old concepts and terms even while they no longer seem to fit well. The original garment has been outgrown.

We have been thinking and writing about adolescence for many years (see, for instance, Novick, J. 1982; Novick, K.K. 1990; Novick, J. and Novick, K.K. 1996, 2001a, 2002a, 2008, 2015, 2016, 2019; Novick, K.K. and Novick, J. 1994, 2005, 2013; Novick, K.K. et al 2020; DeVito et al 1994, 2000; Dowling et al 2013). This interest has continued alongside the construction of our evolving developmental model of two systems of self-regulation (Novick, J. and Novick, K.K. 2001, 2016). Simultaneously with collecting, collating, and digesting the material for this volume we began to examine the interdigitation of adolescence and the two-systems model (Novick, J. and Novick, K.K. 2022 in press). We suggest that our model of two systems of self-regulation may be useful in formulating new ways to think about adolescence and work with adolescents and emerging adults. It is our hope that readers will consider that possibility, add to the ideas, suggest revisions, and use the material of this book to generate ever-expanding ways to meet the needs of the young people who now constitute the majority of the world's population.

Along the way, the inclusion of new models based on the dual-track developmental tradition in psychoanalysis may help us all move beyond the confines of teenism, which relies, like all prejudices, on over-simplified characterizations of those to be dominated as primitive and uncontrolled, thus justifying negative attitudes, judgments and actions. The classical single-track model underlies the whole problem, with its unsubstantiated assumptions of recapitulation of all the so-called 'primitive' stages of development. The dual-track model, which underlies our two-systems model, asserts that everyone, from birth on, has available alternative responses to life's challenges, open- or closed-system solutions.

REFERENCES

Aichhorn, A. Wayward Youth, New York: Viking Press, 1935, also: Northwestern University Press, Reprint 1984

Aries, P. (1965). Centuries of Childhood. New York: Random House.

Aron, L. (2006). Analytic impasse and the third: Clinical implication of intersubjectivity theory. Int. J. Psycho-Anal. 87: 349-368

Basch, M.F. (1983). The perception of reality and the disavowal of meaning. The Annual of Psychoanalysis XI: 125-154.

Bell, A. I. (1965) The Significance of Scrotal Sac and Testicles for the Prepuberty Male. Psychoanalytic Quarterly 34:182-206

Bergman, Anni. (Personal communication, 1988).

Bick, E. (1968). The Experience of the Skin in Early Object Relations. In: Harris Williams M., Ed.) Collected Papers of Martha Harris and Esther Bick. The Roland Harris Trust.

Bion, W.R. (1967) "Volviendo a pensar", Editorial Lumen-Hormé, Buenos Aires, 1970

Blos, P. (1967). The second individuation process of adolescence. Psychoanal. StudyChild 22:162-186.

——— (1972). The function of the ego ideal in adolescence. The Psychoanalytic Study of the Child, 27(1), 93-97.

Braten, S. (1987). Dialogic mind: The infant and the adult in proto conversation. In M. Carvallo (Ed.), Nature, Cognition and Systems (pp. 187-205). Dordrecht, Boston: D. Reidel.

Brazleton, T.B., Koslowski, B. and Main, M. (1975). The origins of reciprocity: The early mother-infant interaction. In M. Lewis and L. Rosenblum (Eds.), The Effect of the Infant on its Caregiver (pp. 49-76). New York: Wiley.

Burlingham, D. (1932). Kinderanalyse und Mutter. Zeitschrift für psychoanalytische Pädagogik, 6(7-8):269-289. (Later published in English as Burlingham, D.T. (1935). Child Analysis and the Mother. Psychoanal. Q., 4:69-92).

Busch, F. (1993). "In the neighborhood": Aspects of a good interpretation and a "developmental lag" in ego psychology. J. Amer. Psychoanal. Assn., 41:151-177

Cardenal, M. (2002). Object relationship vicissitude: towards the acknowledgement of living dependent, young children observation" In: "Create Bonds", Cracovia, 2002.

——— (2014). Belleza, creación y misterio. El conflicto estético. Revista de la Asociación Psicoanalítica de Guadalajara, México.

——— (2017). Las capacidades de la mente para crear. Una perspectiva estética. Revista de Psicoterapia Psicosomática, editada por el Instituto de Estudios Psicosomáticos y Psicoterapia Médica, España.

Chused, J. (1982). The role of analytic neutrality in the use of the child analyst as a new object. J. Amer. Psychoanal. Assn. 30:3-2

Davoine, F. and Gaudillière J-M. (2004). History beyond Trauma. New York: Other Press.

DeVito, E., Novick, J., and Novick, K.K. (1994). Interferenze culturali nell'ascolto degli Adolescente. Adolescenza 3:10-14.

——— (2000). Cultural interferences with listening to adolescents. J.I.C.A.P. 1: 77-95.

Dowling, S., Lament, C., Novick, K.K., Novick, J. (2013). Dialogue with the Novicks. Psychoanal. St. Child, 67:137-145.

Ferro, A. (2006). Clinical implications of Bion's thought. Int. J. Psycho-Anal., 87:989-1003.

——— (2008). The patient as the analyst's best colleague: Transformation into a dream and narrative transformations. The Italian Psychoanalytic Annual, 2:199-205.

——— (2015). A Response That Raises Many Questions. Psychoanal. Inq., 35(5):512-525.

Ferro, A. and Foresti, G. (2013). Bion and thinking. Psychoanal. Quarterly, 82(2):361-391.

Freud, A. (1936). The Ego and the Mechanisms of Defense. Revised Edition. Writings 2. New York: International Universities Press.

——— (1958). Adolescence. Writings, Vol. 5

——— (1965). Normality and Pathology in Childhood. Writings, Vol. 6. New York: International Universities Press.

——— 1967[1953]). About losing and being lost. Psychoanal. Study Child 22: 9-19. And in Writings, vol.4. New York: International Universities Press.

——— (1969 [1966]). Adolescence as a developmental disturbance. Writings

——— (1970). Problems of termination in child analysis. Writings, Vol. 7. New York: International Universities Press.

Freud, S. (1905a). Three essays on the theory of sexuality. S.E. 7:123-243.

——— (1905b). Fragments of an Analysis of a Case of Hysteria. S.E. 7, pp. 1–122

——— (1910) Five Lectures on Psychoanalysis. Fifth Lecture: Transference and Resistance, S.E. 11 p. 49

——— (1916). Some Character-Types Met with in Psycho-Analytic Work. The Standard Edition of the Complete Psychological Works of Sigmund Freud, Volume XIV (1914-1916): On the History of the Psycho-Analytic Movement, Papers on Metapsychology and Other Works, 309-333.

——— (1933). New Introductory Lectures on Psycho-Analysis. St. Ed., Vol. XXII (1932-1936): New Introductory Lectures on Psycho-Analysis and Other Works, (Page 56).

Furman, E. (1981). Treatment via the parent: A case of bereavement. Journal of Child Psychotherapy, 7 (1), 89-101.

Galatzer-Levy, R. M. (2004) Chaotic possibilities: Toward a new model of development. International Journal of Psychoanalysis 85:419-441

Gampel, Y. (1998). Reflections on Countertransference in Psychoanalytic Work with Child Survivors of the Shoah. J. Am. Acad. Psychoanal. Dyn. Psychiatr., 26(3):343-368

Gedo, J.E. (2005). Psychoanalysis as Biological Science: A Comprehensive Theory. Baltimore: The Johns Hopkins University Press.

Gilmore, K. (2019). Is Emerging Adulthood a New Developmental Phase?. J. Amer. Psychoana. Assn., 67(4):625-653

Glasser, M. (1979). Some aspects of the role of aggression in the perversions in Rosen, I. Ed. *Sexual Deviation*, 2nd edition, Oxford: Oxford University Press, pp. 278-305.

Glykys, J. & Staley, K.J. (2015). Diazepam effect during early neonatal development correlates with neuronal CI. Ann Clin Transl Neurol. 12, 1055 – 1070.

Hall, G.S. (1904). Adolescence. New York: Norton.

Heineman, T., Clausen, M. Ruff, S. (2015) Treating Trauma: Relationship-Based Psychotherapy with Children, Adolescents, and Young Adults. Chapter 5. Lanham MD: Rowman & Littlefield.

Holinger, P.C. (2016). Further considerations of theory, technique, and affect in child psychoanalysis: Two prelatency cases. International Journal Psychoanalysis 97: 1279-1297.

Horney, K. (2007 [1936]) The Problem of the Negative Therapeutic Reaction. Psychoanalytic Quarterly 76:27-42

Hug-Hellmuth, H. (1915). Die Kriegsneurose des Kindes Pester, *Lloyd*.15. Mrz

——— (2013). pp. 18-9. A Study of the Mental Life of the Child. Hong Kong: Forgotten Books. (Original work published 1919)

——— (1920). Child Psychology and Education. Int. J. Psycho-Anal. 1:316-318

Hurry, A. (1998). Psychoanalysis and developmental therapy. In: A. Hurry, Editor, Psychoanalysis and Developmental Therapy. London: Karnac.

Igbal, M.I. and Sobham, T. (2002). Effects of Commonly Used Benzodiazepines on the Fetus, the Neonate, and the Nursing Infant. J. Clin. Pharmacology, 53, 39-49.

Jones, E. (1922). Some problems of adolescence. In: Papers on Psychoanalysis. Boston: Beacon Press, pp. 389-406.

Katan, A. (1961). Some thoughts about the role of verbalization in early childhood. The Psychoanalytic Study of the Child 16:184-188.

Kavaler-Adler, S. (2006) From Neurotic Guilt to Existential Guilt as Grief: The Road to Interiority, Agency, and Compassion through Mourning. Part I. American Journal of Psychoanalysis 66:239-260

Kohut, H. (1968). The psychoanalytic treatment of narcissistic personality disorders – Outline of a systematic approach. Psychoanalytic Study of the Child Vol. 23

——— (1971). The Analysis of the Self: A Systematic Approach to the Psychoanalytic Treatment of Narcissistic Personality Disorders. New York: International Universities Press.

Laub, D. (1998). The Empty Circle: Children of Survivors and the Limits of Reconstruction. J. Amer. Psychoanal. Assn., 46:507-529.

Lauer, R.H. (1973). Perspectives on Social Change. Boston : Allyn and Bacon.

Levy-Warren, M. (2008) In a Fast-moving Thicket: Treating Adolescents Today. Journal of Infant, Child & Adolescent Psychotherapy 7:192-198

——— (2016) Paralysis at the Adolescent Gate: Peter Pan Meets Godzilla. Journal of Infant, Child & Adolescent Psychotherapy 15:51-57

Loewald, H. (1957). On the therapeutic action of psychoanalysis. In Papers on Psychoanalysis. New Haven: Yale University Press, pp. 277-301.

Lombardi, R. (2016). Formless Infinity: Clinical Implications of Matte Blanco and Bion. London: New Library of Psychoanalysis.

Meltzer, D. (1965). The relation of anal masturbation to projective identification. Int. J. Psychoanal. 47:335-342.

——— (1967). El Proceso Psicoanalítico. Buenos Aires: Lumen-Hormé.

——— (1973). Los Estados Sexuales de la Mente. Buenos Aires: Editorial Kargieman, 1974

——— (1988). La Aprehensión de la Belleza. Buenos Aires: Editorial Spatia, 1990

Miller, J.M. (2013). Developmental psychoanalysis and developmental objects. Psychoanal. Inq. 33(4): 312-322

Mitscherlich, A. (1970). Society Without the Father. New York: Schocken Books.

Money-Kyrle, R. 1968 Cognitive development. International Journal of Psychoanalysis 49:691-8.

Murray, L. (1991). Intersubjectivity, objects relations theory, and empirical evidence from mother-infant interactions. Infant Mental Health J. 12:3.

Nicolo, A.M. (2016). Transferences in Adolescence. In: Reading Italian Psychoanalysis. Eds: Borgogno, F., Luchetti, A. and Marina Coe, L. London: Routledge.

Novick, J., (1982). Varieties of transference in the analysis of an adolescent. Int. J. Psycho-Anal. 63:139-148.

Novick, J. and Novick, K.K. Externalization as a pathological form of relating: the dynamic underpinnings of abuse. In: Victims of Abuse., ed. A. Sugarman et al. Madison, CT. International Universities Press 1994, pp. 45-68.

——— (1996). A developmental perspective on omnipotence. J. Clinical Psychoanalysis. 5: 124-173.

——— (2001a). Trauma and Deferred Action in the Reality of Adolescence. Am. J. Psychoanal., 61:43-61.

——— (2001b). Parent work in analysis: Children, adolescents, and adults. Part 1: The evaluation phase. Journal of Infant, Child, and Adolescent Psychotherapy 1:55-77.

——— (2002). Parent work in analysis: Children, adolescents, and adults. Part 3: Middle and pre-termination phases of treatment. Journal of Infant, Child, and Adolescent Psychotherapy 2:17-41.

——— (2002a) Two systems of self-regulation. Psychoanalytic Social Work, 8:3-4, 95-122, DOI: 10.1300/J032v08n03_06

——— (2000b). Love in the therapeutic alliance. JAPA 48: 189-218.

——— Soul blindness: a child must be seen to be heard. In: Divorce and Custody: Contemporary Developmental Psychoanalytic Perspectives. Ed: L. Gunsberg and P. Hymowitz. Washington, D.C.: American Psychological Association Books. 2005, Ch.8.

——— Good Goodbyes: Knowing How to End in Psychotherapy and Psychoanalysis. New York: Aronson (Rowman and Littlefield) 2006.

——— (2008). Expanding the domain: privacy, secrecy and confidentiality. Annual of Psychoanalysis 2008-2009, 36/37: 145-160.

——— (2012). Emotional muscle in therapists – a strengths-based learning model for treatment. Bull. Michigan Psychoanalytic Council 8: 3-23.

——— (2013). Two systems and defenses. Psychoanalytic Review, 100 (1), 185-200.

——— (2015). Loneliness in adolescence. J. American Society for Adolescent Psychiatry 5: 3, 174-186.

——— Freedom To Choose: Two Systems of Self-Regulation. New York: IPBooks. 2016

——— What we can learn about confidentiality from children and adolescents. In: Privacy: Developmental, Cultural, and Clinical Realms. Eds: S. Akhtar and A. Abbasi. 2019, Routledge: New York. pp. 46-56.

——— (2022 in press). Adolescence – the fulcrum of development. In: P. Bruendl, Editor, The Yearbook for Child and Adolescent Psychoanalysis: Migration and Transformation in Child and Adolescent Psychoanalysis (German). Frankfurt am Main: Brandes & Apsel

Novick, K.K. and Novick, J. (1994). Post-Oedipal transformations: latency, adolescence and pathogenesis. JAPA, vol. 42, 1:143-170.

——— (2002). Parent work in analysis: Children, adolescents, and adults. Part 2: Recommendation, beginning and middle phases of treatment. Journal of Infant, Child, and Adolescent Psychotherapy 2:1-27.

——— (2002a). Parent work in analysis: Children, adolescents and adults. Part 4: Termination and post-termination phases of treatment. Journal of Infant, Child, and Adolescent Psychotherapy 2:43-55.

——— (2005). Working with Parents Makes Therapy Work. Lanham, Maryland: Jason Aronson.

——— (2013). Concurrent Work with Parents of Adolescent Patients. Psychoanal. St. Child, 67:103-136.

Novick, K.K. (1990). Access to Infancy: Different Ways of Remembering. Int. J. Psycho-Anal. 71:335-349.

Novick, K.K., Novick, J., Barrett, D., Barrett, T. (2020). Parent Work Casebook. New York: IPBooks.

Offer, D., (1969). The Psychological World of the Teenager. New York: Basic Books.

——— (1991). Adolescent development: a normative perspective. In: Greenspan S., Pollack G., (eds). The Course of Life. 4: Adolescence, Madison, CT: International Universities Press, pp.181-200.

Offer, D., Ostrov, B., Howard, K.I. (1981). The Adolescent. A Psychological Self Portrait. New York: Basic Books.

Ogden, T.H. (1995). Analyzing forms of aliveness and deadness of the transference-countertransference. International Journal of Psychoanalysis 76:695-709.

——— (1997). Reverie and Interpretation: Sensing something human. Northvale, NJ: Aronson

Panel (1972). Indications and contraindications for the psychoanalysis of the adolescent. M. Sklansky, reporter. JAPA 20:134-144.

Paniagua, C. (1991). Patient's surface, clinical surface, and workable surface. JAPA 39:669-685

Perrot-Catipovic, M. and Ladame, F. (1998). Adolescence and Psychoanalysis: The Story And The History. Karnac Books: London.

Phillips,A. (1988). Winnicott. Fontana Paperbacks (London)

Pine, F. (1990). Drive, Ego, Object, & Self: A Synthesis for Clinical Work. New York: Basic Books.

Rosenfeld, S. with Scharff, J. S. (2021). Dance and the Creative Couple. Washington DC: Opus.

Sandler, J., Freud, A. (1983). Discussions with Anna Freud on The Ego and the Mechanisms of Defense: the ego and the id at puberty. Int. J. Psycho-Anal. 64:401-406.

Sandler, J. (1977). Countertransference and Role-Responsiveness. Int. R. Psycho-Anal. 3:43-47.

Schafer, R. (1960). The Loving and Beloved Superego in Freud's Structural Theory. Psychoanalytic St. Child, 15:163-188.

Scharff, D. E. and Scharff, J. S. (1987). Families of divorce and remarriage. In Object Relations Family Therapy, pp. 367-393. Northvale NJ: Jason Aronson.

Shengold, L. L. (1979) Child Abuse and Deprivation Soul Murder. Journal of the American Psychoanalytic Association 27:533-559

Sloate, Phyllis. (2021, Personal Communication).

Solms, M. (2021). The Hidden Spring: A Journey to the Source of Consciousness. New York: W.W. Norton and Company, Inc.

Spencer, M. B., & Markstrom-Adams, C. (1990). Identity processes among racial and ethnic minority children in America. Child Development, 61(2), 290-310.

Sperling, M. (1974). The Major Neuroses and Behavior Disorders in Children. New York: Jason Aronson.

Stern, D. (1974). The goal and structure of mother-infant play. J. Am. Acad. Child Psych. 13, pp. 402-421.

Sugarman, A. (2003). Dimensions of the child analyst's role as a developmental object: Affect regulation and limit setting. Psychoanal. Study of the Child 58:189-213

Tahka, V. (1993). Mind and its Treatment: A Psychoanalytic Approach. Madison, CT: Int. Univ. Press.

Trevarthen, C. (1979) Communication and cooperation in early infancy: A description of primary intersubjectivity. In M. Bullowa (Ed.) Before Speech: The Beginning of Interpersonal Communication (pp. 321-347). Cambridge: Cambridge University Press.

Tronick, E.Z. (2002). A Model of Infant Mood States and Sandarian Affective Waves. Psychoanal. Dial., 12(1):73-99.

Tyson, P. (2010). Research in child psychoanalysis: Twenty-five year follow-up of a severely disturbed child. Journal American Psychoanalytic Association 57: 919-945.

Von Goethe, J.W. [1787] (2012). The Sorrows of Young Werther, Oxford World Classics, tr. David Constantine, Oxford University Press.

Williams, P. (2004). Incorporation of an invasive object. International Journal of Psychoanalysis 85:1333-1348.

Wilson,P. (1991). Adolescence. Chapter in "A Textbook of Psychotherapy in Psychiatric Practice." Ed. J. Holmes. Churchill Livingstone: London.

——— (1995). Narcissism and Adolescence. Chapter in "Narcissistic Wounds." Eds. J. Cooper and N. Maxwell. London: Whurr.

Winnicott, D. W. (1949). Hate in the Countertransference. In: In One's Bones: The Clinical Genius of Winnicott. ed. D. Goldman. Northvale, NJ: Aronson, 1993, pp. 15- 24.

——— (1960). The theory of the parent-infant relationship. International Journal of Psycho-Analysis, 41, 585-595.

——— (1965). The Maturational Processes and the Facilitating Environment. New York: International Universities Press.

——— (1971). Playing and reality. London: Penguin.

Wurmser, L. (1994). A time of questioning: the severely disturbed patient within classical analysis. *The Annual of Psychoanalysis*, (Ed.) J.A.Winer, 22, 173-207. Chicago: Chicago Institute of Psychoanalysis.

——— (1996). Trauma, inner conflict, and the vicious cycles of repetition. *Scandinavian Psychoanalytic Review*, 19, 17-45.

Yanof, J. (1996). Language, communication, and transference in child analysis. I. Selective mutism: The medium is the message. Journal American Psychoanalytic Association 44: 79-100.

Young-Bruehl, E. (1996). The Anatomy of Prejudices. Cambridge MA: Harvard University Press.

——— (2009). Childism – Prejudice against children. Contemporary Psychoanalysis 45: 251-265.

——— (2012). Childism: Confronting Prejudice Against Children. New Haven: Yale University Press.

Young-Bruehl, E. and Bethelard, F. (1999). The hidden history of the ego instincts. Psychoanal. Rev., 86(6):823-851.

www.ingramcontent.com/pod-product-compliance
Lightning Source LLC
Chambersburg PA
CBHW062108020426
42335CB00013B/893